# BEHIND THE

# GRAND OLE OPRY®

## CURTAIN

# BEHIND THE
# GRAND OLE OPRY®
## CURTAIN

*Tales of Romance and Tragedy*

# ROBERT K. OERMANN

CENTER
STREET®

New York  Boston  Nashville

Center Street
Hachette Book Group
237 Park Avenue
New York, NY 10017

Visit our Web site at www.centerstreet.com.

Center Street is a division of Hachette Book Group, Inc.
The Center Street name and logo are trademarks of Hachette Book Group, Inc.
Printed in the United States of America

First Edition: October 2008

10 9 8 7 6 5 4 3 2 1

Book Design by Renato Starisic

Library of Congress Cataloging-in-Publication Data

Oermann, Robert K.
  Behind the Grand Ole Opry curtain : tales of romance and tragedy / Robert K. Oermann. — 1st ed.
     p. cm.
  ISBN-13: 978-1-931722-89-6
  ISBN-10: 1-931772-89-7
  1. Country musicians—United States. 2. Country musicians' spouses—United States. 3. Grand ole opry (Radio program) I. Title.

  ML394.O28 2008
  781.64209768'55—dc22                                    2008013720

The Grand Ole Opry has always had that special something that separates it from every other form of American entertainment: its people.

This book is dedicated to the dreamers who, for going on a century, have made their way to the Opry stage, aspiring to lend their voices to the Opry's song. Country music's home has been built upon their dreams, their performances, and their undying commitment.

This book is dedicated as well to those in the pews, cars, and living rooms around the world who have dropped by or tuned in over that same course of time, sharing in the Opry dream while laughing and clapping along.

Indeed, the Opry is set apart by its people. Good people.

# Contents

CONTENTS

# BEHIND THE
# GRAND OLE OPRY
## CURTAIN

# Johnny and June

The Cash family moved to County Road 3, Box 238, in Dyess, Arkansas' Mississippi County in March 1935. Not long afterward, the family acquired its first battery-powered radio. Musical shows beamed from big cities like Memphis, Chicago, Cincinnati, and Nashville fascinated son Johnny—then known simply as J. R.—as did the radio dramas, serials, and comedies. Radio was theater of the mind, he would later recall.

"I scanned the radio dial when I was a little kid on the cotton farm in Arkansas," he once said. "And it was the most wonderful, magical thing in the world to be able to turn that dial and hear different singers in different places."

He vividly remembered how exciting Nashville's Grand Ole Opry broadcast over WSM sounded to him. At the time, its brightest stars included banjo-whacking Uncle Dave Macon, fiddle virtuoso Arthur Smith, the close-harmony team of The Delmore Brothers, Pee Wee King's uptown Golden West Cowboys band, and the show's newest sensation, mountain singer Roy Acuff.

In 1938, when J. R. was six years old, the set began to pick up the sounds of The Carter Family broadcasting over XERA, one of the superpowerful Mexican-border stations. Country music's founding family was from the mountains of Virginia and consisted of A. P. Carter, his wife Sara, who sang lead and played the auto-harp, and sister-in-law Maybelle, who sang the tenor harmony and played lead guitar and was married to A. P.'s brother Ezra. If the sprit moved him, A. P. would chime in with a baritone vocal.

The family's repertoire would become country music's bed-rock. "Keep on the Sunny Side," "Will the Circle Be Unbroken," "Wabash Cannonball," "Hello Stranger," "Are You Lonesome To-night," "I Never Will Marry," and "Wildwood Flower" were all popularized by the trio. Its "I'm Thinking Tonight of My Blue Eyes" became the melody for three future country classics, "The Great Speckled Bird," "The Wild Side of Life," and "It Wasn't God Who Made Honky Tonk Angels."

But little Johnny Cash knew only that those songs gripped him. For the rest of his life, he would turn to the Carter repertoire for inspiration.

"The simplicity of deliverance and the performance in those songs was like my life, you know? Things were pretty cut and dried, black and white, straight ahead. That's the way The Carter Family came at you, right in the face. And it felt good. I loved that kind of music all my life. That kind of music has always been my cup of tea."


MAYBELLE AND EZRA CARTER brought their three daughters—Helen, June, and Anita—to the Mexican border in 1939. Sara and A. P. brought their children Janette and Joe. The kids were expected to stand on their own, musically. Anita and Janette were the best sing-ers. Helen and Joe were the best guitarists. But ten-year-old tomboy Valerie June Carter didn't measure up in either department.

"Well, the Mexican border stations would have been an adventure for anybody," June reflected years later. "It was for me. I'm a simple little girl that has always lived in the mountains of southwestern Vir-ginia. Mother Maybelle, Uncle A. P., and Aunt Sara were very active on border radio. And then they offered us a job, if any of the children could sing. So my mother came home and within about a week's time, I think, taught me to sing. Because I had no idea how to sing.

"Janette could sing. Helen and Anita could sing. I mean, they had kind of perfect pitch at the time. And I'm the one they're looking at like I'm a snake, like they don't know whether I could sing or not. But I did learn to play the autoharp, and I could play the tenor guitar. And so we went, as these little children."

Even at seventy, June Carter could remember the commercials she wrote and recited for Kolorbak hair dye, Peruna tonic, and the other products she sold over the airwaves. The sister trio sang tunes like "Beautiful Brown Eyes" and "Chime Bells," while June's solo repertoire included such sprightly fare as Stephen Foster's "Oh Susannah" or an autoharp instrumental on "Engine 143." She also became a skillful comic.

"Uncle A. P. was the one who encouraged me. He would say, 'Well, we could use a little comedy. You need to do some kind of joke.'" June also recalled being shocked at the size of her listening audience on XERA.

"The room was full of bushel baskets of mail, and I thought, 'These are an awful lot of letters somebody's got to answer.' And I looked, and they were all to The Carter Family!"

Johnny Cash was listening intently. So were the children who became Buck Owens, Waylon Jennings, and Tom T. Hall.

But the homey "family" those boys were hearing wasn't real. Sara had left A. P. in 1933, divorced him in 1936, and married his cousin Coy Bayes in 1939. Although the couple continued to record and broadcast together, this strained situation would eventually tear the group apart. After the 1940 season on the Mexican border station, the group traveled to broadcast over WBT in Charlotte, North Carolina.

"We were working there live every morning, and it was kind of a strained situation," June remembered. "My Uncle A. P. and Aunt Sara had been divorced, and Aunt Sara had remarried. And I think it was maybe painful for both of them.

"So we came back to the Valley for just a little bit [in 1943]. My father bought Helen an accordion. I kept playing autoharp. For my sister Anita he bought a big bass fiddle. Mother was playing guitar.

And we decided, well, we would just continue on and see if we could do our own radio program."

Mother Maybelle & The Carter Sisters were hired by station WRNL in Roanoke, Virginia, in 1944. Two years later, they graduated to the cast of the *Old Dominion Barn Dance* on the same city's WRVA. In 1948, they moved to Knoxville for work on WNOX. There, they picked up guitarist Chet Atkins as a sideman.

"My father said, 'He's absolutely gonna be the best guitar player that's ever been.' So we had a vote—Mother, Helen, Anita, and Daddy and I—and we voted to ask Chet if he would come to be a part of our group. So we hired Chet Atkins."

During a 1949 stint at KWTO in Springfield, Missouri, June Carter scored a major hit by teaming with comics Homer & Jethro on the delightful "Baby, It's Cold Outside." At this point, the troupe was quite an attraction, boasting the silvery soprano of Anita, Maybelle and Chet's dazzling instrumental work, the beauty of the three sisters, June's comedic shenanigans, and creamy female harmony vocals on folk, pop, country, and gospel tunes. The act was invited to join the cast of the Grand Ole Opry in 1950.

"The Opry was a magic place that was my home," June remarked. "I couldn't do any wrong on that stage. It didn't matter. I just did these corny old jokes, but I always felt loved there."

As fate would have it, 1950 was also the year that Johnny Cash first visited the legendary show. He never forgot what he saw that night.

"We took our senior trip in 1950 from Dyess High School, and one of the stops was the Grand Ole Opry on Saturday night in Nashville," Johnny recalled with a smile. "And I was sittin' up in the balcony, in the middle of the left balcony of the Ryman Auditorium with my class, all in there together in two rows.

"And there she was, down onstage. Little Jimmy Dickens and June Carter, that's all I remember. I said, 'One of these days, I'm gonna get her autograph.'"

June always claimed that the then-eighteen-year-old Johnny also vowed, "Some day I'm going to marry that girl." And maybe he did. At any rate, he graduated, joined the air force, married Vivian Liberto, and began his own music career in Memphis.

Mother Maybelle & The Carter Sisters became one of the Opry's most popular and lucrative concert attractions. Anita had big hit duets with fellow Opry star Hank Snow in 1951. A year later, The Carters were chosen to travel to New York for the Opry's network television debut, on *The Kate Smith Show*.

"I think it was a big deal, or it felt like it at the time. That was the very first time that I think anyone from the Grand Ole Opry had ever appeared on network television—Hank Williams and Roy Acuff and Helen, Anita, Mother and I, and Chet. Television was big. It had just started, so it was really interesting and unusual. We had been used to workin' for five thousand people, but we hadn't been on network TV doin' it."

They toured with Opry superstar Hank Williams, who swore he would never follow "those Carter broads." So they always closed the shows.

"He was a sweet man," June said wistfully. "I thought a lot of Hank, and he thought a lot of my family. But he was tortured and had a very bad kind of chemical problem. Anita and I tried hard to manage Hank. But we couldn't. Hank could be funny. But when he was 'using,' it was so painful for my sisters and me." Within a year of the TV appearance, Hank would be dead.

June married the handsome Grand Ole Opry star Carl Smith in 1952. The couple recorded the 1953 duets "Love Oh Crazy Love" and "Time's a Wastin'." Daughter Carlene was born in 1955, but the marriage soon unraveled.

"I was very happy being in the country-music business, but I was very unhappy in my personal life. I had gotten divorced, and it was a very painful thing for me.

"And so I kind of ran away. I was handled by Colonel Tom Parker at that time. And so I went on the road doing shows with Elvis, because it was something for me to hide behind.

"Elvis had a big crush on Anita, but then he got a crush on me. Elvis got a crush on whoever was handy. It was just his thing. He liked women. I decided I wouldn't touch him with a ten-foot pole. Lord only knows where he'd been. He was a sexy man who really thought he could have any woman that he saw. But he couldn't, and I think that was a big shock to his ego."

While on tour opening shows for Elvis, June was spotted by screenwriter Budd Schulberg, who alerted film director Elia Kazan to her talents. Kazan arranged for June to take acting lessons in New York in 1955–1956. She subsequently appeared in such TV dramas as *Wagon Train, Bonanza, Jim Bowie,* and *Gunsmoke.* She continued to commute to Nashville for Opry appearances.

MEANWHILE, SHORTLY AFTER MARRYING Vivian in 1954, Johnny approached Sun Records owner Sam Phillips about making records in Memphis. Sam auditioned Johnny toward the end of the year. Johnny and Vivian's daughter Rosanne was born in 1955, and a month later "Cry, Cry, Cry" / "Hey Porter" was released as his debut single. It hit the charts in November. In February 1956, "Folsom Prison Blues" / "So Doggone Lonesome" entered the charts. It became his first top-ten hit. Shortly after the birth of his second daughter, Kathy, "I Walk the Line" began storming up the charts in the summer of 1956. Johnny figured it was time to come knocking on the Opry's door.

"When I came to appear on the Grand Ole Opry the first time, I waited two hours out in the waiting room before the manager of the Opry [Jim Denny] finally said, 'Come on in.' He looked at my black clothes and long hair and sideburns and said, 'What makes you think you belong on the Grand Ole Opry?' So I said, 'Well, I've got a record in the top-ten best sellers'—which was 'Folsom Prison Blues'—I said, 'I think they'd like to hear me.'"

Johnny Cash made his Grand Ole Opry debut on July 7, 1956. He was introduced, coincidentally, by Carl Smith, who called Johnny "the brightest rising star of country music."

Reporter Ben A. Green wrote in *The Nashville Banner* newspaper, "He had a quiver in his voice, but it wasn't stage fright. The haunting words of 'I Walk the Line' began to swell through the building. And a veritable tornado of applause rolled back. The boy had struck home, where the heart is, with his song that is Number 2 in the nation today. As his words filtered into the farthermost corners, many in the crowd were on their feet, cheering and clapping. They too had taken a new member into the family."

Elvis Presley had just ended his nine-week stay at the top of the pop charts with "Heartbreak Hotel," his first number-one hit. The newspaper article added, "He'll be better than Presley because Johnny's a true country singer, and Presley isn't and never has been." Even so, there was some unease backstage about the punch and rockabilly rhythm in the stark Johnny Cash sound.

There was something else backstage—or rather, someone. Just as he'd promised, he got June Carter's autograph.

"The first time I went to the Grand Ole Opry, she asked me for some of my records. The next Saturday night, I brought them to her and got an autographed picture from her. Gave her my autographed records, two of 'em."

In a photo taken not long after their Opry meeting, June looks ravishing, wearing a dress with a figure-flattering bodice featuring cap sleeves and a plunging V neckline. Her full skirt, fashionable accessories, and coiffed hair all look just perfect. Johnny, dressed in a white jacket with dark piping, kneels at her side, looking up at the camera with a shy expression.

"The first time I ever saw him was backstage at the Grand Ole Opry," June recalled. "He told me later that night that he knew he was going to marry me. The second time I met him, he was with Vivian, his wife, but he told me later that he knew then that 'If there was any possibility that God would allow me to, I am still going to marry you some day.' And I had never even worked with him!"

In his 1997 autobiography, Johnny reported that her response to his prediction was a laugh. "Well, good," she wisecracked. "I can't wait."

June moved back to Nashville in 1957. She met and married Rip Nix, who later became a local police officer. Their daughter Rosey was born in 1958.

In 1961, the Cash family—which had welcomed two more daughters, Cindy and Tara—moved to California. Johnny, by then with Columbia Records, continued to record in Nashville and remained a frequent guest at the Opry.

He also continued to be smitten with June Carter. Well aware of the fact, his manager arranged for her to be a guest star at a Johnny Cash concert in Dallas on December 5, 1961. That night, Johnny asked her to join his road show. She agreed and became a member of the troupe on February 11, 1962, in Des Moines.

By the 1960s, Johnny Cash was deeply into substance abuse, downing amphetamines in massive quantities. Already an imposing "Man in Black," his wild mood swings could make him utterly terrifying to June. She was afraid she was witnessing the Hank Williams tragedy all over again. Almost equally frightening to her was that she was falling in love with him.

"There is a depth to John that is spiritual as well as sexual," she believed. "I think I felt like I was in a 'Ring of Fire' at the time."

Cowritten by June and Merle Kilgore, "Ring of Fire" topped the charts in 1963, remained at number one for seven consecutive weeks, and became her biggest success as a songwriter.

One fall night in 1965, Johnny arrived at the Ryman Auditorium for an Opry show practically out of his mind. In a now-infamous incident, Johnny became enraged when he fumbled with the microphone. He dragged the mic stand across the front of the stage, smashing the footlights and showering those in the front row with broken glass.

Bass player Marshall Grant recalled being told by an Opry manager, "Get him out of here, and don't bring him back." Johnny later reported that he was told, "We can't use you on the show anymore, John."

That wasn't the end of his adventures that night. As he recalled in *Cash: The Autobiography,* Johnny borrowed June's brand-new Cadillac and, fueled by alcohol as well as pills, sped out into a blinding electrical storm with torrential rain. He hit a utility pole head-on, breaking his nose and teeth on the steering wheel. He was worried about telling June that he'd wrecked her car. He didn't have to. One of the investigating police officers was Rip Nix, her husband.

June and Rip divorced in 1966. At the end of his tour that year, Johnny moved back to Nashville, taking an apartment in the suburb of Madison with fellow drug user Waylon Jennings as his roommate. Once a week, June and Maybelle would come over to clean up the "bachelor pad." Accepting Johnny's decision to leave her, Vivian filed for divorce in California.

On the road, June and Marshall Grant struggled to keep Johnny clean and sober. Finally at the end of her rope, June told Johnny that the 1967 tour with him would be her last—this despite the fact that the couple then had their giant hit duet, "Jackson," and that Helen, Anita, and Maybelle were now also part of the troupe. Desperate to hold on to June, Johnny agreed to quit his habit.

He'd bought a house on Old Hickory Lake, north of Nashville. In it, with the help of a team headed by June, her parents, and psychiatrist Nat Winston, he went through thirty days of agonizing withdrawal from drugs in the fall of 1967. But throughout the next twenty years, he had many relapses. Johnny was later in rehab at the Betty Ford Clinic three times as well as several times at similar facilities in Texas and Tennessee.

Vivian's divorce was finalized in January 1968, and that month the troupe went "behind the walls" to perform and record *Johnny Cash at Folsom Prison*. A month later, in London, Ontario, Johnny proposed to June onstage. "Let's go on with the show," she said. "Say yes!" yelled the crowd. She did. Johnny Cash and June Carter were married on March 1, 1968. Mindful of her two failed marriages, June decided to shelve her own ambitions to live in Johnny's shadow.

"I wanted to have a marriage. I wanted to be the best mother I could be. I worked with him, but I had sense enough to walk just a little ways behind him."

*Johnny Cash at Folsom Prison* sold more than three million copies. In 1969 it was followed by the even rowdier *Live at San Quentin*, which featured the smash hit "A Boy Named Sue." These career milestones led to the creation of *The Johnny Cash Show* on the ABC network in 1969–1971. The series cemented its star's status as an American icon.

"I think it's the best show that's ever been done, for all types of music," said June. "And he absolutely represented every field."

In addition to all the major country stars of the day—Merle Haggard, Charley Pride, Eddy Arnold, and the like—Johnny invited a wide variety of artists from other genres on to the show. As a result, Linda Ronstadt, Joni Mitchell, James Taylor, Joe Tex, and others received significant national attention during the crucial early days of their careers. Ray Charles, Stevie Wonder, Eric Clapton, Roy Orbison, and dozens more superstars appeared, as well as the newcomers. And despite the network's reluctance, Johnny insisted the series be taped at the Ryman Auditorium, the home of the Grand Ole Opry.

"The network had all these rules," Johnny reported, "but I had my own. I wanted some real American artists on there, some people with some backbone, some grit. They made a big deal out of [leftist folk singer] Pete Seeger for a while, but they finally said okay. I had Bob Dylan on the first show. We had Neil Diamond, Mahalia Jackson, Creedence Clearwater Revival. The things that I asked for, the network didn't give a hoot about, as far as their ratings were concerned. But I did it, because I wanted something credible on the show."

June missed part of the 1970 season. She gave birth to the couple's son John Carter Cash that year. Perhaps because of Maybelle's exposure on the series, The Carter Family was belatedly inducted into the Country Music Hall of Fame that year as well.

Johnny Cash continued to triumph on the country charts throughout the 1970s with "Sunday Morning Coming Down," "Man in Black," "One Piece at a Time," and other successes. Another flurry of hits occurred when he teamed up with Willie Nelson, Waylon Jennings, and Kris Kristofferson in the 1980s as The Highwaymen.

He was inducted into the Country Music Hall of Fame in 1980 and entered the Rock and Roll Hall of Fame in 1992. His late-career "victory lap" that made him hip with young rock fans came about via the strikingly raw, emotional discs *American Recordings* (1994), *Unchained* (1996), *Solitary Man* (2000), and *The Man Comes Around* (2002).

Over the years, he continued to visit the Opry stage. In fact, today there is a dressing room at the Ryman dedicated to him.

When June issued her Grammy-winning comeback CD *Press On* in 1999, she returned to the Grand Ole Opry to premiere its tunes.

"I felt so good," she said. "It was like being back on the Opry. They were that kind to me. I can't believe how many people care."

Said Opry star Emmylou Harris that night, "I live for moments like this."

As they entered their senior years, Johnny and June looked back at their amazing life together. As Johnny's daughter Rosanne observed, they were "soul mates."

"John is one of those rare people," said June. "I've seen two or three of these people in my lifetime. Elvis was one of them. But John has always had more—the word might be 'presence' or 'charisma' or whatever you want to call it—so when he walks into a room, the whole atmosphere in that room changes. They become as big as the room. They become bigger than life.

"God puts his hand on some people and says, 'You can be Johnny Cash.' "

He gave her the credit: "What June did for me was lift me when I was weak, encourage me when I was discouraged, and love me when I felt alone and unlovable. She is the greatest woman I have ever known. Nobody else, except my mother, comes close.

"The big thing about the music in my life is we shared it. We have a strong marriage. We share the road and the bedroom. We share backstage and onstage. We share the music, the freedom, and the emotion and the joy of it, the pain and the sadness of it.

"She's not only a lady that I've shared a lot with, she is the person responsible for me still being alive. She came along at a time in my life when I was going to self-destruct. She helped bring me back."

June Carter Cash died on May 15, 2003, at age seventy-three. Her husband joined her four months later. During those last months, he sobbed in anguish for her night after night. He picked up the telephone and pretended to talk to her. When his daughter Cindy and his sister Reba took him to see June's grave, he called to her, "I'm coming, baby, I'm coming."

Johnny Cash died on September 12, 2003, at age seventy-one. An all-star tribute concert in his honor took place on November 10, 2003, at the place where he met his soul mate, the Ryman Auditorium.

# The Stringbean Murders

**E**ven today, it is almost unbearably painful to recall.

The Grand Ole Opry comedian and banjo player David "Stringbean" Akeman was beloved by millions, thanks to his Opry appearances as well as his droll segments on TV's wildly popular *Hee Haw*.

On November 10, 1973, knowing that many old-time country performers kept their cash at home rather than in banks, two men broke into Stringbean's house. Finding no money, they turned on the radio to listen to him performing on the Opry that night, drank beer, smoked cigarettes, and waited to rob him in person.

Stringbean and his wife Estelle lived simply but always had a new Cadillac, paid for in cash. Estelle always drove, since Stringbean had never learned how. Once she'd even chauffeured him on a 15,000-mile tour through thirty-seven states and five Canadian provinces. After packing his costume, his banjo, and the gun he always carried into their Caddy's trunk, they left the Ryman Auditorium at 10:40 that night.

Less than an hour later, both were dead.

Stringbean, fifty-seven, was a hunter and an excellent shot. When he encountered the intruders, he drew his gun and fired, but was shot. Estelle, who was parking the car, heard the shots and began to run. The murderer chased her down. He fired at her back. She fell to her knees, begged for her life, and screamed before he shot her execution style.

Around 6:00 the next morning, fellow Opry star Grandpa Jones, who lived nearby, came by to pick up his buddy for a planned hunting expedition.

"As I drove up the lane, I thought I saw a coat lying about seventy-five yards out in front of the house," Grandpa recalled in his 1984 autobiography. "When I got closer, I saw it was a person. I stopped the car and went over. It was Estelle; she had been shot in the back and in the head. I felt her, and she was cold.

"I rushed to their little house and hollered for String. His banjo that he had played the night before was sitting on its side on the little front porch. I opened the screen; the other door was already open. String was lying in front of the fireplace, shot in the chest. . . . This was one of the worst things I have ever witnessed."

The heinous slayings gripped the hearts of the Grand Ole Opry cast and shocked the entire city of Nashville.

"In my travels since String's death, I've been asked thousands of questions about him," Grandpa wrote. "Each person always tells me how much they miss him. There's no way I can tell them what it feels like to lose a friend like String."

Like many of his generation, David Akeman didn't just perform country, he *was* country. Born on June 17, 1916, he grew up in poverty in the hills of Jackson County, Kentucky. That area is known for producing many excellent old-time banjo stylists, and David's father was one of them. Using a shoebox and thread, little David built his first homemade instrument at age seven. When he was fourteen, he traded two prize chickens he had raised to acquire a real banjo.

"I used to imitate my Dad's banjo pickin' when I was little," Stringbean recalled. "And then, when I was fourteen, he taught me to play a real banjo. I learned the old-time mountain pickin' from him, and there's nothing that can match it."

The family was so poor that the boy was often sent into the

woods to throw rocks at birds and kill them to be boiled for dinner. The experience of such need and want never left him. Having also lived through the Great Depression as a teenager, he was tight with a dollar throughout his life, always believing his next payday would be his last. Even after his *Hee Haw* checks had made him more than financially comfortable, he continued to hunt for ginseng in the Tennessee countryside, selling the plants' roots. He also sold costume jewelry out of a fishing tackle box backstage at the Opry to pick up extra cash.

His first job performing was on Lexington's WLAP in 1935–1938, which he landed after winning an amateur contest sponsored by country star Asa Martin. During one broadcast, the star forgot his name, glanced over at the lanky, 6-foot 2-inch youngster, and called him "String Beans." During another show, the banjo player was pressed into service as a comic and discovered he was a natural at it.

On paper, it reads like a corny old joke. But Stringbean's deadpan, laconic delivery made everything sound hilarious—"A drunk man and a lady were arguing. The drunk said, 'You are the ugliest woman I ever seen.' The lady said, 'You are the drunkest man I ever saw.' The drunk said, 'Yes, but tomorrow I'll be sober, and there'll be no change in you.'"

Stringbean honed his act as an itinerant radio barn-dance performer, with stays at WBT, in Charlotte, North Carolina (1938–1939), and WBIG, in Greenville, North Carolina (1939–1941). He also worked as a semiprofessional baseball player. At the time, Grand Ole Opry star Bill Monroe promoted his shows with his Blue Grass Boys band via sandlot games in the various towns they played. He spotted Stringbean, who was a pitcher, and recruited him for his team. Only later did the bandleader realize that Stringbean played banjo.

And so, as a member of the Blue Grass Boys, Stringbean came to the Grand Ole Opry in 1942. While in the group, he played on such classic recordings as "Footprints in the Snow," "True Life Blues," "Goodbye Old Pal," and "Kentucky Waltz."

Cousin Wilbur (Wesbrooks) was the bass player in the Blue Grass Boys when Stringbean was a member. The two worked up "double comedy" routines to add variety to the band's shows. One bit revolved around the two men being competitive farmers. The punch line was that Stringbean's crops were better because they were grown in the town where the band was playing that night.

"And he could never remember the name of the town where we were," recalled Cousin Wilbur. "We'd get the audience to laughing, and he'd ask me out of the corner of his mouth, 'What's the name of this town?' I'd tell him. . . . So we hit a town in Arkansas, and I really fixed Stringbean up that night. We like to tore that audience to pieces! The name of the town was Rector, Arkansas. And Stringbean says, 'What's the name of this town?' out of the corner of his mouth. So I told him it was Rectum, Arkansas.

"That's what Stringbean up and said, 'Rectum, Arkansas. Right here, folks, in Rectum.' And he like to wrecked the audience. They must have laughed for fifteen minutes. And I got so tickled that Stringbean got broke up, and he was not supposed to laugh. . . . I looked backstage, and there was Bill Monroe and Honey Wiles— Honey was a great big fat guy—and they were backstage . . . lying on the ground just holding their stomachs—dying laughing. I'll tell you right now, we really tore that audience apart, and all I had to do the rest of the show was just ask Stringbean, 'What did you say the name of the town was where your farm was?'

"He would play the deadpan part, and I would play the kind of smart alecky part, you know. We worked together for two years. And he was a fine feller. And we never had a cross word the whole time."

As a bandleader, Bill Monroe was a notoriously strict taskmaster, a contrast to the laid-back, lackadaisical Stringbean. In late 1945, String decided to form a duo act with fellow Opry singer and humorist Lew Childre, "The Boy from Alabam." His replacement in the Blue Grass Boys was Earl Scruggs, the man whose revolutionary banjo playing paved the way for the creation of the style we now know as bluegrass music.

By this time, Stringbean's costume consisted of an extra-long nightshirt, pants that buckled at his knees, and a small gray felt hat. He topped it all off with a molasses-mouth delivery and a hang-dog facial expression. With his permanently bewildered visage and Chaplinesque demeanor, people smiled at the very sight of him. "The Boy from Alabam" and "Stringbean, the Kentucky Wonder," as he was billed, worked together for three years, after which Stringbean became a solo entertainer on the Grand Ole Opry. He appeared on Red Foley's NBC-broadcast portion of the show for several years.

"A man who plays the five-string banjo has got it made," he would drawl to delighted Opry audiences. "It never interferes with any of the pleasures of his life."

Veteran Opry star Uncle Dave Macon took Stringbean under his wing, teaching him banjo tunes and gags. At his death in 1952, the old man willed the younger performer one of his banjos. String played it on his Uncle Dave Macon tribute album of 1963.

"Uncle Dave was the greatest entertainer I've ever known," Stringbean said. "He would play to an audience forty-five minutes and then have to go back for seven or eight encores. It takes a hoss to do that."

When Grandpa Jones and his wife Ramona arrived at the Opry in 1946, Stringbean and Estelle became their closest friends. The couples bought a 143-acre farm together with two houses near Ridgetop, Tennessee, at the northern edge of Davidson County. By choice, Stringbean and Estelle lived in the smaller house, a three-room red cottage heated by a fireplace. All four of them loved to hunt and fish, and Grandpa recalled that Stringbean could imitate a quail's whistle so perfectly that any nearby birds would answer him. Offstage, Stringbean was a man of few words who cherished his solitude in the countryside.

"Stringbean really only liked two kinds of people," Ramona Jones remembered, "real country people from the Opry, and other sportsmen, hunters and fishermen."

"Anyplace you'd see Grandpa, you'd see String," recalled *Hee*

*Haw* producer Sam Lovullo. "They played banjo duets on the show, and whenever String was scheduled to be on, he'd come into my office with a pipe sticking out of his mouth and say, 'Hey, boss, I got a letter from home . . .' which I always found hilarious.

"One day I said, 'String, tell you what. You don't need any makeup, just be in the studio at three. I'll put the gang there, you read one of those letters and we'll see how it works.' That's how he became a regular on *Hee Haw* [in 1969]."

This recurring bit began with Stringbean announcing that he had a letter "close to my heart, my heart, my heart," touching first his chest pocket, then various other pockets until he found it in his rear-end pocket. Another of his features on the show had him as a sad-sack "scarecrow" delivering his self-deprecating one-liners in a cornfield with a puppet crow.

Despite his Opry popularity, Stringbean didn't begin recording solo albums until the 1960s. His most popular tunes included "Chewing Gum," "I Wonder Where Wanda Went," "Run, Rabbit, Run," "I'm the Man That Rode the Mule Around the World," "Hot Corn, Cold Corn," and "Y'all Come."

At the time of his death, he was at the peak of his popularity. His appearances on the highly rated CBS TV series and folk musicians' newfound regard for his old-time playing style and repertoire had led to bookings on college campuses as well as at county fairs.

"Kids are goin' for it now," the star observed to an interviewer backstage at his last Opry broadcast. "They know more about the old tunes than I do, and I've been playin' 'em all my life. They dig up the history of them old songs—where they came from—the old folk songs. I don't know where they get it all."

Cowboy star Tex Ritter (1905–1974) introduced Stringbean on that last Opry show. "Since being on *Hee Haw,* his price has gone up and his pantaloons have gone down a little," Tex quipped. He later recalled, "I had to bring him back for an encore. A lot of young people were screaming."

Over the years, backstage, several of the show's cast members had cautioned Stringbean about his habit of carrying large amounts of cash. At the Ryman that night, comic Oscar Sullivan's wife spoke with Estelle about it.

"One time, I saw him with five or six thousand dollars," recalled Opry star Bill Carlisle. "I told him someone might see it and hurt him or steal it."

Bill Carlisle, Tex Ritter, Oscar Sullivan, Porter Wagoner, The Willis Brothers, Ben Smathers, Bill Anderson, Dolly Parton, Roy Acuff, and other members of the Opry cast gathered for the funeral on November 13, 1973. So did more than six hundred onlookers. The news media, understandably in a frenzy about the awful crime, were there in full force, asking the Opry stars about the man they mourned.

"He lived to make people laugh, and he did just that," said Grandpa Jones.

"I never heard him say a cuss word," remarked Bill Monroe, the man who had brought Stringbean to the Opry stage. "Everyone will miss him. He gave everybody a lot of laughs, you know."

Stringbean and Estelle were buried in Goodlettsville, Tennessee. The graves of country greats Hawkshaw Hawkins, Cowboy Copas, Randy Hughes, and Jack Anglin are nearby. All of them had also died violently.

The sadness at the Opry continued for weeks after Stringbean's death. On November 27, 1973, Hank Snow's guitarist, James P. Widner, was robbed and murdered at the downtown Nashville Holiday Inn. On January 2, 1974, beloved Tex Ritter, the man who'd hosted Stringbean's last Opry show, died of a heart attack.

By then, a massive police investigation into the Stringbean case was well under way. This was chronicled in Warren B. Causey's 1975 book *The Stringbean Murders*. Two twenty-three-year-old cousins were eventually arrested, tried, and convicted. As it turned out, all Doug Brown and John Brown stole was a chainsaw, Stringbean's gun collection, one of his costumes, and about $250 in cash. They overlooked the $3,182 that was in the bib pocket of the star's overalls. After he shot Estelle, John Brown walked back to the house grinning, with her handbag in his hand. He'd overlooked the

$2,150 she had tucked in her bra. Stringbean's guns eventually tied the Browns to the murders.

At the trial, the testimony of Grandpa Jones was crucial. The prosecuting attorney laid a trap by almost casually asking Grandpa to identify Stringbean's guns. The Browns' attorney quickly snapped, "Mr. Jones, how do you know those are Stringbean's guns?" The star's response was practically a soliloquy for the jurors.

"Stringbean was my friend," replied Grandpa, his voice welling with emotion. "Every Saturday night after the Opry, he would drive home. During the summer, he would get his fishing gear and head out to the lake. During the hunting season, he would go hunting. He would stay out Sunday and come home sometime on Monday.

"Now, one would think that someone who could perform so well on the banjer as well as Stringbean could, would have the mechanical ability to do all kinds of things with his hands, but Stringbean couldn't. He could not clean his own guns.

"So, every Tuesday morning in the fall, I would go over to his cabin and sit with him on the front porch and clean his guns. See that shotgun there? It has a scar on the stock from a barbed wire fence. There is a chip in the handle of that pistol.

"I knew he could not take the guns apart and put them back together. And I knew if they weren't clean, there might be a misfire or some kind of accident. I did not want to see Stringbean hurt, so I took it on myself to take care of those guns. I have cleaned them hundreds of times.

"You see, Stringbean was my friend."

"It was one of those rare moments in the courtroom when everybody stops breathing," wrote John C. McLemore, who covered the trial for *The Nashville Banner*. "There was absolute silence.

"We had seen a funny old man from television just wring the color out of one of Nashville's top criminal lawyers. Every word was calculated to create high drama, and every word—including the country pronunciation of the word 'banjo'—had hit home.

"It was a performance fit for the London stage. . . . But more than that, I knew I had seen a man who knew what it meant to have a friend and to be a friend."

At another point in the trial, John Brown attempted an insanity defense. His father testified that as a child he'd pulled the wings off birds and cut the tails off cats. The ploy didn't work. Both men were sentenced to life in prison. Both were denied parole in 1993.

In 1997, a reported $20,000 was discovered behind the mantel in Stringbean's chimney. By then, the currency was so mouse-eaten and rotted that it was worthless. A year later, Stringbean's best friend, Louis M. "Grandpa" Jones, passed away at age eighty-four.

Doug Brown died of natural causes in the penitentiary in 2003. Later that year, the Stringbean murders were profiled on the A&E cable network program *City Confidential*. John Brown, the gunman, was scheduled for a parole hearing in July 2008.

Stringbean's pretaped appearances on *Hee Haw* continued to air for several months after his death. During the next twenty-five years of the program's life, the camera would sometimes pan across the cornfield set, pausing silently in tribute at the spot where the lovable comic had stood.

Archie Campbell, his fellow *Hee Haw* cast member, summed up the feelings of many: "String was the greatest guy in the world. I never heard him say one mean thing about another human being. He was really fine."

Cousin Wilbur concurred, stating, "Stringbean was a fine fellow. I never heard him say anything against nobody."

When the new Opry House opened the year after Stringbean's death, a dogwood tree was planted on its landscaped grounds with a marker identifying it as a memorial to the fallen star. The last song that Stringbean sang was "I'm Going to the Grand Ole Opry to Make Myself a Name."

# A Lesson in Leavin'

The Grand Ole Opry's Dottie West was the envy of other female singers for her deeply emotional performances. But one of her most shattering was one she was quite ashamed of, and the performance wasn't sung.

The glamorous star was a proud beauty, but there she was on national television, weeping openly on *Entertainment Tonight* in August 1990. The bank had foreclosed on her Nashville mansion and seized her Corvette and her possessions to satisfy her debts.

"It's just devastating," she said through tears during the broadcast. "I never thought it would come to this. I thought I could handle it. I thought I could pay. This was home. They can't take my songs or my music away. They can't do that. But they've hurt me deeply."

The experience was humiliating. Just days later, Dottie was admitting how sorry she was that people had seen her so defeated.

"I was so embarrassed when the show came on," she said. "When the TV crew got to the house, I was in the middle of packing, and they had just shown the house for the first time. I'd been crying. But it's not like I'm crying every day.

"I'm not saying it's been easy, but I'll go on. I know how to make money, and I'll make it. I'm a survivor. You can knock me down, but you better have a big rock to keep me there.

"So many of my friends have called and offered to help. I have too much pride for that." She did accept duet partner Kenny Rogers's gift of a Chrysler for transportation.

"These are just material things," she added. "I don't love things. I love people. I am going to be fine."

Just a year later, Dottie West was dead at age fifty-eight following an automobile crash en route to the Opry. During her eventful life, she had overcome many adversities. But she was never able to erase that indignity she suffered late in her career.

Born Dorothy Marie Marsh on October 11, 1932, Dottie was raised on a farm near McMinnville, Tennessee, in a community called Frog Pond. She was the eldest of ten children and was expected to take on adult responsibilities at an early age. Despite the backbreaking farm labor, the family remained desperately poor. At one point, the only nourishment the Marshes had for three days were blackberries the children gathered in the woods.

"I knew that we were poor. There were times when I was even embarrassed about it. We were so poor that Mother would ask me to ask for some of the commodities at school. And I just had too much pride to do that. I would pass it on to my brother, and ask him if he would ask. I would help him carry the groceries, but I had too much pride to ask for a handout. I've always been very determined.

"I think I got it from my mother. She was also a real lady. I can remember one day I was whistling while Mama and I were making the beds. She was on one side, and I was on the other. And she told me, 'Ladies don't whistle. Don't you ever let me hear you doing that again.' To this day, when I start to whistle, I'll think, 'Oh, no.'

"The absolute, real country music—bluegrass—is what I first learned to play. I played the upright bass and the rhythm guitar. My dad played the mandolin and the fiddle. I wrote two songs when I was eleven years old."

Music was one of the only good things her father, Hollis Marsh, ever gave her. Hollis drank, and he physically abused his daughter throughout her childhood.

"My dad was a mean drunk. I mean, when he was drinking, he would beat us. And that's just inhuman. I try to forget about that part of my life."

Dottie never spoke of this publicly during her lifetime, but by the time she was in her teens, he was regularly sexually molesting her as well. At fifteen, she miscarried a child by him. On her seventeenth birthday, he informed her that she was quitting school and moving with him to Detroit, where he could find work at Ford. She broke down, sobbing uncontrollably at school, and confessed all to her principal. Hollis Marsh was arrested, convicted, and sentenced to forty years in prison. While incarcerated, he killed a fellow inmate.

Mama Pelina Marsh moved herself and her children into McMinnville. After subsisting on welfare, both she and Dottie took jobs as waitresses. Dottie spent the rest of her high school years doing that as well as singing in her first country band, The Coonskins.

She earned a scholarship to attend Tennessee Tech in Cookeville, where she majored in music. She continued to work in restaurants and clerked in a flower shop to pay her way through school. She also joined The Tech Two-by-Fours, whose steel guitarist was Bill West. Dottie had met Bill her first day on campus, and they were married by the time she was a sophomore. After Bill graduated with his electrical engineering degree, he and Dottie and their two young sons, Morris and Kerry, moved to Cleveland, Ohio. Daughter Shelly was born there in 1958. Shelly would one day emulate her mother as a chart-topping country vocalist.

"There was a TV show called *Landmark Jamboree* in Cleveland, Ohio," Dottie recalled. "Kathy Dearth [billed as "Kathy Dee"] was a singer on it, and so was I. When we would do a duet, they called us The Kay-Dots. Kathy had sugar diabetes. It was diagnosed when she was eleven years old, and they told her she might live to be thirty. She fooled 'em and lived a full life," before dying in 1968 at age thirty-five.

"I came home for a vacation one time from Cleveland, back to Nashville. We would come home whenever we had two weeks off from the show and also Bill's work as an electrical engineer. As we were leaving, we went back north on Dickerson Road, because the freeway wasn't finished. This was in 1959. The Starday Records studio was on the way. And I just said, 'Bill, just pull in right here. I'm going in there, and I hope they'll listen to me.' I took my guitar in there. I said, 'I really am gonna make hit records. I am gonna be a singer in Nashville. And this is the only thing I have to show you. It's a scrapbook of the TV show that I do.' That's the way it started. I auditioned live.

"[Producer] Tommy Hill said, 'Come back with some money, and we will do this.' So we went back to Cleveland, saved some money, borrowed some more, came back, and I went into the studio and made a record. It's funny, looking back, I don't even think I realized how tough it might be. When you're building and you're young, you're not afraid. Especially if you're dedicated and goin' for it. I had no doubt that I could be a top singer. I don't mean to sound self-centered with that. I'm talking about determination and ambition. I'm just not lazy I will go for it. I will work."

"Angel on Paper," her first Starday single, got enough airplay in Nashville to earn her an invitation to appear as a guest on the Grand Ole Opry. She'd been listening to the show all her life and said, "That was when my dream was fulfilled." To further her career, Bill quit his job, and the family moved to Nashville in 1961. A year later, she had her fourth child, Dale. Dottie wanted it all—motherhood, being a wife, having a career, stardom, being a homemaker, having friends. Living in a community of composers inspired her to add another role, songwriter.

"I didn't start writing songs again until 1961, the year I moved back to Nashville. That was after I'd started spending time with writers. During the TV show [in Cleveland], I would get to work with Opry singers, because they would have some as the guest stars every week. I'd get to talkin' with them and would have them out to my house and cook for them. And so through meeting Roger Miller, Red Sovine, Carl Smith and people like that, I started writing.

"Really, the first song I ever wrote was called 'Is This Me.' I finally got enough nerve to put it down on tape one night for [steel guitarist] Pete Drake. And sure enough, I couldn't believe it, Jim Reeves recorded it."

The song became a big hit for Opry star Reeves in early 1963. By then, Dottie had recorded for Atlantic as well as Starday. But she'd still scored no hits as a singer. Even so, Reeves producer Chet Atkins loved Dottie's voice and signed her to RCA Records.

"Dottie really was the best female singer we had in this town," Chet recalled fondly. "And everybody knew it. She sang with so much feeling and musical abandon. When she improvised on a melody, she usually improved it a hell of a lot, because she put so much feeling in it. She was an original."

"I think I was most influenced by Patsy Cline," Dottie said. "There was so much feeling there. At one time or another, she must have helped all of us girl singers who were starting out. Patsy was always giving her friends things [like] the scrapbook of clippings and mementos Patsy gave me weeks before she was killed. When I got home, I was leafing through it, and there was a check for $75 with a note saying, 'I know you been having a hard time.' It was the money I needed to pay the rent. She was the consummate singer, the consummate human being."

The two women shared their deepest emotions and most private secrets. Like Dottie, Patsy Cline had been sexually abused by her father.

A year after Patsy's death in a plane crash, Dottie was on the charts with her first top-ten hit, 1964's duet with Jim Reeves, "Love Is No Excuse." Her second single that year was her self-penned heartache ballad "Here Comes My Baby." It became the first female country record to win a Grammy Award and led to her being invited to join the cast of the Grand Ole Opry.

"I met her in I think it was late 1963 or early 1964," recalls her fellow Opry star Jeannie Seely. "I was living in Los Angeles at the time, and she had come there to do some shows. In fact, Dottie tried to encourage me to move to Nashville before I did. Our friendship is something that I just truly feel blessed with. We shared so many great times. She was like a sister to me. She was somebody I could call late at night after everybody else had gone to bed. She'd wake up and talk to me. She was wonderful, and I miss her." Jeannie's smoldering vocal style was influenced by the passion in Dottie's recorded performances.

Dottie's voice throbbed with heartache and yearning on such hits as "Would You Hold It Against Me" (1966), "Paper Mansions" (1967), "Country Girl" (1968), and "Forever Yours" (1970). She also recorded memorable duets with Don Gibson (1969's "Rings of Gold") and Jimmy Dean (1971's "Slowly"). The Dean association, in particular, fired her ambitions.

"I'm never satisfied. I'm always trying to do better. I guess I've always loved a challenge. I remember that I was really nervous when I played the Landmark Hotel in Las Vegas with Jimmy Dean, with an orchestra, back in '71. That's when I met Elvis.

"I broke into Vegas a little bit at a time. I guess I was ready for it, psychologically. Next, I had to work downtown at The Golden Nugget, the country place. That's where I met Barbara Mandrell the first time. Anyway, I took it one step at a time. I knew I wanted to build a show to where I could be a headliner."

There were setbacks along the way. On April 21, 1967, Dottie was getting ready for an Opry appearance when she learned that her father had died in prison. Burying her conflicting emotions, she went ahead with her performance, telling no one.

In 1969, her home burned to the ground, and her marriage to Bill West ended. She married drummer Byron Metcalf in 1972. He was twelve years her junior. Dottie was afraid the fans would disapprove, but instead she acquired a sexy new image. Her second marriage ended in divorce in 1980.

In the meantime, her recorded performances became ever more saturated with soul. "Careless Hands" (1971), "Lonely Is" (1971), "Six Weeks Every Summer" (1971), "I'm Only a Woman" (1972), and "House of Love" (1974) were examples of the Nashville Sound at its finest. She discovered and boosted younger talents, such as

Steve Wariner, Jeannie Seely, and Larry Gatlin, the last of whom can be heard singing background vocals on her aching recording of his song "Once You Were Mine."

She was unusual in her time as a female country singer who also wrote. Dottie penned eight of her singles, including "Didn't I," "What's Come Over My Baby," "Mommy Can I Still Call Him Daddy," and "Clinging to My Baby's Hand." In the 1970s, she was hired to write and sing a series of ad jingles for Coca-Cola. One of them, 1973's "Country Sunshine," became a big hit single and won her a Clio Award, the advertising world's top honor.

Dottie West was on hand for the Grand Ole Opry's farewell show at the Ryman Auditorium on March 15, 1974. And she was at the new Opry House the following night, when the venerable show premiered there.

In 1976, she signed a new recording contract with United Artists and subsequently enjoyed the biggest hits of her career. In 1978–1984, Dottie topped the charts as the duet partner of Kenny Rogers. Their hits "Every Time Two Fools Collide," "Anyone Who Isn't Me Tonight," "All I Ever Need Is You," "Til I Can Make it on My Own," "What Are We Doin' in Love," and "Together Again" led to Country Music Association awards as Duo of the Year in 1978 and 1979. Daughter Shelly teamed up with singer David Frizzell to earn those same prizes in 1981 and 1982.

"I see a lot of me in her now," Dottie said proudly of Shelly. "She's so gung-ho, so professional."

Dottie made history in 1978 when she and Kenny Rogers co-hosted what was billed as "The World's Largest Indoor Country Music Show" at the Silverdome in Pontiac, Michigan. The four-hour event, which became an NBC television special, drew more than sixty thousand fans.

"This looks to me like we've got a country Woodstock," she quipped onstage. "I've never seen this many people in one place in my life."

In 1980–1981, Dottie West got her first number-one hits as a solo artist with "A Lesson in Leavin'" and "Are You Happy Baby."

She caught the eye as well as the ears. Dottie had a facelift and other cosmetic surgeries. She bought ever more elaborate and expensive costumes, including a memorable white satin cowgirl ensemble featuring skintight pants and an unbuttoned blouse. She wore it on the cover of her 1981 album titled, naturally, *Wild West*. In 1983 she appeared in a peek-a-boo photo spread in the naughty men's magazine *Oui*.

"I have a healthy attitude about sex," she commented. "I do. You know what? I have had not one bad letter [about the *Oui* spread]. Not one. In fact, now I get all these love letters.

"I've grown so much, and I'm still growing. The business is more challenging than it's ever been, and I look forward to it all. It's twenty years later, and I'm still doing three hundred dates a year. I want to do movies and lots more. I just don't feel my age, so don't expect me to act it."

Later in 1983, she married sound technician Alan Winters. He was twenty-eight; she was fifty. She installed a mirror over her brass bed and zipped around Music City in snazzy cars. Also in 1982–1983, Dottie toured as the lead, the bordello madam, in the saucy musical *The Best Little Whorehouse in Texas*. She took acting roles on television's *Love Boat* and *The Dukes of Hazzard,* and she hosted *Solid Gold*.

By this time Dottie West had one of the flashiest and splashiest stage shows on the road. As she had vowed, she was a Las Vegas and Atlantic City showroom star. She spent a reported $100,000 a year on clothes, favoring the custom couture of Cher's over-the-top designer Bob Mackie. She bought a white Rolls Royce. She and Alan were filmed in her mansion for an episode of TV's *Lifestyles of the Rich and Famous*. Dottie pointedly told the camera how drastically her surroundings contrasted with those of her impoverished upbringing.

"Poor wasn't the word," she said. "I picked cotton, stripped cane, shelled beans. . . . My father was an alcoholic."

On April 13, 1985, Dottie West was among the cast members chosen to star at the Grand Ole Opry the night of its debut as a live weekly television show on The Nashville Network (TNN). Fabulously attired, as always, she laughed and gossiped with her fellow Opry stars, her cascading auburn tresses radiant even in the dim light backstage.

"I've been spending more time here lately," Dottie said softly. "I've realized how much I've missed it."

When bluegrass patriarch Bill Monroe approached her, she stood and embraced him warmly. Onstage, Ed Bruce began singing "Everything's a Waltz," so the two Opry stars began swaying to the music in each other's arms in the wings. Others on the TNN cablecast that night included Roy Acuff and Dottie's buddy Minnie Pearl. Onstage, the glamorous redhead offered "A Lesson in Leavin'," "Here Comes My Baby," and other signature songs to the cheering Opry fans.

Sadly, that Grand Ole Opry show was one of the last of Dottie West's triumphs. Her singles stopped making the popularity charts later that year, and after 1986, her concert bookings dwindled. In 1988, she separated from third husband Alan Winters. Then she discovered that her financial manager had horribly mishandled her money.

"I can spend money real quick—I'm real good at that," she admitted in a 1984 interview. "I know ways to use money, yes. The best thing is to learn how to use money and not abuse it. As far as being a businesswoman and all that, I'm a Libra, and we love to spend money. And there's been times that maybe I spent it in a way that I shouldn't. But I've always enjoyed it. And with good health, I'll just keep on working and make more, and hope to make more people happy."

Her third divorce became final in January 1990. She filed for bankruptcy in August and faced money-seeking lawsuits from both her ex-husband and her ex-manager. Her possessions were seized in the summer of 1990 to satisfy a $1.3 million debt to the Internal Revenue Service. Then came the humiliating *Entertainment Tonight* appearance.

In March 1991, officials discovered two storage facilities and a condo full of crates of valuables she'd hidden from the creditors. These were confiscated and auctioned off during that June's Fan Fair celebration. Dottie attended, bidding on her own possessions. In July 1991 she was involved in a car accident that lacerated her nose, resulting in missed concerts whose proceeds she badly needed.

"It's not easy being a woman alone," said manager Wayne Oliver sympathetically at the time. "You work for years, and you wake up one morning and everything's gone."

On August 30, 1991, Dottie West began driving from her West End Nashville condominium to the Opry House for a Friday-night appearance. But the Kenny Rogers Chrysler broke down just a few blocks from home. George Thackston, eighty-one, stopped to see if he could help. Because she was running late for her Opry date, he volunteered to drive her to the show.

As he entered the exit ramp that leads from Briley Parkway to the Opry House, he was going 55 miles an hour, more than double the posted speed limit. Thackston lost control of the vehicle, which went 180 feet across the grass, struck an embankment, flew 80 feet through the air, and nose-dived into the earth. The reckless driver survived. The star lost massive amounts of blood and suffered grave injuries to her liver, spleen, and neck. She died at Vanderbilt University Medical Center during surgery on September 4, 1991.

"I find it hard to even accept right now that Dottie is gone," says her fellow Opry star Jan Howard. "All that talent and all that love for life and for her fellow man, gone. The night that she had the accident, we were both on the same portion of the Opry, or supposed to be. Dottie was supposed to be on first, and I was down toward the last of that segment. They came and said, 'Janny, c-can you go on now?' And I said, 'Sure.' I just thought, 'Well, Dottie's late,' you know? But that's when she had the wreck. I don't accept it to this day that she isn't here. She's going to be here forever. And forever beautiful. So good inside. And so talented, so darn talented. It was so tragic."

Duane Allen of the Oak Ridge Boys said, "It's sad when someone who contributed so much in such a positive way has to die in such a tragic way."

Kenny Rogers eulogized, "What made Dottie unique is that when she sang about pain, she felt pain; when she sang about love, she felt love; and when she sang about beauty, she felt that beauty. While some performers sang words, she sang emotions. She lived her songs."

"It's like losing a member of the family," said Roger Miller. "She was the sister we all loved. Dottie was a songwriter's friend. I remember the early days when Willie [Nelson], Justin Tubb, Hank Cochran, and I would get together at her house and play our new songs. It's hard to lose a member of the old gang."

Larry Gatlin recalled that she sent him the one-way airplane ticket that brought him to Nashville: "She was the first person who believed in me as a songwriter. If it had not been for Dorothy Marie [West], Larry Wayne [Gatlin] would probably have been a bad lawyer somewhere in Houston."

Dottie's best friend at the Opry was Jeannie Seely, who reminisced, "She recorded one of my songs in 1964, before I ever moved here. That gave me the encouragement to move here. I can't walk through my house without seeing Dottie. She's everywhere, from pictures on the wall to the clothes in my closet. Dottie was always my hero."

Dottie hired Steve Wariner for her band when he was seventeen and brought him to Nashville as well. "She went the extra mile for me, when I was just starting out in the music business," Steve recalled. "She taught me a lot about singing, entertaining, and how you should never take your fans for granted. I'll always remember her warmth and kindness."

The funeral was held on September 7, 1991. Johnny Cash, Emmylou Harris, the Gatlin Brothers, Porter Wagoner, Billy Walker, Bill Carlisle, Connie Smith, Hal Durham, and the rest of her Opry family gathered to say good-bye. Steve Wariner stood and sang a lonesome, mournful "Amazing Grace" during the service.

"She said she always wanted to dance with the angels and sing in the angel band," said the Reverend Ray Hughes. "Family, it's happening today."

They buried Dottie West back home in McMinnville at the Mount View Cemetery. Her likeness is etched onto one side of her tombstone with the inscription "Our Country Sunshine." On the reverse of the monument are the opening lines of her hit "Country Girl":

"I was born a country girl.

I will die a country girl.

My world is made of blue skies and sunshine, green fields and butterflies.

I'm so glad I'm a country girl."

# Barbara and Ken

**B**arbara Mandrell was just fourteen years old when her husband fell for her—in most states, that would have made her "jailbait."

"No, it's called 'San Quentin quail' in California," says husband Ken Dudney with a chuckle. "I don't know what I was thinking. I tell everyone that I must have been emotionally retarded back in those days. I was twenty-one years old, and she's fourteen years old. I see this pretty little blonde girl come into the room. I had no idea she was fourteen. She looked a lot older than that. She had legs on her that were a lot older than that, I can tell you. And big bouffant hair."

"Aqua Net hairspray kept it there," Barbara interjects.

"It was unbelievable," Ken continues. "And I was engaged to another girl at the time."

The year was 1963. By then, Barbara was already a semiprofessional country musician. Born December 25, 1948, she was billed at age eleven as "The Princess of the Steel Guitar" when she played Las Vegas with Joe and Rose Lee Maphis, Tex Ritter, Cowboy Copas, and other stars in the summer of 1960. During that summer vacation, she also toured for two weeks in a package show with Johnny Cash, Patsy Cline, George Jones, Don Gibson, Gordon Terry, and

June Carter, and made appearances on the Los Angeles country television show *Town Hall Party*.

Convinced that his daughter could become a full-fledged attraction, papa Irby Mandrell formed the Mandrell Family Band to back her at shows he booked at California military bases. Barbara sang and played steel guitar and saxophone. Irby was the rhythm guitarist and emcee. Mother Mary played bass. Bill Hendricks played sax and clarinet. Brian Lonbeck played lead guitar. College student Ken Dudney was hired to play drums.

Although barely out of childhood, Barbara was wildly jealous of Ken's fiancée, a beautiful ballet dancer his own age. To this day, she becomes green-eyed when she thinks of her.

He explains his wife's temperament by saying, "Barbara is an extremely creative person. I was engaged to a ballet dancer, a creative person. They're very high-strung human beings. They're very self-willed."

"Are you comparing me to your ex?" she snaps. "That fiancée I took you away from?"

> Ken: *"See? Forty-four years later!"*
> Barbara: *"I'm still so jealous of that woman."*
> Ken: *"She was pretty."*
> Barbara: *"But I got him."*

To disguise the fact that they were falling in love, Barbara and Ken pretended not to like each other in front of her parents. He teased her unmercifully.

"In the clubs when we'd be on break or something, he'd say to me, 'Would you like to dance?'" Barbara recalls. "I'd say, 'Yes.' He'd say, 'Keep sitting there, and maybe somebody will ask you.' I fell for it every time!

"I think the reason we would yell and scream at each other is because we very much tried to mislead people closest to us, like my mother, my father and the other musicians in the group. So we would be kind of not nice to each other, so they would not know that we were in love. Then we got in the habit of it. It stemmed from that.

"I'm really happy the way we are. That's very much a Mandrell and Dudney way. We don't clam up. We don't do the silent treatment. We just yell and scream. Get it over with. Say it."

"We're both Type A personalities," adds Ken. "We're even the same blood type.

"We see couples who are just so bland in their personalities with each other. They never argue about anything. It's 'Whatever you want, Dear.' And we're going, 'Man, those are the dumbest boring people I've ever seen in my life.'"

Barbara and Ken's courtship was volatile from the start. They bickered and argued, made up, and bickered again.

"When we were dating, everything I would do, I was thinking about him," Barbara recalls. "I would sit in class when I was supposed to be listening, and I would be practicing writing 'Mrs. Ken Dudney.' 'Mrs. Barbara Dudney.' I mean, I was possessed."

"When we were first dating, I had the most horrendous jealous demeanor," Ken confesses. "Jealousy is a sickness. It was terrible. We would break up because we would fight. I remember she had a date with another guy one time. I stood across the street in the neighbor's bushes waiting for her to come home. How horrible is that? But I got over that. I have no idea how. Maybe with the help of God.

"It's a good thing, too, because there's a lot of hugging in show business."

When she was sixteen, he bought her an engagement ring: "I wasn't going to let her have it, but she just begged me for it. I was going off to navy flight school—the superhuman beings of the world: I was going to be a naval aviator. She wanted something to remember me by when I'm gone. So I let her have it. I didn't know if she'd wear it."

Barbara kept it in her room in a dresser drawer during the day. At night, she put it on to sleep with it. When she went off to high school, back it went into the drawer. One morning, she forgot and left it out. Her mother found it. When Barbara got home from school that day, her parents lit into her. They insisted she return the ring to Ken's mother. Irby called Ken at a navy base in Florida and threatened to get him in trouble with the commanding officer. Ken was instructed not to call, write, or have any further contact with Barbara. Both agreed to date others.

"I was on *The Dating Game* TV show," Barbara reports. "If you count that date, I had seven different guys that I dated in my life. Six of whom—not *The Dating Game* guy—proposed. What can I say?"

"Some of them even proposed marriage," Ken wisecracks.

Just before Barbara turned eighteen, Ken came home on leave. He proposed. She knew the Mandrells were scheduled to return to Vietnam for their second tour entertaining the troops, so she chose May 28, 1967, as their wedding date. It was ten days before her high school graduation and two weeks before she was scheduled to fly to Asia. She spent her honeymoon studying for her science test so she could graduate. Ken tutored her.

She headed for Vietnam. He traveled to his naval assignment in Washington State. Barbara Mandrell made a record that year called "Queen for a Day" that was fairly successful. But when she returned stateside, the eighteen-year-old vowed she was quitting show business to become a navy wife.

Barbara dutifully studied navy protocol and tended to cooking and cleaning while Ken flew jumbo jets off an aircraft carrier. Her housewife days ended in 1968, when Ken was deployed for nine months aboard a carrier in the Mediterranean Sea.

She went to visit her parents, who were in Nashville by then. They took her to the Grand Ole Opry. She saw Dolly Parton there. That was it. Barbara Mandrell decided that she wanted to get back into music. She phoned her husband overseas to tell him of her decision.

"I had no concept of what that was," Ken says. "That didn't mean anything to me. I just thought, 'Okay, she wants to play music again. That's fine.' See, we had no concept, or I had not anyway, of what being a star meant."

"I had done the TV thing, and I had done the tour with Johnny Cash thing, but I didn't realize," she agrees. "I just knew that music was fun, and that I enjoyed it. And people were nice to me and would say nice things. So this is what I want to do. When I saw the Opry, I thought, 'I can do that.' I didn't see the hard work and the sacrifice."

Although he loved the navy, Ken resigned. He joined Barbara in Nashville and began to give flying lessons. Then he became a pilot for the State of Tennessee, in charge of transporting its governors in its private Leer jet. For the first few years of his wife's musical career, Ken Dudney was the family's chief breadwinner.

Fiddler-singer Louise Mandrell joined her older sister on the road in 1969. That was the same year that Barbara Mandrell debuted on the national country charts with her "blue-eyed soul" version of Otis Redding's "I've Been Loving You Too Long."

The family band was barely making ends meet when Barbara learned that she was pregnant, in 1970. She was taking birth control pills but slipped up one day.

"I forgot to take it. So I took two the next day. It doesn't work that way.

"We knew we couldn't afford to have a baby, but God knew differently. It was mixed emotions, because I was so grateful and so excited and yet so scared, because this was at a very critical time for us. If we could get three [show] dates a month, minimum, we could hang on and pay the bills."

"We didn't make any money from her career for quite a while," Ken explains. "Every dime she made went back into the business, back into the show. That's why I went to work as a pilot for the State of Tennessee."

"We didn't have any maternity insurance, because we weren't going to get pregnant," Barbara continues. "We found out that, back then, babies cost around $800 if you shared a room with somebody. We managed to save $800. But then I had to have a Caesarian section, $1,300. We had to pay for Matthew on time!"

"Several times, we tried to give him back," Ken quips. "We've not paid. You take him back."

Not long after son Matt's birth in 1970, Barbara Mandrell had her first big solo hits, "Tonight My Baby's Coming Home" (1971) and "Show Me" (1972). She was invited to join the Grand Ole Opry cast and became a member in July 1972.

"When I first started doing the Opry, Roy Acuff didn't know who I was any more than the man in the moon," she recalls. "But I was very fortunate, because Tex Ritter was still with us. I had known Mr. Ritter since I was eleven. He gave me probably by far the most incredible introductions I've ever received in my life.

"Because of their scheduling, they began putting me on Roy Acuff's portion of the show. As we got to know each other, we became so close. When he and Bud Wendell inducted me, I thought, literally, 'It doesn't get any better than this.'

"I remember, one night [in 1982] the song I had out was 'Till You're Gone.' It had a saxophone part in it. But I wasn't going to sing it on the Opry, because I didn't want to do it without playing my sax."

At the time, the Opry frowned on bringing "noncountry" instruments onto its stage. And of the show's cast members, no one was more traditional than Roy Acuff.

"All of a sudden, there was a knock on the dressing-room door. Daddy says, 'Mr. Acuff wants to see you.' I'm paraphrasing here, but what he said to me was precious. He said, 'I want you to go get that saxophone, and I want you to do that hit song of yours right now.' I said, 'Mr. Acuff, I don't need to. I can do other songs.' He said, 'No, you got that hit record, and you go play it.' He totally made me [take the sax onto the Opry stage]. I couldn't believe it. Mr. Acuff introduced me, and I did the song. If somebody else would have told me that story, or if I hadn't lived it, I wouldn't believe it."

Barbara scored a major breakthrough with the sexually frank "The Midnight Oil" in 1973. To this day, it is considered a landmark recording in the annals of female country music. "This Time I Almost Made It" (1974) and "Standing Room Only" (1975) continued her momentum.

After daughter Jaime's birth in 1976, Barbara's career went into overdrive. "Married But Not to Each Other" (1977), "Woman to Woman" (1977), "Sleeping Single in a Double Bed" (1978), "(If Loving You Is Wrong) I Don't Want to Be Right" (1979), "Years" (1980), and a flurry of other hits led to 1981's "I Was Country When Country Wasn't Cool," another of her signature songs.

She was named the Country Music Association's (CMA) Female Vocalist of the Year in 1979 and 1981 and hosted her own NBC network variety series, *Barbara Mandrell & The Mandrell Sisters,* costarring Louise and her youngest sibling Irlene, in 1980–1982. Barbara became the only woman in history to win back-to-back Country Music Association (CMA) Entertainer of the Year awards (in 1980 and 1981). She developed one of country music's flashiest stage shows, spotlighting her multi-instrumental abilities on steel guitar, sax, banjo, drums, bass, and mandolin. By 1983, she had added dazzling choreography and was a triumph in Las Vegas, billed as "The Lady Is a Champ."

But it all came to a crashing halt for country music's "golden girl" on September 11, 1984. While out on a shopping trip with Matt and Jaime in her silver Jaguar, Barbara was hit head-on by a Suburu driven by a teenager. He was killed. Barbara and her children were spared by their seat belts, but she suffered a broken right femur, a shattered right ankle, a nearly destroyed right knee, and a severe concussion that affected her personality for months.

Her subsequent 1990 best-selling autobiography *Get to the Heart* went into extensive detail about how wild her mood swings became during her recovery. Ken's patience and love were put to the test. Her head injury caused her temper to rage out of control, and she snarled, screamed, and cursed at him while he tried to nurse her back to health. Opry star Bill Anderson shared his stories about caring for his brain-injured wife, Becky, and that helped Ken to understand what his wife was going through.

Son Nathaniel was born in 1985, and the following year Barbara staged her comeback concert. Friend and fellow Opry star Dolly Parton opened for her at the Universal Amphitheater in Los Angeles. Barbara had a pin in her leg and a brace in her boot, but she danced anyway. Even today, she limps at home when she's having a bad day. But Barbara Mandrell has never done so onstage.

By the 1990s, she was playing Vegas and touring steadily again. Through it all, father Irby Mandrell remained firmly in control as his daughter's manager. Ken says he never felt in competition with his powerful father-in-law.

"He was the boss at what he did, and I did what I did," Ken states. "He handled all the road things, and I didn't. I didn't book the hotel rooms and all that kind of stuff. I had nothing to do with it. When they bought the tour bus, Barbara and her dad designed that bus, and I had nothing to do with it."

But as Irby's health declined in the early 1990s, Barbara asked Ken to step into his management shoes. It was not, he notes, an easy transition for him.

"Her dad had open-heart surgery, and he was off the road for five months, to start with. I went on the road for five months. I quit my job at the State of Tennessee to do that. And I absolutely hated the road. That bus is so tiny to me. Of course, it was a huge world to Barbara. That is where her world was. She lived there. I hated every moment of it on that bus."

Barbara remembers, "When Daddy retired and Ken moved in the last few years of my career to replace him, what was neat was he asked me if it would bother me if he went back to college. I said, 'No, it doesn't bother me.' So even though he was a busy man, he went back to get a degree in business management. Yet he had already become my manager."

Ken enrolled in Belmont University in Nashville in 1992–1993. He was, needless to say, the oldest student in his class. But he was also the best.

"It was coming up on the time for him to graduate," Barbara recalls. "But he had to go to New York with me for something concerning my career. So he wasn't there when he won the school's highest honor, Business Management Student of the Year. Why? Because he was managing! I loved it. I did tease him when I saw his graduation picture. I said, 'You look like one of the professors!'

"You can imagine that there have been many times when he's been introduced as 'Mr. Mandrell.' Or people will say, 'How does it feel to be Mr. Mandrell?' Now, there aren't a lot of men, believe me, who wouldn't be bothered by that. And there are some that would really crush."

Secure, steady, and good-humored, Ken Dudney is not one of them. During the height of her fame, he presided over her massive fan-club gatherings of three thousand or more with the aplomb of a circus ringmaster. His charm and wit have endeared him to everyone in her orbit.

Barbara Mandrell retired in late 1997. But she's just as driven as ever, seeking perfection as a gardener, interior designer, and craftsperson. She and Ken still bicker with one another. And they're still in love.

"You not only forgive, you forget," says Barbara of their spats. "There have been times when I absolutely wanted to walk out or leave him or kick him out or get him to leave me. It's over. That's it. I mean, that mad.

"But when it got right down to it, there was no way. I couldn't imagine life without him. To me, it's because God is with us. He helps us to see what's important. We keep our word. We promised 'til death do us part.

"It is so deep that there are no words for it. I've told him this over and over again. And it hasn't been too long ago that I told him again: I really hope I die first, because I cannot imagine my life without him. We are One.

"He is very witty and very funny, and I love to watch him make people laugh a lot. Sometimes he doesn't make me laugh when he's trying to make me laugh. It makes me mad sometimes, because I'm usually the thing he's joking about. But that's one of the things I fell in love with, his sense of humor.

"But most important, truly in my mind, is that God is a part of this. Ken loves our Lord Jesus Christ. He got saved and found the Lord when he was twenty-one years old. I also love it that he is such an exceptional, great father.

"When we were falling in love, 'I Left My Heart in San Francisco' by Tony Bennett was a hit," Barbara recalls. "We both worked in Daddy's band. On breaks, we'd dance, and when that song played, we just loved it.

"The deal we made is—and he's kept to it—no matter where we are, and no matter what's going on, if we hear that song, he is to turn to me and ask me to dance. No matter what. I don't care if it's in an elevator or where it is."

For their twenty-second wedding anniversary, she gave him a tiny cable car that was a music box. It plays, of course, "I Left My Heart in San Francisco." Sure enough, the first time they played it in their candlelit screened porch, he asked her to dance. When the music box wound down, Barbara and Ken woke from their private reverie to find that Matt, Jaime, and Nathan had all slipped from the room to give them their romantic privacy.

Barbara and Ken rededicated their vows on their tenth anniversary and again on their twenty-fifth.

"What are you doing on the fiftieth?" asks Ken. "I will do it then, too."

"I'll race ya," Barbara replies.

# Tribulation and Triumph

The 1980s were not kind to Bill Anderson. The decade began with the loss of his longtime recording contract. Then his fabled songwriting went into eclipse. The following years were marked by tragedy, illness, and death. A financial disaster capped his litany of tribulations.

"One day I was riding into town—and I remember exactly where I was—I was turning off Old Hickory Boulevard in Hermitage and turning onto the interstate, and I actually wondered if I had enough money to go to the grocery store to buy some groceries that I needed," recalls Bill. "And I remember thinking, 'Golly, Bill, how did it come to this?'"

Twenty years of concerts and touring, more than fifty hit records, years of television stardom, more than forty hits written for his fellow artists, membership in the Nashville Songwriters Hall of Fame, nearly fifty record albums, and glittering fame on the Grand Ole Opry stage—had it all been for nothing? He had built his career as a young man. Now he was in his forties, and everything seemed to be in tatters.

Bill's twenty-three-year recording contract with Decca/MCA came to an end in late 1981. But it was his self-imposed retirement from songwriting the following year that was far more spirit crushing.

"I had written a female song that I thought was really good," Bill remembers. "I took it to a major record producer for a major label. He had three or four of his cohorts in his office. I went in there and said, 'I think I have a hit song for a girl singer.' In front of all his friends he said, 'Well, who do you want me to play it for? Kitty Wells? Haw-haw-haw!' And everybody laughed."

Kitty Wells had been a huge country star in the 1950s, but by 1982 she had long since disappeared from the popular charts. Without even hearing the song, the producer had written it off as belonging to a bygone era.

Stung and humiliated, Bill recalls thinking, "Well, they're laughing at me now."

"That really hurt me. It wasn't like he did it in private. It was in front of a whole bunch of people. I can sit and talk about it even now and still feel how bad that hurt with all those people in that room laughing at me. My spirit had been crushed. After that, I just didn't have the heart to write songs anymore. My heart was not in it, because my heart had been broken."

Bill's songwriting heartbreak was only the beginning. In 1984, his wife Becky was critically injured in an automobile accident. She suffered severe brain injuries and spent weeks in a coma. She subsequently endured years of rehabilitation. The experience drained Bill emotionally and financially. In addition, he had to become "Mr. Mom" to their six-year-old son Jamey.

"The morning I told him about his mother's wreck, he said, 'The bad news is Mama's in the hospital. The good news is you and I get to spend more time together.'" Father and son did, indeed, bond powerfully during the next few years. After each of his appearances on the Grand Ole Opry, Bill said, "Good night, Jaybird," to his boy over the radio airwaves.

In January 1985, Bill was felled by agonizing back pain. For months, he could barely get out of bed in the mornings. Later that year, his best friend died.

"Jimmy Gately and I had more than an employer-employee relationship," Bill says. "We had to for it to last almost thirteen years.

Most musicians are gypsies at heart and not many are willing to stay in one job for that long. . . . But Jimmy was special."

Before joining Bill's band as the guitarist, fiddler, and show-opening "front man," Jimmy Gately had been a regular on TV's *Ozark Jubilee* and had written such hits as Webb Pierce's "Alla My Love" and Sonny James's "The Minute You're Gone." He was older and more experienced than Bill, so in the early years, he was the star's mentor. Bill and Jimmy cowrote "Bright Lights and Country Music," which serves as Bill Anderson's theme song to this day. By the 1980s, the two men were fishing buddies and regular golfing companions.

"The last conversation we had was on the telephone in early 1985," says Bill. "Jimmy had just returned home from a stay in the hospital, and I was confined to my bed with back pain. . . . His heart had been causing him some problems, but he felt sure the doctors had everything under control. He sounded happy to be back with his family and assured me that he'd be up and around in no time."

Less than two weeks later, on March 17, 1985, Jimmy Gately was dead at age fifty-three. Bill recalls that he "cried like a baby" when he heard the news.

In the spring of 1986, Bill's twenty-five-year-old daughter Terri was diagnosed with cancer. She survived and has remained cancer-free. But at the time, it was another agonizing episode in Bill Anderson's spiral of misfortune. As the decade ended, he learned that the failure of his PoFolks restaurant chain might ruin him financially.

"When the PoFolks restaurant thing collapsed on top of all this, the despair was certainly there," he comments. "I had been so naïve. My name was on all of these restaurant leases and all of their equipment leases [as a guarantee]. When they all fell in my lap, I thought you had to pay one hundred cents on the dollar, so I did. Then there were no dollars left. Then I found out I could have paid fifty cents on the dollar, thirty cents on some of them. That's the way I got out of the rest of the debts.

"I thought it was never going to end. I fought lawsuits and all kinds of stuff. It cost me two or three fortunes, but I finally paid off everybody I had to pay off. I should have had much better financial advice. I flunked two subjects in school—math and music!

"I don't mean to sound like I'm this much of a hero or something, but I just kept fighting my way through it. I just kept putting one foot in front of the other. . . . I had to work the road. I'd take dates on the road where I'd almost lose money or would just barely break even, hoping I could sell enough pictures and albums. When you're broke, you want to come home with whatever you can come home with.

"I guess maybe I was so focused on all the things I had to do that I didn't have time to sit around and wallow in self-pity. I know there were times when it was awfully rough, but I am just not a 'woe-is-me' kind of guy.

"When Becky was in the hospital and going through all of that, I had reconnected with a Sunday-school class and my church group. I had started going again. I've never been a religious fanatic. I've never worn it on my sleeve. But I have always had a deep and abiding faith. I've always felt there was somebody looking out for me. So my religion helped sustain me.

"And you've got to realize that there were other things going on in my life at that time. It wasn't like I was doing nothing." Throughout the decade, Bill Anderson was a major television presence, both on network and cable shows. Even so, his financial situation was precarious.

"In the back of my mind, I knew that if it finally came down to absolute push and shove, that I could sell my songs. I knew that possibility was there, but it would be like giving your kids up."

That was certainly a devastating thing to contemplate, because songs and songwriting are at the very core of Bill Anderson's being. Born on November 1, 1937, in Columbia, South Carolina, he was devoted to country music even as a tot.

"My mother and dad told me that I could find country music on the radio a long time before I could tie my shoelaces," Bill reports.

"There was no television. I turned on my radio, my little theater of the mind, and I listened to those artists and to those songs, and there was something in there that spoke to me. The songs that I really liked were the story songs, the songs that painted pictures with words.

"I was a big Hank Williams fan. And I noticed on his records that he not only sang the songs, he wrote them.

"I was about ten or eleven years old when I wrote my first song. It was called 'Carry Me to My Texas Home.' I had never been west of Carrollton, Georgia, at the time, but Texas sounded like something a true country artist ought to be writing and singing about. I was fifteen years old and in the tenth grade at Avondale High School [in Atlanta] when three buddies and I decided to form a band."

Bill studied journalism at the University of Georgia and became a newspaper reporter and radio broadcaster. He was writing songs all along. Throughout his youth, he also attended every country concert he could.

"Roger Miller and I met each other when he was stationed at Fort McPherson in Atlanta, and I was working as a disc jockey in Commerce, Georgia. We used to hang out at all the local Grand Ole Opry shows that came to Atlanta. We got to know one another before either of us had had any success. He wanted to be a songwriter. I wanted to be a songwriter. We had many conversations in those days about our dreams."

Bill Anderson's began to come true when he wrote "City Lights" in Commerce at age nineteen. Superstar Ray Price found the song, recorded it, and took it to number one in 1958. Coincidentally, the record's flip side was Price singing Roger Miller's "Invitation to the Blues."

"I got two royalty checks," Bill recalls. "The first one was for $2.52, and then I got about a $400 check. I didn't think there was that much money in the world!"

Signed as a singer by Decca Records, Bill Anderson issued "That's What It's Like to Be Lonesome" in late 1958. He performed it at his first Grand Ole Opry appearance that October. He graduated from college, married his first wife Bette, and moved to Music City in 1959. Daughter Terri was born in 1961, and Jenni followed in 1965.

In 1960–1961, "The Tip of My Fingers," "Walk Out Backwards," and "Po' Folks" became his first top-ten hits. They led to an invitation for Bill Anderson to become a member of the cast of the Grand Ole Opry. He was inducted on July 15, 1961.

"Me? A member of the Opry? That was like asking me if I wanted to go to heaven when I die!"

"Mama Sang a Song" became his first number-one record, in 1962. Then in 1963 came the blockbuster "Still."

"I got up out of bed about three o'clock in the morning and wrote 'Still,'" says the songwriter. "I had been to Atlanta and run into an old girlfriend. I didn't write the song for her, but I wrote it because of the feelings I experienced when I did see her."

Bill didn't think all that much of "Still," but producer Owen Bradley did. He slowed the tempo, encouraged the singer to recite the lyrics, added bell-like harmonies by The Anita Kerr Singers on the title word, and created a sophisticated musical arrangement. "Still" flew up the country charts to number one and crossed over to the pop hit parade as well. Bill's soft-spoken delivery of "Still" and his other early hits led to his nickname "Whispering" Bill Anderson.

By the mid-1960s, Bill was a country superstar. He launched his own syndicated television show in 1965 and put together a top-notch road show. Singer Jan Howard became part of the troupe, and she and Bill scored a series of hit duets in 1966–1972. Jan joined the Opry cast on March 27, 1971.

Few women have had as tumultuous a life as Jan Howard. She told her remarkable saga in her extraordinary 1987 autobiography *Sunshine and Shadow.*

Comments Jan, "When I started, I wrote all the hate and bitterness. That was therapeutic, because later I threw it away. It was better than going to a psychiatrist and a lot cheaper. Once I started again, it was just like rolling back time. One thing brought on another. . . . It was horrible reliving some of the bad parts. . . . Sometimes I would literally pray for the strength to do it."

Jan's story is a testament to the survival of the human spirit. She was born Lula Grace Johnson on March 13, 1930, and raised one of eleven children in desperate poverty in rural Missouri. At age eight she was raped by one of her father's friends. She married at fifteen, bore three sons, and became a victim of domestic violence. When her husband tried to kill her, she fled with her sons and $10 in her pocket.

Her second husband turned out to be a bigamist. Both of her children with him died. Her third husband became the celebrated country songwriter Harlan Howard (1927–2002). They moved to Nashville in 1960, the same year he cowrote Jan's debut hit "The One You Slip Around With." When Jan Howard first sang on the Opry stage, it was the first time she had sung on any stage or in front of any audience.

She was recovering from her bitter 1967 divorce from Harlan when her son Jimmy was killed in Vietnam in 1968. Four years later, son David committed suicide. Jan Howard's book grew out of her subsequent depression and psychological anguish.

"One thing I want to make really clear is that I'm not a martyr," says Jan. "I can't stand self-pity. I don't deserve and don't want any kind of pity. Because I have a lot to be thankful for. There are a lot of people worse off than me."

When *Sunshine and Shadow* debuted, she stated, "I hope this comes across as a hopeful book. . . . It's the story of a hard, real life. It isn't sugar coated. It's not a fairy tale.

"It's the story of a girl/wife/mother who happens to be an entertainer. . . . It almost seems like an accident that I became a singer. And I'm so thankful for it."

Although she was married to songwriting dynamo Harlan Howard, many of Jan Howard's hits were written by Bill Anderson. In addition to their hit duet "If It's All the Same to You" (1969), Bill wrote her solo singles "Bad Seed" (1966), "Count Your Blessings Woman" (1968), and "I Still Believe in Love" (1968).

She wasn't alone. Dozens of country stars had hits with Bill Anderson songs in the 1960s and 1970s. Jim Reeves (1960's "I Missed Me"), Porter Wagoner (1967's "The Cold Hard Facts of Life"), Faron Young (1959's "Riverboat"), Hank Locklin (1961's "Happy Birthday to Me"), George Hamilton IV (1961's "To You and Yours"), The Louvin Brothers (1962's "Must You Throw Dirt in My Face"), Lefty Frizzell (1964's "Saginaw, Michigan"), Cal Smith (1973's "The Lord Knows I'm Drinking"), and Conway Twitty (1979's "I May Never Get to Heaven") are just a few of the stars who sang hits from Bill's pen. Two of his fellow Opry stars have sung so many of his tunes that each has devoted an entire LP to Bill Anderson songs: Jean Shepard and Connie Smith.

"When I was a disc jockey, the first star I ever interviewed was Jean Shepard," Bill recalls. "Jean was traveling with Hawkshaw Hawkins. So I took my little tape recorder to the show to talk to them [in 1956]. I was so green. I had no idea how to end the interview. I was going to sit there and talk forever . . . I was new at radio and so enthralled talking to a big star that I didn't know when to quit.

"Finally Hawkshaw ended it. This is the nicest I've ever been cut off in my life. He leaned in and said, 'Bill, we've taken up enough of your time. We know you've got other things that you've got to do. Thanks for letting us be on and good night.' He was just wanting to get the heck out of there."

Years later, Bill wrote Jean's 1973 comeback hit "Slippin' Away," as well as such follow-up singles as "At the Time," "Poor Sweet Baby," "The Tip of My Fingers," and "Mercy." She expressed her gratitude with the 1975 LP *Poor Sweet Baby and Ten More Bill Anderson Songs*.

Connie Smith's tribute album was 1967's *Connie Smith Sings Bill Anderson*. By then, the prolific songwriter had provided her with such hits as "Once a Day," "Then and Only Then," "Nobody But a Fool," and "Cincinnati, Ohio." Not only that, Bill discovered Connie.

"I was at a little place called Frontier Ranch [just east of Columbus, Ohio], a country-music park, in August of 1963," he recalls. "When they booked the show, they asked, 'Would you mind, between the matinee performance and the night performance, taking a little bit of your time and helping us judge a talent contest?' I said, 'Sure, I'd be glad to do that.' This little girl came out onstage. Just a tiny, tiny young lady with a guitar that was probably as big or bigger than she was, wearing a little homemade cowgirl outfit. When she opened her mouth, I honestly thought she was pantomiming to a record!

"I said, 'There is no way that big voice could be coming out of that little, tiny lady.' She was singing an old Jean Shepard song, 'I Thought of You.' I was totally blown away. When the contest was over, I went backstage and congratulated her. I asked her if she had any desire to come to Nashville. She said, 'No, I've got this little baby boy here. I'm a housewife, and I'm pretty happy. I don't think I want to be in the music business.'

"I said, 'If you do ever want to get in the music business, please give me a call.' In January of '64, she came to see me in Canton, Ohio, at a concert. She told me she was thinking it over pretty seriously. I brought her to Nashville, I think in March, and we recorded some songs. I first took her tape to Owen Bradley at Decca, because I was recording for Decca. Owen listened to her tape and said, 'Boy she sings great, and I know she's probably going to be a big star, but we really don't have room for Connie Smith on Decca right now. We've got this new girl named Loretta Lynn that we're going to put a lot of our promotion behind.' So we took her to Chet Atkins at RCA. He fell instantly in love with her. But he asked me, 'We've got all these girl singers—Norma Jean, Skeeter Davis, Dottie West, this one and that one—where are her songs going to come from?' I said, 'I'll write them.'"

Songs poured out of Bill Anderson in those days. George Jones, Jerry Lee Lewis, Ernest Tubb, Roy Drusky, Kitty Wells, Roy Clark, Brenda Lee, Waylon Jennings, Eddy Arnold, and others were recording them. In addition, between 1960 and 1970, Bill Anderson wrote twenty top-ten hits for himself, including "8x10,"

"I Love You Drops," "I Get the Fever," "Wild Week-End," and "My Life."

He was a workaholic, writing nonstop, recording disc after disc, touring relentlessly and taping his popular weekly TV show. This took a toll on his private life. He and Bette separated in 1968 and divorced the following year. He married his second wife, Becky, in 1970, and their son Jamey was born in 1978.

Bill's weekly syndicated television show ended in 1974, but almost immediately, new small-screen opportunities presented themselves. He was tapped to host a syndicated show called *Backstage at the Grand Ole Opry*. In 1976–1977, Bill Anderson was the host of the ABC network game show *The Better Sex*. In 1979–1981, he had a recurring role on the TV soap opera *One Life to Live,* also on ABC.

His musical career continued to boom as well. In the 1970s, Bill Anderson scored such top-ten hits as "Quits," "World of Make Believe," "Head to Toe," and "I Can't Wait Any Longer." In 1975, he was inducted into the Nashville Songwriters Hall of Fame.

Then came the setbacks of the 1980s. He was no longer topping the record popularity charts. Even so, Bill remained a highly visible television personality. In 1983, The Nashville Network (TNN) cable channel was launched. Bill Anderson was chosen to host its quiz show *Fandango* in 1983–1989 and was the producer of its talent competition *You Can Be a Star* during the same period. He also hosted *Yesteryear* on the channel's radio outlet, TNNR. When the Opry became a weekly TNN program in 1985, Bill became one of the hosts of its companion show *Opry Backstage*. In 1987, he was featured on the TV soap opera *General Hospital*.

The stresses of the decade occasionally surfaced. When Bill was inducted into the Georgia Music Hall of Fame in 1985, he uncharacteristically lost control and burst into tears. His 1989 autobiography *Whisperin' Bill* recounted some of the difficulties he'd been going through.

He generally remained upbeat and optimistic in public. But something was missing—his heart.

"I am a songwriter—I came to Nashville as a songwriter," Bill states. "I wrote hundreds and hundreds of songs for years. And then I got away from songwriting.

"I was still jotting down ideas. I'd sit on an airplane and write three or four lines, or five or six lines. What I was doing was just taking those ideas home and stuffing them in a drawer somewhere.

"Then Steve Wariner had a hit in 1992 with 'The Tip of My Fingers.' I started thinking, 'Golly, I wrote that song thirty-two years ago. Surely I can still contribute something.' But I didn't know all the new people who had come in the ten or twelve years I had been away from it. I was just plain intimidated. . . . I didn't quite know how to get back into it, and I didn't know if I could.

"I had to learn how they do it today. Because it was a whole different thing from what we used to do. Hank Cochran and Harlan Howard and I never wrote together, but we all wrote the same way—at midnight with the shades pulled down.

"Vince Gill got wind of the fact that I wanted to write, and through a mutual friend, we got together [in 1994]. We didn't really know each other well at the time, but we instantly struck up a friendship and realized that we had a lot in common. He loves sports. I love sports. He loves bluegrass music. I love bluegrass music. He loves heartfelt country songs. I love heartfelt country songs.

"I was very, very nervous. He was a superstar at the height of his game. But he made me feel so welcome and so able to contribute. I went in there with the idea for a song called 'The Cold Gray Light of Gone,' and that drew us together. He liked it, and I thought, 'Wow!' The best thing was at the end of the day when we had finished the song, he said, 'This was fun. Let's do it again. Would you like to do it again?' He had some time the following Monday, and that's when we wrote 'Which Bridge to Cross (Which Bridge to Burn).'

"What a thrill that was. I can't tell you what that did for me. It not only helped my confidence, it kind of legitimized me, especially when Vince recorded the song. It was like, 'Hey, if he's good enough to write with Vince Gill . . .' After that, I just kind of eased back into it."

"Which Bridge to Cross" became a major Vince Gill hit in 1995. "The Cold Gray Light of Gone" eventually appeared on Vince's acclaimed 2006 CD *These Days*. Working with a variety of collaborators and making songwriting appointments the "modern" way on Music Row, Bill Anderson was soon back among the top tunesmiths in Music City. He cowrote the 1997 Bryan White hit "One Small Miracle" with Steve Wariner, and the pair also collaborated on Steve's Grammy-nominated "Two Teardrops" of 1999. Mark Wills had a number-one hit with Bill's cowritten "Wish You Were Here" in 1999 as well.

The new millennium smiled even brighter on Bill Anderson. In 2001, his touching "Too Country" was recorded by Brad Paisley, who asked Bill to be his guest vocalist on the CD, alongside George Jones and Buck Owens. The result won the Country Music Association (CMA) Award for Vocal Event of the Year. To top it off, Bill was inducted into the Country Music Hall of Fame that same night. The following year, superstar Kenny Chesney topped the charts with Bill's "A Lot of Things Different." In 2005, Bill returned to the CMA winner's circle as the cowriter of the organization's Song of the Year, "Whiskey Lullaby," as recorded by his fellow Opry stars Brad Paisley and Alison Krauss. In 2006, George Strait hit number one with Bill's cowritten "Give It Away," which won the CMA Song of the Year award the following year. Bill won his first Gospel Music Association award in 2007 for "Jonah, Job and Moses," as recorded by the Oak Ridge Boys. New country sensation Joe Nichols hit number one in 2007 with Bill's "I'll Wait for You."

"To be able to write songs that these young acts will record today, I can't tell you what that does for me inside. After all this time, to get that is just incredible.

"When I write a song, I don't know where it comes from. Sometimes you sit there and look at a blank piece of paper, and thirty minutes later, there's something on that piece of paper. I really think it is a gift. I think it was a shame what I did for ten years and not use this gift. I feel now that I treasure this gift more than I ever did before, and I don't intend to stop using it this time.

"I am very blessed," says Bill Anderson today, "because my life is happier and better and more together right now than it has ever been. I feel like I have so much to be thankful for."

The Opry star's "cursed" decade has had some residual effects on his life. Bill's back agony of the 1980s was eventually eased by an anti-inflammatory drug, but he sometimes wears a support brace to this day. His marriage to Becky had been rocky before her accident. In fact, they had separated. After her long recuperation, the couple finally divorced in 1997. His emphasis on broadcasting during the 1980s led to *Bill Anderson Visits with the Legends,* a radio program on the XM Satellite Radio service that launched in 2001. One thing that never changed, one thing that remained a constant in his life, has been the Grand Ole Opry.

"Let me emphasize that throughout that whole long thing, I never quit going to the Opry," says Bill Anderson. "The Opry was the constant thread in there. I could still go out to the Opry and sing and be with friends.

"I can't imagine my life without country music. My whole life is and has been country music. It's like the blood that flows through my veins."

# It's All Relative

The relationship between Mel Tillis and his daughter Pam Tillis has been fraught with trauma, tears, and tensions, but it found a happy resolution on the stage of the Grand Ole Opry.

Both father and daughter are strong-willed survivors. As a teenager, Pam rebelled against her parents' strict rules. As a young adult, she turned her back on her country-music birthright. She survived a gruesome car accident and eventually became one of Nashville's most gifted singer-songwriters. Meanwhile, Mel was roaring his way through Music City, wrecking his marriage along the way. He survived his escapades and prevailed to stardom despite a speech impediment that would have crushed a man with less drive and determination.

"Dad always said the reason we butted heads so often is that we're so much alike," Pam observes. "For some reason, it wasn't enough for me to just be his little girl. I wanted his respect, too.

"Family is so important for everybody, but it's so challenging. If we're a success, people like that. It's the same reason why people are interested in celebrity marriages. If you're working it out and pulling it off, they gravitate toward that.

"Music is who we are and what we do, but at the same time, I feel like the story of our relationship is bigger than that.

"For Dad to come from literally nothing and do what he's done, it took some sacrifice. When you have this really big dream, people in your world, to a degree, have to accommodate that dream. There's a price tag, and it's not just you who pays it, it's the people closest to you. That's where acceptance comes in, because you can't hold that [dream] against the person. And that's what I had to come to terms with."

Mel's ambition did have an impact on his family life. But it also led him to the Country Music Hall of Fame. Few have climbed so high while overcoming so much. Born August 8, 1932, a childhood bout with malaria left Lonnie Melvin Tillis with a permanent and pronounced stutter. The only time the speech impediment vanished was when he sang.

His father, a baker, left the family when Mel was quite young, and his mother went to work in a canning factory. Her family was quite musical, and she instilled a love of country music in her boy. As a high schooler, Mel was performing it locally.

"I was in the National Guard, and I went to Columbia, South Carolina, to Fort Jackson," Mel recalls. "They had a little band come and put on a dance for all the National Guardsmen there. Someone asked if I could get up and sing with them. They said, 'Don't worry. He can't talk, but he can sing.' I sang the Hank Williams song 'Why Don't You Love Me Like You Used to Do.' I did it one time, and they liked it so well, they asked me to do it again. That was my first time ever performin' with a band. And I was hooked."

He joined the air force. While stationed in Okinawa, he began to perform regularly in a country band. By the early 1950s, Mel was writing songs while making a living with a series of working-class jobs back home in Florida. He met a manager who brought him to Nashville in 1956. Everyone in the music business laughed at his stuttering, and the trip proved fruitless.

"At Acuff-Rose Publishing, Wesley Rose told me, 'We don't need any stuttering singers. We need songs.'

"Ray Price came to Tampa, Florida. I had a manager. He said, 'You wanna meet him?' I said, 'Yes, sir.' I went over there to Tampa,

I believe it was at the Armory. Ray asked me if I had any songs. I played him 'I'm Tired,' and he liked the song. He took it to Nashville, and he was singing it behind the stage at the Opry, the Ryman Auditorium. At the time [1956], he had a big hit out, 'Crazy Arms.' It had been in the charts for six months.

"Webb Pierce heard Ray Price singing my song. He said, 'I like that song. Can I have it? You don't need it. You have "Crazy Arms."' Ray said, 'Yeah, you can have it.' But he only gave him the first verse."

Mel was listening to the radio in Florida when he heard Webb Pierce introduce his new single, "I'm Tired," with two new verses supplied by songwriter Wayne Walker. Mel didn't care. He was on his way as a tunesmith. He married his girlfriend Doris, and they moved to Nashville. Webb sang Mel's "Honky Tonk Song" to the top of the charts in early 1957. Daughter Pam Tillis was born on July 24, 1957.

Songwriting royalty checks take months to arrive. To keep bread on the table, Mel took jobs playing guitar on the road with bigger stars.

"I remember the first time I met Patsy Cline, I was on tour, working for Judy Lynn. This was about 1958. I drove the car. Patsy was in the car, and so was Brenda Lee and Brenda's mama. That's how I became big buddies with Patsy. I've heard every joke, and boy, she had some good ones. I loved her. Patsy Cline was one of the boys. She'd have a beer with you. I think Patsy only recorded about fifty or sixty songs, and I happen to have two of them, 'Strange' and 'So Wrong.' She liked me, you know.

"Minnie Pearl hired me. She said, 'But I need a fiddle player, too.' I said, 'I met one today.' And I hurried on down to the Andrew Jackson Hotel. Roger Miller was in there, and he had his little bellhop uniform on. I said, 'Roger, you said you could play the fiddle. You want a job with Minnie Pearl?' He said, 'Yeah.' I said, 'Well, you already have a job, don't you?' He said, 'Yeah, but I'm gonna give them my two-minute notice!' And we went on the road.

"Minnie was the first one to encourage me to talk onstage. I wouldn't open my mouth, 'cause when I started talking onstage, they began to laugh at me. 'Melvin,' she said, 'they're not laughing at you. They're laughing with you. Find your niche there.' She said, 'Melvin, just be yourself. And they'll either like you or they'll dislike you.' It turned out that they liked me. So Miss Minnie was right. A dear lady."

Mel debuted on the charts with his self-penned Columbia Records single "The Violet and the Rose." But one thorn in Mel's side was that his manager was listing himself as the cowriter of the songs. Mel decided to break their contract. This meant tying up his royalties and the rights to his songs in court. Destitute and disillusioned, the Tillis family returned to Florida in 1959. Pam was two years old, and Doris had just given birth to second daughter Connie. Mel Tillis took a job as a delivery-truck driver back home in Pahokee. Frustrated by his lack of success as a vocalist, Columbia Records dropped him.

He was back on the bottom, but Mel wouldn't stay there for long. Other artists continued to hit the charts with songs he penned, and in 1960, Mel signed as an artist with Decca with the help of benefactor Webb Pierce (1921–1991).

"Red Foley was my idol," Mel relates. "He was the man that inspired me the most to get into the business. I remember one time he came to Nashville to record. He called the office and asked if I would come over to the Anchor Motel and bring some songs. I recorded for Decca at that time, and so did Red Foley. I got over there, and [guitar player] Grady Martin was over there. Boy, out came the jug. We got to drinkin', Grady got to pickin', and Red got to singin'. He did every song I guess he knew, and we set there for three days. I got kicked off the label [because Red missed his recording sessions]."

Mel signed with Ric Records, then Kapp Records. Despite his mellifluous singing voice, recording stardom continued to elude him. But his songwriting remained popular, particularly the blockbuster 1969 pop hit "Ruby, Don't Take Your Love to Town," recorded by Kenny Rogers & The First Edition.

"That's a true story," Mel says. "I was on my way home, and I got stuck in traffic. I had the radio on, and I was listening to the [Johnny Cash] song 'Don't Take Your Guns to Town.' And I sang, 'Ruby, Don't Take Your Love to Town.' I got to thinking about someone I knew down in Florida. In fact, they lived in back of us in a little house. I used to hear them arguing over there. He was a GI who was wounded in Germany. He met the girl in England, a nurse, and he brought her to my hometown. He had some recurring problems with some of the wounds he had. Eventually, he divorced Ruby and married someone else. The ending to this story is that the guy killed himself and his third wife. Very sad."

Mel and Doris's family continued to grow with the addition of daughter Cindy and son Mel Jr., nicknamed Sonny. Then came their fifth child, daughter Carrie. Despite the added responsibilities, Mel continued to pursue his singing career. And when he wasn't on the road raising Cain, he was raising it around Music City.

"Lefty Frizzell would always call me and Wayne Walker. He liked to party with us. I remember one night we was out for three days. He said, 'Melvin, could you go home with me? Alice won't get mad at me if you're there. She likes you.' So we went out there, and he said, 'You better stay out here 'til I make peace.' The next thing I knew, out come a big ol' buffalo head. It came right by me, landed and knocked off one of the horns. And there he stood. Lefty said, 'Melvin, I don't think you better come in, but you can have my buffalo head. She don't want it in the house anymore.'

"So I got the head, and I went home. When I got home, Doris threw the head out and broke the other horn off! Oh boy. And it took me forever to get back in the house. The buffalo head stayed out there two or three days. The dogs drug it off."

His wild-and-wooly behavior sometimes affected his professional life. One brawl in downtown Nashville cost him his job as a member of *The Porter Wagoner Show,* on television and on the Opry. Porter heard about the fight and didn't want anyone in his troupe associated with anything so controversial.

"Porter Wagoner had asked me to become a member of his show," recalls Mel. "It was around the same time he'd hired Dolly Parton. I was on there for six months or so [in 1968]. And then he fired me. The very next day, I get a call from Glen Campbell, who hired me to be on *The Glen Campbell Goodtime Hour*. I went out there, and that exposed me to the world. Glen Campbell [on the CBS network] and all those syndicated television shows helped [country music] to get bigger and bigger and bigger, to what it is today."

Television exposure of his unique personality and excellent singing led to the radio success that had eluded him for so long. At the dawn of the 1970s, Mel signed with MGM Records and began having consistent top-ten hits, including "Commercial Affection," "Let's Go All the Way Tonight," and "Memory Maker." Mel also turned his stuttering speech impediment into a comedic device that delighted millions. The readers of *Music City News* voted Mel their Comedy Act of the Year for six straight years, 1973–1978.

"And then from there, Burt Reynolds put me in the [1975] movie *W.W. and The Dixie Dancekings*. I played a gas station attendant. I only had a few lines in it. He pulled up at my gas station, and I delivered my lines. He said, 'Cut!' and shot me with a water pistol, right in the head. He said, 'Mel, I hired you to stutter in this! You're not stuttering.' I said, 'I've learned my line, so I don't stutter as bad.' He rewrote the line, and the next time, I really stuttered."

In 1976, Mel Tillis was inducted into the Nashville Songwriters Hall of Fame. He was also named the Country Music Association's Entertainer of the Year, much to his surprise.

"I remember when that happened. Tennessee Ernie Ford said, 'The winner is—and I love him—Mel Tillis!' I was in the audience, and I had a pipe. I guess in those days you could smoke in the auditorium. I didn't expect to win, 'cause I was up against [Ronnie] Milsap, Dolly, Willie, and Waylon. I said, 'There ain't no way for me to win this thing.' But I won, and I took the pipe and stuck it in my tux pocket. I got up onstage and, man, it started burnin' up in there! I hurried up my acceptance speech."

Now at the peak of his profession, Mel signed with MCA Records in 1976 and became an even bigger star than ever. But his prolonged absences, carousing, and female flings upset his wife. After several separations and earlier divorce filings, he and Doris finally divorced in 1977. The experience profoundly depressed him. He married second wife Judy in 1979 and had daughter Hannah. Mel and Judy are also now divorced.

Things might have been turbulent personally, but professionally, Mel Tillis rose higher than ever in both music and film. He appeared in several movies, including *The Villain* (1979) with Kirk Douglas and Arnold Schwarzenegger, *Every Which Way But Loose* (1978) with Clint Eastwood, and *Cannonball Run* (1981) with Burt Reynolds. He was also the star of his own showplace in the Ozark Mountains tourist boomtown of Branson, Missouri, from 1990 to 2002.

MEL TILLIS AND HIS daughter Pam Tillis are now mutual admirers, and she cherishes the time she spends with her famous father. But as both will admit, this was not always the case.

Pam was a self-described "melancholy child," a withdrawn loner, a bookish dreamer. Although she lacked self-confidence, she did accompany Mel to the Opry when she was eight and performed "Tom Dooley" on its stage. As a youngster, Pam was fascinated by the Opry's glamorous female stars.

"Ooh they were beautiful, they were fabulous. They would walk into the room, and they smelled good and their hair was big and they sang so great. I remember the first time I heard Tammy Wynette sing, and she had that unbelievable range.

"I don't know if I wanted to be that, or even if I thought I could be that. They were stars. People who were popular back then, they were larger than life.

"The late, great Dottie West—she was a star. They were flashy, they were tragic, they were all these wonderful things. They were elegant ladies. And they were feisty.

"I've known Dolly since I was a little girl. To me, she was just this deity, this country-music diva. She's so beautiful. It was such a thrill to work with her [on the 1993 single "Romeo"]. I told her,

'Dolly, I don't even need money to come over here and work with you. All I want is some hair tips.' She said, 'Oh honey, I'll give you a whole bag of hair.'

"My favorite thing about awards shows is not being nominated or any of that stuff. It's being backstage and talking to these gals who have been around the block."

Pam grew up immersed in music. She took classical piano lessons for nine years and picked up the guitar at age twelve. She was writing songs by age thirteen and performing in Nashville nightspots at age fifteen. Mel was not pleased.

"They were very strict," says Pam of her parents. "We weren't allowed to do a lot of things. So I didn't have to stray too far to be on the wrong side of the law. So if I was rebellious, it's because everything I was trying was outside the bounds of acceptability, for the most part. I remember it was a huge deal to go to concerts or to take road trips with my friends."

Mel would return from concert tours and try to lay down the law. As a teenager, Pam resented it.

"I'm like, 'Who are you to tell me anything? Because you're never here.' Daddy worked so much. I figured it up one time, and from the time I was born to the time I was eighteen, I felt like I had maybe three years of any kind of interaction with him. Now that's pretty crazy.

"It's really hard [for him] to be an authoritarian. . . . That was another rub. I knew for a fact he was telling me not to do a lot of stuff that he was doing. I mean, The Statesiders were infamous. I always characterized them as the Led Zeppelin of country music.

"Plus, my parents had trouble in their relationship, and that rubs off on young kids. It was just a really tough time, and they eventually split up.

"I'm sure he had his own feelings—You're at the top of your game, and everybody tells you how wonderful you are, and then you come home and everybody's got a laundry list of why you're in the doghouse. That's hard to take.

"So there's this whole big aura of uncertainty, and this person who's larger than life. And you don't quite know how to please him. Anyway, in my teenage years, to say I felt alienated from my dad is an understatement."

The advent of the Beatles completely pushed aside any country daydreams Pam might have had. To Mel's dismay, she became completely immersed in pop music.

"Daddy was like, 'Where did I go wrong? What have I done?'"

"It's very painful to say—I knew Daddy loved me, but I was never totally convinced that he liked me. Daddy's real tough. He's not a flatterer. In fact, if you ever got a compliment out of him, that was huge.

"At one point, I couldn't be in the same room with him without feeling so sad. I was just on the verge of tears. I had all these feelings, and I didn't know how to process them. I distanced myself from the situation until I could get a handle on it."

Country-to-the-core Mel strongly disapproved of Pam's musical direction. He also disapproved of her friends. When she was sixteen, she was out partying with them when a car crash sent her face-first through the windshield. Pam's facial bones were shattered in thirty places.

"People ask me, 'What's your fondest Christmas moment?' This is going to sound weird as all get out, but when I had my wreck it was Christmas Eve, and I woke up [in the hospital] Christmas morning. When you're a kid, your very first thought is, 'Well, I'm not gone, now my parents are going to finish me off.' Instead, there was that total look of acceptance. My best gift was knowing that there was nothing I could do that they wouldn't love me and be there for me. Even though they were having a lot of trouble, they worked together as parents."

Five years of plastic surgeries restored her looks. After high school, Pam attended the University of Tennessee in Knoxville.

"My majors in college were music and partying. The first week, I signed up for a rock 'n' roll group and my classes, in that order."

She dropped out after two semesters, determined to make her living with music. Pam sang pop tunes at top nightspots in Los

Angeles, then moved to San Francisco and performed in a jazz group. She also married. She returned to Nashville to have her son Ben in 1979. Almost immediately afterward, she divorced.

"I had gone through a very bad relationship," she recalls. "My first marriage was really bad. So in the process of dealing with that, I went, 'Okay, let's start at the beginning.' I came home and got into counseling. I just laid it all out and looked at it long and hard. What I came to realize is that Daddy is not a bad guy.

"Over time, we did have some really serious, good heart-to-hearts that might have hurt and might have been painful at the time. But we cleared the air."

Mel had taken her on the road as his backup vocalist in 1978, but that had only resulted in a clash of wills.

"I wanted to be Bonnie Raitt. He wanted me to be, like, I don't know, some girl with a gingham skirt on. I didn't hear my music the way he heard it. That was our first rub, professionally.

"It didn't help my self-confidence any, but at the same time, it made me very resolute. So it was really a blessing in disguise that he was really tough on me."

Despite their differences, Mel featured her singing a prominent harmony part on his 1980 hit "Your Body Is an Outlaw." He also signed Pam to be a staff writer for his publishing company. Country stars recorded her tunes, and Barbara Fairchild had a minor hit in 1978 with Pam's "The Other Side of the Morning," but often her biggest successes were songs she wrote for R&B stars such as Chaka Kahn, Rebbie Jackson, Dorothy Moore, Bettye Lavette, and Gloria Gaynor. Pam spent two years singing soul songs herself, working on the motel-lounge circuit in Music City.

"I've sung all of Donna Summer's hits a million times each! I mean, this was working every night until three and four in the morning, doing five sets a night. I feel like that was when I really 'did my time' and paid my dues."

She sang backup for Nashville stars such as Crystal Gayle and Helen Cornelius, recorded ad jingles, and sang hundreds of demo sessions for Nashville songwriters.

"I pounded the pavement of Music Row for what seemed like forever, a young single mother who didn't want to ride the coattails of a famous dad," she later reflected. "I sang in a beer commercial with a tall, skinny kid named Alan Jackson. One of my last sessions was with another struggling up-and-comer, Trisha Yearwood, singing backup on a Paul Overstreet record."

Signed by Elektra Records, she went to Los Angeles to record a disco-flavored single called "Every Home Should Have One" in 1981. She returned there to work on her 1983 pop-rock album for Warner Bros. Records, *Above and Beyond the Doll of Cutey*. She also shot its MTV video, "Killer Comfort," on the West Coast.

"I was in L.A. recording, and I had a three-year-old son," Pam recalls. "I was involved in the pop world, and I just felt like I didn't belong. I'll never forget it. I thought, 'I can't bring a child into this environment. I'm a Southern girl, and my family—imperfect as they may be—are my safety net, because, you know, I'm a single mom. Let's be honest, I don't want a career in L.A. or New York. It's not worth it to me.'

"That was one consideration. And the second consideration was that everybody kept going, 'We like it when you sing all this other stuff, but when you sing country, it just sounds right.'"

Back in Nashville, this time for keeps, Pam Tillis began issuing country singles in 1984. Nothing clicked. She issued "Those Memories of You" in 1986 to no avail. A year later, it became a huge hit for Dolly Parton, Linda Ronstadt, and Emmylou Harris. During this period, Pam also recorded "Maybe it Was Memphis" and "One of Those Things," also to no avail. Both became hits for her five years later. Warner Bros. Records dropped her in 1987. Pam was facing her thirtieth birthday as a failure.

Her talent was the talk of Music Row, but it was getting her nowhere. Everyone in the industry loved her torrid soprano singing, her vivid songwriting, her enchanting wit, and her quirky personality.

"That gave me a lot of self-confidence, at first. Then it started to become a burden, because people started to get angry that it was taking me so long to become what they thought I should be. Seriously, I didn't want to go to the grocery store, the mall, the post office, because invariably I'd run into somebody who'd go, 'Why aren't you a star yet? You're shattering my illusions of order in the universe.' It was like, 'Please. I'm working on it!'"

Pam began reviving country oldies in a series of Nashville nightclub showcases called "Twang Night." She and her female songwriting buddies established "Women in the Round" nights at the Bluebird Cafe.

In 1990 she signed a recording contract with Arista Records, which issued "Don't Tell Me What to Do" late that year. It made her a star, and her *Put Yourself in My Place* CD became a gold record.

"I've gone on and on about Daddy not spoiling me," she said at the time, "and now I think he's finally said, 'Well, she's come this far on her own; I think I'll do something nice for her.' And he gave me a bus."

Professional success was accompanied by personal happiness. Pam married award-winning songwriter Bob DiPiero in 1991. Soon after, she released the platinum albums *Homeward Looking Angel* and *Sweetheart's Dance*. The highlight of the latter album was "'Til All the Lonely's Gone," which she recorded with Mel and her siblings Connie, Cindy, Sonny, and Carrie. She was named the Country Music Association's Female Vocalist of the Year in 1994.

"It just made me so proud," says Mel. "My thoughts immediately went back to when she was a little girl, and she used to do her little imitations of Jack Benny. And she'd sing. She mentioned during the awards show that 'It hadn't been too long ago that my dad stood right here.' I'm awfully proud of her."

Pam became the first woman in contemporary country music to solo produce her own album, 1995's gold-selling *All of This Love*. Its hit singles included "Deep Down," "It's Lonely Out There," and "The River and the Highway." Country Music Television named her its Top Female Video Artist of 1995. The following year she costarred in a groundbreaking all-female country tour alongside fellow "second-generation" performers Lorrie Morgan and Carlene Carter.

Pam and Bob filed for divorce in 1997, but her star shined brighter than ever. Having already appeared in the feature film *The Thing Called Love,* she spread her wings as an actor on episodes of the CBS series *Diagnosis Murder* and *Promised Land.* In 1999, she headed to Broadway to appear in the hit musical *Smokey Joe's Café.*

In the summer of 2000, Jimmy Dickens asked her if she'd like to become a cast member of the Grand Ole Opry.

"Let me think about it—YES!" Pam responded. "This is a special night. This is a lifelong dream to join. I want to send thanks to Dad and God."

On August 26, 2000, Marty Stuart officially inducted her into the Opry cast. "Welcome home, Baby," said Marty.

"I never dreamed that would happen," says Pam. "I didn't think I'd win a CMA Award, either. I'm still just like, 'Wow!' I do like it there so much."

Pam recorded an album of her father's songs in 2002 called *It's All Relative: Tillis Sings Tillis.* The record's supporting cast included Dolly Parton, Rhonda Vincent, Ray Benson, Trisha Yearwood, Emmylou Harris, The Jordanaires, Delbert McClinton, Marty Stuart, and, happily, Mel Tillis.

"My fans have totally embraced that record, and the reviews were incredible," Pam comments. "That, for me, was just a big labor of love and an important gesture. I felt like that was something that I just really wanted to do."

By this time, Mel and Pam had become much closer. He brags about her success, sends her cards and flowers, and sings duets with her.

Mel was making a guest appearance on the Grand Ole Opry in the spring of 2007 when Bill Anderson inquired if he would like to become a cast member. "We'd love to have you," said Bill.

"This is another part of a dream yet to be fulfilled," Mel replied. "The Opry's always been on my mind."

Pam inducted her father into the Opry cast on June 9, 2007. She confided that night that she'd always felt a little uncomfortable about becoming an Opry member before him.

"All week long, people have been telling me they can't believe Daddy wasn't already an Opry member," Pam told the audience. Then she turned to Mel and added, "And that just tells me, 'You belong here.' The best thing about getting inducted first is that I get to induct you. You are now an official member of the Grand Ole Opry."

Mel Tillis had an even greater treat in store. Just four months later, on October 28, 2007, he became a member of the Country Music Hall of Fame.

"You are special, and you are great," Pam told him that night. She also reminded the audience that Mel Tillis is still renowned for his marathon three-hour concerts and penultimate showmanship. Then Jimmy Dickens presented Mel with his official Hall of Fame medallion.

"A true friend is someone who knows all about you and still likes you," Jimmy told the audience. "That's the Mel Tillis I know. When he steps onstage, he upgrades country music. Men like this are hard to come by."

Responded Mel, "I've been a blessed man, and I want to thank this little angel on my shoulder. . . . I love you folks."

# Fatherhood First

No other artist in history so completely dominated his genre as Eddy Arnold did when he was a Grand Ole Opry superstar.

Eddy first sang on the Opry as the lead vocalist in Pee Wee King's Golden West Cowboys in 1942. He became a solo cast member the following year. By the time of his final Opry show, on September 11, 1948, he was even bigger than the most famous country program in the world. He and Minnie Pearl cried in each other's arms after his final Opry broadcast, but Eddy Arnold knew he needed to move on.

"It was a real wrench to leave," Eddy recalled, "but I knew if I were to keep on goin' upward, I had to. . . . My world had changed. I didn't really know whether it was for better or for worse, the night I walked to the center of the stage on the Grand Ole Opry and told the audience I was resigning. I told them it was my last performance, and I felt inside as if it were my last performance, anywhere. I thanked the people for being so kind to me . . . saying all the things everyone expected me to say; then I hurried offstage and cried in the wings.

"Tom Parker was my manager when I left there," Eddy explained. "It took Tom quite a while to convince me that I had to do that, 'cause my ties were emotional there. It just didn't seem right to leave performers and friends like Minnie Pearl, Roy Acuff [and] Uncle Dave Macon. I loved those people. I admired them. For years, my only ambition had been to work with them.

"A lot of people couldn't understand [leaving the Opry]. But we knew there were a lot of other things I could do. And we did 'em. I was a new boy on the scene. I was makin' pretty good money, and I had other deals to make."

At the time, no one in country music was hotter. His 1947 smash "I'll Hold You in My Heart" had remained at number one for twenty-one weeks, and 1948's "Bouquet of Roses" stayed at the top of the charts for nineteen weeks. During 1948, only seven country songs occupied the number-one position, and six of them belonged to Eddy Arnold.

"It's a Sin" (1947), "I Couldn't Believe it Was True" (1947), "Molly Darling" (1948), "Anytime" (1948), and "Take Me in Your Arms and Hold Me" (1949) are other songs of the 1940s that became country standards because of Eddy Arnold. Several of them were also pop-crossover hits.

"All I was looking for . . . is good songs," said Eddy. "That's all I have ever looked for—music that touches people's hearts."

With that simple credo, Eddy Arnold essentially built RCA's Nashville division. In his heyday, his records outsold those of every other artist on RCA, including the company's biggest pop stars. His 1944 recording session for the label launched Nashville as a recording center.

His 1945 single "Each Minute Seems a Million Years" was the first of his ninety-two top-ten hits. That is a tally still unmatched by any other artist. It was also the first of sixty-seven consecutive top-ten hits, again a figure that is unequaled. In 1946, "What Is Life Without Love" became the first of his twenty-eight number-one hits. Eddy Arnold's career total of 145 weeks spent at number one is, again, far in excess of anyone else's.

By the end of his first decade as a recording artist, Eddy Arnold was a national icon. Among the evergreens he introduced in the 1950s were "May the Good Lord Bless and Keep You" (1951),

"I Wanna Play House with You" (1951), "I Really Don't Want to Know" (1954), "Cattle Call" (1955), "You Don't Know Me" (1956), and "Tennessee Stud" (1959).

In 1952, Eddy Arnold became the first country star to host his own prime time network TV show. *Eddy Arnold Time* was unique in that it aired in syndication as well as over all three networks—CBS (1952, three nights a week), NBC (1953, twice weekly), and ABC (1956, weekly).

In the 1960s, Eddy soared even higher. He embraced the sophisticated new recording techniques of the Nashville Sound and created such standards as "Make the World Go Away" (1965), "The Tip of My Fingers" (1966), "Misty Blue" (1967), and "Then You Can Tell Me Goodbye" (1968). All of them landed on pop as well as country popularity charts.

"That was fine," said Eddy of the recording style that revived his career. "That brought the music out of the hills and brought it uptown."

In 1967, Eddy Arnold was named the Country Music Association (CMA) Entertainer of the Year, one year after he'd already been inducted into the Country Music Hall of Fame. That accomplishment is also unduplicated.

He made guest appearances on virtually every television variety program of the era, starred in more than a dozen TV specials, and headlined at the top showcase venues of Las Vegas, Hollywood, and Manhattan. The smooth-voiced balladeer took country music to new heights of sophistication and respectability.

"I do have a wider audience than just the country audience," commented Eddy Arnold. "One of the reasons for that is that I went to Carnegie Hall. I did bookings in Las Vegas and Lake Tahoe, over and over. I appeared with I don't know how many symphony orchestras. I went to New York and courted those people. I did national television." Eddy went on to say that he made no excuses for vastly broadening country's appeal by adding string sections and pop-crossover arrangements to his ballads.

By the end of the 1960s, he was an undisputed country-music

titan. But it all came screeching to a halt on August 1, 1971. On that date, son Dickey Arnold was in a gruesome car crash near Bessemer, Alabama. He was dead on arrival at Birmingham's Lloyd Nolan Hospital but was revived by the staff. Suffering from severe head injuries, he was in a coma for nine weeks. Eddy cut back his concert schedule sharply to remain by his son's side as much as possible.

When Dickey regained consciousness, the young man had little memory of his life, had limited speech, and had lost movement in various parts of his body. Rather than send his boy to a rehabilitation facility, Eddy brought him home. Eddy and his wife Sally rented rehabilitation equipment and supervised a team of therapists.

The superstar was fifty-three at the time, but the hard physical labor of his early years had left him big and strong. He carried his adult son when necessary. Every morning, he hauled a large trough into the house, picked Dickey up, put him in it, bathed him, and gave him rubdowns to restore the feeling in his limbs. Day after day, he nursed him. Step-by-step, he taught him to walk again. Life changed completely for Eddy Arnold. His thriving career was put aside for fatherhood.

When his son was young, Eddy was on the road and missed many important childhood moments. The tragedy made his family his top priority once more.

"I guess I was just trying to be a father," he later reflected about this trying time. "My wife worked very hard, and I tried to be as much help to her as I could."

"Dick's doin' pretty good," Eddy commented fifteen years later. "I call him, and we talk all the time. After Christmas, they put some good things on sale, and I always take him and buy him two or three outfits."

Eddy Arnold's career never regained the momentum it had before the accident. But he never regretted the extraordinary bond he forged with his son when Dickey needed him most, particularly since his own childhood had been so bruised.

Eddy was born near Henderson, Tennessee, on May 15, 1918. His father died of heart and kidney disease when he was still a boy.

"We were a very poor but a very proud family," he recalled. "At one time, my father was a very successful farmer and then lost it. Then he died when I was eleven years old. We were in the Depression. It was beans-and-bread time. I wanted to get away from that farm labor. I wanted to do better, but I didn't really know what better was."

Creditors auctioned off the family farm, its equipment, the furniture, the livestock, and even the family pets. The Arnolds became sharecroppers on what had been their own land. Eddy went to work as a laborer. That meant dropping out of high school at age sixteen.

"I grew up on a dirt road farm. Not a gravel road, a dirt road. I did hard labor. I used to cut timber, a lot of pine timber. You know those big power-line poles? I used to cut them and scale the bark off them in the swamps.

"When I was on the farm, I heard Jimmie Rodgers records, Vernon Dalhart, Gene Autry. I heard the records, but I didn't own them. I didn't even have a record player. We couldn't afford one.

"I had a little guitar. And in the spring and summer, I'd sit on the porch and strum for anybody that came along. There was a man that drove up in front of our place, selling subscriptions to a newspaper in Jackson, Tennessee. And I played him a little tune. He said, 'Son, I probably can get you an audition on the radio station.' And he did, on a station called WTJS. They let me on that station. I didn't make any money. So I got me another job on the side, driving an ambulance."

That was in 1936. By 1939, he was broadcasting on KXOK in St. Louis. He sent a recording of his voice to Pee Wee King (1919–2000), who hired him as a vocalist in early 1940. Eddy was so excited about joining the band, he didn't even ask what he would be paid.

"I learned a lot from Pee Wee—I've always been a student of watching other people perform," said Eddy. "Traveling in the 1940s was tough. The cars were not air conditioned. All we knew to do was just get in the car, tie a bass fiddle on top of the car, let the windows down, and go. It was tough when I look back on it today. Then, I thought, 'Oh boy! This is fun!' But of course, I'd been working in the trenches, cutting timber and working on the farm. And anything was better than that, to me."

During a 1940 radio broadcast by the troupe on WHAS in Louisville, Eddy spotted a petite brunette in the audience who looked like movie star Olivia de Havilland. Struck by his strapping build and dimpled chin, Sally Gayhart chatted with him after the show. They were soon courting. Sally and Eddy Arnold were married in Nashville on November 28, 1941. They were together for life.

"I had an old friend who's dead now, a pop singer named Gene Austin [famed for "My Blue Heaven," "Ramona," and the like]— He came to visit me once and was then living with his fifth wife," Eddy recalled. "He said, 'Eddy, I only made one mistake, and that was getting rid of my first wife.'

"I just figured I might as well stay with the same one," Eddy concluded with a chuckle. Daughter Jo Ann was born in 1945. Son Richard "Dickey" followed in 1949.

Sally prodded Eddy to better his circumstances, so he went to WSM to propose a solo show for himself. When the station agreed, he gave Pee Wee his notice in 1943. The following year, Eddy was given his own Grand Ole Opry segment.

A magazine story about the handsome, square-jawed country youngster caught the eye of carnival huckster and concert promoter Tom Parker. He came from Florida to the Opry to court the up-and-comer, whom he'd met earlier at Pee Wee King shows. Sensing impending stardom, Parker talked Eddy Arnold into signing with him as the singer's exclusive manager. Parker's timing coincided perfectly with WSM executives engineering an RCA Victor recording contract for their radio protégé.

On December 4, 1944, Eddy Arnold went to the WSM studio to record instead of broadcast. He remembered well the session that gave birth to Nashville as a recording capital.

"Well, the first session in Nashville was in a radio studio," he related. "The thing I remember most is that we recorded on what we called a transcription, you know, a record . . . that they used on radio. This was long before tape was ever, I guess, thought of. And of course, at that time, if you made a mistake or one of the musicians made a mistake, you had to do it all over again. You couldn't just do one little part, which you can today.

"We never thought we were doing anything historic. You never think about it being important at the time. All I wanted to do was just make one record. I sang a song called 'Mommy Please Stay Home with Me.' I did 'Cattle Call.' I did a song called 'Each Minute Seems a Million Years.' "

The third title became the first of 145 charting Eddy Arnold discs of 1945–1983. "Cattle Call," re-recorded as a duet with LeAnn Rimes, became his 146th, in 1999.

Tom Parker worked Eddy Arnold and His Tennessee Plowboys band relentlessly throughout 1945. In addition to touring, Parker arranged for his star to perform on a weekday afternoon radio show and a weekly one, both sponsored by Purina on the Mutual network, as well as on a prerecorded program to which three hundred stations subscribed. While Eddy logged thousands of miles traveling from show to show, his record sales were exploding to unheard-of heights in 1946, 1947, and 1948.

"I never felt like I was a superstar," he remarked. "I guess I was too busy then."

His chart-topping hits "Anytime" and "Texarkana Baby" were both recorded at New York sessions in 1947. During that visit, RCA Victor vice president Jim Murray summoned Eddy to his office. The singer went to see the boss with trepidation.

"I thought, 'Golly, what does he want to see me for? What's he gonna do? Tear up my contract?' But it was the opposite. The guy stood up and shook my hand and wanted to give me a cigar. I was scared to death. He said, 'Sit down, son.' So I sat down. He said, 'I wanted to see what you looked like. I see these orders for your records coming across my desk every Monday morning.' He was very nice to me. I didn't realize I was selling. I didn't know anything about the record business. I was so dumb.

"That's how I found out I was outselling everybody else. And see, a country boy had never done that to them.' "

Eddy earned a reported $500,000 in 1949. During that year, Tom Parker arranged for him to appear on Milton Berle's top-rated national television show, booked him for his first shows in Las Vegas, and had him star in two movies that Eddy described as "cheap." Both *Feudin' Rhythm* and *Hoedown* were released to theaters in 1950, and Eddy and his band performed in theaters that screened them.

"You know how I met Elvis? I met him before he ever happened. In '49 I did two movies over in Hollywood. And then when the movies were released, I traveled with them. They'd play the movie, and I'd appear in the theater. I came to Memphis, and Presley came down. I had The Jordanaires on the bill with me. He wanted to meet The Jordanaires. He'd heard them on the radio. And that's when I met Elvis Presley. Tom Parker, of course, was managing me then."

The crude, cheap stunts of his slovenly, uncouth manager increasingly embarrassed Eddy Arnold. In the wake of his TV series that began in 1952, the singer began to aspire to a more sophisticated image. "The Colonel," as Parker had anointed himself, was taking an unethical 25 percent of Eddy's earnings and was violating his "exclusive" agreement by secretly promoting Tommy Sands, Opry star Hank Snow (1914–1999), and others. After a heated argument in Las Vegas, Eddy Arnold fired "Colonel" Tom Parker in 1953. Three years later, Parker signed Elvis Presley to the most notorious management agreement in music history.

The rise of Elvis and rock 'n' roll initially damaged country music's popularity badly. The industry fought back by crafting increasingly sophisticated productions in a style of recording that became known as the Nashville Sound. Eddy Arnold became one of the new style's most enthusiastic proponents.

"At that point, my record sales had dropped off a lot. As far as making country records, I had recorded every way you could think of. I wanted to try that [Nashville Sound style]. I found a song called 'What's He Doing in My World,' and I think we used four violins on that. Violins, not fiddles. It was a good seller, and I realized I'd found something. I had an idea to do an LP called *My*

*World.* Two years before that, a pop singer named Timi Yuro had sung 'Make the World Go Away.' Ray Price had recorded it. Jim Reeves had recorded it. But I just thought it fit this album. The day we did it, we were listening to the playback in the control room, and I said to Chet Atkins, 'That sounds like a single record to me.' So we released it as a single, and it became a big record. It still sells today."

In 1965, "Make the World Go Away" became the biggest hit of Eddy Arnold's career. He finished the 1960s with the major hits "I Want to Go with You," "The Last Word in Lonesome Is Me," "Lonely Again," "Turn the World Around," and eight more top-ten smashes. During this same decade, Ray Charles reintroduced such Eddy Arnold classics as "You Don't Know Me" and "Just a Little Lovin'." On the country charts, Marty Robbins revived "It's a Sin" and "I Walk Alone."

Dickey's tragic accident and Eddy's sacrifice on behalf of his son may have contributed to the cooling of the star's career in the 1970s. But he shot back into the top ten with 1980's "Let's Get it While the Getting's Good" and "That's What I Get for Loving You." His 1999 "Cattle Call" hit with LeAnn Rimes came fifty-four years after his first charted disc, setting yet another record.

*Billboard* magazine's statistics rank Eddy Arnold as the number-one country artist of all time. His lifetime sales have been estimated at $75 million. Notably frugal with his finances, Eddy retired from the road in 1999 as a very wealthy man. His real estate holdings are said to be worth $12 million.

"Oh, I know what all the tour buses say," he chuckled about the fans who pass his home each day. "They say I'm the richest guy in country music, that I drive a Volkswagen, that I donated a church to Brentwood. I've never owned a Volkswagen, and that church was built in 1925! Someday I'm gonna put on a disguise and ride one of those things.

"You need to be careful," he said of his investments. "As a young person, you're selling millions of records, and you get the feeling it's never gonna end. You think it's gonna go on the rest of your life.

One day, there's gonna be another young person out there that the girls are gonna run and squeal over. And they'll forget. That's when they gotta have something in the bank. That's what I think about when I look at a young artist who is very, very successful. And it's tough to be successful. To the public, we make it look like it's so easy. It's not easy. It's hard."

His "retirement" was eventful. In 2000, the White House presented him with the National Medal of Arts. In 2003, he and Sally made the largest single donation of memorabilia in history to the Country Music Hall of Fame. In 2005, he was honored with a Grammy Lifetime Achievement Award. Later that year, he recorded a new RCA collection titled *After All These Years*. It became the one hundredth album of his astounding career.

Sally Arnold died on March 11, 2008. "I want to be with her," mourned Eddy. He died on May 8, 2008, exactly one week before his ninetieth birthday. In tribute, RCA issued the touching "To Life" as his final single. When it hit the charts, Eddy Arnold made history again, as the only artist to place a record on the charts in seven consecutive decades.

In the spring of 2007, an elderly fan approached the living legend to say how much his singing on the Grand Ole Opry had meant to him as a youngster growing up on a Missouri farm. "I left the Opry more than fifty years ago!" Eddy sputtered. But no one who heard his golden voice on the fabled show ever forgot it.

# Garth and Trisha

S ometimes people marry their best friends."

That is how Garth Brooks talked about his blossoming romance with fellow Opry star Trisha Yearwood in 2003. The two married on December 10, 2005.

Speaking to television personality Lorianne Crook two years later, Garth said, "Trisha Yearwood is my morning and my evening. She is my breathe in and my breathe out. . . . Miss Yearwood makes me want to be a better me. I want Miss Yearwood to be so happy that we were married."

Says Trisha, "Everything is in the best perspective of my life . . . I feel wiser. I am just very, very happy."

Garth and Trisha were singing partners for many years before their friendship turned into a courtship. They were introduced to one another in early 1989 by songwriter Kent Blazy, who cowrote Garth's hits "If Tomorrow Never Comes," "Ain't Goin' Down ('Til the Sun Comes Up)," "Somewhere Other Than the Night," "It's Midnight Cinderella," and "She's Gonna Make It." At the time, Trisha was a studio demo singer, making tapes of songs that were played in the hope that stars would record them. Garth was a demo singer, too. Although he had signed a contract with Capitol Records, his first single had yet to be released. Kent believed in

Trisha's talent and had a hunch that her voice would blend well with Garth's. He was right. Garth was floored by her vocal prowess when they sang together at Kent's house.

Garth promised Trisha that if he ever went on tour, he would hire her as his opening act. In the year that followed, he rose to stardom, and she got a recording contract at MCA. While her debut single, "She's in Love with the Boy," was rising to number one in 1991, Trisha was on the road, opening shows on the Garth Brooks tour.

They came to Nashville on very different paths. Born Troyal Garth Brooks on February 7, 1962, he is "to the manner born." Mother Colleen Carroll Brooks sang on the *Ozark Jubilee* and recorded four singles for Capitol Records in 1955–1957. She even guest starred on the Grand Ole Opry. Garth is the youngest of six children, several of whom took up music. He began playing in bands in his hometown of Yukon, Oklahoma, at age seventeen.

He attended Oklahoma State in Stillwater and graduated with a journalism degree. Garth married his first wife, Sandy, in 1986, and they moved to Nashville the following year. By then, Garth was a seasoned stage professional with plenty of nightclub work behind him. When he earned his recording contract in 1988, he was ready to rock.

Trisha Yearwood, by contrast, had very little stage experience. Born Patricia Lynn Yearwood on September 19, 1964, she was raised in Monticello, Georgia, by a banker father and a schoolteacher mother. Trisha idolized Linda Ronstadt and Emmylou Harris and yearned to follow in their footsteps. As teenagers, she and her sister Beth sang duets of Linda's and Emmy's songs. When Trisha moved to Nashville in 1985, it was the farthest she'd ever been from home.

Trisha enrolled in Belmont University's music-business program. She was an intern in the publicity department at MTM Records and after graduation became the office's receptionist. She married fellow Belmont student Chris Latham in 1987. They divorced in 1991.

"We probably would have gotten divorced two years sooner except that I was afraid of what my parents would think," Trisha commented at the time. "And you don't want to admit you've failed at something. Divorce is always difficult. But the good part was, I had the career to really throw myself into.

"That's probably one of the problems that I've had in my personal life . . . my career has always been more important."

After singing studio demo recordings for two and a half years, Trisha was spotted singing in Nashville's Douglas Corner club by producer Garth Fundis. He introduced her to MCA Records. In 1991–1992, Trisha exploded on the popularity charts with such tunes as "The Woman Before Me" and "Wrong Side of Memphis." The latter contained the memorable lyric, "I've had this dream from a tender age/Calling my name from the Opry stage."

By then, Garth's Opry dream had already come true. He first appeared on the show as a guest on June 24, 1989. He wept for joy that night. On October 6, 1990, Garth officially joined the Grand Ole Opry cast. He was inducted by Johnny Russell and sang his hits "Friends in Low Places," "If Tomorrow Never Comes," and "The Dance."

"I've always been treated like family when I was at the Opry," said Garth. "But now to be recognized as a member is among the class of honors that will never be topped, no matter how long or how far my career goes."

In 1992, Garth and Sandy named their first daughter partially after the Opry's Minnie Pearl. The little girl was christened Taylor Mayne Pearl Brooks. A second daughter, August Anna, was born in 1994. Allie Colleen Brooks, born in 1996, carries Garth's mother's name.

Garth and Sandy's marriage weathered some rough spots. Early in his career, she caught him cheating on her and threatened to leave him. He begged her to forgive him, and she did. Garth took his wife and baby on the road with him in 1993. But in 1995, they quarreled over his nonstop working. They separated in early 1999.

TRISHA YEARWOOD MARRIED ROBERT Reynolds of The Mavericks in 1994. The ceremony was the first event held in the newly reno-

vated Ryman Auditorium. Mavericks lead singer Raul Malo ser-
enaded the couple with the Elvis Presley ballad "Can't Help Falling
in Love."

Both Trisha and The Mavericks then entered their most prolific hit-making eras. The band was named the Country Music
Association's Group of the Year in 1995 and 1996 and scored on
the charts with "All You Ever Do Is Bring Me Down." Trisha's
1995–1997 output included "Thinkin' About You," "Believe Me
Baby (I Lied)," and "How Do I Live." She was named CMA Female
Vocalist of the Year in 1997 and 1998.

Trisha and Garth continued to sing harmonies on each other's albums
throughout the decade. In 1997, they finally issued a full-fledged duet,
"In Another's Eyes." It won the team a Grammy Award and led to their
1998 concert tour together. Subsequent duets have included "Where
Your Road Leads" (1998) and "Squeeze Me In" (2001), and they have
often talked about doing an entire album of them.

Ricky Skaggs invited Trisha Yearwood to become an Opry
member during a Ryman Auditorium show on January 16, 1999.
On March 13, 1999, Porter Wagoner inducted Trisha into the cast
of the Grand Ole Opry.

"I've done a lot of things in my life, so far, but this night takes
the cake," she said. "I'm really proud that you could all be here.

"I'm excited to be part of a group of artists who seem to be really
committed to letting people know how important the Opry is,
people like Vince [Gill], Garth, Steve Wariner and Ricky Skaggs,
artists who are going to take this to the next generation, to teach
the younger artists the importance of it, to try to keep it going for
future generations."

At the Opry House induction ceremony, Patsy Cline's widower
Charlie Dick and daughter Julie presented Trisha with a silver neck-
lace that had belonged to Patsy. In the legend's honor, Trisha sang
"Sweet Dreams."

"Right before I started [to sing], I looked down at the circle of
wood [from the Ryman stage], and I definitely felt Patsy was there,"
Trisha said backstage.

Later that year, Trisha and Robert divorced amicably. They have remained friends.

Also in 1999, Garth's mother died of cancer. He had long been dedicating his 1998 inspirational hit "It's Your Song" to her. After her death, Garth began talking seriously of retiring. He made it official at a press conference in October 2000. He stated that he would issue one more album and also indicated that he and Sandy had discussed divorcing. A week later, that became official, too, when divorce papers were filed. The divorce was finalized in 2001.

Garth and Trisha began appearing in public as a couple in 2002. She kept her house in Nashville but started spending more and more time with him in Oklahoma during 2003. Garth moved from Nashville to Claremore, a town northeast of Tulsa, because that is where Sandy had moved with their daughters. He and Trisha built a 30,000-square-foot mansion there, not far from Sandy's house. The Brooks daughters divide their time between the two residences.

On May 25, 2005, Garth went down on bended knee and proposed to Trisha in Bakersfield, California, at Buck Owens's Crystal Palace nightclub. Some seven thousand fans cheered when she said, "Yes."

"What's new with you guys?" Trisha playfully asked the crowd at her concert that summer at the CMA Music Festival in Nashville. She waved her hand playfully in front of her, showing off her engagement ring. "Me? Nothing's really new with me," she added coyly. Thousands roared with laughter. That December, Garth and Trisha wed in a quiet ceremony at their house.

"From the first day that I met her, you knew there was something special," says Garth. "She's as beautiful inside as she is outside. You just love her when you meet her."

"I fought it, and fought it, and fought it, for so long," says Trisha of their romance. "I said, 'Okay, let's explore it and see what happens.' This is the guy. He's it. I feel it's the right place to be."

"She is a dream, she is a doll, an amazing cook," says Garth. "She loves our three girls, and they love her. And she gets along great with Sandy. . . . Everybody gets along great. . . . That's gotta be my biggest thank-you."

"I've met a couple of soccer moms, and we get together three or four times a week," Trisha says of her daily life in Claremore. "We do a four-mile hike on the farm. It's wonderful, because I'm hanging out with women who don't understand chart positions and don't care. We talk about other things, and it's a really nice time for me.

"I've always been a good little Southern cook, but this has given me the opportunity to really do a lot of cooking. These kids know me for my mashed potatoes as much as they do for my music, which makes me happy. The other boring, nerd thing that I do is I crochet. You know, I'm really boring, but very happy."

There is just one little problem: "Being with Garth and him being retired from the road, people sometimes think I am too. And I'm quick to say, 'He's retired. I'm not.' I'm not finished, and I don't know when that time will come for me."

# Loretta and Doo

I know what love is," says Loretta Lynn without hesitation, "because I love Doo."

She speaks of her late husband, Oliver "Doolittle" Lynn, in the present tense, although Doo died more than a decade ago. Doo was more than her husband. He practically raised Loretta. And he is the reason she became a singing star. In the early years of her career, he pushed her onto the stage, into radio stations, and to the Grand Ole Opry.

"When you can't forget somebody, you must love them, right?" adds Loretta. "When I'm down at the ranch, it's really weird, because a lot of times I'll raise up and holler, 'What?' because I'll hear him speak my name.

"I think that's why I keep trying to run from down there. But it's no use running. I go and stay there when I'm off the road. But when I'm on the road, I try to stay away from there as much as possible, because it is hard on me."

Loretta has a house in Nashville where she stays when touring, but her memory-filled antebellum mansion still stands on the grounds of Loretta Lynn's Dude Ranch in Hurricane Mills, Tennessee. The iconic house and her turbulent marriage are familiar to millions, thanks to her best-selling autobiography *Coal Miner's Daughter* and the Oscar-winning film it inspired.

"Doo was really a sweet, tender person when he wasn't out there trying to show off in the public. He tried to hold up his image a lot, and all he'd do was get in trouble. Every time he'd get drunk and carry on, we'd all hear about it. So he couldn't win."

Just as Loretta had her image as a feisty country superstar, Doo had his as a macho roughneck. The interplay between the two fascinated her millions of fans.

Born Loretta Webb on April 14, 1935, in Butcher Hollow, Kentucky, she was famously just thirteen years old when she met and married the love of her life. He was a twenty-one-year-old army veteran with a wild reputation. His family had nicknamed him "Doolittle" because he was such a small baby. In fact, Loretta thought that was his real name until she saw "Oliver" on their marriage license.

"We'd only went together a month when I married him," Loretta explains. "One month! We started going together the tenth day of December, and on the tenth day of January [1948], we got married.

"He asked, 'Will you marry me?' the day before we got married. Mommy and Daddy 'bout died. Mommy cried all night long. Daddy was so tore up. But he'd asked them [for their permission] the night before.

"When I was two months pregnant, he'd already left me. He'd found him a new girlfriend, he said. I found out the kind of girlfriend he was with wasn't really the kind of girl he wanted to be married to. So he was really not what he seemed to be."

Determined to get her husband back, the teenager wrote to her rival and told the hussy in no uncertain terms to "lay off." A contrite Doo was by then offering to buy baby clothes. She was fourteen and seven months pregnant when Doo moved Loretta 2,000 miles across the country to the state of Washington. When his workmates there learned he had smuggled moonshine whiskey back home in Kentucky, they gave him his second nickname, "Mooney."

By age eighteen, Loretta Lynn had four children. Isolated from her family, tied down by motherhood, burdened by ceaseless domestic work, and desperately lonely, she found solace in her singing. Doo listened to her and declared that she was as good as anyone he heard on the radio.

"He's the one that started me singin'," Loretta reports. "He come in one day from work and said, 'Loretta, I've heard you singin' rockin' the babies to sleep, and as I listen to the radio, there's no girls on the radio that cain't sing any better than you. I think I'm gonna try to do something with your voice.' And he did."

He bought her a $17 guitar, and she taught herself to play it. In 1959, he began taking the shy Loretta into local honky-tonks and forcing her to sing in front of audiences. He pushed her to enter a Tacoma talent contest, which she won. Future superstar Buck Owens (1929–2006) began to feature Loretta on his Tacoma country TV show. A Canadian businessman saw her on it and financed a trip to Los Angeles to record her self-penned tune "I'm a Honky Tonk Girl."

"I wrote my first song when I was about ten years old. I started writing songs not even really knowing how to do it when I was just a kid. But when I did really start getting down to writing was when Doo said I was going to sing. Doo bought me a guitar and expected me to write songs. And that was it. He bought me a *Country Song Roundup* [magazine]. I learned how to write in there," by studying the hit song lyrics that the periodical published in each issue.

Doo found a list of country-music radio stations. He took a photo of Loretta in a cowgirl outfit and mailed it with copies of "I'm a Honky Tonk Girl" to each station on the list. Then he piled his bride into his old Mercury sedan and took her from station to station for three solid months. At each stop, she'd change into the cowgirl outfit, go into the station, and charm the local disc jockey into playing her record. At KCKY in Coolidge, Arizona, the DJ was future star Waylon Jennings (1937–2002).

"The first time I ever saw Loretta Lynn, was in Arizona," Waylon later recalled. "I was a disc jockey out there, and this beautiful little girl came in with the thickest accent I had ever heard in my life. But she was just gorgeous you know, and she had this record with her. She brought this record in and asked me if I would play it. It was on the Zero label, that's the reason I remember it. And so we sat there that afternoon, and she talked to me. I gave her a tape of a couple of songs that I had written. She's still got 'em. We've been friends ever since."

Amazingly, Doo's homespun approach to the music business worked. Despite being on the dinky Zero label, "I'm a Honky Tonk Girl" appeared on the national country popularity charts in the summer of 1960. It also brought the couple to Nashville and to the stage of the Grand Ole Opry. On October 15, 1960, Loretta made her Opry debut, singing her against-all-odds hit.

"When I first stepped on the stage at the Grand Ole Opry, they had to push me out on the stage because I was so bashful and backward. I remember patting my foot to my song. I don't remember singing, but I do remember patting my foot.

"Doo was outside [the Ryman Auditorium] trying to get it on the radio," Loretta remembers. "He was out in the alley, and he was trying to get it on his car radio. I came out the back and hollered, 'Honey, I've just sung on the Grand Ole Opry!' And he was still just trying to get it. There was so much static he couldn't figure out what was going on. He never even heard me! But he come running, and we were hugging."

Early in her Nashville career, Loretta was aided by a number of Opry stars. The show's handsome and popular Wilburn Brothers were the first and foremost in this regard. Doo and Loretta approached them for career advice. Doyle Wilburn (1930–1982) and Teddy Wilburn (1931–2003) were then at the peak of their success. Since joining the Opry in 1953, the duo had racked up eight top-ten country hits, including "Sparkling Brown Eyes" (1954) and "Somebody's Back in Town" (1959). Astute businessmen, the brothers also owned a song-publishing company and a management firm. Loretta signed with both, and the brothers instantly went to work.

Teddy had Loretta record a tune from their company called "The Biggest Fool of All," and Doyle played the result for Decca Records executive Owen Bradley. Owen said Loretta sounded too much like his label's star, Kitty Wells, but that he wanted the song for another Decca headliner, Brenda Lee. The Wilburns insisted that if Owen took the song, he had to offer Loretta a recording contract. So Brenda got the retitled smash "Fool #1," and Loretta got a major-label deal.

"Loretta was real timid and real bashful," Owen Bradley recalled. "I told her, 'You sound like a female Hank Williams.'"

Produced by Owen, "Success" became her first Decca hit in 1962. On the strength of that, the Wilburns successfully lobbied the Opry to add her to its cast. Loretta Lynn became an official Grand Ole Opry member on September 24, 1962. "Before I'm Over You" (1963) and "Wine, Women and Song" (1964) were Loretta's next big hits. The Wilburns featured her on their nationally syndicated TV series. Even so, she was very much a newcomer when her next Opry booster stepped into the picture.

By the 1960s, Ernest Tubb (1914–1984) was unquestionably a country superstar. Ernest was one of the great innovators. He was a founder of the post–World War II honky-tonk style, popularized the electric guitar in country music, took the Opry to Carnegie Hall for the first time, campaigned against the use of the term "hillbilly," created the still-thriving late-night radio show *The Midnite Jamboree,* and built the Ernest Tubb Record Shop into an international retail phenomenon. In the early 1960s, he decided he wanted a female duet partner. He could have had his pick of any of country's women. But he chose the relatively unknown Loretta Lynn.

They debuted as a team with 1964's "Mr. and Mrs. Used to Be." It was the first of their four big duet hits. They also recorded three albums together in 1964–1966.

"I learned a great deal from Ernest Tubb. He said to me, 'Now hon, I'm gonna tell you something in this business. Tomorrow you may not have a hit record.' And, of course, for twenty-five years, I had records in the charts, so I couldn't complain. And for twenty-five years I kept looking for 'em to flop out of the charts, you know. But that's something that every artist should know. That they're not gonna be up there forever, and tomorrow may be their last big hit record.

"Ernest Tubb helped more people in this business than anybody else. Ernest was probably never given the credit for helping as many people as he has. He put me on the Ernest Tubb Record Shop's *Midnite Jamboree* radio show and helped me get on the Grand Ole Opry for the first time that I was on.

"Decca Records asked Ernest Tubb, 'If you could record with anybody you wanted to, who would you like to record with?' I was just the new girl on the block at the time, but he said, 'If I could record with anybody, I would love to record with the little new girl called Loretta Lynn.' So they called me and asked me if I would do it, and I said, 'Oh, I don't believe this.' He's the only one that ever did come on the radio—when Daddy had the old Philco radio—that just about every song he sang, I would cry. I don't know why to this day. But I can still listen to Ernest Tubb and cry. He would be singing 'It's Been So Long Darling,' and I would cry. Then when he sang 'Rainbow at Midnight,' I would cry. I was just a little girl, and I never dreamed I'd ever, ever sing with Ernest Tubb. And the last time that I stood up and sang with Ernest Tubb was like the first time. Never got used to ever singing with Ernest Tubb, because he was such a great hero to me. I can't even explain it. He was a monument to me. They just don't make 'em like Ernest Tubb anymore."

The third Opry star who mentored Loretta was the great Patsy Cline. Patsy taught the youngster how to dress, apply makeup, and style her hair. She taught her about backstage jealousy and about onstage finesse. Loretta idolized and adored Patsy.

"I wanted to be just like Patsy. But how could you be like Patsy? She was twenty-five years ahead of her time, and everybody thought I was twenty-five years behind my time. Patsy, bless her heart, she done everything she could to help me.

"Patsy was a person that said her words perfect. If you've ever listened to her singing, you'll notice that ever' word that she says in her songs are perfect. Right? Well you might ought to think how it was for me and Patsy to sit down and carry on a conversation. She would be laughing at everything I would say. And I'd say, 'What's wrong?' I thought, you know, maybe I'd told a joke or something. She'd say, 'The way you just said so-and-so,' and she'd laugh.

"Patsy taught me how to do a lot of my dressing. She bought a lot of my clothes for me. She would give me clothes to wear. I didn't have much. She'd tell me how to go onstage and how to come offstage."

Patsy was also responsible for Loretta learning to stand up for herself. The superstar went toe-to-toe with her ne'er-do-well husband Charlie Dick. As Loretta grew to womanhood, she became more feisty with Oliver Doolittle Lynn. His philandering led to Loretta writing more and more self-assertive songs and becoming increasingly outspoken about women's issues. "Don't Come Home A-Drinkin'" (1966) wasn't fictional. It was the truth.

"He liked to drink, but not backstage. He liked to drink, but he didn't want nobody to watch him. You can't blame him. It seemed to me like I knew how to [pick a fight] when it came to Doo. Because if I was tired or wanted to be left alone, one or two little things would just set him off. Well, I wouldn't have to worry about him for the rest of the evening, because he'd go get drunk and stay that way for a day or two.

"You know, before I started singing, and I lived out in the state of Washington, I swore if I ever got away and got back to Kentucky where I could leave and be on my own again, I'd do it. But I didn't. I thought to myself, 'Don't get too big for your britches. Don't act like you're better than he is.' You have to love somebody really well and respect them. If you don't respect them, there's no use loving them.

"And I did respect Doo. He kept me grounded. And I could always look to him if I had a record out or if I done a good job onstage or whatever. I could always depend on him telling me the truth.

"When I was writing the song 'Fist City,' he said, 'You're gonna have to speak them words real plain when you sing, "gonna tell you gals to lay offa my man if you don't wanna go to Fist City." He said, 'It sounds like you're saying, "gonna tell you GUYS."' I feel like he was probably what made me do things as well as I did. He was the reason I tried to do better. It made me more nervous if he was backstage at a show. Because I felt like I had to be perfect around him.

"So he kept me pretty straight on a lot of things. I miss that right now. It's hard to find somebody to do that, because everybody around you is going to say, 'Yeah, you did great,' because they don't want you to be mad at them.

"That's what I really miss about him, is the way we played off each other. I think he was good for me. I think we were both good for each other."

Not that every day was peaches and cream. "Fist City" (1968) and "You Ain't Woman Enough" (1966) came from a very real place. Yes, there were "other women."

"Behind my back, he was out with the guys pulling that stuff. You can't win, can you?

"I was out in Vegas, and at the Aladdin Theater the tables are right up next to the stage. This ole gal kept hollering that she was going out with Doolittle. She kept hollering, 'I went out with your old man. I was out with him on Monday when I went to the Dude Ranch.' And blah-blah-blah. She kept carrying on like that. I said, 'Well, I'll just come out and see if you're woman enough to take my man!' I just laid the microphone down. I started walking on the tables! It cost me a lot of money in spilled drinks getting to her. They drug her out before I got to her table. So Doo and I both probably had our faults when it came to stuff like that [fighting]."

The Wilburn Brothers tried to polish her countrified image. Producer Owen Bradley disagreed, telling them to let her be her natural self. He was the wise one, because Loretta's Appalachian twang, natural sense of humor, and blunt-spoken honesty charmed everyone.

Loretta recalls one incident early in her career with typical candor—"The first time that I got heels was when Teddy Wilburn locked my boots up in the trunk of the car. We were on tour. He locked my boots up in the trunk of the car and went out and bought me a pair of heels about that high. So that was all I had to wear on the stage. And I went on the stage in Salt Lake City, I'll never forget it if I live to be 150 years old—which I will. I went onstage and had my guitar on my back. There was a little gate that you had to walk through to get up on the stage, and I couldn't even get through that gate with them high heels on and my guitar. The disc jockey had to help me get up onstage. I walked on the stage, and I know the people thought I was drunk. For the first two or three songs I was standing there, and it was killing me. I thought, 'I've got to let 'em know I'm not drunk,' 'cause I don't drink. So I pulled off my shoes, and I said, 'Friends, I don't wear high heels. This is the first pair I've ever had. Teddy Wilburn has my boots out in the trunk of his car and won't give 'em to me. I can't wear these shoes. If you don't mind I'll just finish my show barefooted.' And that's the way I finished my show."

She buck-danced barefooted in her concerts for many years to come.

By 1964, Loretta had tallied six straight hits and was working continually. When she found out she was pregnant again, she burst into tears. She feared her burgeoning career was coming to an end. Doo, on the other hand, seemed pleased with his accomplishment.

Her older children, Betty Sue, Jack Benny, Ernest Ray, and Cissie, were joined by twins Patsy and Peggy in 1964. From the start, Doo doted on them. Loretta went back to work, and he became "Mr. Mom." He also got a vasectomy. "When they start coming in pairs, it's time to quit," quipped Loretta.

Loretta Lynn was named the Country Music Association's Female Vocalist of the Year in 1967. By the end of the decade, she had sixteen top-ten hits. It was only the beginning. Her star ascended even higher in the 1970s. On the strength of such hits as "Coal Miner's Daughter" (1970) and "One's on the Way" (1972), she was again named CMA's Female Vocalist in 1972 and 1973. In 1972, she became the first woman to win the CMA's Entertainer of the Year award. "After the Fire Is Gone" (1971), "Lead Me On" (1971), "Louisiana Woman, Mississippi Man" (1973), and other hits led to CMA Duo of the Year awards for Loretta Lynn and Conway Twitty in 1972, 1973, 1974, and 1975.

"Me and Conway Twitty were over in London, and we were playing the Palladium. He'd be in one dressing room singing, and I'd be in the other one singing just as loud as I could, trying to drown him out, just for meanness. So him and I got together with some harmony over there. We recorded for the same label, so he said, 'Loretta, why don't we record together?' And I said, 'Well, let's see what the label has to say.' The hardest part for me was that I was still singing with Ernest. But the label really wanted us to go ahead and record together.

"Conway was such a great man. My husband loved him too. Him and Conway got along so good. Doo would of never, ever thought of me recording with anybody else after me and Conway started recording together.

"I loved Conway like a brother, with all my heart. We had a duet going like nobody else, because when we would get in the studio we tried to out-sing each other. We would come out doing our best. We sang together better than we did apart."

Her infectious personality charmed Conway Twitty (1933–1993) just as it did everyone she encountered in those days. During the 1970s, Loretta became a big favorite on the TV talk-show circuit. She was featured on the covers of *Newsweek* (1973), *Redbook* (1974), and other mainstream periodicals. The 1976 publication of her autobiography *Coal Miner's Daughter* made her story familiar to millions. Like everything else about her, the book was characterized by her wit and honesty.

"Take me as I am, because I couldn't change," she comments. "There wasn't no way for me to change. I was having a hard enough time being me. So why should I change? Why should I change the way I say a word because somebody else wants me to? When I wrote my book, [cowriter] George Vecsey would come out on the road with me. He would put everything on tape. He'd go back home, and he would send me the chapter and tell me to work it over. Well, I'd work it over, and I'd write the words like I'd say 'em. I'd spell 'em exactly like I said 'em. So he got a little upset about this at first. He said it would never sell."

*Coal Miner's Daughter* topped *The New York Times* best-seller list. Its dedication reads "To Doo, who had an idea."

Loretta Lynn was then a certified superstar. Concert offers poured in, and she threw herself into her work. Her devotion to her fans became legendary, but it came at a price. The pressures of stardom, the constant travel, and the unending work took a toll on her physical and mental health. In 1976, she suffered a complete breakdown while onstage in Illinois. She was hospitalized several times for exhaustion. Each time, Doo was there to pick up the pieces.

When *Coal Miner's Daughter* was made into a film, in 1980, Loretta became a national icon. Star Sissy Spacek won an Academy Award for her portrayal of the country legend.

"Sissy was on the road with me for a year, off and on. She liked to kill me. I was doing two shows a night, and then working with her until four in the morning. I was learning her all the songs. We'd pin the lyrics up with clothespins on lampshades. I'd go in front of her with a guitar and sing, and she'd come up behind me. This is what we did every night, just about, while I was working. And at that time, I was working every night. That's the way they did back then: two shows a night, and if you couldn't do it, get out of the business."

Doo, on the other hand, kept actor Tommy Lee Jones at arm's length. He hated it when Tommy Lee imitated his walk and his mannerisms. Eventually, he did offer to help the actor portraying him. But Loretta says it was too little too late, and that's why Doo had no right to complain when Tommy Lee's acting wasn't awarded.

Loretta clung to Doolittle more than ever after son Jack Benny Lynn drowned in the Duck River, near their home, in 1984. She has no memory of the accident's aftermath, nor of the funeral. Similarly, she can recall the days leading up to her mother's death in 1981 but has no memory of the funeral. While she completely blocked these events from her mind, Doo took charge.

She dealt with her grief by returning to work and by attending a plethora of awards banquets held on her behalf. Loretta's achievements won her dozens of honors in the 1980s. She was inducted into the Nashville Songwriters Hall of Fame in 1983. In 1988, she was inducted into the Country Music Hall of Fame. In 1993, her *Honky Tonk Angels* trio album with Dolly Parton and Tammy Wynette (1942–1998) earned Loretta renewed acclaim.

But by then she was facing her darkest days. Doo developed diabetes. Instead of being her caretaker, she became his. Between 1991 and 1996, she was almost constantly by his bedside.

"I took care of him for six years," she says sadly. "He was in bed. I just forgot about everything else, and that was all I thought of, trying to take care of him. When they started taking his legs off, one and then the other one, I knew it was bad.

"Ain't that awful? It just tore me up. I don't remember much about that first year [after his death in 1996]. I really don't. I lost a complete year of memory. I come here to Nashville and stayed in this little house. Do you know I was there for a year and really never even called about the kids?"

Numb with grief, Loretta began writing songs again. In 2000, she released a CD titled *Still Country*. It contained "I Can't Hear the Music Anymore," a tribute to her late husband. On the recording, she is audibly sobbing. The album's "Country in My Genes" made the popularity charts. When it did, sixty-five-year-old Loretta made history by becoming country's senior charting female star. She published a second memoir in 2002, *Still Woman Enough*. In it, she reminisced often about her life's companion.

"He thought I was something special, more special than anybody else in the world, and never let me forget it," Loretta wrote. "Doolittle Lynn was my husband; my soul mate from the time I was thirteen years old. He was my everything. When you lose everything, you are a lost person. I got lost for quite a while after Doo died in 1996." Again, she dealt with the profound loss by returning to the road.

"It's a good thing, too. Because if I hadn't I would have been nuts by now. I would have been completely nuts."

Incredibly, she once more became the center of a firestorm of acclaim. Jack White of the rock band The White Stripes had long professed himself a fan. In 2004, he produced Loretta's album *Van Lear Rose*. It revived her career, inspired a hit video, and won two Grammy Awards. Again, Loretta included on the album an ode to Doo, the sad lament "Miss Being Mrs."

"Doo could always stand up to me, and stand beside me, too. And I always loved that in him. He was always there. And I would do what he said 99 percent of the time. I may not like his criticism and I would get mad. But I would weigh it out when I'd get to myself and think about it. And Doo would always have the right decision for me. I think a woman oughtta listen to that. Because a man usually does have the right decision for his woman, because that's his woman, and he loves her.

"We fought like cats and dogs and everything else. Doo and I fought, and we loved. We fought, and we loved. We fought, and we loved. But I think both of us loved each other. That's what kept us together. That's what love is."

# No-Show Jones

By the 1980s, it seemed almost certain that the life of George Jones was going to play itself out as one of country music's greatest tragedies. Chronically skipping shows, mentally unstable, practically destitute, and enslaved by drugs and alcohol, George was on a slide toward the bottom of a very deep pit.

Hailed as one of the greatest country vocalists in history, George Jones was recording some of the best performances of his career. But away from the studio, his life had become a living hell.

"God knows how many prayers I got from the fans," George reflects. "If I hadn't quit drinking, I'd be dead. Because I was at the point where I couldn't even drink a glass of wine without getting drunk. That's the way my system was. It had gotten to the point where it couldn't take any more."

There is a one-word answer to his salvation and rehabilitation. And that word is Nancy, the steadfast and loyal woman who not only became his wife but literally saved his life.

As chronicled in terrifying detail in his autobiography *I Lived to Tell It All,* Nancy's journey with George has been difficult. They met in 1981, and he was soon missing shows in order to be with her in Shreveport, Louisiana. At the time, George's reputation was at its nadir, with him being known as "No-Show Jones." At his invitation, she quit her factory job to become his constant companion. When his brain was inflamed by cocaine, he beat her.

"When we went through the tough times, a lot of people said, 'Well, why did you stay?'" Nancy comments. "Because I knew there was a wonderful guy in there when he wasn't drinking and all that.

"I was kind of shocked at some of the things—I never knew about the drugs and all of that drinking. But I knew in there was a nice guy, once we got the Devil out of him. And we definitely did that."

"One thing that has kept us together is that she is down to earth, just like I am," says George. "We were both raised up without anything, out in the country. We never had anything. And when we first met, we had just $20 apiece.

"She helped so much with the solvency. The no-show things and the lawyers had to be taken care of. She'd call them up and explain things to them. We did some make-up dates here and there. And she got it all worked out. We saved. Just by her jumping in there, I had a manager."

Nancy had no experience with drugs and alcohol, yet she took it upon herself to battle them. She had no experience with show business, yet she learned to book shows, manage concert percentages, and renegotiate recording contracts.

Whether she was aware of it or not, Nancy was stepping into the world of one of the most legendary country entertainers in history. Born in East Texas on September 12, 1931, George Jones began singing as a child and was on local radio as a teenager.

"Roy Acuff was the first man I ever heard sing a country song," he recalls. "I've got a picture of me and him by my bed at home and a picture of me and him on the bus by the bed. I even recorded a whole album of Roy Acuff songs with the Smoky Mountain Boys. But I never could get my record label interested in putting it out."

George was an eighteen-year-old with his own afternoon radio show in Beaumont, Texas, when he met his other idol, the man known as "The Hillbilly Shakespeare."

"The program director knew Hank Williams personally and invited him to come down and do a song on the show, 'cause he was appearing that night in Beaumont. 'Wedding Bells' was what he had out at the time [1949]. I was gonna play lead guitar for him and kick it off. He just started singing and, boy, I never hit a lick, not a note. I just stared and gazed at him. Couldn't believe he was standing there."

George married his first wife, Dorothy, in 1950. Following their separation, she bore him a daughter, Susan. After serving in the marines and getting a divorce, he married his second wife, Shirley, in 1954. They have two sons, Jeffrey and Bryan. They divorced in 1968.

George issued his debut single, "No Money in This Deal," in 1954 and scored a top-ten hit with "Why Baby Why" the following year. "What Am I Worth" and "You Gotta Be My Baby" both hit the top ten in 1956. As a result, he was invited to become a member of the Grand Ole Opry on August 25, 1956. George joined the show again on March 31, 1973.

In a striking display of longevity, George Jones remained on the country-music popularity charts every year between 1955 and 1998. And in each of those decades, he created bona fide country classics. His 1950s chestnuts include "White Lightning" (1959) and "Color of the Blues" (1958). From the 1960s came "She Thinks I Still Care" (1962), "The Race Is On" (1964), "Love Bug" (1965), and "If My Heart Had Windows" (1967). From the 1970s came "A Good Year for the Roses" (1970), "The Grand Tour" (1974), and "A Picture of Me (Without You)" (1972). His 1980s classics include "He Stopped Loving Her Today" (1980) and "Who's Gonna Fill Their Shoes" (1985). In the 1990s he unforgettably sang "You Don't Seem to Miss Me" (1997, with Patty Loveless) and the Grammy Award–winning "Choices" (1999). Since then, he has teamed with Garth Brooks on 2001's "Beer Run" and Shooter Jennings on 2005's "Fourth of July."

Among George's most memorable collaborations were those with Tammy Wynette, who was his third wife, from 1969 until

1975. Fans called them "The President and the First Lady" when they were country music's most famous married couple. They had daughter Georgette. Because of George's well-chronicled battle with the bottle, their union didn't endure. But it left fans with a host of colorful anecdotes and a string of unforgettable recorded duets. Tammy's death in 1998 at age fifty-five brought their story to a sad end.

In the wake of their 1975 divorce, George spiraled out of control. He was arrested for assault, sued over missed concert bookings, bankrupt, and hospitalized for substance abuse. In spite of all this, his recording career continued to move forward. And, amazingly, he found true love.

George married Nancy in Texas on March 4, 1983. Despite her predecessor's fame, Nancy says she has never felt like she is in Tammy's shadow. "The fans accepted me, and they still do," she says.

"The fans love her to death," adds George. "And she loves them. She loves people. She gets out there and kids around with them at the concession stand, talking to all those people. I say, 'Honey, you don't need to be doing that.'"

"But I love to," she protests. "I love people, and I think the people know when you're sincere.

"People ask me how you live with an alcoholic. It's plain, and it's simple. If you turn your back and don't talk to them, that's wrong. That was a lot of George and Tammy's problem. She wouldn't talk to him. You can't do that. You're not going to build a relationship, a marriage, that way. If the man is drinking, and you sit there and don't talk to him, well, that just makes it that much sadder."

With Nancy's guidance, George gradually eased up on his consumption. With her loving aid, he began to put his demons behind him and forge a whole new career as a senior citizen. He was elected to the Country Music Hall of Fame in 1992 and underwent a successful coronary bypass operation in 1994. During this same period, he staged his serious bid for sobriety.

"I went through them withdrawal symptoms for about the first two years, just like the doctor said I would," said George in 1993.

"I thought I was dying. It scared me to death. I would just get down on the floor and roll. It was awful."

Nevertheless, he relapsed. In the end, it was a brush with death that led to full sobriety. On March 6, 1999, a backsliding George was involved in a major car crash, driving his Lexus into a bridge abutment near his home, south of Nashville. He was unconscious for eleven of the thirteen days he spent in the hospital. He had a lacerated liver, a collapsed lung, and internal bleeding. He developed pneumonia, and a tube from a ventilator damaged his vocal cords. His weight dropped drastically.

"That bad wreck I had really opened my eyes and put the fear of God in me," George comments. "I was slowing down a lot in my drinking. I still hadn't quit completely. After I had that bad wreck, I couldn't get nothing to stay down. I thought, 'This is it, this time.' I said a lot of prayers, and I finally got to eating. I just made up my mind to quit [drinking]. While all this was going on, I threw the cigarettes away. Now I can't stand the smell of smoke at all."

Ironically, just weeks before the accident, he had prayed, asking God to "straighten me up, or hit me in the head with a sledgehammer, or do something to make me see the way and quit doing all the drinking and things I've done in the past.

"I just didn't know He was gonna hurt me that bad!"

Nancy thinks George hid his shyness behind the bottle. By facing the world with clear eyes, George has become the man she fell in love with. In 2008, the Joneses celebrated their twenty-fifth anniversary.

"I think he wanted a family, but I don't think that he knew how to be around one unless he had to have a drink," Nancy observes. "He thought that was the way to make himself funny or likable or whatever. Now, it's not that way. He knows that he has a family."

"I don't think we'd have stayed together if I hadn't gotten a little sense," says George. "I guess it's just that I quit my rowdy ways.

"We're so much alike, both contrary at times. Neither one of us can put up with anybody else. She's got a great personality. It just happened to strike me. What we felt for each other got stronger and stronger, and turned into true love, I guess. We're so much alike. We're down to earth. We don't try to be something we ain't. That's what I love about her more than anything."

"I think we have like a Johnny Cash–June Carter relationship," says Nancy. "Because one of us can't do without the other. If I'm gone too long, he's worried to death. We're just so close to one another that one of us can't exist without the other."

"I've sure felt better these last few years, for sure," says George Jones. "We got hundreds of letters from people who drank and had nothing but troubles. And they said, 'If George Jones can stop drinking, I can.' They let us know at the shows that we do. And that's just great. You feel like you're good for something else besides just singing.

"If I've helped other people, that's the greatest thing in the world."

**11**

# An Opry "Curse"

March 5, 1963, will always be remembered as one of the most tragic days in the history of the Grand Ole Opry. That is the date of the airplane crash that took the lives of Patsy Cline, Hawkshaw Hawkins, Cowboy Copas, and manager/pilot Randy Hughes. Jean Shepard, who was married to Hawkshaw, has an especially vivid memory of that date.

"I haven't shared this with a lot of people," Jean begins. "The day of the plane crash I had a fifteen-month-old son, and I was eight months pregnant. We lived in this kind of old-fashioned home. And I was so huge with child that I couldn't bend over the bathtub to give my fifteen-month-old a bath. In the kitchen we had this real old-timey sink, about three feet long. So that evening, I was bathing him in this sink.

"Randy Hughes's wife Kathy had called me and told me that Randy had called her from Dyersburg [in West Tennessee] to say that they were coming on in. The weather looked rough, but they thought they could make it. And she said she heard Hawkshaw holler in the background, 'Tell Kathy to call Jean for me.' So she called me.

"Well, I was giving the baby a bath, and all of a sudden I thought I was going into labor. It really scared me. I got so weak that I couldn't stand up. I started shaking all over. I broke out in a cold sweat. I had a little kitchen step stool, and I reached and pulled it over and sat down so the baby wouldn't fall. I sat there for what must have been fifteen or twenty minutes. I was literally so weak and shaken that I couldn't control myself. It was just a horrible feeling."

As Jean later learned, "It was just about the time of the plane crash that I had this feeling come over me.

"I went on and put the baby down and went to bed about 10:30 or so. About 11:00 or 11:30 the phone rang, and it was one of Hawkshaw's fan club representatives from Minneapolis, Minnesota. She called me and said, 'What are you doing?' I was pretty irritable, being eight months pregnant, you know. I said, 'I am doing what all good people should be doing this time of night. I'm sleeping.' She said, 'Oh my God, you don't know.' When she said that, I knew something was very bad and wrong. She started crying, and she was getting pretty hysterical. I said, 'I have to get off the phone. I have to call somebody. I'm here by myself.'

"So I got up and switched on the little bedside radio. Grant Turner, I think, was on the air. I called Smiley and Kitty Wilson, some very dear friends of ours. They came to the house. And we sat the rest of the night out, by the television set.

"It was a nightmare. It was hell."

Meanwhile, Kathy Copas Hughes and her mother Lucille had driven to Nashville's small Cornelia Fort airfield to get its lights turned on in anticipation of the plane's arrival. Kathy was Randy's wife and Cowboy Copas's daughter.

"We sat in the car and waited and waited," Kathy recalled. "It shouldn't have taken Randy more than forty-five minutes to get home. We began to suspect something had gone wrong. We asked the attendant if he'd heard anything. There was no word. Then something snapped in me. I knew immediately something had, indeed, gone wrong. The attendant suggested it might be better if we went home and waited for further news or in case someone was trying to reach us."

At home, they too heard the news of the missing flight via broad-caster Grant Turner on WSM. The phone began ringing just after 8:00 p.m., and soon the house began to fill with friends.

Patsy's husband, Charlie Dick, was playing with their children Randy and Julie early in the evening. Around 7:30 he began to get worried. Around 8:00 some friends arrived at the house. They had heard the news of the vanished flight on the radio. Dottie West, Billy Walker, Mother Maybelle Carter, Roger Miller, June Carter, and other close friends were soon by Charlie's side.

Future Grand Ole Opry star Jan Howard was roused from her sleep by a telephone call around midnight. It was songwriter Hank Cochran, who'd penned the Patsy Cline hits "She's Got You" and "I Fall to Pieces," and he was spooked. Two record albums had suddenly fallen off a shelf, one of Jan's and one of Patsy's. When he heard from Jan that everything was okay at her house, he said he knew that there was "something wrong" with Patsy. Like the others, Jan turned on the radio.

"An all-night disc jockey . . . was saying something about a plane being lost," Jan recalls. "Then he mentioned the names of the passengers. Oh my God. It was Patsy, Hawkshaw Hawkins, Cowboy Copas, and Randy Hughes. . . . The phone rang again. Before Hank could talk, I said, 'I've just heard. I'm going over to Jean's.' Jean Shepard was married to Hawk and was expecting a baby at any time.

"Driving over, I thought, 'God! How could this be happening? We were playing cards with Jean and Hawk just a few nights ago.'"

Meanwhile, over at Hawk and Jean's house, the Wilsons called her physician. Jean was in a daze. The doctor had to give her a sedative and began monitoring the baby's heartbeat every half hour. Minnie Pearl and her husband Henry Cannon arrived and began keeping vigil with Skeeter Davis and Jean's other Opry friends.

Things got worse. The next day, gawkers and sightseers began showing up outside Jean and Hawk's house. Governor Frank Clement ordered the Tennessee Highway Patrol to post guards to watch over her and the other victims' families.

Searchers found the plane's wreckage near Camden, Tennessee, on the morning of March 6, 1963. A 6-foot crater on a hillside where the plane had hit was filled with water. Clothing, personal effects, plane wreckage, and pieces of flesh were strewn over a 60-foot area. One police officer described it as the most gruesome accident scene he'd ever seen. No one survived. The victims had to be identified by their wallets.

Returning from Kansas City, Randy Hughes had landed with his famous passengers at Dyersburg, Tennessee, to refuel. He was told there that proceeding any farther was extremely dangerous because of severe weather conditions. Instead, he blundered onward into the turbulence. He was not an experienced enough pilot to fly by instrument readings when visibility became impossible.

"It was a crash that never should have happened," says former WSM disc jockey Ralph Emery. "The weather was bad and showed no sign of clearing despite Randy's assurances to Patsy when they set down in Dyersburg, Tennessee. Bill Braese, the airport manager, even pulled Randy aside and warned him not to take off. But Randy was a daredevil at heart." Randy Hughes was well known at the Grand Ole Opry, because in addition to being Patsy's manager, he was a guitarist who'd backed many of the show's stars, both onstage and in the recording studio.

GRAND OLE OPRY STAR Bill Anderson was particularly affected by the loss of Cowboy Copas, whom he greatly admired. "He was a jewel of a human being," Bill recalls. "Once, on a tour of Michigan, the promoter had not provided a band for several of the acts who were working as singles, and Cope stayed out onstage every night after his part of the show was over and picked guitar behind me and all the others. I never forgot his unselfishness and true professionalism." Bill also remembers Cowboy as an amusing mimic and a hilarious storyteller.

At age forty-nine, Cowboy Copas was the oldest of the accident's victims. He was also the first to become a star, having rocketed to fame in 1946 with his debut single, the World War II–themed "Filipino Baby." Born Lloyd Estel Copas on July 15, 1913, he was a native of Blue Creek, Ohio, a small town in the southern part of the state, near its Ohio River boundary with Kentucky. Cope, as he was called by his friends, began his musical career after dropping out of school at age fourteen. He was an excellent flattop acoustic guitarist who teamed up with fiddler Lester Vernon Storer, known professionally and costumed as "Natchee the Indian." Accordingly, Cope took the nickname "Cowboy" and was advised to say he was born on a ranch in Oklahoma to add to the image.

He married Lucille Markins Copas in 1934 in Covington, Kentucky, which is across the river from Cincinnati. As Cope went from show to show, from radio station to radio station, the newlyweds literally lived in their automobile. He eventually joined the cast of the *Boone County Jamboree* at WLW in Cincinnati. But his biggest early career boost came when he began touring as a vocalist in Pee Wee King's Golden West Cowboys, then one of the flashiest and most successful road attractions in country music.

In the wake of "Filipino Baby," Cowboy Copas was invited into the Grand Ole Opry cast in 1946. In 1948, he sang the classic "Signed, Sealed and Delivered" and had the first hit version of the immortal "Tennessee Waltz." In 1951–1952, Cope had big hits with "The Strange Little Girl" and "'Tis Sweet to Be Remembered."

The flip side of "The Strange Little Girl" was a tune called "You'll Never Ever See Me Cry," which the star recorded as a duet with his sixteen-year-old daughter, Kathy Copas. They also recorded duets such as "Copy Cat" and "I Love You (My Darling, I Love You)" in the early 1950s. Kathy joined her father on the Opry stage and became a part-time member of The LaDell Sisters at Opry shows.

Because "Signed, Sealed and Delivered," "Tennessee Waltz," and such Cowboy Copas favorites as "Tennessee Moon" and "Kentucky Waltz" were all in 3/4 time, WSM announcers dubbed the singer "The Waltz King of the Grand Ole Opry." He sang "Signed, Sealed and Delivered" and "Blue Pacific Waltz" in the 1949 feature film *Square Dance Jubilee*.

"These were good years," son Gary Copas reminisced. "It wasn't uncommon for Dad to have two and sometimes three records on the nation's top-ten country song listings. In one week's time more than 3,000 people wrote WSM for a picture of Dad. He was traveling 150,000 miles a year and singing to thousands of fans. In 1948, he was voted the #1 country and western performer by *Cash Box* magazine. Then the good years turned to lean years."

Cowboy Copas scored no more hits in the 1950s decade. But in 1960, he surged back with the number-one success "Alabam," the biggest hit of his career. It sat at number one for three solid months. In 1961, it was followed by the back-to-back hits "Flat Top" and "Sunny Tennessee," then a second recording of "Signed, Sealed and Delivered."

"Perhaps the greatest single thing that can be said about Dad was that he was a friend to man," Gary Copas said. "He was always ready to say a kind word of encouragement, shake a hand, or work a benefit show in order to help others."

Like Hawkshaw Hawkins, Patsy Cline, and a number of other Opry stars, Cowboy Copas had traveled to Kansas City to put on a benefit show for the widow and children of country disc jockey Cactus Jack Call, who'd been killed in a car crash. Unlike most of the other stars, Cope, Hawk, and Patsy had elected to fly there in a plane owned by Cope's son-in-law, novice flyer Randy Hughes. Because of Randy's call to his wife, Kathy was the first to realize that a tragedy had occurred. She lost both her husband and her father on March 5, 1963. Their son Larry Hughes later became a successful country-record promoter for MCA Records and other labels.

On the Friday before he left, Cope delivered his newest single to WSM disc jockey Ralph Emery and made an appointment to appear on the broadcaster's Monday-night show. That night, Ralph stared at an empty chair. But he played the final Cowboy Copas recording, just as he'd promised. It bore the prophetic title "Goodbye Kisses."

HAWKSHAW HAWKINS ALSO HAD a posthumous hit. In fact, it became the biggest hit of his career. In late 1962, Hawk had recorded "Lonesome 7-7203," written by fellow Grand Ole Opry star Justin Tubb (1935–1998). It first appeared on the country-music charts just three days before the fatal plane crash. The tune occupied the number-one spot on the country charts for a solid month in the spring of 1963.

Hawkshaw Hawkins was just forty-one years old at the time of his death. He was born Harold Franklin Hawkins on December 22, 1921, in the Appalachian Mountains of West Virginia. As a boy, he reportedly traded five rabbits he'd trapped to get his first guitar. He also picked up his nickname "Hawkshaw" as a youngster. Hawk won a talent contest in Huntington, West Virginia, at age fifteen. This got him a spot on the city's WSAZ radio station. Early in his career, he also worked at WCHS in Charleston, West Virginia, and at WCMI in Ashland, Kentucky.

During World War II, Hawk earned four battle stars for combat in the Battle of the Bulge in Europe. Then he was shipped to the Pacific. While in the Philippines, he performed on a Manila radio station.

After the war, he signed a 1946 recording contract with King Records and joined the cast of the *Wheeling Jamboree* on WWVA. His smooth, rich baritone voice, good looks, and commanding stage presence made Hawkshaw Hawkins an immediate favorite in the Mountain State. In his cowboy boots, he stood more than 6 feet 6 inches tall.

During 1947, WWVA received five thousand requests for Hawkshaw Hawkins photos. That was also the year that the CBS radio network picked up the *Jamboree* for nationwide broadcasting, furthering his fame. As an emerging country heartthrob, Hawk appeared on the cover of *National Hillbilly News* in July–August 1947. He had his first big hit the following year, his rendition of the Hank Williams tune "Pan American." Later in 1948, he became one of the first country musicians to broadcast on television, appearing on an ABC regional network that hooked up Philadelphia, Boston, New York, Washington, D.C., and Baltimore to his *Hayloft Hoedown* Saturday-night appearances in Philly.

By the early 1950s, Hawkshaw Hawkins had scored a number of top-ten hits, among them "Dog House Boogie," "I'm Waiting Just for You," and "Slow Poke." He also popularized "Sunny Side of the Mountain" and used it as his theme song a decade before the tune became a bluegrass standard. In 1953, he signed with RCA Victor, and in 1954, he joined the cast of the *Ozark Jubilee*. It became a national TV show the following year.

"I met Hawkshaw when he first came to the *Ozark Jubilee* in Springfield, Missouri," recalls Jean Shepard. "With a wonderful man, Mr. Red Foley, we did the *Ozark Jubilee* together. And then he came on to Nashville to join the Grand Ole Opry [in 1955], and I followed a few months later.

"Hawkshaw had become a member. I had moved to Nashville, and I talked to him about becoming a member. Mr. Jim Denny, who was the head of the Grand Ole Opry at that time, got up in the middle of this meeting. It was at what we called the Disc Jockey Convention back then. He said, 'We would like to welcome the newest member of the Grand Ole Opry, Jean Shepard! Happy birthday, Jean.' That's why I can never, ever forget the day I became an Opry member. It was November twenty-first, my birthday."

At the Opry, Hawk became close friends with Don Gibson and Marty Robbins. His friendship with Marty was particularly strong. The two would take turns sneaking into each other's performances and deliberately playing off key. They also competed on the baseball diamond, Hawk being a particularly fearsome batter. Despite his height, Hawk also raced micromidget autos opposite Marty. Neither man drank alcohol.

Like Marty, Hawkshaw Hawkins was a master showman. He told jokes easily and was always comfortable in front of a crowd. And he eventually incorporated trained horses, rope twirling, gunplay, and whip tricks into his act. Opry manager Jim Denny booked Jean Shepard into Hawk's touring package. Although signed to Capitol Records, she also surreptitiously sang harmony on Hawk's RCA discs.

"We began to work a lot of dates together. And, um, it was

just inevitable. Hawkshaw and myself, we got married in Wichita, Kansas, at the Forum, onstage there. Hap Peebles was a great country-music promoter, and he arranged it. They broadcast the ceremony on the radio, too. Except I wouldn't let them broadcast it when we went into the 'I do' parts, when the real personal stuff came in. So, yeah, we shared it with the fans, and I still see fans all over the country who say, 'I saw you and Hawkshaw when you got married in Wichita, Kansas.' "

With approximately four thousand in attendance, the wedding day was November 26, 1960. The couple named their first child Don Robin, after Hawk's buddies Don Gibson and Marty Robbins.

"Hawk was strictly a man's man," Jean recollects. "He liked to hunt, he liked to fish, he liked to ride horses. Strictly an outdoorsman." The couple socialized with Opry stars Wilma Lee and Stoney Cooper, Hawk's old friends from WWVA. "We played canasta, and me and Wilma Lee would whip 'em every time," notes Jean. When Stoney suffered a heart attack, Hawk visited him often to help nurse his friend back to health. On one trip to the house, he brought a chicken, wrang its neck, made chicken soup, and fed it to Stoney.

They called Hawkshaw Hawkins "Eleven and a Half Yards of Personality," but capturing that charisma on disc eluded him through most of his recording career. Hawk had moved to Marty's label, Columbia Records, in 1959. "Soldier's Joy" was his most successful song with that company.

In September 1962, Hawkshaw Hawkins returned to his original label, King Records. In a three-day period, he recorded what turned out to be his last twelve songs. "Lonesome 7-7203" was originally intended for Jean Shepard, because songwriter Justin Tubb thought it sounded more like a woman's song. She recorded it, but Capitol never issued her version. Hawk heard his wife's recording and immediately sensed that the song was a smash. Before he left for Kansas City in 1963, he gave a copy of his version of the tune to WSM disc jockey Ralph Emery with the inscription "Play the hell out of this, Hoss."

"Lonesome 7-7203" went on to become a country standard. It

has been revived on the charts by Burl Ives (1967), Tony Booth (1972), and Darrell Clanton (1984) and has appeared on albums by Roy Drusky, Hank Snow, Loretta Lynn, Brian Gale, Carl Smith, Webb Pierce, Don Walser, Ernest Tubb, and Tex Williams, among many others.

On April 8, 1963, Jean had their second son, Harold Franklin Hawkins II. Marty Robbins wrote a touching song for the fatherless kids called "Two Little Boys" and assigned its copyright to them. Jean recorded it on the flip side of her 1964 smash hit "Second Fiddle."

Alas, today Hawkshaw Hawkins and Cowboy Copas are known to most casual country fans as "the guys who died in the Patsy Cline plane crash," their memories forever overshadowed by a towering legend  Patsy is arguably the greatest female country vocalist in history. More than forty years after her death, she continues to be the standard by which every female country talent must measure herself.

Patsy's *Greatest Hits* album, released in 1967, has sold more than ten million copies. It is the largest-selling hits package by any woman in any field of music. She was the first solo female inducted into the Country Music Hall of Fame (1973). The Grammy Hall of Fame includes her recordings of "Crazy" and "I Fall to Pieces," and she has been given a posthumous Grammy Lifetime Achievement Award (1995). She has been honored with a U.S. postage stamp (1993) and a star on the Hollywood Walk of Fame (1999). In 2002, she placed first on the CMT countdown of the Forty Greatest Women in Country Music. Her life has become the basis for several TV documentaries, four stage productions, eight books, an Oscar-nominated feature film, and a number of tribute albums.

Her recorded performances have stunned listeners for decade after decade. You can hear her breathe, cry, and ache on her discs. You can feel her emotions in the anguished tension-and-release of her vocal phrasing. The little heart-tugging "cry" in her delivery remains vividly affecting. Patsy's performances include dramatic volume control, stretched-note effects, sobs, pauses, and a distinctive way of holding back, then bursting into full-throated exclamation.

"Patsy Cline has an extraordinary voice," says Grand Ole Opry star Emmylou Harris, who revived "Sweet Dreams" in 1976. "I mean, there's nobody that sounds even remotely like her. I'm very drawn to her. She has a voice that is in touch with emotion. And you put that together with those great straightforward songs that country music is so known for, it is an unbeatable combination. Because, ultimately, music is supposed to touch you where you live. Basically, we want somebody to shake us up inside our hearts, and she certainly had the voice to do that."

"There was nobody who could ever touch Patsy Cline's voice," says Opry star Loretta Lynn. "She could sing it country. She could sing it pop. She could yodel. She could do anything with her voice she wanted to, and do it to perfection. I just admired this girl so much. When she walked out on that stage, she had everybody's attention. It was like, 'I demand respect.' I've never seen nobody like that afore her or after her. The people just loved her. I've seen her get three standing ovations. It was really something. She demanded respect, and she got it. How she done it, don't ask me."

"I was a fan of Patsy Cline long before I ever came to Nashville," says the Opry's Jan Howard. "Her voice just stood out all by itself, far and above any others I'd heard. . . . Her voice will live forever. Her recordings are timeless."

Patsy was born Virginia Patterson Hensley in the mountains of Virginia on September 8, 1932. Mother Hilda Hensley was only sixteen when she had her first daughter and throughout Patsy's life was almost more like a sister to her than a mother. The family moved nineteen times while the little girl was growing up. As she neared puberty, her father began to sexually molest her. Shortly after the family moved to Winchester, in 1948, he left the family, which now included a younger brother and sister, and Patsy dropped out of high school.

She was obsessed with the Grand Ole Opry radio broadcasts

she heard from Nashville. Even as a kid, it was her ambition to one day join the show's cast. In 1948, she wrote to WSM, requesting an audition, and talked her way into a singing job at her local radio station, WINC. In 1952, she joined Bill Peer's band, a fairly well-known regional attraction. The bandleader changed her name from Virginia to Patsy, derived from her middle name, Patterson. In 1953, she married Gerald Cline, but this event had no effect on her ambition. Later that year, she traveled to Nashville to sing on Ernest Tubb's *Midnite Jamboree* radio show on WSM. The following year, she signed a recording contract.

Armed with "A Church, a Courtroom and Then Goodbye" as her debut single, she got a guest spot on the Opry in 1955. Later that year, she joined the cast of the Washington, D.C., television show *Town and Country Time*. She used this as a stepping stone to Arthur Godfrey's nationally telecast *Talent Scouts* program, which was then one of the most popular shows on network TV. In January 1957, she triumphed on the show, singing the bluesy "Walkin' After Midnight" and the Hank Williams standard "Your Cheatin' Heart."

"Walkin' After Midnight" became her first national hit. She divorced Gerald Cline in 1957 and married Charlie Dick seven months later. Their relationship was depicted in the 1985 film *Sweet Dreams,* costarring Jessica Lange and Ed Harris as the tempestuous lovers.

Patsy finished 1957 by winning *Billboard* magazine's Most Promising Female Country Artist award, *Cash Box* magazine's Most Promising Female Country Vocalist award, and *Country & Western Jamboree* magazine's Best New Singer honor. Daughter Julie was born in 1958, and the family moved to Nashville the following year. On January 9, 1960, Patsy Cline fulfilled her childhood dream by becoming a member of the Grand Ole Opry cast. With her saucy manner, salty language, blazing red lipstick, and tight, sexy clothes, Patsy Cline was quite a departure from the show's demure, "country sweetheart" expectations.

"When I came to Nashville, I wanted so much to meet her," recalls Jan Howard. "But I was very, very shy. Seems unbelievable, but I really was. I would go to the Opry, and I would do my spot. And then I'd leave. Because I didn't want to bug anybody. Sometimes I'd hang around backstage to hear certain ones, and always if Patsy was on. But I had never met her. We changed clothes in the ladies' restroom [at the Ryman Auditorium]. That was our dressing room. I remember one night Patsy was on, and she had on a fringed cowgirl outfit, with the boots. I did my spot. Then I went to the side of the stage and stood until Patsy sang. And then I went in to change clothes.

"All of a sudden the door flew open and in walked Patsy. She stood there with her hands on her hips and she said, 'Well, you're a conceited little thing.' Only she didn't say, 'thing.' And I said, 'Uh, what?' And she said, 'Well, you just waltz in here and do your spot and leave. You don't say hello, kiss my—foot—or anything else to anybody.' Only she didn't say, 'foot.' I said, 'Now wait just a minute!' That's when my Irish and Indian temper came up. I said, 'You know, where I'm from, it's the people who live there that's supposed to make the newcomer feel welcome. And there isn't anybody who's made me feel welcome here.' She laughed, and she said, 'You're all right, honey. Anybody that'll talk back to The Cline is all right. So we're gonna be good friends.' And we were. We were good friends." Jan recorded the original demo versions of "I Fall to Pieces" and other tunes written or cowritten by her then-husband Harlan Howard so that Patsy could learn them.

"I'm a very straightforward person," says the Opry's Jean Shepard. "I'll tell you exactly what I think. Patsy was pretty much that way, yeah, she really was. I got along great with Patsy. I admire anybody who tells it like it is."

"Patsy was funny, too," adds widower Charlie Dick. "We had a ball. We enjoyed life. It was Christmas every day. I partied a hell of a lot. Patsy and I, we didn't hold anything back. If we had something to say to each other, we said it."

"Patsy was someone that I saw on TV," recalls Loretta Lynn, "and I really wanted to meet her when I came to Nashville. We were together for only two years. She was just one year older than I was, but she was like my sister, my mother, my friend. I mean, she was all this to me. She meant so much to me."

"Did I like Patsy Cline?" asks former WSM broadcaster Ralph Emery. "Yes. Patsy and I were the same age. She did some things that annoyed me, because I tried to interview her a number of times, and I would catch her at the end of her evening when she'd been out partying. She would be with Charlie and some friends, and they'd come in and, wouldn't be drunk, just be happy, really happy. If I asked a question, I didn't get a straight answer, and they would punch each other with their elbows and say, 'Ha, ha, ha.' So that annoyed me.

"Except one night she came up to the station, and I wish I'd had the presence of mind to roll the tape. I got to go one-on-one with her, and I remember it was great. That was the interview I had been after for a long time. But, yeah, I liked her. I found Patsy to be down to earth and very open.

"I felt sorry for her. I remember one night we were down at the old Methodist film studio, and Faron Young was making some sort of military-recruiting show. Hubert Long had put the talent together, so Patsy, who was getting some bookings through Hubert, came in. I guess she was gonna be a guest. But she was really down. This was before 'I Fall to Pieces.' She'd been in Nashville I guess for about a year, and she couldn't seem to make anything happen. I think Patsy knew she could sing. And, boy, could she. So she was frustrated."

She waited for the follow-up hit to "Walkin' After Midnight" for three long years. In late 1960, Patsy recorded "I Fall to Pieces," which became a smash in early 1961. It was around this time that producer Owen Bradley began surrounding the star with the cushioning voices of The Jordanaires quartet, adding strings to her sessions, creating zephyr-soft arrangements, recording in stereo, and pushing Patsy to sing torch songs and ballads. As a result, she became the ultimate female singer in the style that became known as the Nashville Sound.

The follow-up to "I Fall to Pieces" was the classic "Crazy." As a result, Patsy Cline was named *Billboard*'s Favorite Female Country Artist of 1961.

Son Randy was born in early 1961, but Patsy's personal and professional momentum were both stopped cold that spring, when she was nearly killed in a car accident in Nashville. She suffered a dislocated hip, a fractured arm, multiple contusions, and a horrible gash that began at her right eyebrow, ran across the bridge of her nose, extended across her left brow, and ended at the top of her skull. She spent a month in the hospital in traction.

Wearing the heavy, scar-hiding pancake makeup that she used for the rest of her life, Patsy returned to the Opry stage in a wheelchair, and then on crutches. By July, she was back out on the road, notably at a Cimarron Ballroom show in Tulsa that became a posthumous live CD.

"She was beat up pretty bad," recalls the Cimarron's then-manager Peck Allen, "and she was on crutches, and she couldn't stand up to sing. So I got her a stool to sit on. Of course she still had large scars on her face, but she could sing. . . . She just put on a great show. I've never had a show in there that was any better. She shut the house down. It was a great night."

In November 1961, she costarred at an Opry show staged at New York's prestigious Carnegie Hall. The following summer, she was cobilled with Johnny Cash at the Hollywood Bowl. Next, she conquered Las Vegas with a monthlong engagement at The Mint casino. She was going where no woman in country music had ever gone before.

In the wake of the aching "She's Got You," "When I Get Through with You," "Imagine That," and "So Wrong," Patsy won *Billboard*'s Favorite Country Female Artist of 1962, plus *Music Reporter*'s 1962 Star of the Year award. "Leavin' on Your Mind" was in the can and poised to become her next top-ten hit in the new year.

She bought her suburban dream home and proudly showed it off to such girlfriends as Loretta Lynn, Brenda Lee, and Dottie West. She loaned money to Dottie and Loretta and shared her deepest emotions with them, as well as with Jan Howard, Del Wood, and June Carter. She doted on child stars Brenda Lee and Barbara Mandrell. Several of these close friends reported that the superstar had premonitions of her death. Patsy gave her career scrapbook to Dottie, saying that she'd never live to see thirty. She dictated her funeral wishes to June when the two were traveling between shows in California.

"She said, 'I'm gonna go out, and I'm gonna go out really fast,'" June recalled. "She'd said that to me before, and every time she did, I'd say, 'Just shut up. Don't be that way.' But for some reason, I wrote it down." There was one other such premonition. After she finished what turned out to be her final recording session, she uncharacteristically called Jan and Dottie to her side.

"I never would attend a recording session unless I was invited, because I always felt that that was business," says Jan. "I know that when I recorded, it bugged me when a lot of people were there. But Patsy called me and said, 'Are you coming to the session tonight?' I said, 'Well, I hadn't planned to.' She said, 'Well, I'd like for you to be there.' Several people were there. Dottie West was there. When Patsy sang, she literally lived a song. We went up to Owen Bradley's office after the session, and all of us were sitting around listening to the playbacks. She was so happy. She was so proud.

"'Sweet Dreams'—Who can listen to that without getting cold chills? 'Faded Love' is another. . . . I was in awe of Patsy. You know, afterward you're supposed to say something nice. I couldn't talk. I was dumbfounded.

"Suddenly, she got up and went into the adjoining office and brought out a record of 'A Church, a Courtroom and Then Goodbye.' That was her first record. And she said, 'Well, here it is, the first and the last.' I said, 'Don't say that!' She said, 'Don't get in an uproar. I just meant the first recording and the most recent recording.' But it was the last. I think that was the last time I saw her." It was February 7, 1963, the conclusion of four days of recording that included such breathtaking performances as "Always" and "He Called Me Baby" as well as "Faded Love" and "Sweet Dreams."

During the next few weeks, Patsy performed concerts in Ohio,

Louisiana, and Alabama. Following her Saturday, March 2, show in Birmingham, she flew back to Nashville with Randy, dropped husband Charlie off, and picked up Cowboy Copas and Hawkshaw Hawkins to head for the Sunday benefit show in Kansas City.

"We were together all day on Thursday, and she made curtains for my house," Loretta remembers. "I didn't have any furniture for my livin' room, and she was gonna buy me somethin' for my livin' room. I was so excited. She was givin' me $50, and she knew I needed it. She said, 'Oh gal, me 'n' you will always stick together.' I was goin' to go with her [to Kansas City], and in the meantime, there was a place in Memphis that offered me $75 to come and work four shows. Patsy told me to go and get the $75. We were going to go shopping together after she got back home."

The Kansas City show included a number of other Grand Ole Opry greats. But Patsy Cline, thirty, was indisputably the biggest star.

"She did close the show," said Dottie West. "She *was* the star. I walked out and watched. . . . And I will never forget that white chiffon dress. As I watched her, I thought, 'My God. She sings like an angel, and she looks like one.' She was in this draped chiffon dress, and she was just beautiful." Backstage, country fan Mildred Keith took the last known photo of Patsy Cline, wearing that white dress that Dottie recalled so clearly.

On Monday, March 4, the weather was so bad that no planes could take off. Dottie tried to talk Patsy into driving back to Nashville with her.

"The last thing I said to her was, 'I'm really going to be worried about you flying in this weather.' She said, 'Don't worry 'bout me, hoss, when it's my time to go, it's my time.'" After waiting a day in Kansas City, Randy Hughes decided to fly on March 5.

"The night that she died, all durin' the night the wind blew," remembers Loretta Lynn. "I would wake up, and it would be soundin' like Patsy singin' 'Sweet Dreams' in the wind.

"The next morning, when I got up, my husband went off to work. I laid my hand on the telephone. I was gonna call Patsy up, and I was gonna say, 'Patsy, you get your lazy butt up and let's go shoppin'. It was weird that it happened like this, but just as I touched the phone, it rang. The people that were bookin' me said, 'Uh, Loretta, are you listenin' to the radio?' I said, 'No. Me and Patsy's goin' shoppin'. Who wants to listen to the radio right now?' She said, 'Loretta, turn your radio on. Patsy died in a crash last night.' My husband came walkin' through the door about that time. He'd heard it, and he'd started back to the house. And nobody could make me believe this. It was like a dream for a while, you know?"

As she'd specified to June Carter, Patsy Cline's remains were brought to her dream home for the visitation. June arranged for heaps of food to be brought and took the children to her house while mourners gathered.

"I was sittin' in the front room where her coffin was," Loretta recalls. "Her picture was sittin' on the floor, right by the coffin. I was by myself. Everybody else was in the kitchen. I looked over at Patsy and said, 'Gee. I'm cold,' mentally, in my mind. Patsy says, 'Well get up and turn the damn heat on,' just like that. I got up and turned the heat up and sat back down. All of a sudden, I thought, 'How could that have been Patsy? She's not here.' But I heard it."

A prayer service was held in Nashville for Patsy on Thursday afternoon, March 7. As it was concluding, there was a commotion as word spread among the mourners that Jack Anglin of the Opry duo Johnny & Jack had been killed in a car wreck while en route to the service. Singing partner Johnny Wright and Johnny's wife Kitty Wells were given the news at the funeral home.

JOHNNY, BORN ON MAY 13, 1914, and Jack, born on May 13, 1916, were native Tennesseans who shared a birthday. The men teamed up in 1938, the same year that Jack married Johnny's sister Louise. The duo failed three Opry auditions before their temporary breakup, while Jack served in the army during World War II. Johnny & Jack finally became members of the Grand Ole Opry in 1947. Kitty was the "girl singer" in their show, who planned to retire until "It Wasn't God Who Made Honky Tonk Angels" catapulted her to stardom in 1952.

Meanwhile, Johnny & Jack scored plenty of hits of their own, including "Poison Love" (1951), "Cryin' Heart Blues" (1951), "Three Ways of Knowing" (1952), "(Oh Baby Mine) I Get So Lonely" (1954), and "Goodnight, Sweetheart, Goodnight" (1954). Johnny & Jack also originated the country chestnut "Ashes of Love" (1951), which later became a big hit for Dickey Lee (1972) and The Desert Rose Band (1987). The duo's hit streak extended with such later successes as "Stop the World (And Let Me Off)" (1958) and "Slow Poison" (1962).

After Jack's tragic death at age forty-six, Johnny Wright continued to tour with Kitty and their children. In 1965, he scored a number-one solo hit with the topical "Hello Vietnam."

Now numb with grief, the Opry community soldiered onward in that grim month of March, 1963. While Patsy's body headed home to Virginia for burial, a joint funeral service was held on Friday morning, March 8, for Cowboy Copas and his son-in-law, Randy Hughes. A service for Hawkshaw Hawkins was held on Friday afternoon. Jack Anglin's funeral was on Saturday, March 9.

There was talk of canceling the Grand Ole Opry that weekend. Instead, new Opry manager Ott Devine greeted the crowd at the Ryman Auditorium with a spoken tribute to the fallen stars. The Jordanaires, who backed Patsy on all her hits, closed the tribute segment with an emotional "How Great Thou Art." The rest of the cast joined in, many of the Opry stars sobbing in song. And then the show was to go on as normal. People in the audience were still sniffling and holding handkerchiefs when Minnie Pearl bravely took the stage to do her comedy. Despite the aching hearts, she got the folks laughing. Announcer Ralph Emery recalls that Minnie had tears streaming down her face as she came off the stage. "She had wept virtually throughout her comedy routine, and the audience never knew," says Ralph in admiration.

★     ★     ★

JUST THREE WEEKS LATER, former Opry singer Texas Ruby perished in a trailer fire while her husband, fiddler Curly Fox, was playing on a Friday-night Opry show. Her name lived on in the 1980 Waylon Jennings hit "I Ain't Living Long Like This," wherein a woman was so rough, she "made Texas Ruby look like Sandra Dee."

The brassy, sassy Texas Ruby was born Ruby Agnes Owens in Wise County, Texas, on June 4, 1908. She grew up to be a strong, hefty gal with a deep, almost masculine alto voice that could bellow through even the rowdiest crowd noise. In 1930, she accompanied her father and brothers on a cattle drive to Fort Worth. There, she was heard singing by an executive from the Kansas City radio station KMBC. He offered the husky-voiced brunette a job. Because of her booming vocal style, Ruby was billed as "The Sophie Tucker of the Feminine Folk Singers." She soon teamed up with singer-songwriter Zeke Clements (1911–1994), who brought her to the Grand Ole Opry in 1933.

She and Zeke traveled to Los Angeles in 1936. Walt Disney was desperately seeking singing voices for his mining little people in his history-making full-length cartoon *Snow White and the Seven Dwarfs*. Zeke wound up as the yodeling voice of Bashful. Ruby got inebriated and missed her audition. Her hard drinking eventually wore Zeke Clements out.

In 1937, she hooked up with Tennessee trick fiddler Curly Fox (1910–1995). They married two years later. They were an Opry team from 1944 to 1948. After stints in Texas and California, the two returned to Nashville in 1962. Curly resumed his Opry entertaining, but Ruby made only occasional appearances. They recorded a comeback LP in Music City in early 1963.

On March 29, 1963, Curly Fox arrived home after his Opry performance to find firefighters battling the flames that engulfed their mobile home. Ruby, fifty-four, died. In all likelihood, she nodded off or passed out while holding a cigarette and lit her bed on fire. She was the sixth Opry personality to die that month. People began to talk of there being an Opry "curse."

"A lot of people seem to think our industry is cursed by a jinx," said Opry star Bill Anderson. Ralph Emery also recalls this kind of hex talk at the time. There was no curse, of course—just a lot of broken hearts.

"I thought about not going back to the Opry," recalls Jean Shepard about that painful time in her life. "One day, this line of cars pulled up in the driveway. Jack DeWitt and the powers-that-be from the Opry came out to see me. They really wanted me to come back. I had always been onstage with Hawk. We were a team. It was rough walking in the backstage of the Ryman that first time."

# Gentleman Jim

There was no such phrase when he was alive, but Jim Reeves was a "control freak." By the time of his early death, he was his own manager and song publisher. He built his own recording studio in his home. He invested his money in real estate and radio stations to lock in financial security. He guided himself to the status of an international music icon. He built himself into a pop-crossover star by pioneering the then-new "countrypolitan" style that became known as the Nashville Sound.

He trusted no one, except perhaps his wife, Mary. Because he didn't like depending on others, he learned to fly—and that would prove to be his downfall.

One explanation for his uptight personality might be found in his childhood spent in suffocating poverty. Born in East Texas on August 20, 1923, James Travis Reeves was the youngest of nine children. Nine months after his birth, his sharecropper father Tom died of brain cancer. Mother Mary Beulah collapsed, physically and emotionally. She never really recovered, so Jim was mostly raised by his older brothers and sisters.

The children planted and harvested cotton. Their garden provided almost all of their food. The onset of the Great Depression in 1929 only worsened the family's dire circumstances.

The East Texas oil boom of the early 1930s saved them. Oldest brother Beuford Reeves went to work for the United Gas Company and bought his mother and siblings a house in DeBarry, Texas, when Jim Reeves was nine years old. It was around this time that the youngster found the two passions of his life, baseball and music. By his early teens, he'd become proficient on the guitar and was an ace right-handed pitcher who threw a mean curveball.

Following his graduation from Carthage High School, Jim was offered a baseball scholarship to the University of Texas in Austin. Strapped for cash, he didn't even last a week in the state capital. A bout of rheumatic fever during childhood had damaged his heart, so he was classified as 4-F during World War II. He signed up to play minor-league ball for the St. Louis Cardinals in 1942.

In 1946, the pitcher fell in love with a Marshall County High student named Mary White. They met at a dance.

"Jim came into the dance by himself, and he was looking around to see if there was anybody there he knew," Mary recalled. "I had a date with a guy that had gone to school with Jim. . . . Well, he joined up with my date and me, we were introduced, and during the course of the evening, Jim and I danced together. While we were dancing, he asked me for a date. I accepted.

"We danced so long the boy I was with got mad at me. I never did see him anymore, so that ended that romance. I don't blame him, though, 'cause I did act ugly."

Jim injured his leg the following summer, and that ended his baseball career. Even though he had neither prospects nor a job, he impulsively proposed. Jim and Mary Reeves were wed on September 3, 1947. It turned out to be the first of several wise career moves, for Mary would become invaluable to his entertainment future.

Jim tried out for spring training in 1948 but failed. He took a job at radio station KGRI in Henderson, Texas. As was common at small-town stations, his job required him to wear many hats. He read the news, called local baseball and football games, operated the control board as his own engineer, and spun records as a disc jockey.

With his naturally smooth, resonant, deep voice, he was soon a regional celebrity.

His first recordings were made on KGRI's tape machine, for he realized that his radio work could be a stepping stone to a music career. He joined a small country band and began playing in clubs around East Texas. In 1949, Jim Reeves and his group recorded his debut single, "My Heart's Like a Welcome Mat," for Houston's fledgling Macy Records label. He later recalled that the session cost him his life savings at the time. The pleasant ditty became his calling card for bigger and better show bookings.

Even so, it was Mary's bookkeeping job that was bankrolling the couple. So it took a real leap of faith for her to quit it to accompany Jim to Shreveport, Louisiana, to audition for an announcing job at the powerhouse KWKH. Program director Horace Logan said he liked Jim but had no openings.

Returning to scrambling for radio jobs at backwater East Texas stations, Jim had his back to the wall. Fortunately, Tom Perryman at KSIJ, in Gladeville, was a fan of "My Heart's Like a Welcome Mat" as well as of the singer's live performances. In 1952, he persuaded Abbott Records executive Fabor Robison to catch a Jim Reeves show at the now-legendary Reo Palm Isle Ballroom, in Longview, Texas. Jim was signed to the label on the spot. Although the company launched his career, he would soon come to despise Fabor Robison.

KWKH offered him a job that same year. After his second audition for the station, he was hired as both a disc jockey and as one of the four announcers on the nationally broadcast *Louisiana Hayride* Saturday-night barn dance. Horace Logan said in his memoir that Jim was first invited to sing on the program when Hank Williams was too drunk to perform. But most other accounts disagree. In fact, when Jim Reeves had "Mexican Joe" as his first hit record, in 1953, he was initially given the humiliating assignment of introducing cast member Billy Walker to sing a competing version of the song on *Hayride* broadcasts.

That all changed when the Jim Reeves version of the jaunty

"Mexican Joe" became a number-one record on May 9, 1953. It remained at the top of the country charts for nine weeks, ensuring Jim's transition from announcer to singing star on the *Louisiana Hayride*. On May 23, 1953, he was invited to sing his smash hit on the nationally broadcast portion of Nashville's Grand Ole Opry. He reportedly brought down the house at the Ryman Auditorium.

Meanwhile, the California-based Fabor Robison was reveling in Jim's first national hit. To the surprise of Jim Reeves, the executive had no intention of sharing the hit's proceeds with its singer.

"Deep in the sludge . . . skulks the memory of Fabor Robison," writes Jim Reeves biographer Michael Streissguth. "Performers who worked under his umbrella complained of lost royalties, missing concert payments and sexual harassment, as well as Robison's brow-beating, violent style. He was known to brandish a revolver and would flout any wishes but his own. Cunning just dripped from his greased-back hair onto his beige summer suits."

The executive openly bribed radio stations with payola. He stole his artists' touring income. He controlled when, where, and what they recorded. To Jim's dismay, the novelty "Mexican Joe" was followed by the even more frivolous "Bimbo" and "Penny Candy," both of which became big hits in 1954.

Fabor Robison put Jim on the road on the West Coast with his label mates, The Browns, then experiencing their first hit with "Looking Back to See." Maxine Brown remembers the experience bitterly.

"God, how we hated that SOB," she says of Robison. "Since it was on his side of the continent, Fabor came along to manage everything—and collect all the money. He met with everybody on the tour and told us he would pay for all our road expenses. When the tour was over, he continued, he would pay us the money we had coming from the dates. We should have smelled a rat right then.

"Jim Reeves's wife, Mary, was a godsend. She helped sell tickets, counted heads in the crowd to make sure we got our fair percentage of ticket sales, and generally kept our spirits up. She suffered right beside Jim through those long and lean first years, and I don't think anyone ever heard her complain. If there is a synonym for courage, it surely is Mary Reeves."

Maxine's brother Jim Ed Brown developed pneumonia from the dreadful working conditions. Everyone on the tour was malnourished. Robison accused The Browns of being lazy and ungrateful, fired the singers, and refused to pay them. Jim and Mary Reeves gave the green kids enough money to get them to the next town. Next, Jim and the rest of the performers went to Robison and threatened to quit the tour if The Browns weren't hired back.

When the tour was finally over, the demoralized cast met in Jim and Mary's living room in Shreveport. Fabor Robison arrived, criticized all the artists, and started handing out money. To The Browns' shock, they were given just $234.

"Instead of apologizing, Fabor was getting meaner and madder, as if we were the lowest scum he'd ever come across," recalls Maxine. "At last, Jim Reeves stood up, holding the paltry bills in his clenched fist, and called Fabor a lowdown sneak and cheater. They got into a cussing match and pretty soon some punches were flying. Jim went into his bedroom, got his gun, and pointed it right at Fabor. We just knew he was going to kill him. Mary knew it too, but she was able to convince Jim that the sorry SOB wasn't worth it—but not until he fired one shot at Fabor and missed. We were all wishing he'd go ahead and kill the bastard."

Meanwhile, back at the *Hayride,* a mother ushered her daughter into Horace Logan's office and accused Jim Reeves of impregnating the girl. Horace knew the girl slept around with a lot of the *Hayride* musicians. He gathered the entire *Hayride* staff in the auditorium and confronted the mother and daughter in front of them all. Jim loved children, and he and Mary had been trying to conceive. They were unable to, because Jim was sterile and could produce a doctor's statement to prove it. So the potential paternity suit ended then and there. Mary evidently learned to accept her husband's infidelities.

"Jim Reeves was one good-looking hunk of a man," says Maxine Brown, "and to tell the truth he'd always had his share of road honeys."

"Jim had an eye for the ladies," confirmed Jim's confidant Buddy Killen. "Women always seem to be drawn to entertainers, making it easy to have casual encounters. It's important, of course, to keep one's sense of humor about these dalliances, something that Jim was particularly good at."

At the time, there wasn't much humor to be found in his professional life. Things finally reached the boiling point between Jim Reeves and Fabor Robison at what turned out to be the star's last recording session for Abbott Records, in January 1955 in Los Angeles. This time, it was Fabor who was waving around a pistol while ranting at the musicians. When he put it down, Jim grabbed it and took hold of Fabor's collar.

"You got six or eight songs of mine on the shelf," Jim hissed at Fabor. "I'm gonna sign a contract tonight and give you those songs, royalty free. You're also going to sign a contract releasing me from your record company, or I'm gonna shove this damn pistol down your neck."

Finally free of Fabor, Jim Reeves signed with Nashville's RCA Records in March 1955. Several of his early contacts in the city reported that he seemed mistrustful of the music business. Tree Publishing executive Buddy Killen attended Jim's first RCA session, bringing along some contracts allowing his firm to publish the singer's songwriting efforts.

"Mr. Reeves, I really appreciate you placing your songs with Tree," said Buddy.

"I might as well place them with you as anybody else," snapped Jim. "You're not going to pay me anyway." Buddy reported that he felt stung by the suggestion that he'd cheat anyone.

At that same session, when songwriter Cy Coben made a suggestion about how Jim might approach a lyric, the singer snarled, "Don't tell me how to sing," and never recorded one of Cy Coben's works again. Producer/guitarist Chet Atkins recalled that Jim seemed to mistrust him as a record producer. Apparently, the experiences with Fabor Robison had left some scars.

Even so, Jim Reeves advanced rapidly in Music City. On October 22, 1955, he became a member of the Grand Ole Opry cast. Jim and Mary moved to Nashville that fall, initially living in a humble trailer park.

By then, Jim's folksy composition "Yonder Comes a Sucker" had emerged as the hit from that first RCA session. It also became Tree's first chart topper as a publishing company. The number was still very much in the mode of his up-tempo Abbott hits. Fabor had relentlessly forced Jim to sing high and fast. The singer had to fight for every ballad he wanted to record.

Producer Chet Atkins now encouraged him to lower his vocal register and sing slow songs. Furthermore, he recognized that Jim's years of radio work had made him a master of microphone techniques. Over the audio engineer's objections, Chet allowed Jim to move his lips to within kissing distance of the mic, creating an extraordinarily warm and intimate baritone purr. In early 1957, this paid off with the caressing ballad sound of "Am I Losing You," which was Jim's finest songwriting effort.

Back in the studio to record a follow-up, Chet surrounded Jim with a small, hushed instrumental combo featuring his lightly chiming guitar, tinkling Floyd Cramer piano droplets, and lovely choral harmonies. The result, the gorgeous "Four Walls," has stood the test of time as one of the definitive Nashville Sound ballads.

In April 1957, Jim Reeves became the first Nashville star to headline a European tour. Although confined to U.S. military bases in Germany, it was still a beachhead for country music overseas.

Maxine Brown remembers the tour as being unorganized and chaotic, with misplaced luggage, bungled hotel reservations, and chronically late transportation. Still, everyone enjoyed it, despite Jim's constant complaining. His mood brightened when he learned that back home, "Four Walls" was a titanic number-one country smash, his biggest-selling record to date and a crossover hit on the pop charts.

"Four Walls" led to a rash of network television appearances, his own variety radio series on ABC, an eight-week run as the host of the national TV series *Country Music Jubilee,* and offers to play Las

Vegas showrooms. But success had a darker side for Jim Reeves. He became haunted by fears of failure. His mood swings became erratic. In the middle of performances, he would suddenly lash out at band members, right in front of audiences. He berated and belittled Mary at gatherings in their home. Even Chet Atkins was not above an icy rebuke in the studio. The star's soothing singing style had gotten him the nickname "Gentleman Jim." Privately, he was anything but.

Buddy Killen, who cowrote songs with Jim Reeves and became one of the singer's best friends, recalled that Jim "had real bouts with depression." In time, he sought help from a psychiatrist.

"Jim was victimized by the roller-coaster mood swings that often haunt creative or talented people," Buddy said. "He'd be laughing one minute and moaning the blues the next. . . . Other times, he'd make a cutting remark about someone."

His temperamental outbreaks weren't seen by everyone. And there are many who testify to his kindness and generosity. On the road, he always took care of his band before paying himself. There are many accounts of his love for children. Many associates remained fiercely loyal to him, despite the outbursts.

He brought conductor/arranger Bill Walker to Nashville. He launched the careers of producers Ray Baker and Bud Logan. He brought Dottie West to Chet Atkins's attention, which resulted in her being signed by RCA. He went to bat for The Browns, also securing them an RCA contract and an escape from Fabor Robison.

"There never was a better man than Jim Reeves at keeping his word," says Maxine Brown. After signing with RCA, The Browns made history with "The Three Bells" as a number-one country and pop smash of 1959.

On Jim's own musical front, Cindy Walker's gentle ballad "Anna Marie" followed in the footsteps of "Four Walls." But Boudleaux Bryant's "Blue Boy" of 1958 was a teen-type tune with a "walking" bass line. Roger Miller's "Billy Bayou" reverted to Jim's upbeat novelty style. And Danny Dill's "Partners" of 1959 was an eerie story song about a miner who murders his gold-mining companion.

Everyone who attended these recording sessions remembers a man who approached his work with deadpan seriousness. Unlike the shenanigans at, say, a session with Marty Robbins or Faron Young, there was no good-natured banter or kidding around when Jim Reeves was in the studio.

"Even today, we have to wipe a smile off our face when we talk about Jim Reeves, because there wasn't anything funny on his sessions," recalls Gordon Stoker of The Jordanaires. "You hardly cracked a smile, because he would have thought you were laughing at him. The biggest hit we did with him was 'Four Walls.' Everything was very serious. You couldn't joke around. You couldn't tell any jokes, couldn't laugh. He concentrated strictly on the song. He watched that clock. He wanted to at least turn out three songs per session. We were told by RCA that Jim's records had all been up high and hard driving country. Once he did [ballads], it was a whole new world. That's the way he got that 'Gentleman' name."

"Jim Reeves was one of the great artists of all time," recalled Chet Atkins (1924–2001). "He's a fellow that worked harder than anybody at finding good songs. He would look the country over, then he'd get in his studio and record the songs and he would decide which ones he liked, which ones he might have a problem chord-wise or range-wise in his voice. So he was always prepared, well before we got into the recording studio. I found about half and he found the other half of the hits we had."

Jim's and Chet's song quests led them to "He'll Have to Go" in 1959. This time, Gentleman Jim's velvet vocal was accompanied by teardrop notes from a vibraphone and the sighing of The Anita Kerr Singers. When he asked "to turn the jukebox way down low," Jim dropped his voice an octave on the word "low," creating an unforgettable sound. In the early weeks of 1960, "He'll Have to Go" spent fourteen weeks at the top of the country charts and crossed over to become a major pop hit as well. In addition, the ballad became the first of the singer's many British pop hits.

On April 23, 1960, Chet Atkins walked onto the Ryman Auditorium stage during Jim's Grand Ole Opry performance. In his arms, Chet held a framed gold record, which he presented to Jim for "He'll Have to Go."

In keeping with his pop stardom, Jim Reeves changed his image. He and the band ditched their western duds and donned sport coats or tuxedos, depending on the engagement. Jim renamed his group The Blue Boys—after his 1958 hit title—and donated its previous name, The Wagonmasters, to fellow Opry star Porter Wagoner.

"He'll Have to Go" was followed by the hit 1960 ballad "I'm Getting Better," then a remake of "Am I Losing You" that added a lilting string section and then the gently lulling "I Missed Me," the last-named written by Bill Anderson, who would join Jim as an Opry cast member in 1961.

But chafing at the Opry's performance requirements, Jim quit the cast in 1962. The demanding perfectionist was spending more and more time on the road, as though insecure about his financial future.

Unlike most of his country contemporaries, Jim Reeves became hugely popular overseas. In 1962, he headlined a tour of South Africa, where his records outsold Elvis Presley's. Upon arriving, Jim and his entourage were mobbed at the airport by fans. Hysteria greeted him at his Johannesburg hotel, where frenzied crowd members tore at his clothes, and his hand was bloodied by one who tried to strip a ring from his finger. At shows, he endeared himself to attendees by singing two songs in their native Afrikaans. The following year, he returned to South Africa to star in the feature film *Kimberly Jim*.

Also in 1963, Jim Reeves toured Ireland and England. His Irish concert promoters put Jim and The Blue Boys on a punishing schedule and booked them at substandard rural dives with broken-down pianos. Jim retaliated by cutting shows short and curtly refusing to sign autographs.

Back at home, he began 1963 by issuing the hit "Is This Me." This was the first songwriting break for Dottie West. Jim touted her talent to Chet Atkins, and after her signing with RCA, Jim aided the newcomer by becoming her duet partner on "Love Is

No Excuse." Written by Opry star Justin Tubb, the song became Dottie's first top-ten hit, in early 1964.

Jim followed "Is This Me" with the melodic ballad "Guilty." Its author, songwriter Alex Zanetis, was a licensed pilot. When Alex arrived on the Nashville scene in 1962, he reportedly inspired others to take flying lessons. Session musicians, executives, and stars such as Faron Young and Roy Drusky all began buying planes. One person that Alex felt did not belong behind the controls of an airplane was the high-strung, impatient Jim Reeves.

"He was very skittish and nervous," Alex said. "He had no business flying. . . . He was not plane-minded, but he still wanted to do it."

"I frequently hire a commercial plane to get from one place to another," Jim said in 1963, "and generally it is piloted by someone whom I have never seen before or know anything about. . . . I just want to be prepared to land the plane in case something should happen to the pilot while we're airborne." At the time, regulations required licensed pilots to have only six hours of practice with an instructor.

The band continued to travel by bus. However, Jim Reeves could fly to the shows and avoid the long, weary miles on the road. After the March 5, 1963, plane crash that killed Opry stars Patsy Cline, Cowboy Copas, and Hawkshaw Hawkins, many in the country community sold their airplanes and gave up flying. But Jim Reeves continued to fly.

"Guilty" was followed in 1963 by another career-defining ballad, "Welcome to My World." In England, it became Jim's first top-ten pop hit. Between 1961 and 1964, he scored nine pop hits in the British Isles. In addition to "Welcome to My World," they included the songs "I Love You Because," "You're the Only Good Thing," "Whispering Hope," and "There's a Heartache Following Me," none of which were issued as singles in the United States.

This activity inspired yet another overseas tour, which found him headlining a bill that included Bobby Bare, Chet Atkins, and The Anita Kerr Singers. The troupe toured Germany, Austria,

Denmark, Sweden, Norway, the Netherlands, and Belgium in the spring of 1964.

The European tour's grueling schedule frayed nerves. The volatile Jim snapped several times, sometimes resulting in bad publicity. He complained about the working conditions in practically every interview he did. In Berlin, a suitcase containing his hairpiece was stolen. Somewhere along the way, the world-weary singer confided to Chet Atkins that he didn't believe he'd live to see age fifty.

Back in Nashville, an exhausted Jim took off most of the month of July 1964. He golfed, vacationed with Mary, and did some recording. Then he decided to look at investment property near Batesville, Arkansas. Piano player Dean Manuel had grown up in that region, so he accompanied his bandleader on the trip. Jim leased a plane and took off on July 30. Later that day, the men examined the land. The next afternoon, Jim and Dean headed back to Music City.

A summer thunderstorm popped up as the plane approached Nashville. Instead of flying around it, Jim foolishly decided to fly through it. At 4:52 p.m. on July 31, 1964, the plane disappeared from the airport's radar screen. When no one had heard from Jim by 8:00 p.m., fears began to spread that the worst had happened.

It took days to find the crash site in the heavily wooded hills of suburban Brentwood. The plane had crashed at such a steep angle that few tree limbs were broken. Finally, on Sunday, August 2, searchers found the remains of the aircraft and the dismembered bodies of Jim Reeves and Dean Manuel.

The long delay in confirming the accident gave Jim's widow Mary time to compose herself and prepare his funeral arrangements. His service was held in Nashville on August 4. Chet Atkins, Skeeter Davis, Eddy Arnold, Red Foley, and dozens of other Opry stars attended. Then the body was taken for burial to Carthage, Texas, where Mary erected a handsome memorial statue of Jim Reeves. He was just forty years old at the time of his death.

Next came the most amazing part of the Gentleman Jim saga. Mary's astute business skills and the quality and quantity of her husband's home recordings ensured that the late star's record releases could continue for years to come. Between the remaining months of 1964 and the dawn of 1967, Jim Reeves had eight top-ten country hits, six of which reached number one. Included were such immortal performances as Leon Payne's "Blue Side of Lonesome" and Cindy Walker's "Distant Drums." When songwriter Cindy heard the throbbing percussion, haunting bugle, and shimmering strings that Chet Atkins had dubbed onto Jim's vocal of her song, she burst into tears. In 1967–1970, Jim Reeves had six more consecutive top-ten hits, including the classic "When Two Worlds Collide," penned by Bill Anderson and Roger Miller.

"I realized when Jim died that it was up to me to carry on the business that Jim had started, that we both loved so much," said Mary. "Like a song, so the business must go on. Why should I throw away everything that we have built up through the years together?

"I know Jim would want it this way," she continued. "The heritage that Jim left me is indeed priceless . . . and I want to keep the image there as long as possible in good taste."

RCA continued its overseas marketing of Jim Reeves as well. Between the time of his death and 1972, Jim had twenty more hits in England, with "Distant Drums" becoming a number-one pop smash there in 1966. He remained a favorite in numerous other nations around the world. Many overseas fans believe that he is still alive.

In 1972, Jim crooned "Missing You" into the country top-ten. By the time of 1973's "Am I That Easy to Forget" and 1974's "I'd Fight the World," his hit streak had become longer in death than it was during his lifetime. In 1979–1980, newcomer Deborah Allen overdubbed harmony vocals onto Jim's performances to create three more top-ten hits, "Don't Let Me Cross Over," "Oh How I Miss You Tonight," and "Take Me in Your Arms and Hold Me." In 1981, the voices of the late Jim Reeves and the late Patsy Cline were spliced together for a hit "duet" of "Have You Ever Been Lonely."

Mary bought a two-hundred-year-old historic home called Evergreen Place and opened the Jim Reeves Museum in it in 1981.

It was the most elegant, serene, and beautiful of all the country-star museums in Nashville. Unfortunately, developers illegally tore down the historic museum building in 2005, after Mary's death in 1999.

The music of Jim Reeves continues to enthrall listeners today. In India, his Christmas album remains an annual favorite. In the Netherlands, three of his hits were among that country's most popular radio tunes of 2003. A Dutch Jim Reeves fan club has been operating continuously since 1975. He is still reportedly the best-selling Western artist in Nigeria and Kenya. Fans in Tanzania have made his "Christmas Polka" a holiday evergreen. Sri Lankan officials once launched an investigation to determine whether Jim was still alive. He sells steadily in the Caribbean, South America, Australia, and Germany. And he remains a legendary figure in South Africa.

Gentleman Jim Reeves has been a member of the Country Music Hall of Fame since 1967. His worldwide record sales are said to exceed eighty million. As recently as 2004, his estate was earning $400,000 a year in royalties, forty years after his death.

"Jim Reeves was born to sing," wrote Cindy Walker in her liner notes to *The Jim Reeves Way*, "as sure as the sun was made to shine. . . . Keep this album, and any other Reeves album that you have, for your children and for their children, as you would a treasure, for treasures they will be. If ever there was a voice destined to remain a favorite with generations of listeners, this is it, the voice of Jim Reeves."

# Dolly's Mystery Man

The whole world might be in love with Dolly Parton, but she's a one-man woman.

"I doubt that I would ever marry again if something happened to Carl," Dolly says. "I doubt that either of us would ever marry again. We've always hoped that we'd die at the same time.

"I was his first true love, and he was my first true love. I just can't imagine that I would want to live in a house with somebody else or sleep with somebody else. One never knows what life's going to bring, but I certainly would never love anybody in all the ways that I love Carl.

"We're in this for the long haul."

"Carl" is Carl Dean, Dolly's husband of more than forty years. Theirs is one of the most enduring marriages in country music. Yet Carl is a celebrity's husband whom few have seen and even fewer have known well. Some have even questioned his existence. But Carl Dean has been by Dolly's side since 1966, throughout her meteoric rise.

She was born Dolly Rebecca Parton on January 19, 1946, and was raised in Appalachian poverty in East Tennessee. She was the fourth of twelve children, not all of whom survived. Her father was a sharecropper who paid the physician attending Dolly's home birth with a sack of cornmeal. The one-room cabin had no electricity, telephone, or indoor plumbing.

The family, particularly on Dolly's mother's side, was highly musical. Dolly was making up songs before she could read and write. At age ten, she became a regular on radio and TV in nearby Knoxville, Tennessee. She recorded a single for Goldband Records called "Puppy Love" at age fourteen and parlayed it into a guest appearance on the Grand Ole Opry. Even more obscure is "So Little I Wanted, So Little I Got"/"Forbidden Love," a pair of duets with her uncle Bill Owens issued on Circle B Records. She first recorded on Music Row at age sixteen, the result being "It's Sure Gonna Hurt" on Mercury Records. A 1963 album called *Hits Made Famous by Country Queens* on Somerset Records featured Dolly singing six songs popularized by Kitty Wells.

In 1964, Dolly became the first member of her family to graduate from high school. The graduation ceremony in Sevierville, Tennessee, took place on a Friday night. On Saturday morning, she boarded a bus for Nashville carrying sacks of dirty clothes, her songs, and her dreams. On her first day in Music City, she took the clothes to a Laundromat, dropped in her coins, and went outside to look around.

Nashville native Carl Dean spotted the pretty blonde while driving by. He honked his horn. She waved. He stopped. They chatted. Every day for the next week, he visited her at the home where she was babysitting. She fell for the handsome, lanky, 6-foot 2-inch Carl at once.

Carl Thomas Dean was born in Nashville's Saint Thomas Hospital on July 20, 1942. He attended Central High School with his friend Ronnie Shacklett, who later became Brenda Lee's husband. After graduation, Carl went to work for his father's asphalt-paving business.

"I met him the first day I got here," Dolly recalls. "I think one of the things that made me feel real attached to him was because he made my heart happy. He made me laugh a lot. This is when I first came to Nashville, and I was kind of sad because I had left home.

My heart was lonely. That's in addition to the fact that he was very handsome. And Carl's very deep and very sensitive. So he had a lot of qualities that just suckered me in. The thing that made me love him at the start is the same thing that keeps us together through the years—we make each other happy.

"I found this out later. Before he even talked to me, he said, 'There's the girl I'm going to marry.' At the end of that first week of babysitting, the first date we had, he took me to his mamma's house and said, 'This is the girl I'm gonna marry. Fix her a plate,' because they were having supper. I thought, 'Well, how bold of you! You didn't say any of this to me.' Then I thought, 'Well, is he kidding?' Because I knew he had an off-the-wall sense of humor. But he said he wasn't kidding. And he evidently wasn't."

Carl enlisted in the National Guard, and during his two-year duty, Dolly visited him at military bases. She also continued to pursue her dreams. She took part-time jobs as a receptionist for a neon-sign company, a waitress in a family restaurant, and a singer on local early-morning TV. But she kept her focus on promoting her songwriting.

Bill Phillips recorded Dolly's "Put It Off Until Tomorrow" and featured her singing a prominent harmony vocal on it. The disc became a top-ten hit in the spring of 1966. In early 1967, Skeeter Davis had a hit with Dolly's "Fuel to the Flame," and Hank Williams Jr. released Dolly's "I'm in No Condition."

In the meantime, Carl had returned to Nashville, and he and Dolly were courting like never before.

"How did he propose? I was living over in Madison, and he was working in the pavement company. He was staying over at my house until two and three o'clock in the morning every night, because we were so in love. You know how that goes. He was going to work, and he was just wore out. So the way he proposed to me was this: 'You're either going to have to move on the other end of town, or we're going to have to get married.' That was his proposal. I said, 'Well then, I guess we'll just get married.' And that's how that happened."

They went to the no-waiting Southern marriage capital of Ring-gold, Georgia. Carl and Dolly married on Memorial Day, May 30, 1966.

At first, she kept the news to herself. Thanks to her songwriting success, Dolly had signed a recording contract with Monument Records, and she knew that the label's Fred Foster would not approve of her marrying. Monument was noted for pop-music success with such artists as Roy Orbison and Boots Randolph. Early Dolly singles for the company, like "Happy, Happy Birthday Baby," "Busy Signal," and "Don't Drop Out," were aimed at the teen market by producer Ray Stevens. In early 1967, Dolly switched to her true style and began to attract attention with country singles such as "Dumb Blonde" and "Something Fishy."

"Put It Off Until Tomorrow" earned Dolly her first professional accolade, a Broadcast Music, Inc. (BMI) songwriting award. New husband Carl dutifully put on a rented tuxedo and accompanied his wife to the 1967 ceremony. The photographers and crowds of well-wishers startled the reticent Carl. On the way home, he told Dolly that he'd support her music dreams in every way but that he would never be in the spotlight with her again. A man of his word, Carl has remained in the shadows ever since. He can be seen, however, in the background on the cover of his wife's 1969 LP *My Blue Ridge Mountain Boy*.

"He's got tremendous pride and integrity," says Dolly. "He don't give a damn for show business or this 'Dolly Parton' business.

"I think he was so happy to have someone to love and someone to love him. And he knew that I had come here to do this very thing. He sensed right on that it wouldn't do him a bit of good to tell me not to do something, because I'm going to do what I'm going to do. I came here to do what I felt was my calling in life, so he never stood in the way of that.

"Carl is pretty giving. He's actually catered to me all of our whole relationship. I guess one of the reasons we have got along so good is that I stay gone enough to make it interesting. That and the fact that he don't try to boss me around."

If country fans thought at all about any romance for Dolly, they probably assumed it was with her flamboyant TV costar and recording duet partner Porter Wagoner (1927–2007). The superstar's "girl singer," Norma Jean, had left his troupe to get married and retire. Porter had taken note of the vivacious newcomer and invited Dolly to join his show in 1967. It was a stupendous opportunity for the still-green twenty-one-year-old Dolly. When he hired her, Porter called a meeting with Carl Dean to assure him that his intentions with Dolly were honorable and to warn Carl that rumors were always spread about country duet partners.

At the time, Porter Wagoner was one of the biggest stars in country music. Born August 12, 1927, in West Plains, Missouri, he had risen to prominence in his home state on the *Ozark Jubilee*. Such hits as "Company's Comin'" (1954), "A Satisfied Mind" (1955), "Eat, Drink, and Be Merry (Tomorrow You'll Cry)" (1955), and "Uncle Pen" (1956) led to an invitation to join the Grand Ole Opry cast. Porter's induction was on February 23, 1957.

"The first night I joined the Opry, Roy Acuff come up and shook hands with me," Porter recalled. "He said, 'We really need people like you. You have a great rapport with the fans and the people.' And he handed me a little piece of paper and said, 'This is my home phone number. If I can help you in any way, just call this number.' You can imagine what that meant to me, a kid five hundred miles from home who didn't know anyone here. Even though I didn't have to use the number, it gave me a feeling of confidence that I belonged.

"Well, years later, on Roy's eighty-fifth birthday, we had a party for him. I reminded him about that night at the Opry. I said, 'You've meant more than you'll probably ever know to me and my career.' We had a wonderful evening, and we all had dinner. I went over to say good-bye to him. He said, 'I'm glad that you came.' And he handed me this little piece of paper. I opened it, and it said, 'If you need anything, call me.' It just hit me right in the heart.

"I've thought a lot of times how fortunate I've been to have been associated with people I love and respect so much. People like

Roy, Ernest Tubb, Red Foley, and Minnie Pearl, all these immortal country-music stars. I got to know them and work with them. What a gift."

Porter launched his syndicated television program in 1960. At its peak, *The Porter Wagoner Show* was seen in more than a hundred markets. For many people, it was the first time they'd seen country music performed. Porter's road show was a state-of-the-art ensemble of flashy instrumentalists, comedy, elaborate costuming, and sincere presentation that played 230 concerts a year to packed houses. Gospel records recorded with The Blackwood Brothers had earned Porter Grammy Awards in 1966 and 1967 (he'd earn another in 1969), and his more than twenty classic recordings prior to hiring Dolly included "Misery Loves Company" (1962), "I've Enjoyed as Much of This as I Can Stand" (1963), "Sorrow on the Rocks" (1964), "Green, Green Grass of Home" (1965), "Skid Row Joe" (1966), and "The Cold Hard Facts of Life" (1967).

In 1968, Dolly Parton scored the first top-ten hit of her career by singing a duet with Porter of "The Last Thing on My Mind." It was the first of twenty-one hit collaborations by the pair. Porter and Dolly won Country Music Association (CMA) Awards for their partnership in 1968, 1970, and 1971. He brought her to RCA Records, where she soon began having solo hits as well. Her top-ten streak began with "Mule Skinner Blues" (1970), "Joshua" (1971), "Coat of Many Colors" (1971), and "Jolene" (1973). Porter also brought Dolly to the Opry cast, which she joined on January 4, 1969.

All of Dolly's early RCA records were produced by Porter. But his name isn't listed as such on any of them.

"The reason they couldn't put my name on them as producer is because RCA Victor had a rule where they didn't have any outside producers, just 'in-house' [employees]," Porter explained. "Bob Ferguson was 'in house,' so that's why his name is on all the things I produced on myself. Same on Dolly's things, our duets and everything. Had Bob Ferguson's name [on them]. He wasn't even there.

Credit really didn't bother me. I just wanted to get it done the best it could be."

Although Porter was her mentor and producer, Dolly was just as strong-willed as he was. As she gained confidence and built a catalog of her own hits, she began to resist his control and domination. Dolly left Porter's employ in 1974, penning the unforgettable "I Will Always Love You" as her farewell song to him. Their last show together was on June 9, 1974. He remained her record producer until 1977, when she made the break final.

"Me and Porter did have our love-hate relationship," she reflects. "We fought like cats and dogs, but we loved every minute. . . . We were very bonded and very bullheaded. There was a lot of passion in that relationship. I don't know that it broke his heart [when she left him]. I think more than anything, it broke his pocketbook. He sued me for a million dollars . . . and got it. It took me a while to pay it off, but he got the first million dollars I ever made.

"But I always loved Porter, and I'm sure there was a part of him that always loved me. When we grew older, all those old hurts and aggravations faded away, and it turned into a pure kind of sweet love, peaceful and nice."

Porter's national television show continued until 1981. His further solo hits included "The Carroll County Accident" (1968), "Big Wind" (1969), "What Ain't to Be Just Might Happen" (1972), "Highway Headin' South" (1974), and "Ole Slew Foot" (1978). In 1971, he recorded the cult-favorite insanity song "The Rubber Room." Porter was also notable for making concept albums about prisoners, alcoholics, and farmers, often illustrating their jackets with vivid portraits of himself in costume.

He created controversy in 1979 by bringing soul superstar James Brown to the Opry stage. He produced an album for R&B singer Joe Simon in 1981. In 1982, Porter appeared in the Clint Eastwood movie *Honkytonk Man*. In the 1990s, he became the unofficial ambassador of the Opry, flashing his toothy smile and $8,000 rhinestone suits for visitors. He was elected to the Country Music Hall of Fame in 2002.

On May 19, 2007, Porter Wagoner celebrated his fiftieth anniversary as a Grand Ole Opry member. Dolly sang "Just Someone I Used to Know" with him and sang "I Will Always Love You" to him.

A month later, Porter's acclaimed *Wagonmaster* comeback CD was issued. Produced by Marty Stuart, the collection led to Porter performing in July at Madison Square Garden, opening for the star rock band The White Stripes.

But the "victory lap" was short-lived. Diagnosed with lung cancer, Porter Wagoner entered hospice care on Friday, October 26, 2007.

"I went over on Sunday afternoon and spent the last few hours with Porter and his family," Dolly recalls, "so I was able to say good-bye. I sang for him and prayed with him. It felt good that I had the opportunity to say good-bye properly." Porter died that night, on October 28, 2007.

The funeral took place at the Opry House on November 1. Opry stars Marty Stuart, The Carol Lee Singers, Ricky Skaggs, The Whites, Patty Loveless, and Vince Gill sang for Porter. The gospel song "Drifting Too Far from the Shore," Dolly's final duet with Porter, was played over the loudspeakers. He'd been sending her a lot of gospel tunes during the previous year.

She commented on that at the funeral. "I said, 'Porter, are you cramming? After all those years living like we did?' He said, 'Yeah, I guess I am cramming.' He was ready to go home. It's a sad day for everybody but Porter."

Mourners included Porter's Opry cast mates Garth Brooks, Trisha Yearwood, Hal Ketchum, Jan Howard, Jeannie Seely, Bill Anderson, Jim Ed Brown, Jimmy Dickens, Martina McBride, Charlie Louvin, Steve Wariner, Del McCoury, and George Jones. Dolly led them in singing "I Saw the Light," then looked at the flower-topped casket at the foot of the Opry stage and said softly, "Good-bye, Porter."

"When Porter died, it was like a piece of me died with him,"

Dolly told *People* magazine. "We were always so attached, musically and emotionally."

When Dolly Parton left Porter Wagoner in 1977, she was ready to put wings on her dreams. She was poised to go where no country star had gone before. She hired a Los Angeles manager and staged an all-out assault on mainstream show business.

"I'm not leaving country," she replied to her narrow-minded Nashville critics. "I'm taking it with me."

Musically, she began aiming at the pop hit parade. In 1977, the jaunty "Here You Come Again" topped both pop and country charts and earned her a Grammy Award. "Heartbreaker," "You're the Only One," and "Starting Over Again" were all glossy ballads that were played in both formats as well. The propulsive "9 to 5" of 1980 was another pop and country chart-topper. It earned Dolly two Grammy Awards and was nominated for an Oscar as the theme song from the film of the same title.

*9 to 5,* costarring Jane Fonda and Lily Tomlin, became Dolly's big-screen debut and a career triumph. She followed it with 1982's *The Best Little Whorehouse in Texas,* opposite Burt Reynolds; 1984's *Rhinestone,* opposite Sylvester Stallone; and the 1986 hit TV movie *A Smokey Mountain Christmas,* opposite Lee Majors and John Ritter. *Wild Texas Wind* (1991), *Unlikely Angel* (1996), and *Blue Valley Songbird* (1999) have been among her other made-for-TV starring vehicles.

In 1989, Dolly held her own amid an Oscar-caliber cast including Sally Field, Olympia Dukakis, Shirley MacLaine, Julia Roberts, and Daryl Hannah in *Steel Magnolias.* In 1992, *Straight Talk* costarred her opposite James Woods.

With her wit and glitz, she became a huge favorite on the TV talk-show circuit. Dolly's over-the-top beauty, business savvy, quotable interview skills, and musical talent landed her in the pages of such mainstream publications as *People, Time, Good Housekeeping, Vanity Fair,* and *Rolling Stone.* She posed in a bunny outfit on the cover of *Playboy* in 1978, which drew a rebuke from Porter.

As she promised, she took country music to places it had never been accepted before. She teamed up with fellow pop-country crossover star Kenny Rogers for the international smash duet hit "Islands in the Stream" in 1983. She reclaimed her Appalachian heritage with her acclaimed *Trio* album with Linda Ronstadt and Emmylou Harris in 1987. It won another Grammy. So did a track from their second get-together, *Trio II,* in 1999.

Dolly was also showered with awards at home. The CMA named her its Female Vocalist of the Year in 1975 and 1976. She was named CMA Entertainer of the Year in 1978. *Trio* won a CMA Award in 1988. Her recording of "I Will Always Love You" as a duet with Vince Gill won a CMA Award in 1995, as did her 2006 collaboration with Brad Paisley "When I Get Where I'm Going." She was inducted into the Nashville Songwriters Hall of Fame in 1986 and into the Country Music Hall of Fame in 1999.

Dolly Parton's last solo chart-topping country hit to date occurred in 1991. Ironically, it was after that when she achieved some of her greatest commercial and artistic successes. In 1992, actor Kevin Costner suggested to his *Bodyguard* film costar Whitney Houston that she should record "I Will Always Love You." The resulting single from the movie's soundtrack became a gigantic smash, remaining at number one on the national pop charts for fourteen weeks. Dolly reportedly earned $6 million in royalties from that disc. In 1986, she'd opened Dollywood, and in the 1990s, the East Tennessee theme park became one of the most visited and profitable vacation destinations in the United States.

Musically, she teamed up with fellow country queens Loretta Lynn and Tammy Wynette for the 1993 album *Honky Tonk Angels.* She scored a disco hit with her 1997 single of "Peace Train" and an adult-contemporary hit in 2004 with "Baby, It's Cold Outside," a duet with Rod Stewart. The return-to-her-roots CDs *Hungry Again* (1998), *The Grass Is Blue* (1999), *Little Sparrow* (2000), and *Halos and Horns* (2002) were hailed as masterpieces. *The Grass Is Blue* won Dolly her sixth Grammy Award. "Shine," a track from *Little Sparrow,* earned her a seventh.

And this is where the reclusive Carl Dean reemerges from the shadows. Carl is a rock-music fan, and his taste in music has occasionally influenced his famous wife in recent years. On her 1996 *Treasures* CD is her version of the Katrina & The Waves pop hit "Walking on Sunshine." *The Grass Is Blue* contains a bluegrass version of the Blackfoot rock song "Train, Train." Dolly's Grammy-winning version of "Shine" was a 1994 pop hit for Collective Soul. *Halos and Horns* contained an acoustic arrangement of Led Zeppelin's "Stairway to Heaven." Her 2008 CD *Backwoods Barbie* contains her version of the Fine Young Cannibals classic "She Drives Me Crazy." She learned all of these because of Carl's listening preferences.

"He'll always be a rock and roller at heart," says Dolly. "I get a lot of good ideas by listening to his music, like 'Shine.' I'm always hearing him playing his music, and I get all these great ideas. So it works out for us.

"Carl is funny. He loves so many odd types of music. He'll go from Frank Sinatra to loving a certain song of Merle Haggard's. He'll be listening to Bob Wills, then he'll listen to acid rock.

"He loves a lot of those old Broadway musicals. Every now and then, I'll hear him singing songs from *State Fair* or *Oklahoma!* So I asked him, 'Would you like to hear a couple of the things that I'm writing for the *9 to 5* Broadway musical?' He said, 'Well, yeah.' Man, was he floored. He couldn't believe it. He was just in tears. He said, 'Now I may not know much about stuff, but that's damn good. For you to have never done this before or to even know that world, this is as good as anything.' So that really built my confidence and made me feel like I was on the right track. And it made me want to write more and more.

"After a while, he said, 'Do you got any more of that stuff from *9 to 5,* the musical?' He's never been as involved in anything I've done like he has been with this *9 to 5* stuff. I was surprised, but he really encouraged me. Because I know he knows that world, that helped me a lot.

"One of the things that has kept us together is our good sense of humor, and the fact that we make each other laugh, and that we're just naturally funny. He just kills me. He's a character of the world. That's one of the things that made me fall in love with him to start with is his off-the-wall, crazy sense of humor.

"And he still makes me laugh. It's like we get funnier and better at that as the years go by. We both have the kind of humor that really gets to the other one. It's like he thinks I'm the funniest person, and I *know* he is.

"He loves his alone time, as I do. He's very much a loner, and he doesn't really like to be around anybody but me. And he don't even want me under his feet all the time. So we're very safe and secure in our relationship. It just works out the way that it does.

"He does not want me to schedule anything around him. He wants me to do exactly what I please. And I want the same for him.

"It's just that when we are together, we have a great time. We have a lot to catch up on. We have a lot to talk about, because sometimes so much time has gone by. I still don't like being away from Carl more than two weeks. I usually ain't, if I'm in the States. The only time we're really apart for more than two weeks at a time is if I'm on tour, like last year when we went to Europe for four weeks. That's pretty hard. That's when I'll start calling twice or three times a week, as opposed to our usual Sundays when I'm gone. I miss him. I miss mostly that he makes me feel good and safe and secure. I sleep better in the house when I'm with Carl than I do anywhere else, because I know I'm safe and I'm home."

Dolly reports that she and Carl seldom have confrontations or strong disagreements. She believes his upbringing is partly the reason why.

"Carl was the oldest in a family of three children. His father was in the war when Carl was born, so he was always much closer to his mom. I think he and his dad bickered a lot, because when he came home, his dad thought he was going to raise his son. But Carl was already four years old and already kind of set in his ways. So I think they had that love-hate relationship where they bickered back and forth a lot.

"He still lived with his mom and dad when we got married. I really think that Carl was so glad to get the heck out of that house. He and his dad were in business together, too. They had the asphalt-paving company. So he loved his dad, of course. But they did argue.

"I learned years ago, during our first days, don't argue with Carl Dean, because you are not going to win. 'Cause he's stubborn as a mule, and so am I. So we just never did get into that arguing thing.

"If we do get under each other's nerves, and we see it coming, Carl will say, 'Ain't you needin' to go somewhere?' Or I'll go, 'Why don't you go to the barn or something?'

"See, it would kill me if we got to a point where he really said something hateful that just cut my soul. I'm so sensitive, I never get over hurts like that. And the last thing on this earth I would want to do would be to hurt him in a way that he couldn't get over it. So we've never done that."

Considering her beauty and charm, Carl is remarkably not a jealous man, Dolly reports. She has been on the road and away from her husband with everybody from Porter Wagoner to Kenny Rogers. She's starred in movies with hunks from Burt Reynolds to Sylvester Stallone. Carl takes it all in stride.

"If he was ever jealous, he never showed it, and he never acted it," says Dolly. "He just sensed that I was always coming home. He knows that I flirt, have friends, and have great relationships with people. He's always said, 'I think a man would be crazy not to love you. You're a very likable person. I'd be crazy to be jealous of your friendships or your relationships with other people.' So he just never got into that, and we've never had trouble over that.

"What he meant was, I'm so easy to know, and I like people. He knows I have a motherly instinct. I take everybody under my wing, whether its musicians or bandleaders, whoever I'm working with. I'm gonna cook for them. I'm gonna baby them. I'm gonna notice if they don't feel good and make sure they go to the doctor. He knows I'm like that. But he's never been threatened by any of that.

"Our love has always been strong and deep-seated enough that I know Carl is always going to be there for me. He knows I'm going to be there for him, and he knows I'm always coming home. No matter what I have going anywhere else, whatever the type of relationship it may be, I've never ever once thought that I would ever want a divorce or want to be married to anybody but Carl."

Carl was also unfazed when it turned out that Dolly was unable to bear children, because "he's pretty much of an independent loner," she explains.

Dean Paving stopped being Carl's business in the mid-1970s. Since then, he has been a "horse trader," as Dolly puts it. He is particularly astute in real estate. She remembers being surprised when he bought a tract of land in the middle of nowhere near Spring Hill, Tennessee. Today, the Saturn car–assembly plant sits on that site. But although Carl is savvy, he never gives her career advice.

"He doesn't try to give me advice, no," she says. "He knows better than that. I'd say, 'Hey, you're not in this business. I know what I'm doing.' That would be my thinking on that.

"But he's got good insight on things. If I ask him an opinion on something, he usually has a good one. I feel like sometimes God channels his answers through Carl, because I pray about stuff, and God does answer prayers. It's funny: I'll be wondering about something, and he'll just up and say, 'Well, did you ever think about so-and-so?' or 'Wouldn't so-and-so be a good idea?' So I think God does work through him with me.

"I'm very open to him. He's very much like a father and a brother and an advisor. He really does have good suggestions. I wouldn't say it's 'advice.' It's just stuff that he says in our general conversations. He'll say something, and I'll go, 'Wow, that's exactly what I needed to hear,' or 'How did he know that?' There's a lot of that comes just by him knowing me so well. He senses a frustration or a need of some kind. It just seems that he knows what to say."

As a general rule, Carl does not attend his wife's shows—not even when she is in town and playing the Opry.

"He's taken me to the Opry, but he's never gone in. Years ago, he had this big ol' tandem truck. There was some bad snow and weather, and I couldn't get to the Opry. Carl had on his work clothes, and I had on my show clothes, and he drove me down to the Opry in the tandem truck. He pulled it right into the alley at the Ryman by the stage door. Then he listened to the Opry in the truck. Then he pulled back into the alley and picked me up in the truck.

"But, no, he wouldn't in a million years dream of getting backstage in all that chaos. Lord, that would drive him nuts. He'd think, 'How in the heck do you stand that?' He don't like crowds at all. He's seen me perform very few times in our whole relationship. There's been a couple of times when he'll come to a fair.

"One time, for a joke, he got up on the back of the stage at a fair date and started singing 'Higher and Higher' with the background group. I thought, 'That sounds awful.' I turned around, and Carl was there. We even took pictures. As my own joke, I called security and said, 'There's a man onstage that I don't know. Get him off of there and hold him.' So they pulled him off the stage. Because I was going to act like they were going to take him to jail. But [road manager] Don Warden said, 'Oh, that's Dolly's husband. He's all right.'

"Carl loved the song 'Higher and Higher' and I guess he thought he'd sound good. Carl has a beautiful voice. But he was not in tune with them. He can sing on his own, but he don't know harmony parts."

When they're at home, Dolly dresses to please Carl. That means he's one of the few people who have seen her without her trademark wigs.

"Unless I'm sick, if I had surgery or am just feeling puny, I clean up every day. I get up. I plug in my hot rollers while I'm making coffee and put on a little makeup. I don't overdo it, but I don't like to run around the house looking like a hag. I think he deserves better. So I like to look good for him. I usually don't go the full-blown wearing wigs when I'm home, because I can fix my hair cute, the way he likes it. He calls me 'Little Miss Sunshine.' I usually pull it up on top in a little scrunchy, and he thinks I look cute that way.

"I try to wear little things that I know he likes, and I try to do little things that I know he enjoys. He'll say, 'Whatever happened to that shirt with them leaves on it, that autumn-looking shirt?' or 'You still have that green thing?' He'll call out every once in a while if I ain't wore something he likes. He wants to make sure the housekeepers or the people taking care of my clothes ain't throwed away some of his favorite little things he likes to see me wear.

"And I'm the same with him. He's gray now, so he looks great in blues and grays. He knows the stuff I like. So when I'm coming home after I've been gone a long time, I'll notice he's wearing one of those shirts he knows I love.

"So that's the way we are with each other. I think that if you're conscious of the little things that the other likes, and you pay attention to those little things, I think you can always be happy together."

Dolly Parton was awarded a Living Legend medal by the Library of Congress in 2004, in part because her Dollywood Foundation supports her much-acclaimed literacy program, Dolly Parton's Imagination Library. A year later, she won a National Medal of Arts, which is the highest accolade that can be given by the U.S. government for excellence in the arts. In 2006, Dolly was honored by the John F. Kennedy Center for the Performing Arts for her lifetime of contributions. She also has a star in the Hollywood Walk of Fame, which was presented in 1984.

But when the accolades are over and the spotlight dims, Dolly goes back to her home, south of Music City. That's where Carl Dean is always waiting.

"I think we were destiny," she says of her life's one true love. "God has always laid right in my path and in my arms the things that were going to nurture me in the work that I really believe was my calling and has been more like my ministry. It's just like Judy [Ogle], my best friend, and how we've been together since we were little, and we are still together. And like me and Carl will be together all of our lives. It's like they completely know and understand me before, during, and after I'm a star. I think that God put the two perfect people in my life.

"I knew the second that I saw him that he was the one. I honestly believe—as the years go by, and I see the ways we've been so good for each other and so good to each other—that we've really enriched each other's lives. I just know that it was meant to be. Either that, or we're just the luckiest two people in the world.

"But we both believe it was destiny."

# Marty's Greatest Treasure

The evening of July 8, 1997, was tranquil on a Native American reservation in the hills of Pine Ridge, South Dakota. Standing on a dirt road in the wilderness, two people exchanged wedding vows.

"It seemed like the perfect setting," says Marty Stuart of his marriage ceremony with his fellow Grand Ole Opry star Connie Smith. "It was a very private affair. It was hard not to include our families. It was hard not to include friends and neighbors. But it was something that was deep, to us. It was highly spiritual.

"We were married on a buffalo path that we used as a symbol for how far we've come and how far we have to go. After the ceremony, we went way up on a ridge and danced to Buck Owens & The Buckaroos singing 'Your Tender Loving Care.' The thing I remember most about it was how the lightning was popping in all directions. It was so beautiful, and it didn't make a sound. The moon came up, and it was gorgeous. And an eagle flew over our ceremony. All the right symbols were sent down from Heaven to tell me that I was at the right place at the right time, doing exactly the right thing."

"It was just like a light show," agrees Connie.

"We love the deep spirituality of the Native American people," explains Marty of their unusual wedding setting. "The other thing was the peacefulness of it and the non-celebrity of it. We were simply two people in love trying to make our lives work together. It was not about an 'event,' other than the event of two people consummating their love."

"I'm probably Marty's biggest fan," Connie adds. "I think he's a genius. I can't sing his praises too much. His mind is constantly creating, and he has a great heart. And that's why I fell in love with him."

Marty and Connie walked into their marriage with their eyes wide open. As Marty puts it, "I gave her every excuse not to say yes." Both have been married before. Both had vowed they'd never marry again. Connie is seventeen years Marty's senior. They work in the same business, which can sometimes strain a relationship.

"It looked strange on paper, and I wrestled with all of that and tried to make logical sense out of it," comments Marty. "But my heart was bigger than all of that. The love that was coming at me kept flooding over me. It's bigger than all that stuff, those 'statistics.' Yeah, we talked them out.

"When in doubt, go see Mama. I called my mother and said, 'Mom, I need to come talk to you.' I told her everything and kind of ran down the 'statistics' and my fears and my concerns and all that stuff. I said, 'What do you think?' She looked at me and said, 'Five minutes of the real thing is better than fifty years of, "It ain't right." ' So there you go."

Connie's first marriage was to Ohio steelworker Jerry Smith. Born Constance June Meador on August 14, 1941, she was one of fourteen children raised in dire poverty. She was a young housewife when Opry star Bill Anderson discovered her at a talent contest and brought her to Nashville in 1964. Her very first single, the Anderson-penned "Once a Day," catapulted her to instant stardom. Connie's Opry debut was on July 18, 1964.

Billed as "The Cinderella of Country Music," she turned in a series of searing, passionate performances like "Then and Only Then" (1965), "Nobody But a Fool" (1966), "Ribbon of Darkness"

(1969), "Just One Time" (1971), and "Just for What I Am" (1972). They made her the queen of the hit parade. She joined the Opry cast in 1965.

"The music business just kinda took me where it wanted," she remarks. "I was so unready to be here. I didn't know what I was doing. . . . I was terrified. I was miserable."

Unhappiness enveloped her. Under the pressure of show business, her marriage disintegrated, leaving her alone to raise a son, Darren. Her marriage to guitarist Jack Watson survived just over a year and left her with a second son, Kerry. Every time she left her children to travel to do a concert, her heart ached with guilt and misery.

One of those concerts was on July 24, 1970, in Philadelphia, Mississippi. Marty Stuart, then eleven years old, was in the audience, completely smitten.

"Momma's favorite country singer, Connie Smith, was booked to come to our town and sing at the Choctaw Indian Fair," Marty later wrote in his book *Pilgrims*. "She looked like an angel.

"The day of her concert, I had Momma take me into town to Seward's department store. I picked out a yellow shirt to wear to the fair, hoping it would make me stand out in the crowd enough for Connie Smith to notice me.

"I talked to her musicians, watched her sign autographs for the fans, and waited for her to notice me. She never did. In a last-ditch attempt for recognition, I borrowed my momma's camera and went to the car where Connie was sitting to ask if I could take her picture. She said yes. As it turns out, it was the first photograph I'd ever taken. On the way home, I told Momma I was going to marry that girl."

He now adds triumphantly, "It took me a while, but I did."

Marty Stuart began his own music career at age twelve. Born September 30, 1958, Marty was a mandolin prodigy who began playing locally with the bluegrass-gospel group The Sullivan Family. When he was thirteen, he was hired by bluegrass superstar Lester Flatt. Completing his schooling via correspondence courses, Marty toured with Lester from 1972 to 1979. He was in Johnny Cash's band from 1980 to 1986 and was married to Johnny's daughter Cindy Cash from 1982 to 1988. Marty made solo LPs for the labels Ridge Runner (1977), Sugar Hill (1982), and Columbia (1986). But stardom eluded him.

During this same period, Connie Smith was increasingly troubled. She was contemplating suicide and seeing a psychiatrist when she found Jesus in 1968. She married electrician Marshall Haynes in 1972 and had daughters Julie, Jeanne, and Jodi. Now the mother of five, she was trying to juggle an even busier home life with the demands of her career. She couldn't even fulfill her Opry performance obligations.

"I got dropped from the Opry because I didn't make my Saturdays. So I was off the Opry for a couple of years. I think I left about 1970, and then I came back in 1972 and have been there ever since. And I'm really proud to be a part of the Grand Ole Opry.

"The Grand Ole Opry is like a home to me. . . . All the guys are my brothers, and all the girls are like sisters. If you're not there for a while, it's just like going back to a family reunion. I think some of the greatest people in the world are in the dressing rooms at the Grand Ole Opry."

Connie's last major hit was 1978's "I Just Want to Be Your Everything." After she won the *Music City News* award as Gospel Act of the Year the following year, she said, "I've done my last country show and cut my last country record. I've wanted to quit ever since I got into this."

"I have never regretted that decision," she later commented. "I was sick and tired of it all. There just wasn't enough of me to go around. . . . I couldn't keep doing what I was doing in church and with the family and the career. . . . So the only thing I could give up was the singing. And I never really thought that I'd go back to it as a career."

For the next ten years, Connie was content to sing just on the Opry. She did a little recording in 1986, but mainly stayed home to raise her children. She and Marshall divorced in 1990. By then, the country-music business had changed a great deal. A whole new crop of artists had emerged, attracting much younger fans.

One of those new performers was Marty Stuart. He first made the charts with a flurry of singles in 1985–1989, then rose to stardom on the strength of such MCA Records discs as "Hillbilly Rock," "Tempted," "Burn Me Down," and "You Can't Stop Love" in the 1990s. Marty joined the Opry cast on November 28, 1992. His 1992 duet with fellow Opry cast member Travis Tritt won the team a Grammy Award. Marty earned a reputation for honoring country's history and traditions while creating strikingly contemporary sounds.

As she had promised herself, Connie gave show business a backseat to her family. But eventually, all five kids had "flown the coop."

"I was by myself. I was divorced. The kids were grown and doing their own things. I thought, 'I better get a life.' The only thing I know and love is music. But if I did go back into it and if I recorded again, who would produce me? I needed somebody who appreciates what I've done, where I've been, where I'm coming from.

"The only person I could think of to work with in this whole town—who would accept me for who I was, but who had their finger on the pulse of what is going on today—was Marty Stuart."

Backstage at the Opry in 1993, she approached him with the idea. He suggested that they write songs together. When they did, sparks flew.

"It was Country Music Romance 101," says Marty. "You write songs with her, and you can't help falling in love with her. You just can't."

"I remember the first day he came over to the house," recalls Connie. "He got ready to leave. And like hillbillies do, we hugged each other. I said, 'You're my kid.' He said, 'No, I'm not.' It didn't take long before we were in love. Anybody that's been around Marty for more than five minutes is going to fall in love with him."

"I had been over to her house one day," Marty remembers. "I was driving home and something bigger than me just turned the wheel around, and I called her on the phone and said, 'Will you meet me in the parking lot of the Kroger in Brentwood?' She had no idea why we were meeting. And I really didn't either. I just knew I wanted to see her. When she got there, she was talking, because she talks a lot. She talks a whole lot. I finally said, 'Shut up and come here.' And I kissed her. I expected her to slap me, but she didn't. After a long kiss, she looked at me and said, 'Let's do that again.' So that's how our love affair took off."

Ironically, "One of the reasons I thought Marty would be good to work with was that he was younger, and I wouldn't have to worry about him being 'interested' in me," says Connie. "And I knew I wasn't interested in nobody.

"After my divorce in 1990, I thought, 'That's it for me; never again.' I never had any intention of looking for romance again. I thought, 'I don't deserve another chance, and I don't think I want to put forth the effort.' I don't know what happened. It musta been the moon."

Following his divorce, Marty Stuart had also decided he'd never marry again. But after he and Connie had been seeing each other for more than three years, he proposed.

"Pretty clumsily," he explains. "We were sitting on the front porch of the house, and I wasn't very good at it. She says that when I really asked her, I said, 'Go find that rock your birth certificate is carved on, and let's get this thing over with.' I don't think I was that clumsy, but I probably was."

MARTY STUART AND CONNIE Smith are not the longest-married Opry cast members. Nor are Garth Brooks and Trisha Yearwood. That distinction belongs to Ricky Skaggs and Sharon White of the family band The Whites. Ricky and Sharon were married on August 4, 1981.

Ricky and Sharon have had parallel careers. Both became country stars around the same time. Both were professional musicians as teenagers. Both are steeped in country tradition. Both work on the bluegrass festival circuit.

Ricky Skaggs was born in Kentucky on July 18, 1954. Sharon's birth date is December 15, 1953, and she was raised in Texas. Ricky became a member of Ralph Stanley's band at age fifteen. That's around the same time that Sharon and her younger sister Cheryl (born January 27, 1955) told their father, Buck White, that they were ready to hit the road as a band. Sharon plays guitar. Cheryl plays upright bass. Buck, who was born January 13, 1930, is proficient on mandolin, guitar, and piano.

"We met in 1971," says Sharon. "It was the first summer that Ricky traveled with Ralph Stanley. And it was the year that Cheryl and I said to Dad, 'Whenever you're ready, let's put the house up for sale and go for it.'"

"I flipped out when I saw her and heard her," recalls Ricky. "I wanted to meet her so bad. Went up and kinda flirted with her a little bit. I was sixteen years old."

"We moved to Nashville in September 1971, and I saw him again in October when he came to town for the Country Music Convention," Sharon remembers. "We started working the festivals on the bluegrass circuit. We ran into him a lot then. . . . We just gradually got to be pals during that time."

"Sharon was just someone I could talk to," says Ricky. "I could relate to her because we both had the same goals. You know, we both wanted to make it in the music business."

Emmylou Harris discovered The Whites' abilities. In 1979, she invited them to join her on tour as her opening act and harmony singers. Ricky joined Emmylou's band, too. In January 1980, Sharon was divorced from her first husband, banjo player Jack Hicks. Eight months later, Ricky was divorced from his first wife, Barbara, with whom he had two children, Mandy and Andrew. The divorces drew Ricky and Sharon together.

"I was hurtin', and she was hurtin'," Ricky recalls. "We started hangin' really close together."

At first, "there was nothing really romantic happening," Sharon reports. "When it started becoming a romantic thing, it scared us both. We were afraid it would ruin our friendship."

Ricky had his first hit records in 1981. He produced the records that made The Whites stars the following year. He joined the Opry cast on May 15, 1982. The Whites became members on March 2, 1984. Since then, Ricky and Sharon have had two children, Molly and Luke.

In 1987, Ricky Skaggs and Sharon White won a Country Music Association (CMA) Award for their duet "Love Can't Ever Get Better Than This." Twenty years later, Ricky and The Whites teamed up for their first full CD together, *Salt of the Earth*. On February 10, 2008, it won them a Grammy Award.

SHARON IS PARTICULARLY CLOSE to Connie Smith. The two women share a deep Christian faith and often pray together. Sharon is also a fan of her friend, and she's not alone in her admiration for the emotion-drenched singing of Connie Smith. Connie's fellow Opry star Dolly Parton notably once said, "There's really only three female singers in the world: Streisand, Ronstadt, and Connie Smith. The rest of us are only pretending."

Marty Stuart's recording-studio work with Connie Smith resulted in her comeback album in 1998. Since then, Connie has enthusiastically reembraced the career she once walked away from.

After he took his first snapshot of Connie, Marty developed a passion for photography that has led to two books and several exhibitions. Marty has also collected music memorabilia for many years, and he is now the curator of a traveling museum exhibit called *Sparkle and Twang*. But nothing he has ever "collected" compares to his wife, he says.

"Connie is so authentic, and that applies to any generation," says Marty. "Connie's voice is a true part of America's atmosphere. She sings better washing the dishes at the sink than most people's best records. I'm married to Connie Smith, and that's the *standard*. My baby is a country-music *essential*. I am often asked, 'Marty, what is your favorite treasure in country music?' Why, Miss Connie Smith!

"The thing that makes our marriage work is we both go back to what we went up to Pine Ridge for, the spirit . . . and the fact that we've both been down these roads before. Experience helps. Wisdom helps. Counsel helps. I think even music helps. But at the end of the day, it's the love and respect and looking to God and having a sense of humor underlying the whole thing.

"When Connie and I have a bad day, the thing that comes up is, 'You wanna go again tomorrow?' What is love? Love is going again tomorrow."

## 15

# Vince and Amy

If you ask Vince Gill why he loves his wife, Amy Grant, he just might look at you like you're insane.

"Have you ever *met* her?" he asks incredulously. "That's all you have to do. Really, all it takes is to spend just five minutes with her and have a conversation with her, and you can't help but love her. It's kind of amazing."

The outrageous New York radio personality Don Imus began making wisecracks about Amy after she and Vince wed in 2000. Vince recalls making a special trip to New York to confront him.

"After Amy and I got married, Imus really turned on me. He really liked me before that. On his show, he was just ragging us every day for getting married. He just started hammering us. So I went on his show after my next record came out. We were talking for a little while, and finally he brought her name up. I said, 'You know, I heard you said some things about my wife.' I said, 'I've got to be real honest. That's the reason I came up here. I didn't really come up here to promote my record. I came up here to tell you we need to straighten this thing out. Because we're either going to straighten this out, or I'm going to come across this desk, and I'm gonna whip your butt.'

"He started grinning and said, 'Well, let's straighten this thing out.' I said, 'You've never met her, have you?' He said, 'No.' I said, 'If you'd ever met her, you would never say those things about her.' Afterward, somebody called me and said, 'That is the greatest thing you could have said to him.' Just my saying, 'You never met her.' "

Vince avers that to know her is to love her. He explains that Amy Grant is not only glowingly beautiful and immensely talented as a singer-songwriter, she is unfailingly gracious, considerate, kind, compassionate, and warm. She is also the largest-selling Christian-music artist in history. And it turned out that her music community made their relationship much more difficult than Don Imus ever could.

In the 1990s, rumors swirled in Nashville about the two celebrities, particularly in highly judgmental Christian-music circles. But Vince states that he and Amy were simply great buddies and not romantically involved during most of the time the gossip was being whispered.

"It was rumored and so public, long before we really did become a couple," he says. "There was an awful lot of damage done by the tongue-waggers who really thought the worst of us. They were incorrect.

"It was like meeting my oldest and dearest friend when I met Amy," Vince recalls. "I think a lot of people assumed we orchestrated our getting together, and they couldn't be more wrong. It was never even discussed between the two of us. We just tried to maintain a great friendship. We did the best we could with the high road."

Vince Gill taped his first Christmas television special at the Tulsa Performing Arts Center in Oklahoma on November 29, 1993. His guests on that Nashville Network special were Michael McDonald, Chet Atkins, and Amy Grant. She and Vince dueted on her song "Tennessee Christmas," and they "clicked" as personalities at once.

The two first recorded together at Amy's request. In 1994, she had a tune called "House of Love," and thought his high voice would sound good singing with hers. He was such a fan of hers that he agreed to her request without even hearing the song first. Their duet became a big pop hit single. On his *When Love Finds You* album of the same year, she returned the favor by cowriting and singing background vocals on "If I Had My Way." Prophetically, that album also included the torn-between-two-loves ballad "Which Bridge to Cross (Which Bridge to Burn)," a song Vince cowrote with his fellow Grand Ole Opry star Bill Anderson.

At any rate, by 1996, Vince Gill and Amy Grant were fast friends. Each encouraged the other musically. In his case, the result was his brilliant 1996 album *High Lonesome Sound*. That Christmas, Vince appeared at the Nashville Arena as a guest at her "Amy Grant's Tennessee Christmas" concert. She called their close friendship an "investment" in one another.

"My investment has been criticized and called into question and everything else," she said when asked about the gossip surrounding them. "I just go, 'I'm not responsible for everybody's opinion of the people I choose to be friends with.' I think the world of my friends."

Complicating and intensifying the rumors about them was the fact that both celebrities were married to two other public figures. Vince's crumbling eighteen-year marriage was with Janis Gill of the country duo Sweethearts of the Rodeo. Amy's troubled marriage was with Christian singer-songwriter, humorist, and TV personality Gary Chapman. Amy and Gary married in 1982 and were in marital counseling as early as 1987–1988.

Still, it was Vince who went through a divorce first. His marriage to Janis ended in 1997. During that year, the troubled star found solace at the Opry. For several months, he performed on the show almost weekly.

"When I went through my divorce, I spent most of my time out there," he comments. "The amount of time I've been out there is for the investments I've made in all those folks as people, not as stars. That's the real beauty of the Opry, getting to know the people. It's even a better thing than knowing them as the big stars that they are.

"All those people know how much I revere them. Part of my getting to know those folks was as much out of respect for my parents as anything else. They loved that music, probably even more so than me."

VINCENT GRANT GILL WAS born April 12, 1957, in Norman, Oklahoma. His father, Stan, was an attorney and judge who played piano, guitar, and banjo. Both he and Vince's mother, Jerene, were big country-music fans who sang around the house. By the time he graduated from high school, in Oklahoma City, Vince was an excellent guitarist and the veteran of a high school bluegrass band called Mountain Smoke. An invitation to join Bluegrass Alliance led him to move to Louisville, Kentucky, after graduation. Following a subsequent and brief stint in the band Boone Creek with future Opry star Ricky Skaggs, Vince moved to California.

On the West Coast, nineteen-year-old Vince joined Byron Berline and Sundance. While in that group, Vince met Rodney Crowell, Guy Clark, and Emmylou Harris, who became lifelong friends of his. It was also while in Sundance that Vince first encountered the sister duo Sweethearts of the Rodeo. In 1979, he became the lead singer for the established pop-country group Pure Prairie League. The following year, Vince sang the group's biggest hit, "Let Me Love You Tonight," and married Janis Oliver of Sweethearts of the Rodeo.

In 1981, Vince joined The Cherry Bombs, the band that backed Rodney Crowell and Rosanne Cash. Daughter Jenny was born in 1982. Former Cherry Bombs member Tony Brown offered Vince a solo recording contract in Nashville, so the Gills moved to Music City in 1983.

"After I moved here in '83, I took my dad and my sister to see the Opry. I'd never been to an Opry performance. It was pretty unique to see it for the first time. What's so neat about the Opry, to me, is that so many of those artists are my family's favorites. When my dad met Jimmy Dickens for the first time, he said, 'Hey, I cannot find a copy of "Country Boy" [Jimmy's 1949 hit].' Jimmy said, 'Give me your address, and I'll just send you one.' I had no idea why my dad brought that up.

"My favorite story of all is when my dad called me up after I had sung 'May the Bird of Paradise Fly Up Your Nose' with Jimmy Dickens. He said, 'Now you've made it. Now you've done something.'

"At my dad's funeral [in 1997], I brought a boom box out and started playing some of his favorite songs. The first song I played was 'Country Boy.' After I played that, I asked my dad's brother to speak. He was kind of in shock. He said, 'I cannot believe Vince picked 'Country Boy' to play. He probably has no idea of this, but when we were little boys, we got a little record player for Christmas, and the first record we ever had was that!'

"So you just can't help seeing the connection, that circle, and thinking of me as a kid listening to all those records that those Grand Ole Opry stars made."

In the wake of such hits as "Oklahoma Borderline" (1985), "Cinderella" (1987), "When I Call Your Name" (1990), "Never Knew Lonely" (1991), and "Pocket Full of Gold" (1991), Vince Gill was invited to join the Opry's cast. The date of his induction was August 10, 1991.

"That was pretty great," Vince recalls. "How many artists can say that Roy Acuff inducted them? Not many, I'm sure. I always had such a reverence for that place. There's a side of me that feels like some of the young Turks need to stick up for these people. They need to tell other people who these stars are. It's like me discovering Eric Clapton and Eric telling me, 'Hey, Robert Johnson is where I got all this.' That's the way you teach. George Jones will tell you that Roy Acuff was how he learned to sing."

Vince's fame and acclaim grew dramatically throughout the 1990s. But he always maintained his loyalty to the Opry. "When

Love Finds You" (1994), "Worlds Apart" (1996), "If You Ever Have Forever in Mind" (1998), and the rest of his more than twenty-five top-ten hits have delighted Opry audiences as well as millions who have seen his concerts.

Many of his songs come from deeply personal places. "Go Rest High on That Mountain" was written to commemorate the 1994 passing of his older brother Bob. His moving 1998 song "The Key to Life" saluted his late father. "Pretty Little Adriana" (1996) was inspired by the tragic shooting death of a young Nashville girl. "I Still Believe in You" (1992) was written as an apology following a fight with Janis.

He has sung duets with several of his fellow Opry stars, notably Dolly Parton (1995's "I Will Always Love You"), Patty Loveless (1999's "My Kind of Woman, My Kind of Man"), Ricky Skaggs and Steve Wariner (1991's "Restless"), Reba McEntire (1993's "The Heart Won't Lie"), and Alison Krauss (1996's "High Lonesome Sound"). The Opry's Emmylou Harris enlisted him as her harmony vocalist for her 1987 gospel collection *Angel Band*. So it was no surprise that Vince found comfort in his frequent visits to the show in 1996–1997, when his marriage was ending.

"I am going to be fine," he said at the time. "I am going to get through it. I am just trying to treat [the divorce] with as much class and respect as I have everything else in my life. So I'm being respectful of Janis and protective of myself. It doesn't need to be an open book."

"My marriage dissolved because it should have," he reflects today. "It needed to. Not because of Amy, but because of Janis and me.

"What my friendship with Amy did more than anything was to shine a light on what was really true, that we were both in places that weren't great, weren't healthy, weren't a lot of things. In all honesty, I don't think I ever believed that we would wind up together."

They collaborated professionally again during the production of Vince's 1998 Christmas album. Its title tune, "Breath of Heaven," was one of Amy's songs. Originally written for a female voice to sing about the Virgin Mary, Amy agreed to change a few words so that Vince could sing it from a male point of view.

Amy and Gary separated in 1998 and divorced in 1999. Inevitably, her community blamed Vince for the breakup.

"They had a scapegoat, and it was me. I felt like every Christian in the world didn't like me. All that stuff, in a sense, probably made us withdraw more than normal. I knew those feelings [of love] were there. So we tried to be respectful by not being out in public too much, too soon.

"One of my favorite memories was from when we first started dating. One of the first things we did together was go to one of her niece's graduation from [the private Nashville girls' school] Harpeth Hall. I was a little apprehensive about going. I said, 'Man, the whole West End community is going to be there.'

"But we're going to go. So away we go. We're running a little bit late, as we normally do. We round the corner going into this big courtyard area where all the parents are sitting and waiting for the girls. I did not know this, but back farther behind us, the girls were lining up to come out. Everybody was really looking, honestly, where the girls were coming out. And I thought it was me. I was looking at Amy as we were walking up, and I go, 'This is really uncomfortable. I feel like the whole zip code is staring at me.' She goes, 'Me, too.' Then we turned and saw the girls were behind us, and we go, 'I think we're okay.'"

In 1999, Amy was one of the participants in his annual charity golf tournament, The Vinny. They were seen dining together, attending church together and, especially, golfing together. Vince Gill is so good at the sport that he could have been a professional. Amy Grant's enthusiasm for golf helped draw them closer together. After several sightings of them on the links, she told the press that they were a couple, in late 1999.

He proposed the old-fashioned way, on bended knee. On March 10, 2000, Vince Gill and Amy Grant were wed outdoors at a farm in rural Tennessee, south of Nashville. She wore a cream-colored floor-length dress with a matching cape and flowers in her hair. He wore a black formal suit. They wrote their own vows.

"The view from the hilltop that day made me think I could see forever, which is how a man feels when he's finally complete," he said later. "I tell Amy all the time, 'You have no idea how amazing it is to be whole again.' There is just no overestimating the power of a second chance, which is what I feel I got by marrying Amy."

Today, he reflects, "She just made things more peaceful. What's beautiful about our relationship is we don't argue. We don't fight and yell or any of that. We really never have had any cross words."

Vince brought Amy to the Opry on April 21, 2000. Although she'd grown up in Nashville, this was the Christian-music superstar's debut at the city's most famous institution.

AMY LEE GRANT'S FAMILY'S roots were in Nashville. She was born on November 25, 1960, in Augusta, Georgia, but the Grants moved back to the city when she was a girl. Her great-grandfather, A. M. Burton, was a multimillionaire philanthropist who founded the Life & Casualty Insurance Company. The firm's skyscraper is one of the most prominent features of Nashville's skyline to this day. Amy's father, Burton, became a prominent Nashville physician, and her mother, Gloria, raised Amy and her sisters to be proper young ladies. Amy attended the elite Ensworth and Harpeth Hall schools and majored in English at Vanderbilt University.

While at Harpeth Hall, she began writing and performing pop songs with religious lyrics. The leader of her Bible study group took a tape of them to Word Records, which signed her at age sixteen. *My Father's Eyes* (1979) and *Never Alone* (1980) paved the way for her breakthrough album, 1982's *Age to Age* and its hit "El Shaddai." She first crossed over from the Christian to the pop charts with 1985's "Find a Way." Then, 1986's "Next Time I Fall" (a duet with Peter

Cetera) and 1991's "Baby Baby," "Every Heartbeat," and "That's What Love Is For" made her a mainstream pop star. She continued to make the pop charts throughout the 1990s.

"I have become the most blessed man, I think, on this earth, to marry my best friend," said Vince in introducing Amy to the Opry audience. "And I want her to come out and sing a song all about tomorrow. Would you please welcome Miss Amy Grant."

She and Vince sang "How Great Thou Art" together. They brought the house down. The Opry cast was thrilled to meet her.

"They're crazy about her," beams Vince. "That community mind-set out there is really beautiful. She has a tremendously long history of her family in this town, and a connection that I think is as big a part of that place as anybody who's gone through those doors. She was willing to meet all the people that make up my life, and vice versa. I've met so many of the people who shaped and formed her faith and her life. It's been pretty neat for both of us. It's broadened both of us in a beautiful way."

On the home front, things were a little more strained. Vince's daughter Jenny was a teenager during his divorce and remarriage. Amy's children, Matt (born in 1987), Millie (born in 1989), and Sarah (born in 1992), all entered their rocky teenage years during the early years of their mother's new marriage.

"It was not an easy road," Vince admits. "There were a lot of issues. But I just told Amy, 'Time is going to take care of all of this. It's not going to be right today. Maybe not next year, not two years from now, but just with time all of these kids will see who you are. And your kids will see who I am. Regardless of what they've been told or taught to believe, they'll see who I am, and they'll see how I treat you. And time has been a great thing. Everybody's great. I think everybody realizes that things are the way they ought to be."

The birth of their daughter Corrina Grant Gill in 2001 was a major turning point. She blended the family in a profound way.

"What's beautiful about Corrina is she gives everybody in our family the connection. My daughter has a sister, and Amy's three kids have a little sister, and it's ours. So she kind of connected all of us.

"She's just a little twin of Amy. She's full of kindness and sweetness. She cares about animals and all things and people, too. Her prayers at night should be songs or books. That she would think of what she thinks of is pretty inspiring."

Corrina's birth coincided with Vince and Amy's blossoming as a beloved couple in Music City. Both of them have long been noted for their civic involvement and commitment to charity work. Their collaborations as artists have endeared them to throngs of fans in recent years.

Vince and Amy were together on holiday concert tours in 2001, 2003, and 2004. He played guitar in her touring band in 2002. They costarred on Christmas TV specials in 2002 and appeared together on a PBS Independence Day special in 2004. Amy sang back-up vocals on Vince's 2004 single "In These Last Few Days." He appeared at the Nashville Symphony gala honoring her in 2006. She toured with him in 2007. He coproduced her albums *Legacy Hymns & Faith* (2002) and *Rock of Ages Hymns & Faith* (2005). Since the latter won a Grammy Award, Vince is unique as someone having earned Grammys as a singer, songwriter, instrumentalist, and record producer.

"Working together in the studio is really easy," he says. "It's never hard if you're respectful. To me, that's the whole key to working with anybody, but especially with your best pal.

"I don't think she has any idea of how great she is. There's beauty in that. It was interesting that she asked me to do them [traditional hymns]. I never heard of them, you know. She said, 'This is what will be neat. You won't have forty-five years of singing this in church to guide your wife on how to do this song.' I'm sure I ruffled a few feathers with some of the more soulful and funky grooves I put on some of these old hymns.

"If I write any songs of faith, I have to go to her and ask, 'Is this really accurate or not?' She's a great help. We don't write a lot together. Once again, that's as much a respect factor as anything else. She had a twenty-five-year career before I showed up. And I did too. Just because we got married, we don't have to be Sonny & Cher.

"But I think people sense it, could feel it, and can see it, that we are two people who are just so amazingly right for each other."

# Funny Love

Blessed with a droll, dry wit, the husband of the Grand Ole Opry's most famous comic was just as funny as she was. Sarah Ophelia Colley, known to millions as Minnie Pearl, married pilot Henry Cannon in 1947, and they were still together when she passed away forty-nine years later. Lost without her, Henry died the following year. Theirs was truly one of Nashville's greatest love stories.

"The fact that Henry is one of the funniest men I have ever met makes him even more attractive," Minnie reflected. "He *thinks* funny. He has a dry wit, and his timing is absolutely perfect.

"We will be having a discussion about something, and he'll make one of his wry observations, and I will absolutely *fall out*. He's not trying to be funny. I'm very conscious of people who try to make me laugh, and Henry has never done that. It's just his natural way of expressing himself—and has been since the day I met him."

She once observed, "I've always said that he is funnier than me."

He was also completely and utterly unimpressed with show business, which could lead to hilarious consequences. During a 1952 trip to New York, the couple went to see the hit musical *Guys and Dolls*.

"Henry was seated on the aisle," Minnie recalled. "Just as the overture started, I heard whispering all around me. I knew someone famous had arrived. Being from the country, I turned to look. There stood Elizabeth Taylor at her most devastatingly beautiful. She had just married Michael Wilding, and she was absolutely glowing. I said, 'Henry, Henry, here comes Elizabeth Taylor!' 'Oh mercy,' he mumbled, and turned around and stood up to say hello. He thought it was someone he had met and was supposed to know!

"He had no idea who Elizabeth Taylor was. I tugged on his coat and said, 'Henry, *sit down!* She's a *movie star,* the most beautiful woman in the world!' He said, 'Well, she does look pretty good,' and then went right back to his program."

When Minnie met Henry Cannon, he was a pilot who owned a charter-airplane business in Nashville. At the time, neither of them was an innocent youngster. He was a twenty-nine-year-old veteran of World War II. She was thirty-four and had been a theater professional for more than a decade.

"I had been on my own for a long time and had already become set in my ways," she recalled. "I was also as stubborn and independent as the dickens. Considering all this, it's amazing to me that there was never any question as to who wore the pants in our family."

She added, "I think women deserve to have as much pay for an honest day's work as men, but I don't go all to pieces over women's lib. My husband is the boss in our household. He tells me what to do, and I like it that way."

After he married her, Henry was shocked to learn that she had no investments or even a savings account. He sold his company, eventually flying Minnie to all her shows, and became the entertainer's business manager. From that time on, they were practically inseparable.

That Minnie was irresponsible with money is somewhat surprising, because her father had a lumber business that was wiped out during the Great Depression. She was born Sarah Ophelia Colley on October 25, 1912, in Centerville, Tennessee, a small town west of Nashville. Her mother had been the belle of nearby Franklin, Tennessee, and had raised all five of her daughters to be well-educated ladies. Sarah Ophelia, the baby, was doted on, pampered, and praised when she played the piano and play acted. Her mother took her along on shopping trips to Nashville, which is where the little girl unwittingly witnessed her future.

"I used to go to the Princess Theater," she remembered. "Back then, you could put a child in a theater and leave 'em there while Mama did her shopping. Elviry Weaver used to come there and do her act with her 'brothers.' I sat there and learned every one of Elviry's lines."

Elviry Weaver was vaudeville's pioneering rube comedienne. Minnie was also influenced by the shenanigans of Lulu Belle, a star of the *National Barn Dance* on NBC radio, and the films and broadcasts of the hokum comic Judy Canova. All of these ground-breaking country-comedy women would eventually be featured in Minnie's Nashville museum.

Because of the reversal of her father's fortunes, there wasn't enough money to send the baby to college when she became of age. There was just enough to put her through Ward–Belmont ladies' finishing school in Nashville for two years. After failing as a drama, piano, and dancing teacher in Centerville, she hit the road in 1934.

The Wayne P. Sewell Company of Roscoe, Georgia, sent actors to towns throughout the South to organize community theatricals with amateur talent in conjunction with Lion's clubs and the like. The aspiring thespians would work from scripts purchased from the firm.

In the winter of 1936, Sarah arrived in northeastern Alabama to put on a production of a trifle called *Flapper Grandmother*. She boarded with a mountaineer woman and became fascinated with the way she talked, her folk expressions, and her rustic stories.

"When I got to the next place, I got to tellin' people about this woman. By 1938, I was 'doing' her, but I hadn't named her. So

Johnny and June Carter
Cash perform on the
1977 CMA Award Show.
*Photograph by Les Leverett,*
*© Grand Ole Opry*
*Archives.*

David "Stringbean"
Akeman. *Photograph*
*by Les Leverett, ©*
*Grand Ole Opry*
*Archives.*

The glamorous Dottie West performs on the Opry. *Unattributed photograph, Grand Ole Opry Archives.*

An excited Barbara Mandrell accepts the 1980 CMA Entertainer of the Year Award. *Photograph by Les Leverett, © Grand Ole Opry Archives.*

Bill Anderson and Brad Paisley perform "Too Country" during the Grand Ole Opry's 80th anniversary concert at Carnegie Hall. *Photograph by Curtis Hilburn, © Grand Ole Opry Archives.*

Pam Tillis welcomes dad, Mel, to the Grand Ole Opry cast on his induction night. *Photograph by Chris Hollo, © Grand Ole Opry Archives.*

Eddy Arnold with wife, Sally, and baby daughter, Jo Ann. *Unattributed photograph, Grand Ole Opry Archives.*

Garth Brooks and Trisha Yearwood share the Opry stage in 1998. *Photograph by Donnie Beauchamp, © Grand Ole Opry Archives.*

Loretta poses with husband, "Doo" Lynn, backstage at the Opry. *Photograph by Les Leverett, © Grand Ole Opry Archives.*

George Jones steals a birthday kiss from wife, Nancy, onstage during his 70th birthday celebration at the Opry. *Photograph by Chris Hollo, © Grand Ole Opry Archives.*

Patsy Cline chats with Randy Hughes backstage at a show.
*Photograph by Les Leverett, © Grand Ole Opry Archives.*

Gentleman Jim Reeves
performs on WSM's
Pet Milk radio show.
*Photograph by Gordon
Gillingham, © Grand
Ole Opry Archives.*

Dolly Parton celebrates Porter Wagoner's 50th anniversary as a Grand Ole Opry member, singing the song she wrote for him, "I Will Always Love You." *Photograph by Chris Hollo, © Grand Ole Opry Archives.*

Connie Smith and husband, Marty Stuart, come together for a duet on the Opry stage. *Photograph by Chris Hollo, © Grand Ole Opry Archives.*

Amy Grant and Vince Gill. *Photograph by Chris Hollo, © Grand Ole Opry Archives.*

Henry Cannon with his bride, Sarah Ophelia Colley Cannon (aka Minnie Pearl) on their wedding day. *Photograph by Henry Schofield Studio.*

Little Jimmy Dickens gets a little help from a stepladder as he invites Trace Adkins to join the Grand Ole Opry cast. *Photograph by Chris Hollo, © Grand Ole Opry Archives.*

Martina sings songs from her *Timeless* album on a special Opry broadcast. *Photograph by Chris Hollo, © Grand Ole Opry Archives.*

Patty Loveless is welcomed to the Opry family by her mentor, Porter Wagoner. *Photograph by Donnie Beauchamp,* © *Grand Ole Opry Archives.*

Faron Young performs on the Grand Ole Opry in 1954. *Photograph by Gordon Gillingham,* © *Grand Ole Opry Archives.*

Garth Brooks and the rest of the cast welcome newest Opry member, Clint Black, during the 65th Anniversary television special. *Photograph by Dan Loftin, © Grand Ole Opry Archives.*

*Marty Robbins. Unattributed photograph, Grand Ole Opry Archives.*

Charley Pride and wife Rozene pose backstage at Charley's 1993 Grand Ole Opry induction. *Photograph by Donnie Beauchamp, © Grand Ole Opry Archives.*

Alan Jackson. *Photograph by Chris Hollo, © Grand Ole Opry Archives.*

Emmylou Harris duets with her special guest, Elvis Costello, during an Opry at the Ryman show. *Photograph by Chris Hollo, © Grand Ole Opry Archives.*

Johnny Paycheck excitedly accepts the invitation to join the Opry cast from then-General Manager, Bob Whittaker, and Steve Wariner. *Photograph by Donnie Beauchamp, © Grand Ole Opry Archives.*

Ronnie Milsap.
*Photograph by
Chris Hollo,
© Grand Ole
Opry Archives.*

Willie Nelson makes an Opry guest appearance. *Photograph by Chris Hollo,* © *Grand Ole Opry Archives.*

Dierks Bentley and his dog, Jake, on the night of his induction. *Photograph by Chris Hollo,* © *Grand Ole Opry Archives.*

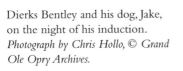

DeFord Bailey,
The Harmonica
Wizard. *Unattributed
photograph, Grand
Ole Opry Archives.*

Hal Ketchum reads
the poem he wrote for
his Opry induction.
*Photograph by Donnie
Beauchamp,* © *Grand
Ole Opry Archives.*

Opry patriarch, Roy Acuff, welcomes Randy Travis to the stage.
*Photograph by Donnie Beauchamp, © Grand Ole Opry Archives.*

Hank Williams.
*Unattributed
photograph, Grand
Ole Opry Archives.*

I just picked out two nice women's country names," Minnie and Pearl.

The costume was the result of $10 spent in a thrift store in Aiken, South Carolina—the organdy dress, the white cotton stockings, the Mary Jane strapped shoes, and the famous tacky hat with its flowers. Once when she replaced the silk flowers, Minnie mistakenly left the price tag on them. During her show, it dangled down. And that $1.98 price tag completed the ensemble.

The Sewell roadwork eventually dried up. She limped home to Centerville as a twenty-eight-year-old failure. It was up to Minnie to support her now-widowed mother. Desperate for any kind of theatrical job, she auditioned her comedy persona at WSM in November of 1940. Worried that this woman with a "drawing-room" upbringing might seem to be mocking the Opry's rural listeners with her Minnie Pearl character, station officials scheduled her debut on the show for 11:05 p.m., when many would have turned off their radios or left the auditorium.

After Minnie finished her routine, her mother offered this encouragement: "Several people woke up." But three hundred pieces of fan mail arrived during the next week. Minnie was offered a job. Two years later, in February 1942, she was put on the NBC national-network portion of the Opry.

"I have never gotten over the debt that I owe the Opry," she said. "I was a failure at twenty-eight. The Opry was a marvelous break for me that I will always remember. The Opry pulled me out of the slough that I was in. Or whatever that word is. The miasma?

"When I came in 1940, most of the people who listened to the Opry were considered country people, hillbillies, at that point. Most people believed that nobody listened to it except country people. Nowadays, you don't know where you're gonna find a country fan. The Opry, and country music, have become worldwide. That's very exciting to me.

"And when I walk out onto the stage, the Opry audience is different from any other audience. There's a special feeling that you get from an Opry audience that you don't get, for example, when you tape a TV special in that same hall. The Opry audience is people who have sent in for those tickets and have come here especially for the Opry. Some are there for curiosity, but I think the majority of them are there because they care."

She always greeted them the same way. "HowDEEE! I'm jest so proud to be hyere!" she'd holler with her arms flung wide.

Delighted crowds shouted "HowDEEE!" back at her for fifty years.

Minnie Pearl initially gained fame as a member of Pee Wee King's touring troupe during World War II. On the road, often entertaining men in the armed forces, Minnie became brasher, louder, more uninhibited, sillier, and a little racier. She played the man-hungry "old maid" with a glint in her eye. She was the homely wallflower with an eternal optimist's outlook. She was plucky and foolish.

She gossiped innocently about the fictional residents of Grinder's Switch. Miss Lizzie Tinkum, Brother, Uncle Nabob, Aunt Ambrosy, Mrs. Orson Tugwell, Doc Payne, Moonshine McGinny, Poker Face Perkins, Hezzie, and the rest of her "neighbors" populated her corny jokes. And the cornier she was, the more embraced she was.

Although she hadn't grown up with country music, Minnie Pearl soon came to love her fellow Opry cast members. She even romanced them.

"There had been several love affairs in my life—naturally— before I met Henry. He would be the first to say that a woman who didn't marry until she was nearly thirty-five was bound to have had some romances. I did, and I'm glad that I did. I profited from all of them. I cried some, but that helps me appreciate 'the good life.' Only by comparison can you come to a point where you can say, 'This is *the one*!' I'm glad I felt deeply for one of the musicians who joined Pee Wee in 1943. He taught me to truly appreciate this beautiful, pure country music. . . . The sound of the fiddle . . . still sends me."

At this same time, her future bridegroom was seeing the world.

Born on August 11, 1912, Henry Cannon grew up in a well-to-do family in Franklin, Tennessee. He enlisted in the Army Air Corps in World War II and served in the Pacific theater. Henry's best boyhood friend married Minnie's Nashville roommate in 1946, and the couple immediately began a matchmaking campaign. While still in Japan, Henry was bombarded with letters about Minnie. At the boardinghouse for women, Minnie was nagged about meeting Henry.

"Henry was no more interested in meeting me than I was in meeting him," she recalled. "I was perfectly satisfied with my social life, and I was tired of friends trying to marry me off. I was having the time of my life! If some people saw me as an old maid at thirty-four, I figured that was their problem."

In May 1946, Henry came home from the war. He and Minnie were introduced at a party at the newlyweds' apartment one night after an Opry performance. Sparks did not fly. They continued to meet at such get-togethers throughout the summer. All the while, the newlyweds kept pressuring them to date one another.

"They weren't about to give up, even though it was obvious no great explosion had taken place between us. He was attractive, and the more time I spent around him, the more I realized that he was one of the funniest men I'd ever met."

At one party, Henry impulsively kissed her and instructed her to get rid of the man who was her date that night. She obeyed. After her date dropped her off at home, Henry pulled up in his car to take her back to the party. They kissed again in the moonlight.

"Baby, after the Lord made you, he sure must have buffed his nails," said Henry. Back at the party, he announced, to Minnie's surprise, "We just made up our minds we're going to get married." They had never even been on a date.

Nevertheless, after Minnie finished a concert tour with Ernest Tubb, she married the love of her life on February 23, 1947. Only a few close friends were in attendance. The bride wore a beige gabardine suit rather than a gown of white.

Initially, she tried to give up her gypsy touring ways. But every time she played the Opry on Saturday nights, she realized how desperately she missed traveling to shows. When she confided this to Henry, he understood completely. And to her surprise, Henry was completely at ease among her country-music buddies.

"Although he'd never been around show people, he fit in perfectly. . . . He has such a natural, spontaneous sense of humor. All my friends thought he was much funnier than me. . . . They admired his honesty and his kindness and the fact that he wasn't impressed by celebrities."

"How does it feel to play second fiddle to your wife?" a man asked Henry Cannon backstage one night.

"I don't play a musical instrument," Henry dryly replied.

In no time, he was flying country stars to shows in his chartered plane. Among those who hired him were Elvis Presley, Roy Acuff, Carl Smith, Webb Pierce, Faron Young, and Hank Williams.

As for Minnie Pearl, she was in the right place at the right time. In the postwar era, country music boomed, and Nashville became its undisputed capital city. Between 1947 and 1961, she appeared at New York's Carnegie Hall and Washington, D.C.'s Constitution Hall, was profiled on *This Is Your Life,* and costarred with Elvis Presley at a benefit show in Hawaii to raise funds for the battleship *Arizona* monument.

By the 1960s, Minnie Pearl was an icon herself. One often-told Opry anecdote is of songwriter Joe Allison mailing a letter in Los Angeles in 1960 with just a drawing of her hat as an address. The post office delivered it to the Grand Ole Opry.

Minnie Pearl became the country industry's goodwill ambassador. Her well-bred graciousness and her genuine affection for her less-schooled costars made her their mother confessor, chaperone, and spokesperson. Hank Williams cried on her shoulder. She mentored June Carter as a comic. She gave Roger Miller his first job as a road musician. She encouraged a shy Mel Tillis to use his stutter to humorous advantage. She taught Jimmy Dickens how to deliver jokes. She memorably shared routines with Rod Brasfield, Grandpa Jones, and Roy Acuff. Backstage, she patted scared youngsters on the back, hugged the troubled, consoled the dejected, and cheered the successful.

The recitation "Giddyup Go—Answer" earned her a top-ten hit in 1966. She recorded both songs and comedy routines for Starday, RCA, Liberty, Decca, King, Bullet, and other labels on Music Row. As a writer, she published cookbooks, Christmas stories, joke books, and a 1980 autobiography.

Minnie quit doing one-night stands in 1967 in the aftermath of a harrowing emergency landing by Henry. But her star was undimmed. In 1969, she joined the cast of *Hee Haw,* the longest-running syndicated show in television history. In 1975, she became the first comic inducted into the Country Music Hall of Fame. In 1977, she began headlining in Las Vegas.

At home in Nashville, she became renowned for her charity work. Minnie worked with United Way, Big Brothers Big Sisters of America, the March of Dimes, the American Cancer Society, Vanderbilt Children's Hospital, the Nashville Humane Association, the W. O. Smith Nashville Community Music School, the E.A.R. Foundation, the Red Cross, the Veterans Administration, and dozens of other causes.

"When I got this job and moved to Nashville, people asked me to do what was called 'public service' then," she commented. "I was so indoctrinated by my mother, I just immediately fell into it."

Because of her "many years of service and devotion," she became the first female recipient of *Billboard*'s Country Man of the Year award in 1966. Twenty years later, she was costarring with Billy Crystal, Robin Williams, George Carlin, Whoopi Goldberg, and others of an entirely new generation of humorists in *Comic Relief,* the nationally televised fund-raiser for the homeless.

The *Comic Relief* telecasts of 1986 and 1987, her weekly "Minnie's Memories" column in *The Nashville Banner,* and her many Opry appearances during those years were done despite her undergoing a double mastectomy in 1985. Following her reconstructive surgery, she quipped that she was "an eighteen-year-old from the waist up." Henry said she looked like a curvaceous *Hee Haw* "honey."

In the operation's wake, she became a crusader for breast-cancer awareness. Henry Cannon objected to his wife's publicity campaign. She said that was because he considered her condition a private matter. More than likely, he was simply terrified at the prospect of losing her and couldn't bear to hear her talk about her disease.

"I'm fine," she insisted. "I can't 'languish on a bed of pain.' I've gotta get out, and I did. I don't recommend that every lady in her seventies with two mastectomies do that. I did it, because that's my way of coping. I did it, but I don't advocate that much activity."

In the 1980s, the new medium of cable television was born. On The Nashville Network (TNN), she became a regular on *Nashville Now*, doing a popular weekly bit called "Let Minnie Steal Your Joke." The mailroom boy who sifted through the gags sent to her was future Grand Ole Opry star Alan Jackson.

The honors continued to pile up. Tennessee governor Lamar Alexander invited her to the governor's mansion for a seventieth birthday party in 1982. Minnie and Henry didn't have far to travel. Their house was next door. A country who's-who attended, and Roy Acuff led the singing of "Happy Birthday to You."

"Minnie Pearl is only forty-five years old, but Sarah is seventy," said the honoree. "Minnie will never grow old. When I met her, she was in her 'early flirties'—young enough to flirt with men, but too old to have 'em flirt back! And she has stayed that way."

Her career museum opened in 1984; it moved to the Opryland theme park five years later. In 1986, she set up the Minnie Pearl Scholarship Fund to give financial assistance to hearing-impaired students seeking higher education. In 1987, President Reagan gave her the American Cancer Society's Courage Award, and the annual Minnie Pearl Humanitarian Award was inaugurated the following year.

Minnie collapsed during a luncheon at the Nashville restaurant Midtown Cafe in March 1990 and was taken to Centennial Hospital. She was operated on and got a heart pacemaker as a result.

"The doctor must have put it in wrong," she said with a twinkle in her eye. "Every time my husband kisses me, the garage door goes up."

That same year, her cancer returned. She underwent lymph-node removal and radiation treatments. But she sailed onward indomitably. On November 7, 1990, she celebrated her fiftieth anniversary on the Grand Ole Opry.

On January 22, 1991, the Sarah Cannon Cancer Center was dedicated at Centennial Medical Center in Music City. It remains a monument to her breast-cancer campaign to this day.

Minnie Pearl played what turned out to be her last Grand Ole Opry show on June 14, 1991. Three days later, she suffered a major stroke. Her left arm was paralyzed, and she was unable to hold her head up thereafter. But her speech, though weakened, was not impaired. After intensive physical therapy at home, she moved to the Richland Place Retirement Center in Nashville, with Henry still by her side. Friends such as Barbara Mandrell, Ralph Emery, and Roy Acuff visited the legend there.

She was unable to attend when President Bush presented her with the National Medal of Arts in 1992. Later that year, she watched, bedridden, as TNN aired its two-and-a-half-hour television extravaganza *Hats Off to Minnie: America Honors Minnie Pearl*. It featured more than a hundred performers.

"The show has affected her," Henry reported. "It made Minnie cry, because every one of those people came to the show because of their love for her, people from all over the country. I can't hardly talk about it," he added, choking with emotion. "I thought it was poignant."

At the time, Minnie was unable to sustain long conversations or to concentrate for extended periods of time. Some days, she talked only of the past. At other times, she was more engaged with friends and well-wishers.

"I don't want to talk about the future," Henry said. "I don't want to speculate. But we had a lot of great years. We've had more than our share of good times. We're way ahead of most people."

In 1994, she was announced as the first female inductee into the Comedy Hall of Fame, in Tampa, Florida. This was the last honor she received during her lifetime. In February 1996, Minnie Pearl suffered a stroke from which she never regained consciousness. She died on March 4, 1996, at age eighty-three.

More than 1,500 people attended her funeral, including many of her fellow Opry stars and four Tennessee governors. At Minnie's request, Connie Smith sang "In the Garden," accompanied by a string band featuring Marty Stuart. Amy Grant performed "Fairest Lord Jesus" and "It Is Well with My Soul," backed by Gary Chapman and Ruth McGinnis.

Henry was now battling cancer himself. But he personally cut magnolia boughs in their yard to mingle with the lilies on her casket. He greeted attendees one by one for over an hour. He reportedly offered as much consolation as he received to the grief-stricken throng who loved Minnie Pearl so much.

That weekend, he attended an Opry tribute show in her honor. Backstage, he said he imagined her walking up to the pearly gates and shouting, "HowDEEE! I'm jest so proud to be hyere!" The female stars of the cast gathered to sing Minnie's favorite song, "Have I Told You Lately That I Love You," each holding a yellow rose, Minnie's favorite flower.

"She was a ray of sunshine in everybody's lives," said Jean Shepard. "This is for the grandest lady of them all."

Henry Cannon died in his sleep on November 7, 1997, at age eighty. He and Sarah Ophelia Colley Cannon are buried side-by-side at Mount Hope Cemetery in Franklin, Tennessee.

"The best thing that ever happened to me was marrying Henry," she said. "When the lights go down, the applause is stilled, the laughter is a memory, the show is over—you've got to go home. And there's got to be somebody waiting there for you who cares. . . . Henry has been greatly responsible for whatever personal and professional happiness I have attained."

"Minnie and Henry were the most beautifully matched pair,"

said former neighbor and governor Winfield Dunn. "He lived for her, and she couldn't have survived a day, probably, without him."

"They had a love affair that was almost unheard of," eulogized Porter Wagoner.

# For the Rest of Mine

There have been plenty of romances behind the Grand Ole Opry curtain, but only one Opry star has proposed to his wife in front of it.

While making his Opry singing debut on November 23, 1996, Trace Adkins went down on bended knee in front of his girlfriend Rhonda. He asked her to marry him with the show's audience and cast as his witnesses. Everyone cheered when she said, "Yes."

"Who knew if I'd ever be invited back on that sacred stage?" Trace recalled in his 2007 memoir *Trace Adkins: A Personal Stand*. "So I decided to ask Rhonda to marry me right there on the Opry stage. I knew I wanted to pop the question somewhere special, but I needed it to be something truly spectacular and memorable. That's how much playing the Opry meant to me."

Trace adds, "There's no way I'll ever forget that night. She didn't have a clue. She had no idea. I had the ring in my little coat pocket, and my coat was hanging in the dressing room, Mr. Acuff's old dressing room. I went to do makeup, and somebody told me it was time to go on. She said, 'I'll go get your jacket,' and I said, 'No! No!' She kind of thought that was weird, but she didn't know why I acted that way. But that was about the only surprise that I've ever pulled on her."

At an outdoor ceremony in the garden at Nashville's historic Belle Meade Plantation, Trace and Rhonda were married on May 11, 1997. After they exchanged rings, he sang "The Rest of Mine" to her with a lump in his throat. Trace had cowritten the ballad with Kenny Beard, who played guitar accompaniment for him at the event. That fall, it became Trace Adkins's fifth hit single. Listeners loved its memorable tagline: "I can't swear that I'll be here for the rest of your life/But I swear I'll love you for the rest of mine."

The performance proved that roughneck Trace Adkins has a softer side, and in the case of Trace, the term "roughneck" applies in the classic definition of the word—oil field worker. He dropped out of Louisiana Tech after his sophomore year studying petroleum engineering to take a job laying pipe in an oil field.

Next, he signed on for offshore drilling work. During the lonely downtime at night on the rig, Trace played his guitar and wrote and sang country tunes. His fellow roughnecks liked what they heard. One knew a successful country band in Lafayette, Louisiana.

"On my two weeks off, I went down there and met these guys. They had entered a contest, the Wild Turkey Battle of the Country Bands. They'd won the local competition and were going to the regionals in Dallas. They wanted me to come to the regionals and sing this song I had written called 'Bayou Sunrise.'"

Billed as Bayou Speak Easy, the band won the regional contest and came in second at the national competition in Nashville. Despite the loss, Bayou Speak Easy recorded and released "Bayou Sunrise" by "Tracy Adkins" in 1986. A booking agent who'd spotted them in Dallas soon had the band on the road three hundred days a year.

Performing was not new to Trace. As a teenager, he recorded two albums with gospel group The Commitments but abandoned the genre when Pentecostal preachers objected to his long hair.

"My mother was just horrified when I wasn't singing gospel anymore. We did everything else. I had to run the spectrum from George Jones to Kool & The Gang and everything in between. They expected you to be a breathing jukebox."

Many of the honky-tonks that hired Bayou Speak Easy were rough joints. Trace's face is a roadmap of the route he took to stardom. It has faded scars from punches, kicks, and knife wounds. When you're a 6-foot 6-inch, 245-pound ex–college football player in a redneck roadhouse, you don't have to look for trouble—it has a way of finding you.

"I never picked a fight in my life," says Trace. "There'd be a little bitty guy in a club who would get really drunk [and] they'd want to fight the biggest guy there. And sometimes that would be me."

No wonder Trace Adkins calls his style "combat country." He lived on "the wild side of life" for four years on the road, boozing and brawling when he wasn't evolving into one of the greatest country entertainers of his generation. The long separations destroyed his marriage to his high school sweetheart. But Trace won custody of their daughters Tarah, born in 1985, and Sarah, born in 1989.

Disillusioned with the music business, Trace returned to oil-rig work in 1989. A couple of years later, the Texas booking agent telephoned to ask how he was doing.

"He said, 'Do you sing anymore?' I said, 'I don't even sing in the shower.' He said, 'One of these days you're gonna look in the mirror and are gonna go, "I wonder what would have happened if I had really applied myself to music and gone to Nashville." Son, don't ever ask yourself that question. Take it from someone who knows.' I thought about that. And the thought of being sixty years old and asking myself that question scared me a lot worse than selling my house and moving to Nashville and giving it a shot."

Trace arrived in Music City in August of 1992. He worked construction jobs and began performing on weekends at a bar outside Nashville called Tillie's.

A second marriage proved even stormier than his first. It ended during a heated argument in 1994, when his wife shot him through the lungs and heart. Incredibly, he survived. Even more incredibly, this was not Trace's first brush with death. He was in a nearly fatal car crash when he was a junior in high school, and there were at least two accidents on the oil derricks that could have ended his life.

On the mend from the shooting, Trace returned to Tillie's. One night in 1995, he took a job entertaining at a real estate convention in a Nashville hotel. Rhonda happened to be there.

"She was back in the back of the room with [music producer] Blake and Jan Mevis," Trace recalls. "I knew Blake and Jan. So I just walked back there to see who those two hot chicks were, standing there with Blake. I went back there and introduced myself."

Rhonda not only liked what she saw, she liked what she heard. At the time, she was working for producer and record-label executive Tim DuBois. Rhonda brought Tim to Tillie's. Tim agreed to finance some recording sessions but wound up not signing Trace to his label. Undeterred, Rhonda next brought producer and record-label executive Scott Hendricks to Tillie's. That night, Trace finished his set, put his guitar down, and turned to find Scott standing right in front of him. On the spot, the producer offered him a Capitol Records contract.

"That's how it went down," relates Trace. "I was floored. I had to call him the next day to reassure myself that it wasn't a dream."

Trace Adkins signed with Capitol on March 29, 1996. After that, things moved quickly. On April 13, the gently rhythmic, self-penned "There's a Girl in Texas" debuted on the charts as his first single for the label. His last performance at Tillie's was on June 22. *Dreamin' Out Loud* was released as his debut album on June 25. "Every Light in the House" became his first top-ten hit that fall. Then came his proposal to Rhonda on the Opry stage. While "No Thinkin' Thing" was en route to becoming his first number-one hit in early 1997, Trace was hard at work on another song.

"I had been commissioned by Rhonda to write something to sing at the wedding," he recalls. "It was a daunting task. Kenny Beard and I were just trying to come up with something. 'The Rest of Mine' just kind of fell in our lap.

"I proposed in November, and I think I wrote that in January. I just put pressure on myself to write a positive love song. I had never written one before that I thought was any good. I've always been in a better frame of mind to sink my teeth into a painful song rather than one that was really happy. So I really set about trying to write a good, positive love song that was serious without being mushy and trivial. I'm glad I was watching that movie *Phenomenon,* because that's where it came from.

"That was one of those 'Eureka!' moments, one of those epiphanies. I mean, as soon as we heard that line, we both knew it was a song. I remember when we played it for Scott Hendricks. He said, 'It only has one verse! Can't you guys write two verses?' I told him, 'Scott, we have already said, "I will love you 'til I die." I can't go any farther than that. Another verse would be redundant. We said all that we needed to say.' So then he let us get by without another verse."

"The Rest of Mine" went on to become one of the great country wedding anthems. Many others have since used it in nuptial ceremonies.

As a gag, Trace had his management company send Rhonda's parents a concert contract and a $7,500 bill for performing "The Rest of Mine" at the wedding. "I ain't cheap, baby," he remarked at the time. "I still haven't been paid," he wisecracks now.

Trace and Rhonda have three daughters—Mackenzie, born in 1998, Brianna, born in 2001, and Trinity, born in 2004. Counting Rhonda and his two older daughters, Trace is surrounded by six females at home.

"I was really hoping for a son, but not for the reasons everybody might think. I'd just like to have somebody that I can boss around. I've got a girl who just looks at me when I tell her to do something. What do you do with that? I'm 6-feet 6-inches, and I'm completely defenseless!

"I don't call the shots at my house. And when we go to the mall, I'm just the pack mule, there to carry the credit card and all the stuff that they're buying. I work up a lather by the end of the shopping trip."

Trace wasn't home all that much during the early years of his

Nashville career. Hits such as "I Left Something Turned on at Home," "Lonely Won't Leave Me Alone," and "More" led to ever-increasing concert bookings. He won the 1997 Top New Male Vocalist award from the Academy of Country Music. He picked up even more steam with raucous, party-hearty hits like "Hot Mama" (2003), "Rough and Ready" (2004), and "Ladies Love Country Boys" (2006). His macho bass-baritone is deep and sonorous enough to rattle window glass, and onstage he has the physical charisma to match it. Trace often punctuates his shows with hip-swiveling dance moves on the up-tempo numbers.

Offstage, Trace finally confronted the fact that he had an alcohol problem. In one way or another, the bottle had been behind most of his trips to the emergency room and most of the scars on his body. Following an intervention staged by Rhonda, his manager, and others, in December 2002 he entered a treatment facility.

"The whole first week I was there, I was like, 'It's come to this. I've been institutionalized.' But then after about a week or so, my head cleared up.

"It wasn't as hard as I thought it was going to be. Everything's going so great it's a little scary, actually. You can buy into the whole 'one-day-at-a-time' philosophy. It really is easier if you do it that way. You just wake up in the morning and go, 'Well, I don't think I'll drink today.' And every day is 'today.'

"I thought I was a smart alcoholic. I didn't do shows plastered. I didn't drink at music-industry functions. I was an isolationist. I would get away from everybody for two or three days.

"Quitting was easier than I anticipated it being. And I'm not patting myself on the back, because I've abstained for long degrees of time in the past, just to prove to myself that I could. But it feels different now."

Since his sobriety, Trace Adkins has become even more popular. His shows are routinely sold out. His *Dreamin' Out Loud, Comin' on Strong,* and *Greatest Hits Vol. 1* albums are now all platinum records, and *Songs About Me,* which contains "Honky Tonk Badonkadonk," is a double-platinum disc.

Since Trace Adkins is country music's tallest male star, he was memorably asked to become a member of the Grand Ole Opry cast by its shortest, Jimmy Dickens. On June 14, 2003, the 4-foot 11-inch Jimmy climbed a small stepladder on the Opry stage in order to be eye-to-eye with Trace.

"I have a very serious question for you," said Jimmy. "Just how bad would you like to become a member of our Grand Ole Opry family?"

Trace placed his hand on Jimmy's shoulder and replied, "I want it bad."

"I asked for Ronnie Milsap to induct me," says Trace. "He's one of my heroes, somebody that I've looked up to and wanted to kind of emulate. I've said it jokingly many times, but it's true, I came to Nashville to make Ronnie Milsap records. I just always loved the way Ronnie incorporated all different styles on the records he made. You get one of his records, and he hits you with this stone-country ballad. And then the next thing would be something he might do with The Pointer Sisters. You just didn't know what was coming. What a great roller-coaster ride his records are.

"I've been influenced by all kinds of music, too. And that's kind of what I'd like to do. If I want to do an R&B tune, I'll do it. If I want to sing the blues, I'll sing the blues. If I want to rock, I'll do it."

On August 23, 2003, Ronnie Milsap introduced Trace Adkins as the newest member of the show's cast. "I feel like I'm king of the world tonight," said a grateful Trace. Jimmy Dickens carried Trace's guitar onto the stage, a reference to a remark Trace had made to a reporter that he'd be happy to do anything the Opry asked him to do, even if it meant cleaning Porter Wagoner's dressing room or carrying Jimmy's guitar.

"I still see Jimmy in the Home Depot every now and then," he chuckles. "And I'll offer to pick him up so he can see what's on the shelf.

"I just love the Opry. I love the spirit of the place. I like the people out there, the camaraderie, the family atmosphere. I just like everything about it.

"It's kind of hard to explain. But I can tell you this: I've probably played the Opry seventy times, if not more. And I've never had a bad experience out there. It's not the time that I spend onstage that's the most special to me. It's the time that I'm backstage getting to hang out with the legends and rubbing shoulders with those men and women.

"The kids go with me quite often. That kind of worries me a little bit. I grew up listening to the Opry and then watching it on television on Saturday nights. I never would have allowed myself to dream that I would ever get to walk out on that stage. And now my kids are growing up backstage at the Opry. I'm thinking, 'How weird are they going to be?' They're totally comfortable when they're there. All kids love Jimmy, because he's their size."

TRACE ISN'T THE OPRY'S only star who has been romantic on the show's stage. In 1996, his little buddy Jimmy Dickens renewed wedding vows with his wife Mona on that same stage. The romantic gesture was in celebration of their twenty-fifth wedding anniversary.

Born December 19, 1920, James Cecil Dickens was the oldest of thirteen children of a poor West Virginia farmer. Captivated by mountain music at an early age, he dreamed of becoming a country singer.

"All my people were coal miners, but I never wanted to go into the mines," says Jimmy. "From my childhood on, I always wanted to be an entertainer. And I set out to do that early on, while I was still in high school. I was getting on every show that I could get on or an amateur contest or whatever. I knew I wanted to be in country music some way."

After apprenticing on West Virginia radio stations, Jimmy began headlining on various stations in the Midwest. He credits Roy Acuff for his breakthrough in Nashville.

"Mr. Acuff and I became friends when I was working at WLW in Cincinnati. I was doing an early-morning program there in

1945, and Mr. Acuff came to Cincinnati for a concert. I got backstage and was telling him that I was in radio. He said, 'Would you like to do a song on the show?' I had my guitar with me, just in case he asked. I did a number and encored, and Mr. Acuff talked about that for ages, about me stealing the show from him. But he liked what I did.

"Then later on in 1948 I was in Saginaw, Michigan, working at WKNX, and he came there in concert. I opened the show for him that day. It was in February, and it was awfully cold. He said, 'What are you doing in this cold country?' I said, 'It's a job. I'm making a living.' Then he mentioned if I would like to come to the Grand Ole Opry. Of course, this was a dream for me. A month or so later I got a call from WSM. I came in and did a guest spot on the Red Foley show. Went on back to my job in Michigan and a month or so later I got another call to come back and do another guest appearance.

"The second time I came, Mr. Acuff said, 'We are just gonna keep you here on a trial basis. I'll use you on my program and so forth.' So I moved down here to Nashville. I stayed at Roy Acuff's house for the first six months. Mr. Acuff was responsible for basically everything I ever did in country music. He was my advisor, teaching me the do's and don'ts. I tried to do the things that Mr. Acuff taught me."

Jimmy Dickens became an Opry cast member on November 6, 1948. His Opry appearances led to a contract with Columbia Records, which was Roy Acuff's label as well. "Take an Old Cold Tater and Wait" hit the charts in 1949. The energetic novelty tune set his style and led to his nickname, "Tater." He followed it with the bouncy "Country Boy," the first hit written by future Country Music Hall of Fame members Boudleaux and Felice Bryant.

In addition to launching the Bryants, Jimmy Dickens is responsible for a number of other breakthroughs in country music. He was the first Opry star to sport the flashy rhinestone stage attire that gave country music its classic look. Jimmy recalls that his first such suit, designed by Nudie the Rodeo Tailor, was mustard yellow with horseshoe-shaped pockets outlined with green stitching, and his initials were embroidered on the shirt's bib.

The twin electric-guitar leads by his band members Jabbo Arrington and Grady Martin on his hot, brash, up-tempo hits of the 1950s made Jimmy a forerunner of the rockabilly movement. Grady later became a top Nashville session musician. Jimmy also discovered Opry star Marty Robbins. In the spring of 1964, Jimmy Dickens became the first country star to circle the globe on tour.

"It was all American military installations, all over the world," Jimmy recalls. "Hawaii, Tokyo, Okinawa, Tai Pai, Bangkok, Vietnam, and from there to Copenhagen, Denmark, and Istanbul, Turkey, and from there over to Germany, Italy, and Spain. It was educational for me. The greatest audiences I think I ever worked to were those people. I was in Saigon at Christmastime, and I don't think I've ever seen a bunch of guys so happy to see an American entertainer."

Jimmy achieved fame way beyond country music's audience, thanks to "May the Bird of Paradise Fly Up Your Nose," a 1965 novelty tune that crossed over to the pop-music hit parade.

"Boy, I have never been so surprised by a hit record," says Jimmy of his most famous number. "I just thought it would be a good piece for my stage show. [Neal Merritt] had put a melody to an old comic poem. Hap Wilson and I had been friends for years. He brought the tape to the studio and asked me to take five minutes to listen to it. We went back in the studio and ran it down. On the first take, we got it.

"Johnny Carson had been kicking that phrase around on *The Tonight Show*. So I wound up singing 'May the Bird of Paradise Fly Up Your Nose' on the Carson show.

"I got branded with that novelty material after 'Old Cold Tater.' But I did a lot of ballads that kind of got lost. In my shows, I'd always do both."

In fact, his most requested number is his 1970 tear-jerking, lump-in-throat recitation "Raggedy Ann." Jimmy also introduced such serious evergreens as "Life Turned Her That Way," "We Could,"

"Farewell Party," "The Violet and the Rose," and "Take Me as I Am."

Jimmy Dickens entered the Country Music Hall of Fame on October 10, 1983. He retired from the concert trail on November 29, 1997, after a performance in Columbia, South Carolina. He celebrated his fiftieth anniversary as an Opry star on November 7, 1998.

"I'd play the Opry for free," says Jimmy Dickens with a chuckle, "and in the beginning, it was as close to playing for free as you can get!"

# Small-Town Gals

Every marriage is a partnership, but Martina McBride's is something more.

Martina's husband John McBride is her sound engineer, both in the studio and on the road. He also comanages his wife's career (along with the Canadian Bruce Allen). He is her constant companion and biggest cheerleader. They live together, work together, raise children together, and tour together.

"We've always had a relationship where we have been able to relate on a lot of different levels," comments Martina. "I think it surprises a lot of people. I don't think a lot of people really understand it until they see us together.

"John and I have a great sense of respect for each other. I really respect his talent, and he respects my talent. We have different talents, but they complement each other. We spend every day together in the studio making a record, and we go home. We're just together a lot.

"He's the one person I can trust to be really honest with me. He doesn't try to butter me up or pat me on the back. I mean, he gives me praise when things are good, but I need somebody to give me the bottom line.

"He's my favorite person in the world to be with. He has

such great instincts. Really, he's just amazingly talented. . . . He's wonderful.

"John is actually probably a bigger music lover than I am," Martina adds. "I like quiet. I'm like, 'Turn that radio off. Let's have some peace and quiet around here.' He just lives, eats, and breathes music. He approaches it from a real heartfelt place. Whereas I'm probably a little more clinical when it comes to my producing. So it's a really great combination.

"His enthusiasm is priceless. He just immerses himself in everything he does. That's the way he is. So we are very different, but it ends up working out."

"It's interesting," agrees John McBride. "Martina and I work together, and we spend a lot of time together. I hope I can give her a comfort level in the studio, do a great job for her that makes her happy, so that she doesn't have to think about anything except making music.

"She is the best friend and the best partner I could ever have. No question about it. She's the most stable, rational person I've ever met in my life, which drives me insane. I'm a wreck, normally. I'm a passionate guy, and I burn a little hot.

"Martina's not nearly as competitive as I am. She doesn't worry about awards and how many records she sells. She just loves music. She loves singing and performing, and that's why she does this. I am the more competitive one. I worry about it more than she does.

"The longer we're together, I'm thinking I'm getting a little more like her, and she's getting a little more like me. We're able to do this work together."

John is eight years older than his wife. In the beginning of their relationship, he was the "big-city sophisticate" living in Wichita, Kansas, a town of 300,000. Martina, by contrast, hails from tiny Sharon, Kansas, population 250. Her high school graduating class contained ten of the town's residents.

"We grew up on a farm. There was nothing to do. We had three channels on the TV, one of which was fuzzy, so we had two channels. No video games. No running down to the Quick Trip or the convenience store. No playing with neighborhood kids. It was just us, really. We'd come home from school, and we were isolated on the farm. So we always had musical instruments. Our playtime was sitting around making music and singing and playing together.

"The Shiffters were a band that my dad had ever since I can remember. There was always rehearsing in the living room and music around us all the time. I started singing in the band when I was about seven years old. We would play wedding dances, VFWs, American Legion halls, and things like that.

"It was our family thing to do. My mom ran the soundboard. My dad played guitar and sang. I played keyboard. My brother played guitar. We worked our way up to where we were playing four-hour dances every Saturday night. It was just a lot of fun. I did that all through, until I graduated from high school.

"I was singing Reba McEntire, Juice Newton, Patsy Cline, Jeanne Pruett, Connie Smith. My dad would teach me the [country] standards, and then I would pick up whatever song was on the radio. Linda Ronstadt—I was a big fan of hers. The area where I'm from is pretty rural, so country music wasn't uncool at all.

"I was always encouraged, had a real optimistic outlook and always believed this could happen if I was in the right place at the right time. I was raised to believe in myself. It was pretty ideal."

There was never any question in Martina's mind that she wanted to make music her profession. After graduating high school, she moved to Wichita, where she sang in a rock band called The Penetrators. Martina was so innocent, she didn't grasp the sexual innuendo of the group's name.

"I was pretty naïve. I went to a big city and realized that you can't trust everybody. You have to lock your doors, and everybody isn't always what they say they are. It was real new for me, because where I was from, everybody knew everybody. Everything was so down to earth. So I guess we were real sheltered.

"Most of what I remember about those days is traveling around in a van with a hole in the floor and having no money. I'd go into these little dives and scream my head off singing Pat Benatar. It was a good experience, but I don't miss it at all."

She formed a second band called Lotus, driving them around in a converted ambulance.

"She was trying to put together a band to travel around," recalls John McBride. "That's when we met. I had a rehearsal hall, and she rented it. Of course, she didn't pay me, so I had to track her down."

She didn't pay because she couldn't. The band was falling apart. Martina began telling her troubles to John, who was living in the warehouse rehearsal hall. To her shock, she realized she was falling in love with him.

"Here I was, crying on his shoulder about my band not coming together, and I thought, 'I'm in love with this guy. This is crazy. He lives in a warehouse.'"

After taking time off to heal her rock-ravaged vocal chords, Martina returned to singing country music. She and John married on May 15, 1988. Their romance began the couple's round-the-clock togetherness.

"Actually, I can't imagine it being any other way," says Martina. "I mean, for us it's real natural. We both live, eat, and breathe the music business. For a long time, I never thought I would get married, because I didn't think I could ever find anybody that was so involved and supportive, and could understand what this business is all about, all the traveling and everything. But when I found John, it just clicked. We're just like a really great team.

"He started his sound-system business with two speakers and a mixing board and two microphones. He built it up from there and was trying to run it out of Kansas, which is not exactly the musical center of the universe. It was kind of hard, but we both looked at each other one day and said, 'If we really want to pursue this in a big way, we really need to move [to Nashville]. So three months later [in 1990], we packed up everything in a long trailer and moved.

"I always knew John would do well. He moved here with nothing and has really built up a huge company."

In Kansas, John had toured with such rock bands as Steppenwolf and Bad Company. In Nashville, he found work at once as a sound man and went on the road with Charlie Daniels, Ricky Van Shelton, and other country stars. Martina waited tables and bided her time. John soon built up his sound company to one of the most prominent in the U.S. touring industry, with his gear on the road with dozens of top stars. When John became Garth Brooks's production manager on a 1991 tour, Martina went along to sell T-shirts.

"It was an easy job," she recalls with a chuckle. "I'm telling you what, when people hit that door, they were ready to *BUY* T-shirts and hats and all that stuff."

Back at home, John continued to badger Music Row and local clubs about his wife's singing talent. Finally, he struck pay dirt.

"I heard that they were looking for a new female artist at RCA," recalls Martina. "I went and bought a big, bright purple envelope and put in the tape and a bio and a picture. At RCA they have this sign that says 'No unsolicited material.' That means that they don't take anything that they haven't requested. So—actually this was John's idea—he took a big pen and wrote 'Requested material' on the envelope and dropped it off. And it got through! They called us about three weeks later, and then we did a live showcase for them."

RCA Records introduced her in 1992 with the singles "The Time Has Come," "That's Me," and the devastating anti-alcohol ballad "Cheap Whiskey." Martina sang its chilling lyrics with incendiary force. Her harmony vocalist was Garth Brooks, and when she went out on Garth's 1992 tour, she graduated from merchandising to being the superstar's opening act. Her powerful voice and striking song choices impressed more than a million fans on the road that year.

"I get people in interviews who ask me all the time, 'So they let you pick your own songs?' I didn't really know how things were done, so I just kind of barged in and said, 'These are the songs I want to do.' Maybe that kind of helped me."

"Martina picked those songs," says her proud husband. "No one else picked them. She made all the decisions, because she's got such a strong sense of what she wants."

"I was so concerned about being taken seriously," Martina explains. "I didn't want to be a fluffy 'girl singer.' I think the material that I pick is very strong-woman material."

Many of her hits have reflected her happy private life—1995's "Safe in the Arms of Love" and "Wild Angels," 1997's "Valentine," 1998's "Happy Girl," 1999's "I Love You," and 2001's "Blessed." But many others have striking, socially conscious lyrics, such as the 2002 anti–child abuse song "Concrete Angels," "Anyway," which Martina co-wrote, and her powerful anthems against domestic violence: "A Broken Wing" (1997) and, unforgettably, "Independence Day" (1994).

"I love lyrics that ring true and that are honest. Something that kind of opens your eyes and opens your heart and makes you want to do something to make a difference. I think the songs I sing should stand for what I believe. I like to sing songs that portray people, and especially women, with dignity, strength, and respect."

Most of these songs were accompanied by striking videos. Martina's luminous, ice-blue eyes and chestnut hair are highly photogenic. And everyone was struck by the larger-than-life voice coming from that petite 5-foot 4-inch, 100-pound frame. By 1993–1994, she was a star.

The transition did not come easily for her. Offstage, Martina is a shy woman who doesn't make small talk easily. Onstage, she gradually warmed to her audiences and began to relax. One recurring gag in the early days came when she'd introduce the guitar player in her band: "This guy and I slept together for about four years," she'd say. "Then we got rooms of our own." It was, of course, brother Marty Schiff, who remains in his sister's band to this day.

"I don't feel comfortable talking about myself," Martina comments about her reserved, introverted nature. "John is much more of a people person. We get in a cab, and I just sit back and look around. John's like, 'So how long have you been driving a cab? What's going on?' By the time we get to the hotel, he's made fast friends with the cab driver. It's amazing.

"Sometimes we'll go to a business dinner, and he's kind of my secret weapon. He takes a lot of the pressure off of me."

On October 14, 1995, Martina was invited to be on the Grand Ole Opry on the night the show celebrated its seventieth birthday. No one told her that her time onstage was to be brief. She sang too long, which meant that the cast's "Happy Birthday" singing couldn't air on the televised portion of the show. When other stars criticized her, she burst into tears. Backstage, she was comforted by Jeanne Pruett.

Nevertheless, Martina was invited to become a member of the Opry cast. On November 30, 1995, she was inducted by the legendary Loretta Lynn. Loretta has subsequently "adopted" Martina and taken her under her wing.

"I love her," says Martina of Loretta. "She's amazing to me. What she's done is opened herself up to me. I'll find myself in a corner with her, and her just telling me all this stuff. Does she do this to everybody? I've got to remember it all. It's unbelievable

"Becoming an Opry member was the most thrilling moment of my career. I'll try to make the Opry proud and do my best to continue the tradition of country music and the tradition of the Opry."

Despite her increasing stardom, Martina retained her humility and stuck to her small-town values. Motherhood, not her career, is her main focus. Martina schedules her tours and her promotional appearances around her daughters'—Delaney, Emma, and Ava Rose—schooling and schedules.

"That just seems to make the most sense to me. Being a good mom, that's important, definitely. As long as you have that priority set, then it all just kind of takes care of itself. I feel like I'm successful and I'm happy. I don't have a desire to be the world's biggest superstar. I'm happy with my life just the way it is. I want to be able to go to the grocery store. I want to be able to raise my kids in a way that's sane and normal.

"I really wouldn't want to have this immediate kind of superstardom that so many acts have. You'd have to put everything in your life aside, and I can't do that. I have a family that I adore. I won't make those sacrifices. I don't care enough about being a big star to do that. I can't imagine these people who can't even walk down the street. I don't have the desire to be on the cover of every magazine. Maybe I'm just lazy."

John disagrees. He says his wife's career has been the result of determination, a solid work ethic, and a continuous drive for self-improvement. In 2005, Martina began producing her own records, a rarity for a woman in country music.

"Martina is very, very hands-on," says John. "Starting with her second album, she received a coproducer credit, and she took that very seriously. She did at least 50 percent of the work. Her ears are incredible. She hears better than anyone I know. She knows what she wants, and she'll work and work and work until she gets what she wants.

"Martina has really built her career the old-fashioned way. She came out with her first album, which did okay but not great over-all. The second album, she had a little more radio success and a few more hits. The third album, she finally got her first number one. She's really had to fight every inch of the way.

"The first time that Martina received the Female Vocalist of the Year award [in 1999] was a magical, magical night. Of course, I felt like she should have gotten it the previous five years in a row. As a matter of fact, I think I threatened that if she didn't win, I was going to light myself on fire and run out of the auditorium. Thank God that never happened."

Martina was also named the Country Music Association (CMA) Female Vocalist of the Year in 2002, 2003, and 2004. She and her idol Reba McEntire are the only stars who have won this award four times. The two women costarred in the landmark, all-female country tour Girls' Night Out in 2001, alongside Sara Evans, Jamie O'Neal, and Carolyn Dawn Johnson. It came about because of Martina's experience on the road with female pop stars in the 1998 Lilith Fair tour. She approached Reba about creating something similar for country music's women.

"That Lilith Fair experience was life-changing for me," says Martina. "I never knew a tour could be like that, with all that ca-maraderie. The whole vibe was really cool." Girls' Night Out was just as much fun, she reports.

Behind the scenes, John's star was rising just like his wife's. He built Blackbird Studio and an accompanying equipment-rental business in Nashville. The facility is now one of the top studios in America, hosting sessions for country and pop stars alike. The complex also houses the McBrides' song-publishing business. Naturally, Martina records there, with John engineering by her side.

"My husband doesn't do anything halfway," says Martina. "He is passionate about audio. Blackbird Studio has a great vibe. It's got a great energy about it that everybody comments on when they come to work here. It's really palpable. You can just feel it when you walk in."

"They built a paradise where we all get to hang out and make music," comments producer/guitarist Paul Worley. "John is there to help Martina and support her on the roller-coaster ride of being an artist. And she has been there for him as he's built his own dream, this wonderful, wonderful studio. Kudos to them.

"John and Martina, they've got the most wonderful relationship of any man and woman together I've ever seen. They both have huge dreams and huge lives. They pursue their dreams, and they don't get in each other's way. I hope it goes on forever."

"It's an unconditional kind of love," says Martina McBride. "It's really rare. I feel lucky that I found it."

COINCIDENTALLY, THE OTHER MAJOR Opry star whose career is managed by her husband is Martina's idol, Reba McEntire. And like John McBride, Reba's husband, Narvel Blackstock, is an empire builder. The couple's business interests have included real estate, song publishing, transportation, concert promotion, a clothing line, racehorses, and recording studios.

Also like Martina, Reba is a product of small-town America,

growing up near Chockie, Oklahoma. The community (population 754) is so small, it doesn't even have a post office. Reba was raised on a 7,100-acre ranch to herd cattle and compete in rodeos. She was discovered singing at a rodeo and was signed to a Nashville recording contract in 1975, at age twenty.

She married rodeo champion Charlie Battles in 1976, the year her first major-label single hit the charts. It took four long years of hard work before she scored her first top-ten hit and two more beyond that before she got her first number-one record.

"I didn't know absolutely anything when I came to Nashville," says Reba. "I didn't know what the music business was like. All I'd ever been associated with was ranchin' and rodeoin'."

Reba listened and learned. In 1987–1988, she moved from Oklahoma to Nashville, fired her manager, divorced Charlie Battles, and took charge of her career. Steel guitarist and road manager Narvel Blackstock divorced his wife shortly afterward. He and Reba married on June 3, 1989. Son Shelby Steven McEntire Blackstock was born on February 23, 1990.

By then, Reba seemed to be at the top of her game. The CMA had voted her its Female Vocalist of the Year in 1984, 1985, 1986, and 1987. In 1986, she was inducted into the Grand Ole Opry and received the CMA's Entertainer of the Year award. Reba's Opry induction date was January 17, 1986.

She was just beginning. Reba released a white-hot streak of hits in the 1990s. Her road show became one of the flashiest in country music, incorporating costume changes, choreography, elaborate sets, lighting effects, and video screens. She emoted powerfully in her music videos, which led to film and television acting roles.

But tragedy struck on March 16, 1991. Reba's band was killed when her leased jet crashed on takeoff after a concert in San Diego. Believing that work was the best healer, Reba sang on the Oscar telecast nine days later and resumed touring two weeks after the accident. She took roles in more feature films and television shows. By the end of the decade, she was said to be the most successful female artist in country-music history.

Reba freely admits to being enterprising, determined, and devoted to her career: "I'm always greedy. I want to do more. I'm very competitive, very ambitious."

In 2001, the multimillion-selling redhead earned critics' raves in the role of Annie Oakley in the Broadway revival of *Annie Get Your Gun*. She became a TV ratings champ, starring in her own situation comedy *Reba* in 2001–2007. Her return-to-music *Reba Duets* album of 2007 became yet another major success for her.

"My one essential rule for survival is work hard," says Reba McEntire. "When you're done, continue to work hard. When you're done with that, keep working hard."

# It Takes Two

G rand Ole Opry hit maker Patty Loveless says her music isn't hers alone.

"I feel that the music I have done, Emory Gordy is as much a part of that music as I am," states Patty. "That's just the way I feel. He wouldn't put it that way."

Emory Gordy Jr. is Patty Loveless's producer. He is also the husband she kept secret from the public for nearly two years after they married. He is twelve years her senior and has a wealth of show-business experience and expertise. Emory was a member of Elvis Presley's TCB band; toured with Emmylou Harris, Neil Diamond, and Rodney Crowell; produced successful records for dozens of stars; and is a former Music Row record-label executive.

Emory plays bass, guitar, accordion, mandolin, piano, percussion, and organ and is also a string and/or horn arranger. He has performed as a studio instrumentalist for a staggering number of stars, ranging from Reba McEntire to John Denver to Billy Joel. Also an accomplished songwriter, he cowrote Martina McBride's "Cheap Whiskey" and Wynonna's "When I Reach the Place I'm Going," among others, as well as 1969's pop standard "Traces," which has been recorded by more than fifty artists.

Patty, born Patricia Lee Ramey in Pikeville, Kentucky, on January 4, 1957, began writing songs and performing locally as a young girl. At fourteen, she and her older brother Roger came to Nashville and were befriended by Opry great Porter Wagoner. Patty has fond memories of riding in the superstar's tour bus and singing songs with him and his duet partner Dolly Parton. The three would gather on Dolly's bed in her room in the back of the bus.

"I'm probably the only guy in the world who spent the night in a bed with Dolly Parton and Patty Loveless," laughed Porter. "Of course nothing happened. We just sang until we fell asleep."

The Opry duo The Wilburn Brothers also took an interest in Patty, signing her to their song-publishing company and taking her on the road as the female vocalist in their troupe. She replaced Loretta Lynn, who is her distant cousin. Patty worked for the Wilburns during her last three years of high school. She was sixteen years old when she first saw the man with whom she would eventually share her life and music.

"I was working in a record store called Music Mart USA—Doyle Wilburn was a part owner of the business," recalls Patty. "It used to be across the street from the Ryman Auditorium, on Fifth Avenue. I worked there part-time. Anyhow, through the store, I managed to get tickets to an Elvis concert. This was the first time I had gotten to see Elvis. I was really into Elvis, so I was very excited about seeing the concert.

"I have to say that I did notice the musicians in the band. I noticed that they all dressed alike, in these jumpsuits. I thought the band was just awesome, and I was just really into the music. I do recall seeing Emory playing bass. But all that I remember is that his hair was shoulder length and that he was the bass player. That's really all I noticed about him at the time. I also took notice of all the other artists who were there—directly behind me was Brenda Lee."

Emory Gordy was unaware that his future bride was in the audience at Nashville's Municipal Auditorium on July 1, 1973. But he was delighted to learn that his schoolboy crush was in the crowd.

"Brenda and I are the same age," says Emory. "I grew up in

Atlanta, and I can remember seeing her on *TV Ranch* on WAGA. I was only eight years old at the time, and I'll never forget my mother saying, 'You ought to marry that girl.' Isn't that something?"

"He has mentioned that to me many times," chuckles Patty. "And, actually, Brenda Lee and I have talked many times about it. I love her."

Emory's "Traces" was recorded by Brenda Lee on her *Johnny One Time* LP in 1969, and he wound up coproducing Brenda's superb *Feels So Right* album in 1984.

While Emory was building his career as a songwriter, producer, and instrumentalist, Patty was taking a detour. Instead of pursuing her Grand Ole Opry contacts, she went in an opposite direction. After her high school graduation, she married a drummer and moved to North Carolina. For the next eight years, she fronted rock bands.

Around 1983, she resumed writing country songs. In 1985, brother Roger took a tape of her tunes to producer Tony Brown.

"Roger convinced Tony Brown that he had the best girl singer in the whole town of Nashville," laughs Patty. "Roger can sell ice to the Eskimos.

"So I was going to my meeting with Tony. I was going to go in and sing a couple of songs that I had written. I was on my way to his office in the elevator. Emory was in the elevator, and he was dressed very casually, in a pair of white overalls. He was looking at me, and I was looking at him. His thoughts were, 'That mousy little thing is an artist?' I was looking at him, going, 'This is a producer?' I still have those white overalls! They're pretty messed up, but I have them.

"We went into Tony's office together and sat down. Of course, I was very nervous, because I am not a great guitarist. I kind of know how, because I taught myself. I play at it enough to write, but I'm really not a picker. So I played for them. We talked. Then I started becoming comfortable with Emory, because he was very sensitive to the way that I was feeling and knew that I was nervous. I began to really like him."

Tony and Emory decided to coproduce Patty's debut album. While preparing to make the record, Emory was the one who worked most closely with her.

"Tony turned it over to Emory to do the preproduction with me in order to prepare me to go into the studio. We really got so much done during this time and ended up really liking being with each other, having fun and talking about a variety of music. Not just country, but many varieties of music. At first, I didn't really know much about him. I remember I thought his first name was 'Gordy.' Then when I started checking into it, I said, 'Oh, how stupid are you?' A lot of the artists that I was very much influenced by—Linda Ronstadt and Emmylou Harris—Emory had been a part of them.

"When I was like fifteen or sixteen years old, I had started becoming more interested in the musicians and who they were. There was the artist, but the music that was made behind them was made by 'unknown artists.' That is the way I called them, 'unknown artists.'" Patty soon realized that her coproducer was one of the top recording-session musicians in America.

Coproduced by Emory, "Lonely Days, Lonely Nights" appeared as Patty's debut single at the end of 1985. "Wicked Ways" succeeded it in 1986. "After All" and her self-composed "I Did" appeared in 1987, as did her debut album, *Patty Loveless*.

"I had gone on the road [to promote the early singles], and when I was on the road, I was missing him a lot," Patty recalls. "Emory called me and talked to me many times. I think he was starting to fall for me. He finally admitted it to me after the record was finished. He expressed his feelings for me. Here he was telling me he was falling in love with me. I was going, 'I can't really say that I don't feel the same.' A part of me felt like I had feelings for this man. But I was just so shy of getting into a relationship, especially since my divorce wasn't final. I was afraid. But, you know, a heart can't help how it feels.

"When people fall in love, I think it's real important to be friends first and then let love take over. Your heart knows. The more we worked together, I just knew."

None of the early records became hits, but Emory and Tony joined her again in the studio to create 1988's *If My Heart Had Windows.* The title tune, Patty's revival of a 1967 George Jones favorite, became her first top-ten hit, and the album also contained her second, "A Little Bit in Love." For her third album, 1988's *Honky Tonk Angel,* Emory Gordy stepped out of the picture, both as a producer and a musician. He was also absent on 1990's *On Down the Line.*

"He was very nervous about becoming involved with his artist," Patty explains. "I mean, I couldn't even get Emory to listen to what I was doing until it was completely finished. He said, 'No, that's between you and Tony. Tony's your producer. I don't need to be stepping into Tony's territory.' But even during the two records that I did with Tony, Emory was actually helping me with the road band."

Those two records yielded such career-building hits as "Don't Toss Us Away," "Timber I'm Falling in Love," "Chains," "On Down the Line," and "I'm That Kind of Girl." As her star rose, concert offers poured in.

"Emory enjoyed working with the band and helping me put the shows and the music together. He'd show up and either play keyboards, guitar, or bass, just fill in wherever he was needed. He traveled to Europe with me, on that USO tour I did."

Among the many events that consumed her time during this star-making period was Patty's induction into the cast of the Grand Ole Opry. On June 11, 1988, she was welcomed to the Opry stage by her old mentor, Porter Wagoner. Because the Opry had been part of her life for so long, she was thrilled by the honor. Her only regret was that Emory was back in Georgia and couldn't attend that evening.

"It was a shame," she comments, "because Emory just loves everybody at the Opry. I think they feel the same way about him. His whole family has such high respect for the Opry and its artists.

"We did get to go to his twenty-fifth high school class reunion together that spring. We actually were just starting to date each other. They had a DJ there. I went up there to make a request. I said, 'There's a guy here who wrote "Traces," and I want you to play it. He said, 'But that wasn't part of the music at that time [Emory graduated in 1963].' I said, 'Well, it is now. It is tonight.' He pulled out the record and played it. I said to Emory, 'I want to slow dance with you.' So they played 'Traces.' "

He proposed. But there was no time for a wedding.

"We had talked about getting married in '88, but we decided to wait. There was a lot going on. I had started really touring a lot to get my face out there and be known. I just felt like we didn't have time to really break away and get married. So finally in '89, we just decided to elope. We called our mothers, but we didn't have any family with us at all [at the wedding]. We just went to Gatlinburg."

They were wed in the East Tennessee mountains on February 6, 1989. Surprisingly, they were able to keep their marriage from the public for almost two more years before finally revealing their relationship in September 1991.

"Well, one of the reasons was that I didn't want to flaunt it," Patty says. "I mean, I was in the press so much anyway. I didn't want to make a big deal of it because of my ex. He was still having a hard time over the divorce. We were just trying to be sensitive to other people's feelings.

"Another reason was that I didn't want people to think, 'Oh, yeah, she married the producer, and that's the reason things are really happening now.' That wasn't the case, because Emory was not producing recordings on me."

After their marriage, Emory rejoined the production team to make 1991's *Up Against My Heart*. It contained such hits as "Hurt Me Bad (In a Real Good Way)" and "Jealous Bone." Now Patty Loveless underwent a metamorphosis. During the preparation for her next album, she discovered her vocal cords were damaged and in need of emergency surgery. Singer Kathy Mattea had undergone the same operation a few months earlier, so she counseled and encouraged the frightened Patty. After recuperating, Patty Loveless reemerged with a sleek new image, flame-red hair, and an album titled *Only What I Feel.* Produced by Emory, the 1993 collection contained such giant successes as "Blame It on Your Heart" and "How Can I Help You Say Goodbye" and became her first platinum record.

"He's not hard to work with," says Patty of her producer/ husband. "I think I'm the one who's hard to work with. I ask him all the time, 'Am I tough? Do I give you a hard time?'" She adds that some of her biggest hits have been songs that she was reluctant to try but recorded at his urging.

By the mid-1990s, Patty and Emory were inseparable. Their platinum-selling 1995 creation, *When Fallen Angels Fly,* was named Album of the Year by the Country Music Association (CMA). "I Try to Think About Elvis," "You Don't Even Know Who I Am," and its other singles made her a massive country-radio favorite. "You Can Feel Bad" and "Lonely Too Long" both became number-one hits in 1996. They were on *The Trouble with the Truth,* the record that earned her the CMA's Female Vocalist of the Year award.

"I'll share a little secret with you. I prayed for an award for the music, because Emory works so hard. . . . And prayers do work, don't they? He was proud of the fact that we won it together."

Patty won two more CMAs for her collaborations with George Jones and her frequent vocal partner Vince Gill. Emory continued to produce her albums, including *Strong Heart* (2000), on which the couple collaborated as songwriters on "Rise Up, Lazarus," and her roots-music masterpieces *Mountain Soul* (2001) and *Bluegrass & White Snow* (2002). Subtitled *A Mountain Christmas,* the 2002 CD contained "Santa Train," "Christmas Day at My House," and "Bluegrass, White Snow" as Patty/Emory songwriting collaborations. Is it difficult to collaborate so intimately and to be together constantly?

"We have a really large house. If we want to get away from each other, we can. It is true that one of us can start to make a statement, and the other one will take over. He goes, 'And you're finishing my sentences for me?' I'll say, 'Yeah.' Because we know each other that much."

Their technique for not mixing the music business with their private life is simple: "Once we're at home and out of the studio, we have this thing to say, 'My office is closed for the day.' That was our thing.

"We don't fight, but we do have disagreements. If we do, and it's getting heated, I just go, 'Let's not go there' or 'Let's talk about this later.' I don't like confrontation. It makes me very uncomfortable. I never enjoy hearing people fight or even raise their voices. I don't like being yelled at. If that happens, you can bring me to tears. I can even be brought to tears if people I care about are arguing."

In addition to being an artist he produces and his songwriting collaborator, Patty Loveless has fulfilled another role for Emory Gordy in recent years. By necessity, she has become his nurse. Since 1996, he has been through four major surgeries, three for abdominal problems and one for a collapsed lung.

"He no longer has a gallbladder. He no longer has a spleen. They had to do a whole reconstruction. He was pretty much staying a mess, but he's doing a lot better. He is doing really great these days. I was telling him, 'Maybe it's because I'm at home with you.' I've nursed him through quite a bit."

The couple moved back to Emory's home state of Georgia to be near his children from his first marriage and to allow him to recuperate from his health problems. Patty has declared that she plans to live the rest of her days in their rural home in Dallas, die there, and haunt it afterward. Located northwest of Atlanta, the expansive home sits on 150 secluded acres next to 8,000 acres of protected forest. It has five fireplaces, a huge vegetable garden, and a lake. It also has a home studio, in which they prepared music for Patty's albums *On Your Way Home* (2003) and *Dreamin' My Dreams* (2005).

Emory Gordy Jr. was inducted into the Georgia Music Hall of Fame in 1992. Because of her longtime residency in the state, Patty Loveless joined him as a member of that hall of fame in 2005.

"To tell you the truth, the music truly comes from both of us," she says. "With all these songs, we really put our heads together.

"I've always been kind of shy and humble. I never wanted to

be the center of attention. I sing because I want to touch people. I want to make you feel. If you're buying that ticket . . . I want you to come for the music, not for the flash.

"For me, singing is almost like a crying out from the heart. Songs and music have a way for me to connect to people. They're my way of communicating about myself. He's a shy-type person, too. I tend to open my feelings to him more so than to anybody else. I think we both feel these songs. That's why he's an awesome producer.

"Sometimes I look back on it all, and I think we were meant to be. It took a long time for us to come together. I really believe that Emory and I were meant for each other. It just seems like we were brought together for a reason."

# Some Memories Just Won't Die

**M**arty Robbins believed himself to be ugly.

Perhaps equally surprising, the Grand Ole Opry's most dashing and charismatic showman was private and not very sociable offstage. He was terrified of pain, yet participated in the dangerous sport of auto racing. He had both an outrageous sense of humor and a temper with a short fuse. His concerts were like parties, but he didn't even drink. His image was of a man with a healthy ego and dazzling self-confidence. In reality, he was shy and humble.

These are just a few of the contrasts in the personality of one of the most gifted and complex men in the history of country music. The final irony is that no one seemed more vibrant and alive than Marty Robbins, but he died too young, at age fifty-seven.

"I'm not satisfied at all with what I have done," he said not long before his death. "I want to do more. I haven't lost the drive."

It was typical of his restlessly creative spirit that he still felt that way after placing more than seventy-five titles on the country charts. More than fifty top-ten country hits, two Grammy Awards, six gold records, seven top-twenty pop smashes, membership in the Nashville Songwriters Hall of Fame, and election into the Country Music Hall of Fame never dulled his desire to succeed. During his astonishing career, he became a master of a staggering range of musical styles, meeting every challenge with ease.

Broadcaster Ralph Emery aptly dubbed him "Golden Throat" and recalls, "Marty overflowed with energy and ambition."

In the beginning, Marty Robbins had nowhere to go but up. Stories of childhood poverty are common in country music, but what Martin David Robinson overcame was truly extraordinary. He was born on September 26, 1925. "Home" was a series of shacks and tents in the Arizona desert. Marty had eight brothers and sisters. There was no electricity. There was no running water. There was no indoor plumbing.

"People who think they're poor now never had it any worse than I did, *never*," he recalled. "I know what it is like to be laughed at because your shoe doesn't have a sole in it and because your pants have holes in them. Not only other kids, but I know what it's like to be ridiculed by a teacher. That used to hurt me so much. I was poor, and there was nothin' I could do about it."

There were few toys, but Marty found entertainment in the yarns told by his maternal grandfather, Texas Bob Heckle. Texas Bob's wife Anna was a Paiute Indian, and she was just as colorful as he was.

"Grandfather was a drummer in the Civil War, or so he told me. He sold patent medicines. . . . The old man could really tell stories. He was a Texas Ranger, or so he told me. He was a poet. My love for the Old West came from him. He died when I was six, but I remember him *very* well."

Marty's father John Robinson, on the other hand, was an abusive alcoholic. Even many years afterward, the star seldom spoke of him.

"He would whip me for no reason," Marty said in one of the rare occasions when he talked about his father. "I wasn't one of his favorites. His favorite was one of my younger brothers. I remember my brother and I got into it one time, and he called for my father. My dad had a bad temper. I ran away and wouldn't come back. He chased me and threw a hammer at me like a tomahawk. I picked it up and threw it back as hard as I could and hit him in the chest. He never bothered me after that."

Mother Emma separated from her husband when Marty was twelve. The family moved into a shack near the railroad tracks in Glendale, Arizona, and she took in laundry to support them.

"I'm not sure what happened to him," said Marty indifferently. "I never looked into it. My mother was always the one who took care of me."

Marty worked in cotton fields for twenty-five cents a day. He idolized Gene Autry (1907–1998), and would save his earnings so that he could see his hero on the silver screen each week. School did not interest him in the least.

"I went to high school for three years without passing a single subject. Usually, I didn't even bother to show up. I ran with a rough crowd, just one step away from reform school. . . . The police were always talking to me about something."

It was difficult for Marty to speak about this part of his life, but by age fourteen, he was a juvenile delinquent committing petty crimes. He stole, jumped freight trains, and got into fights. After one boy he beat up wound up in the hospital, Marty outran the law by fleeing into the countryside to live on a friend's goat ranch.

At age seventeen, he enlisted in the navy. It was the height of World War II, and Marty saw combat in the Pacific. He piloted landing craft on beaches and came under fire during the campaign for the Solomon Islands. While in the service, Marty began playing guitar. This is also almost certainly when he fell in love with Hawaiian music. Another navy pastime was boxing, which he continued to do briefly, semiprofessionally, after his honorable discharge in early 1946.

Settling in Phoenix, the youngster flailed around aimlessly throughout 1946 and 1947. He took and quit one menial job after another—mechanic's helper, electrician's helper, well driller, and driver of milk-, brick-, and ice-delivery trucks.

"I never knew what I wanted," he admitted. "I'm lazy. . . . I had never considered anything close to work, because I didn't like to work. I had eight jobs in six months. I only got fired from the last one. I quit all the others. I'd only work long enough for a payday. I found out that work was just not what I was suited for."

While listening to the radio in his brick truck one day, he decided that he could sing as well as the guy who had the country show on the Phoenix station. He took the next day off, hopped on his motorcycle, drove to KOY, auditioned for the station manager by singing "The Strawberry Roan," and got the job.

Marty married Marizona Baldwin about a month later, on September 27, 1948. He'd met her at the soda fountain where she clerked. While they were dating, he didn't tell her he was singer "Marty Robbins." When he finally did, Marizona was thrilled. Like him, she'd grown up poor, and she'd always dreamed that someday a romantic singing cowboy would come to her rescue. Son Ronny was born in 1949. The former ne'er-do-well was now a happy man.

"I got a job in a nightclub . . . and I played three nights in a row and made thirty bucks. And that was great: Getting paid that much for doing something I loved! Pretty soon, I was making sixty bucks a week. There's no way I could have made that much otherwise. I really wasn't skilled labor." By 1952, he was making $750 a week.

For a while, Marty Robbins lived it up as a local celebrity. But a car wreck in December 1950 led him to quit drinking. He remained sober for the rest of his life. In later years, Marty also told a story about Ronny falling gravely ill. He promised God he would quit drinking if Ronny's life was spared. The boy immediately recovered, and Marty kept his word.

By 1951, he was appearing on KPHO in Phoenix. When it opened the city's first TV station that year, Marty became the host of its *Western Caravan* show. At this point, he was so averse to doing television that he threw up before every broadcast.

"I'm not pretty enough," he commented about his reluctance to be on camera. "My face—especially my nose—looks like I've been a boxer all my life and received quite a few knockout blows." Throughout his career, handsome Marty Robbins would refer to himself as "ugly." He was also somewhat sensitive about his 5-foot 7-inch height.

The Grand Ole Opry's Jimmy Dickens was a guest star on Marty's Phoenix TV show. Impressed, Jimmy recommended Marty to his label, Columbia Records. Former Opry executive Harry Stone was another who reportedly scouted Marty for the "big leagues." Columbia signed Marty on May 25, 1951.

Marty Robbins had begun copyrighting his songs in 1950. In 1952, he signed with Nashville's Acuff-Rose as his song publisher. His self-penned heartache tune "I'll Go on Alone" became his first number-one hit. As a result, he was invited to become an Opry cast member on January 19, 1953. The family moved to Music City.

Alabama songwriter Melvin Endsley was crippled by polio, but he managed to get backstage at the Ryman one night to give Marty his composition "Singing the Blues." Marty added a yodel to the word "cry" and wound up with a number-one country smash in late 1956. Marty returned to Melvin Endsley for "Knee Deep in the Blues," placing both Endsley songs with Acuff-Rose. He later realized that he could have formed his own publishing company for them and pocketed the profits himself. As a result, Marty Robbins formed both a short-lived record label as well as his own song-publishing business and booking agency. For most of his career, Marty managed himself and booked his own concert dates. Many of his valuable song copyrights remain in the family's hands to this day.

At his next recording sessions, Marty aimed squarely for the pop hit parade. Under the guidance of Mitch Miller and Ray Conniff in New York, he recorded the prom-themed "A White Sport Coat."

"I wrote 'A White Sport Coat' in eleven miles in 1956," Marty reported. "We were driving somewhere in Ohio, and I just happened to look up and see this sign that read eleven miles to the next town. And I had the song finished by the time we got to that town. Where the idea came from, I have no idea. I'd never heard of a white sport coat and a pink carnation!" Son Ronny thinks his dad passed a teen school dance and was inspired.

"A White Sport Coat" was an unqualified pop and country smash in 1957. Marty followed it with the similarly themed "Teen-Age Dream," "Just Married," "She Was Only Seventeen," and the bouncy "The Story of My Life." But at thirty-two, Marty was too mature for this kind of material. It was time for a change.

In late 1957, he showed his love of Hawaiian music by releasing one of Nashville's first "concept" LPs, *Song of the Islands.* He followed this in 1959 with a nod to his kinship with Texas Bob and a salute to his boyhood hero Gene Autry, recording his landmark *Gunfighter Ballads and Trail Songs* album in one day. It included "El Paso," a saga of romance and death in West Texas that became the first number-one pop hit of the 1960s.

" 'El Paso' I wrote in one day when I was driving through [Texas, en route from Nashville to Phoenix]. I never even got it down on paper until I got to Phoenix the next day. But I couldn't forget it, because it was like a movie, and I didn't know how it was going to end. I must have been going one hundred miles an hour when I ended it. It was so exciting! I did not know how it was going to end, but once I got started, it just rolled out. I never changed a word." His unforgettable recording is now enshrined in the Grammy Hall of Fame.

In 1961, the throbbing "Don't Worry" became his next pop and country smash. It was not only one of his most beautiful melodies, it introduced a new sound. During the recording session, Grady Martin's guitar was distorted by a malfunctioning preamp in the mixing console, resulting in fuzztone. This was the first time this sound was ever recorded. It was later adopted by The Doors, Jefferson Airplane, and many others making "psychedelic" rock music.

"I wrote that one night in the four miles that it takes to drive from the Grand Ole Opry to where I lived then," said Marty of "Don't Worry." "I had started it when I left and had it finished by the time I ever got home. I went right in and played it on the piano. I never even put it down on paper until copyright-filing time, after I sang it [in the studio]."

Marty continued to top the charts and by the mid-1960s had

settled into his tradition of closing Opry shows. Initially, this was because he wanted to come to the Ryman after he'd finished dirt-track racing at Highland Rim Speedway, north of Nashville. But soon it became a habit for him to perform well after the broadcasts ended, doing encore after encore. He mugged for the fans, posed for pictures, clowned around, and shamelessly milked crowds for applause. His showboating endeared him to thousands. Marty soon amassed "Marty's Army," one of the largest fan clubs in country-music history.

"When I'm onstage, I'm having such a good time, and I'm so happy to be there that there is no way the audience can't have a good time, too," he explained. "I like to kid around with the people in the audience, carry on conversations with them and have a big time. I talk *to* an audience, not over their heads. And that makes them feel appreciated."

But after the shows were over and the applause fell silent, Marty went home to be with his family. There were no Music Row parties, just quality time at home. Daughter Janet had been born in 1959, and he wanted to be the father to her and Ronny that he had never had.

"Other than relatives, I've really only had two people over to my house as guests in the last twenty years," he once admitted. "That was Eddy Arnold and Roy Wiggins, the steel guitar player. I'm just not much of one for parties and that sort of thing."

"He had another life, offstage," says son Ronny Robbins. "Music was not a big part of Marty Robbins, to me. To me, he was 'Dad.' As kids, we never thought much about the Opry or the TV shows or the concerts. That was just what he did, something that took Daddy away from us for several months out of the year.

"When he was home, he tried extra hard to be a good father. Partly because he was gone so much and partly because of his own upbringing, he didn't know what a father was supposed to act like.

"Daddy was real protective of that home life. He was always home for Christmas. I don't grieve for Marty Robbins the star, because I probably didn't know him that well. I knew Marty Robbins the father very well." Marty kept Marizona and the children out of the limelight. Ronny and Janet never saw a Marty Robbins show until they were teenagers. Both kids were rock 'n' roll fans, so they didn't watch his syndicated TV series *The Drifter* (1965) and *The Marty Robbins Show* (1968–1969), nor the seven movies he appeared in during the 1950s and 1960s.

Ronny does remember music drifting through the air ducts in the Robbins home late at night. Marty was an insomniac who frequently stayed up in his music room, writing songs. Later, he became a regular visitor to disc jockey Ralph Emery's all-night radio show on WSM. On these occasions, he would reel off song after song on the air. Marty knew more than one thousand songs and could easily sing all night without repeating himself.

In 1964, the Gallup Poll named Marty Robbins one of the most admired men in America. That was the year he campaigned for conservative Republican presidential candidate Barry Goldwater. In 1968, he worked for the presidential campaign of Alabama governor George Wallace.

This was also the period when Marty began racing on the NASCAR circuit. One often-told tale had him running in second place at the Nashville Speedway during a 1968 race but pulling over and withdrawing so that he could make it to the Opry on time.

"I drive for the fun of it," he said. "I try to stay out of the way of these other fellows, who are out there trying to make a living. I just love to be on the track with them."

As the 1960s drew to a close, Marty's popularity was undimmed, but a shadow began to fall over the star. In 1968, he'd had an undiagnosed and untreated heart attack while racing at the Charlotte 500. A year later, he collapsed after a show in Vegas. He checked himself out of the hospital after promising his doctors he'd fly to Nashville to see his own physician. Instead, he flew to Ohio to fulfill a concert date. He had a heart attack on his tour bus, yet played the show anyway. He was hospitalized in Cleveland but was soon on the road again.

On January 27, 1970, Marty underwent a then-experimental

triple bypass surgery in Nashville. While recuperating, he received 22,000 pieces of fan mail.

After the operation, he called newspaper reporter Larry Woody and invited him to bring a photographer to the hospital to "make a picture of the most carved up chest in Nashville." Kidding aside, the experience had deepened the superstar's faith. Marty was always religious but seldom spoke about his beliefs in public, which was in keeping with his private side.

"I know a lot of things don't seem fair in life," he said of his chronic heart condition. "But it all comes down to how you believe, how you accept life. I don't like to get off on religion, but I have my beliefs. I don't ask anybody else to believe the way I do; but then again, no one else could ever change the way I feel."

His self-composed "My Woman, My Woman, My Wife" returned him to the top of the charts in 1970 and led to his second Grammy Award. "Love Me," written by future Opry star Jeanne Pruett, was a top-ten hit in 1973, and he penned his 1974 hit single "Twentieth Century Drifter" about his love of auto racing.

Marty's best finish in a NASCAR race was fifth at Michigan International Speedway in 1974. Four months later, a Charlotte 500 crash resulted in thirty-seven stitches to his face and a broken nose. He'd purposefully crashed into a concrete wall at 150 miles an hour to avoid hitting and possibly killing star drivers Richard Childress and A. J. Foyt.

Later he quipped, "You've heard of stars putting their footprints in concrete? Well, I tried to put my face print in a concrete wall, only the concrete had already dried." He crashed again at Daytona and Talladega in 1975. He said he'd give up racing but didn't.

He also continued to write hit songs, including the lilting "El Paso City," a number-one hit in 1976 that completed the unique trilogy of thematically linked tunes following 1965's "Faleena (From El Paso)" and the original "El Paso." Like many of its predecessors, "El Paso City" came to Marty while he was traveling.

"Every time I flew over El Paso, I was usually getting some sleep. Well, it never failed that I would always wake up about five minutes before the pilot would say, 'And off to the left is the city of El Paso.' So I thought about writing that song for so long. And one time when I heard the pilot say that, I asked the stewardess for a pen and a paper. And I had that song written before we even got across the state of New Mexico. By the time I was in L.A., I had the tune and everything."

After "Among My Souvenirs" became his second number-one hit of 1976, he decided to try television again. *Marty Robbins Spotlight* ran for three years, 1977–1979. On the road, he teamed up with Merle Haggard, who so admired him that he named his son Marty Haggard after the living legend. Opry stars Marty Stuart and Marty Roe of Diamond Rio are also named after Marty Robbins.

At the Opry, he continued his show-closing ways. The program had relocated to the Opry House in the Opryland theme park in 1974. The bigger facility allowed Marty to expand his activities. Now, following his encores and kidding around, the Pied Piper led the crowds to the building's front lobby. There he'd pose for snapshots, answer questions, sign autographs, and mingle with "Marty's Army," sometimes until past 3:00 a.m.

The year 1982 began with his third triumphant tour of Great Britain. In April, *Esquire* magazine declared him "a national treasure." At June's Fan Fair celebration in Nashville, he threw a "Marty Party" for two thousand fans at the Opryland Hotel. He performed for two and a half hours, then signed autographs until 2:00 a.m. In August, "Some Memories Just Won't Die" returned him to the top ten. On October 11, 1982, Eddy Arnold inducted Marty Robbins into the Country Music Hall of Fame.

"I was really surprised when I got it," Marty remarked afterward. "I thought Jimmy Dickens should get it and *would* get it before I did. . . . But I got it," he added with a mischievous laugh, "and I'm not gonna give it back!"

On December 2, 1982, he was scheduled to be at the world premiere of Clint Eastwood's movie *Honkytonk Man* in Nashville. Marty appeared in the film and sang its hit title tune. He returned from a concert in Cincinnati that morning complaining of chest pains. Marizona checked him into the hospital, and he was rushed into surgery. A week-long vigil followed as Marty clung to life. The damage to his heart was too great. Marty Robbins died the night of December 8, 1982.

At Marizona's request, Brenda Lee sang "One Day at a Time" at the funeral service. "I think a lot of people thought Marty Robbins was bigger than life," mused Brenda, "and a lot of others probably thought he was bigger than death, too. That's what has made this so tragic. It's hard to imagine anyone who was more *alive* than Marty."

# Live Fast, Love Hard,
# Die Young, and Leave a
# Beautiful Memory

Faron Young, who starred on the Opry from 1952 to 1964, was one of country's most colorful characters and biggest hit makers, but he believed himself to be forsaken and forgotten when he committed suicide in 1996.

"The industry is not trying to help the older artists anymore," Faron had complained a few years earlier. "They've hired these young boys to come in who really don't know anything about what we did or what we stood for. Back in the day, Ernest Tubb and myself and Carl Smith, Webb Pierce, Ferlin Husky, and Hank Snow were beatin' that road, making this business what it is today. Thanks to us old bastards, there's still a country-music business to be in.

"They have big buses and airplanes to travel in. We drove around with cars pulling trailers. We were more of a family. We'd get together at each other's homes and have cookouts and things like that. We toured in package shows together. It was a family affair. But it ain't no more. There's no camaraderie about it anymore.

"There's no use in me recording anymore. I don't have the heart to do it."

In the later years of his life, Faron Young was alone. Wife Hilda had divorced him in 1986, but friends said he never stopped loving her. He developed emphysema and was despondent when he had to acquire and use an oxygen tank. Dismayed that younger performers were paid so much more than he was for concerts, he let his band go in 1994. The week before his death, he was treated for a chronic and painful prostate condition. He became more and more isolated.

"I tried to call him, but he stopped returning my calls," reported Opry star Jeannie Seely. "When I saw him, I asked him why, and he said, 'because you'll want me to do something, and I don't want to do anything.' Faron was sending out every signal, when you think about it."

He sold his tour bus and gave away many of his belongings. He cleaned out his storage room and even found a new home for his only companion, his dog. Still, no one anticipated what happened next. On the morning of December 9, 1996, Faron Young, sixty-four, put a .38-caliber revolver to his temple and shot himself. He left a suicide note with the day's date and a time of 11:40 a.m.

Former band member Ray Emmett came to visit his old friend at 12:30 p.m. When Faron didn't answer his calls at the back door, Ray entered the house and found the critically wounded star on his bed. Faron was taken to a nearby hospital but died of his injuries the following day.

"He said it best, himself," said Jeannie Seely. "'I'm gonna live fast, love hard, die young, and leave a beautiful memory.' It turned out to be his prophecy. He certainly left some beautiful memories for us."

The Faron Young stories told in Nashville are endless. He drank alcohol in epic quantities, was a world-class smart aleck, could cuss longer and better than anybody, got into brawls, wrecked cars, was overbearingly sassy and cocky, had numerous run-ins with the law, was usually the proverbial life of the party, boasted one of the quickest wits in Music City, and was notoriously frank and outspoken. His wild escapades and frequent misbehavior only fueled his legend.

And no matter how obnoxious he could be, everybody loved him dearly.

Just as numerous as stories of his hell-raising are tales of his kindness and generosity. Faron was known as "the softest touch in Nashville." He'd hand a complete stranger $50 if the fellow looked needy. He reached out to help Roger Miller, Kris Kristofferson, Willie Nelson, Bill Anderson, Roy Drusky, Johnny Paycheck, Don Gibson, Sonny James, Johnny Cash, The Wilburn Brothers, Charley Pride, and many others when they were unknowns trying to make it on Music Row.

He was also regarded as one of the finest showmen of his era. And his tally of more than forty top-ten country classics speaks for itself.

Faron Young was born on February 25, 1932, the youngest of six children. As a boy, his home was a dairy farm on the outskirts of Shreveport, Louisiana. The children were expected to milk the cows at the crack of dawn and again when they returned home from school.

"I developed my voice from calling the cows up," Faron said with a chuckle. "I was singing ever since I was a little boy. I sang pop music until I was about a senior in high school. My football coach had a little country band, so I sang with the band. My desire was to get off of a farm. I didn't care if it was music that got me away from there. It might have been bank robbery. Whatever was more convenient."

Shreveport was the home of KWKH and its *Louisiana Hayride* country show. Faron was enthralled with the show's star, Hank Williams.

"A bunch of us kids went up to the *Louisiana Hayride* in a convertible one time. Hank Williams Sr. was standing out on the balcony there, out in back of the building. And I hollered up at him. I said, 'Hey Hank! I'm gonna be on that stage with you one of these days!' He said, 'I hope you do, boy.' After I came to Nashville, I got to meet Hank. I was surprised that he did, but he remembered the incident."

Up-and-coming Shreveport singer Webb Pierce took Faron Young under his wing. Faron began making guest appearances with Webb's band and on Webb's radio broadcasts in 1951.

"Webb had that high, high, really country corny sound. At that time, that's what country music was. I sang a little bit more mellow than he did. But what he was doing was happening. He was having hit records. And I wasn't until I got to singing something like him and Hank Williams."

Capitol Records producer Ken Nelson heard Faron singing on the radio when he was traveling through Shreveport en route to Dallas. Sensing an opportunity, the executive turned his car around and drove to KWKH. At age nineteen, the singer was too young to sign a recording contract, so his parents signed it for him.

One of his early records was heard by Jack Stapp and Jim Denny of the Grand Ole Opry. They invited Faron Young to come to Nashville and do a two-week trial run on the program in the spring of 1952.

"The first time I was on the Grand Ole Opry, I was so nervous I could have threaded a sewing machine with it running. I was scared to death. When I got through with the song, I ran off the stage. Ernest Tubb grabbed me. He said, 'Get back out there. You're getting an encore. Get back out there and milk that audience by bowing and bowing. I was off of a dairy farm, and I had never heard this. I thought, 'What in the world is he talking about—milk the audience?'

"Then when I came off, Hank Williams Sr. came over and said, 'Hey, boy, you know you just might make it in this business. You're pretty good, boy.' That was like Jesus himself saying, 'Boy,' when Hank told me that."

For the trip, Faron brought along his girlfriend, the beautiful Billie Jean Jones. After Faron's Opry debut, Hank invited the couple out for a night on the town. At some point during the evening, Billie Jean became Hank's date, not Faron's. That fall, Hank and Billie Jean were married.

"I was gonna quit the Opry and go back to Shreveport," Faron recalled. "Roy Acuff called me into the dressing room and said, 'I can tell by lookin' at you that you are fixin' to leave here and not come back, aren't you?' I said, 'Yes, sir, that's exactly what I had in mind.' He said, 'You've really got what it takes to be a star, and if you go back to Shreveport and back into the clubs, that's exactly where you'll be the rest of your life.' He was right. I'd still be makin' $300 a week in Shreveport, I believe, if it hadn't been for Roy Acuff talking to me."

Not long after his third Nashville recording session, Faron Young was drafted into the army. He was in basic training in Georgia when a song from that session, the bopping "Goin' Steady," began scampering up the popularity charts. In early 1953, it became his first top-ten hit.

"I cried like a rat eating a red onion," said Faron of his draft notice. "I had just went in the army when Hank and Billie Jean got married onstage in Birmingham, Alabama. I remember my company commander called me down [two months later] and said, 'Faron, why don't you take the day off? One of your good friends passed away last night.' I said, 'Who?' He said, 'Hank Williams.' I thought, 'My goodness. That's two favors he did for me. He took Billie Jones off my hands, and he got me a day off in the army.'"

Actually, Faron Young's time in the service wasn't much of a hardship. The Korean War was on, but he was kept stateside to sing at recruiting shows in the South. His Capitol publicity photos pictured him in his private's uniform. He appeared on TV wearing it in a series of recruitment programs. He also wore it when he returned to the Opry stage, often including a recruiting pitch with his appearances.

While in the army, he fell in love with German-born teenager Hilda Macon. They were married in 1954, while he was still in uniform. They eventually had four children together, Damion (born 1955), Robyn (1957), Kevin (1967), and Alana (1969).

Faron Young's discharge in late 1954 coincided with his next big hit, "If You Ain't Lovin' (You Ain't Livin')." The honky-tonk tune got a second lease on life when George Strait revived it in 1988.

Faron's first number-one hit came in 1955, "Live Fast, Love Hard, Die Young."

His good looks made him a natural for the movies. In 1955, he was contracted to act in the low-budget western *Hidden Guns*. His part in the film led to the nickname "The Singing Sheriff" as well as to him dubbing his band The Deputies.

"I went out to Hollywood preparing for a six-month movie. Eight days later, the movie was shot, in the can, and ready to show in theaters. The girl who played my girlfriend in it was a young, beautiful girl. I kept trying to get them to write a love scene. They said, 'Look, boy, this is a western. You might get to kiss somebody, but if you do, it'll be that horse sitting over there. You don't kiss girls in western movies.' This was her first movie, a girl by the name of Angie Dickinson. And I sure wanted to have a love scene."

Faron would go on to star in ten more B movies in the 1950s and 1960s. Back in Nashville, his recording career caught fire during the next few years. Successful singles such as "All Right" and "I've Got Five Dollars and It's Saturday Night" paved the way for his first hit as a balladeer, 1956's "Sweet Dreams."

"The way I found 'Sweet Dreams' is Webb Pierce had heard Don Gibson's record of it. At that time, Don had not been heard of yet. Webb called me and said, 'I want you to come over to the house,' and he had this record. He played it. He said, 'You need to record this song. It's a hit.' So when I cut this thing, it immediately went to number one. Then Patsy Cline cut it, and it went to number one again. Then Emmylou Harris cut it, and it went to number one. Don Gibson redid it. When I go out and do 'Sweet Dreams,' some of these younger kids will come up and say, 'Boy, you sure did a heck of a job on that Patsy Cline song.' I say, 'Wait a minute! I had it first!'

"But I loved Patsy Cline. I think I loved everything about her. She took no guff off of nobody. She'd get in with a bunch of guys, and if somebody'd start smarting her off, she could smart you off right back. I remember her sitting backstage crying [when she had no hits]. I said, 'Let me tell you something, little girl. I'm gonna carry you on some road shows with me.' So I used to hire Patsy. Patsy worked for me at least a hundred to a hundred fifty times. When I first bought her, I could get her for $75 a day. Later on, $150. Then she got a couple of good things going and went up to $600, $700. I said, 'I can't afford you no more!' She's still one of the greatest girl singers that was ever in this industry. But she was tough. And I loved her for it.

"Roger Miller was always asking me for a job. I said, 'Well, I need a drummer. You play drums?' He said, 'If you'll get me a set, I'll play 'em.' I gave him some money. He went down to a pawn shop and bought a set of drums. Went on the road with me for two years."

"The only thing bigger than Faron Young's mouth is his heart," said a grateful Roger. In addition to carrying him in his road band, Faron Young boosted the struggling songwriter's career by making hits of "That's the Way I Feel" (1958), "Last Night at a Party" (1959), and "A World So Full of Love" (1961).

Songwriter and future Opry star Roy Drusky got his first breaks when Faron recorded his "Alone with You" (1958), "That's the Way it's Gonna Be" (1959), and "Country Girl" (1959). Faron made hits of early songs written by future Opry star Bill Anderson (1959's "Riverboat" and "Face to the Wall"). He hired Kris Kristofferson to work in construction at his office. He hired Johnny Paycheck for his band. Most famously, Faron Young gave the struggling Willie Nelson his first big hit.

"When Willie Nelson came to this town, he was just about penniless," Faron recalled. "We had a little watering hole called Tootsie's Orchid Lounge where me and all the guys always hung out. Willie came down, and he was singing his songs. He come and told me, 'You and George Morgan are two of my favorite singers,' because we sang behind the beat. He says, 'I've got a couple of songs I want to sing to you.' And he sang me 'Hello Walls' and 'Congratulations.' I said, 'I'm recording in a couple of weeks. I'll just take 'em both.' He said, 'Are you kidding me? These songs have been turned down by everybody in town.'"

Willie offered to sell him the songs outright. Faron refused and instead loaned the struggling songwriter $500. Years later, Willie paid him back by presenting Faron with a $50,000 prize bull.

"So we get in the studio, and everybody started making fun of the song. You know, 'Hello guitar. Hello microphone.' I said, 'Well, y'all go ahead and make fun of this thing. I think it's a hit record.' So I put it out."

In 1961, "Hello Walls" sat at number one for nine consecutive weeks. It became Faron's biggest pop-crossover hit and is now in the Grammy Hall of Fame.

Hotter than ever, Faron Young was courted and signed by Mercury Records. He continued delivering hits through the 1960s, including the classic country drinking song "Wine Me Up" (1969), which was revived by Larry Boone (1989), Gary Allan (1996), and other young stylists. Faron was also delighted with George Strait's 1988 revival of "If You Ain't Lovin'."

"It's a real shot in the arm to me," he said. "I don't mind seeing these young kids come into the business. I'm tickled to death to see someone have success, because if you can't enjoy someone else's success, you can't enjoy your own. The U.S. Mint is printing money twenty-four hours a day, and there's plenty for us all!"

"I've helped a lot of kids," said Faron nonchalantly. "It don't hurt. It didn't cost me a nickel to help 'em."

He could afford to be generous. Faron cofounded the successful country magazine *Music City News,* built the profitable Young Executive Building in Nashville, owned four song-publishing companies, founded a booking agency, and made real estate investments.

But redneck Faron wasn't exactly a socially enlightened individual. When African American Charley Pride appeared on the country scene, he was advised, "If you can make it past Faron Young, you'll be okay." So Charley tracked Faron down at a bar and sang to him. Soon, they were trading tunes. "I can't believe I'm singing with a jig and don't mind it," blurted the blunt Faron. "I was waiting for you to call me worse," Charley replied. "And if you did, I was ready to call you a pucker-mouthed banty rooster son of a peckerwood." One of the great friendships of country music was born. Faron Young became Charley Pride's champion and defender.

"When he first started, I carried him as part of my road show," Faron recalled. "I always told him if he was gonna ride in my bus, he had to get in the back. He said, 'It ain't like that no more, you little banty rooster.'"

One radio station threw out Charley's records when the station manager found out that Charley was African American. "Do you have any Faron Young records at your station?" asked Faron. The radio man assured him that he did. "Well, throw 'em out along with Charley Pride's, then," Faron snarled. "If I ever hear of your station playing one of my songs again, I'll come back and burn the damn place down!"

Faron was reported injured in a poolroom brawl in 1966, but most of his wild-and-wooly behavior was hushed up. However, a late-1969 car accident was too serious to keep quiet.

"I know a thing or two about comebacks," Faron said. "In fact, my career was almost over in 1970. I had a head-on collision in my car that practically ripped my tongue off. Even after four different operations, I still talked with a lisp, and I figured I would never sing again.

"But I gradually got to the point where I could sing reasonably well. Jerry Chesnutt wanted to write me a song. I said, 'Just don't write one with a lot of S's, because I lisp on S words.' He came up with '[It's] Four in the Morning.'"

In 1972, "It's Four in the Morning" became a number-one smash in the United States as well as a giant hit overseas. The waltz topped hit parades in Ireland, England, Australia, New Zealand, and elsewhere. His European bookings soared. Hits such as "Some Kind of a Woman" (1974) and "Here I Am in Dallas" (1975) carried Faron Young through his third decade on the charts.

But things began to unravel in the late 1970s. In 1979, he shot holes in his kitchen ceiling. Hilda and their daughter locked themselves in a bedroom and called the police. Faron entertained them when they arrived. He later wisecracked, "I figure it's my house; if I want to shoot holes in it, I can do it." Hilda separated from him.

"I was miserable during those years," he admitted. "Me and my wife was having a squabble, so I moved out for the time being. I broke up with her for five years. Later, we went back together. We were together three years. All of a sudden, we think it ain't workin' out again, so I took off again. We get too used to each other. When I slowed down on my travelin,' that's when we started havin' our trouble. The more I was gone, the better we got along."

In the early 1980s, he was arrested three times for driving under the influence. Women charged him with assault. His records no longer made the top of the charts. The concert bookings began to fall off.

He signed with MCA Records in 1979 but left the company bitterly in 1981, with three years remaining on his contract. He said the label wasn't interested in promoting his records properly. In truth, he was still singing magnificently.

"I smoke cigarettes, but I drink very expensive whiskey," he said of his voice's remarkable endurance. "That's it, I think. I remember tellin' George Jones one time, 'If you ever quit drinkin' and smoking, you won't be able to sing a note.' And I believe that's the same thing with me. I never did fool with the pills or the dope. Thank God. Because I am really too weak of a person. If I'd ever got started, I'd-a been hung."

In 1985, his old friend Willie Nelson contacted him about doing a duet album together. The result, *Funny How Times Slips Away,* temporarily lifted the fading star's spirits. He appeared that summer at Willie's gigantic Fourth of July Picnic in Texas.

"He's such a sweet person," said Faron of Willie. "We've loved each other for all these years. I know if I ever really needed anything, I could call Willie. When I was a big star and he wasn't, I was always good to him, and he's never forgot it. Now that he's a big star, he could fluff me off. But he doesn't. He treats me just like the day we met."

In later years, Faron Young appeared in public less frequently. But on the occasions when he did take the stage, he invariably proved he could still entertain with the best of them.

"When he was clicking on all cylinders, there were few acts that could touch him," says Bill Anderson. "He could take an audience and hold them in the palm of his hand.

"I learned a whole lot of what I know about show business from watching Faron Young. I would stand over to the side of the stage and just marvel at the ease with which Faron Young could entertain. He could be funny. He could be warm with the audience. He could really, really sing."

Charley Pride was another who studied at the feet of the master showman. He remembers, "When I was starting out, I had a lot of help from established singers, who took a chance by taking me onstage with them. . . . [Faron Young] was one of my best supporters in the early days, and that helped break some ground for me. When someone who is considered a die-hard redneck stands beside a black man and says, 'I like this guy,' it disarms people who might have been reluctant to associate with him.

"Young invited me to parties at his house, took me for rides in one of his old antique cars, and introduced me to a lot of people in the industry. We had some good times together, and I've always appreciated what Faron Young did for me."

In 2000, the two newest inductees into the Country Music Hall of Fame were announced. They were the late Faron Young and his lifelong friend Charley Pride.

# The Houston Cowboy
# and the Hollywood Star

If it weren't for show business, one of the Opry's sweetest love stories never would have happened. Lisa Hartman attended a high school for the performing arts, then became a pop starlet and a famous Hollywood film and TV thespian. During the same period, Clint Black dropped out of high school, went to work in construction, and performed in Lone Star State honky-tonks. Although both were raised in Houston, Texas, their paths wouldn't have crossed at all.

Fortunately, Clint Black was discovered and brought to Nashville in 1988. His career exploded in 1989. By the end of 1990, he was a superstar and headlining a huge New Year's Eve show back home in Houston.

A friend had given Lisa a copy of Clint's debut album. She liked it and as a lark decided to attend that New Year's Eve concert.

"I was in Houston promoting a movie," Lisa recalls. "I knew his music. It was New Year's Eve, and Mom and I booked a dinner, and then we went to see the show. And I was blown away."

"I didn't know anything about her at all," says Clint. "When I was introduced to her in Houston at the show, I was told she was on *Knots Landing* and everything."

Friends who knew them both played matchmakers. It was a Nashville music manager who'd given Lisa Clint's album and urged her to listen. A television executive gave Clint Lisa's phone number on the condition that the singer call her. He promised he would.

"Next time I was in L.A., I did," he remembers. "I was doing *The Tonight Show.* I had one night off, so I called her and took her to dinner at Gladstone's at the beach. We sat across from each other and yawned the whole night. She did six movies that year, I think. I was on the road constantly. We were both pretty tired."

"I remember that when we went to the beach for dinner, he would not laugh because he was on voice rest," Lisa reports. "You can imagine how dry that date was. You take laughter out of a conversation, and that's a pretty awkward evening."

Still, a spark had flickered. When she was making a film in Toronto a few weeks later, he had his tour bus deposit him there when he had three days off.

"We went to dinner with Robert Stack," Clint reminisces. "We went and saw Michael Bolton in concert. We went to Cirque du Soleil. She really brought me out of my shell, because you couldn't have gotten me to go into a crowd of any kind at that point. I had become overwhelmed with just being recognized.

"Having a wife who has been famous longer than I have been turned out to be a big benefit for me. She recognized things that I was going through and helped me through them. She helped me to have a better life than I might have had otherwise, because she just refused to change her life because she's a celebrity. She would just go and do. Period. I thought I was a pretty cool cat with my newfound fame, but really I was reeling trying to deal with it, and having so much anxiety just going to a mall or something. She got me out going and doing things."

After filming finished in Toronto, Lisa was booked for an appearance on *The Oprah Winfrey Show.* Also on that broadcast was country star Tanya Tucker. She was a matchmaker, too.

Says Lisa, "I remember she said, 'You know who's really tough? Clint Black!' That's what we used to say, 'He's so tough,' meaning 'cool' or 'hot.' Anyway, I had already been out with him, but we weren't yet a couple to the public. So I went, 'Really? Is he really?' I just totally played dumb."

Next, Lisa flew to Salt Lake City, Utah, to meet Clint at a show. By this time, both were completely infatuated.

"We had some serious discussions about our philosophies of life and where we were going," says Clint. "I knew exactly who she was. I knew who I was, by that point. I had always said, 'I'm not going to get married until I'm thirty,' because I had this belief that you can't know yourself before you're thirty. So how can you know what you're willing to say about the rest of your life? So I was twenty-nine, and it just hit me: 'Why should I waste any more time thinking about this?'

"I had a show that night on the university campus, and it was a Sunday. The campus was empty, and we went for a walk. I knew that it wasn't a chief objective in her life to get married. So I don't think I would have been overconfident. The butterflies were there. [The proposal] was pretty exciting, and when she said yes, I couldn't wait to tell the world."

At a tour stop down the road in Tucson, Arizona, they brought their mothers on the bus to share the happy news. Observant reporters at the American Society of Composers, Authors and Publishers (ASCAP) music-industry banquet in Nashville on September 8, 1991, noticed Lisa's ring, cornered the couple, and announced their engagement in the next day's newspapers. Lisa and Clint were married in a small ceremony on his Texas ranch house's porch on October 20, 1991.

Clint Black was born on February 4, 1962, and raised in Houston as the youngest of four music-making brothers. As a teenager, he initially worked as a back-up musician for his brother Kevin, playing bass, harmonica, and guitar. In 1981, Clint started a six-year stint fronting his own band on the East Texas honky-tonk circuit. He was discovered by the manager of the rock band ZZ Top in 1987 and recorded his first Nashville album the following year.

He shot to fame in 1989 with such hits as "A Better Man,"

"Killin' Time," and "Nobody's Home." He was named the Country Music Association's Male Vocalist of the Year in 1990 and joined the cast of the Grand Ole Opry on January 10, 1991.

"All these things were happening to me, my career exploding and all of this unprecedented success and all this stuff. And then you've been asked to become a member of the Grand Ole Opry. I knew a lot of the Opry stars, but I didn't have that much Opry experience. I was inducted as part of a big CBS TV special [celebrating the sixty-fifth anniversary of the Opry]. There were three days of rehearsals, so I got to hang out with all of the different Opry stars, joking around, hanging around backstage.

"Everybody was there—The Jordanaires, Grandpa Jones, Minnie Pearl, and Roy Acuff. It was great. I got to hear all kinds of great stories. . . . I don't want to sound corny, but I think the best way to describe it is, it was like you were being invited to join a family."

To date, Clint Black has had thirty top-ten hits, thirteen of which became number-one hits. The most recent of those chart-toppers came in 1999, when he sang the marriage anthem "When I Said I Do" with wife Lisa Hartman Black. It won the couple an Academy of Country Music Award and a Grammy nomination.

Actually, Lisa was a professional singer before Clint was. Born June 1, 1956, she is the daughter of nightclub singer Howard Hartman and Hollywood publicity agent Jonni Hartman. Jonni, who became her daughter's manager, recalls that Lisa told her she wanted to be a star as early as age four. As a kid, Lisa modeled, did local theater, and made commercials. At age sixteen, she fronted her own Houston rock band. She was discovered by noted pop songwriter Jeff Barry.

"I was doing 'Proud Mary' and all these songs with my band," Lisa recalls. "He said, 'I want to see if you can really sing.' So he played me a song called 'Room Without a Door' that he had written. It was beautiful. It was a cool song. He said, 'Can you sing this?' And I did. In March of 1975, I went to L.A. In March of 1976, my first album was released."

*Lisa Hartman* (1976), *Hold On* (1979), *Letterock* (1982), and *'Til*

*My Heart Stops* (1987) all appeared before Clint released his first album. None of them yielded any pop hits for Lisa, but that scarcely mattered, because her acting career caught fire instead. During the 1976–1977 TV season, she starred in the series *Tabitha,* a spin-off of the long-running hit *Bewitched.* In 1982–1986, Lisa rose to stardom as a "bad girl" on the hit nighttime soap opera *Knots Landing.* She had recurring roles on *Love Boat* (1979), *Matlock* (1988), and *2000 Malibu Road* (1992). Most significantly, Lisa Hartman Black has become the queen of made-for-TV movies. To date, she has starred in more than two dozen of these, including 1987's *Roses Are for the Rich,* 1981's *Jacqueline Susann's Valley of the Dolls,* and 1991's *The Return of Eliot Ness.* Lisa and Clint costarred in 1998's *Still Holding On: The Legend of Cadillac Jack.*

The atmosphere in the Black household in suburban Nashville is remarkably serene. Daughter Lilly was born in 2001, and both parents dote on her. Clint and Lisa never raise their voices to one another, seldom argue, and are still lovebirds.

"When he's really stressed, I go into this calm," Lisa reports. "When I'm really stressed, he goes into this calm. We've never exploded at each other. We're both very strong, very opinionated, and a little bull-headed, but we're very considerate of each other. We presume the best of each other. We never take each other for granted."

Says Clint, "When Roy Rogers found out we were getting married, he said, 'I'll give you one piece of advice: Don't ever go to bed angry.' And it's true.

"The joke I always say is that we figure out the things that irritate one another, and then I don't do them anymore."

In addition to maintaining his career as a singer, songwriter, and performer, in recent years Clint Black has become a Music Row business mogul as well. In 2001, he formed his song-publishing company, and it has had such huge hits as Blake Shelton's "Some Beach" and Billy Currington's "Must Be Doin' Somethin' Right." In 2003, he became the coowner of the record company Equity Music Group. It distributes his discs as well as those of such favorites as Mark Wills, Carolyn Dawn Johnson, and the million-selling Little Big Town. He produced singer Buddy Jewell's top-selling debut album. Clint also owns his own recording studio. He says he's able to juggle all of this because of Lisa's steadying presence.

"She recognizes my breaking points before I do," he comments. "When the stress gets to be too much or I'm exhausted and have no energy to give, she says, 'Look, you've done this and this and this, and you haven't stopped. That's why you're feeling this way.' . . . And then I'll go into strategy mode: 'How am I going to manage this?'"

CLINT AND LISA AREN'T the only Opry-and-Hollywood combination. In 2003, the show's Brad Paisley married national television star Kimberly Williams.

Brad, a West Virginia native born on October 28, 1972, rose to stardom in 1999–2000 on the strength of such hits as "He Didn't Have to Be," "Me Neither," and "We Danced." After making forty-three guest appearances on the show, he was made a member of the Grand Ole Opry's cast on February 17, 2001.

Like his fellow cast members Clint Black, Steve Wariner, and Vince Gill, Brad is a "triple threat" as a songwriter, singer, and hot-shot guitarist. He has collaborated vocally with fellow Opry stars ranging from George Jones to Dolly Parton. His award-winning 2004 duet with Alison Krauss, "Whiskey Lullaby," was cowritten by the Opry's Bill Anderson.

Fiddler and singer Alison is one of the reasons that bluegrass music has enjoyed its recent resurgence in popularity. She also led the invasion of female artists into this formerly male-dominated genre. Alison, born July 23, 1971, is a native of Champaign, Illinois, who became a child prodigy on the fiddle. She recorded her debut album when she was only sixteen. She became an Opry cast member on July 3, 1993.

In 2002, her "Whiskey Lullaby" duet partner scored his third number-one record with "I'm Gonna Miss Her (The Fishin'

Song)." Its video featured blue-eyed brunette Kimberly Williams. The story goes that Brad first spotted Kimberly in 1991's *Father of the Bride,* her debut film appearance. After he broke up with his girlfriend, he wrote a song called "Part Two," wherein he wished that romances could have sequels like Hollywood hit movies. Kimberly did, indeed, make *Father of the Bride Part II* in 1995. So Brad contacted her about appearing in his video for "Part Two." Truth be told, it was a ruse to meet her. There was no video for that song.

Kimberly was born September 14, 1971, in Rye, New York. In addition to the *Father of the Bride* movies, she has been featured in such films as *Indian Summer* (1993), *The War at Home* (1996), *Simpatico* (1999), *Shade* (2006), and *We Are Marshall* (2007). She is best known for her work in the long-running ABC sitcom *According to Jim.*

After several telephone conversations, Kimberly asked Brad out on a date. He proposed in 2002, and they were married on March 15, 2003. She added his last name to hers in order to differentiate herself from a *Playboy* model also named Kimberly Williams. The Paisleys divide their time between homes in Los Angeles and Nashville, where son William Huckleberry "Huck" Paisley was born in 2007.

# Kiss an Angel Good Mornin'

Charley Pride often says that his wife Rozene has more sense than he does, and she is the more educated and outgoing of the two. But the truth of the matter is that they're both very bright and very dedicated.

"She went to college, and I only had an eleventh-grade education," says Charley. "I always felt that I was sharp, and she is a pretty sharp lady.

"We only dated for five months before we were married. So sometimes things just happen, and they work out."

And how. On December 28, 2006, the couple celebrated their golden wedding anniversary. What is the secret to having a fifty-year marriage?

"We don't really have a remedy," Charley says. "We've always done what fit us, what we thought we could live with. We try to give each other enough space. We try to let each other be themselves. Marriage comes down to two people being one. It's not 'Mine is mine, and yours is yours,' none of that kind of stuff. We never fought over any money, which we didn't have when we first got married.

"From the time we got married, we just kind of did it little by little. We just got used to each other more and more.

"She has a good sense of humor, and I think I do too. We get on each other's nerves a lot of times. But deep down, we love each other. Plus, we kind of like each other quite a bit."

As for Rozene, she thinks there are three secrets to a long marriage: "One is space. He has his space, and I have mine. His space consists of golf every day, and my space means going to the office and taking care of business so he can golf every day. Two is communication. Very important. He communicates. I listen. Three, the main reason for such longevity is that neither of us has died."

As she indicates, throughout Charley's career, Rozene Pride has been working behind the scenes on the business side of things. She coordinates his fan club and concert-tour activities. She handles the finances. She calls him "Pride," not Charley.

"Pride's career is definitely a full-time job for all of us," she says.

"She runs the show," he says with a chuckle.

In 1997, Rozene told *Jet* magazine, "Maybe part of our secret has been that we have worked together, and we each have our area. . . . I have no desire to be in the public eye. I am perfectly happy working in the background and doing what I can for him.

"Of course, we disagree at times, because we both think. If there are two people in the house and they don't ever disagree, somebody isn't thinking. I will admit that I am very strong willed, and so is he."

Charley had to be strong willed to come from where he did and get where he is. Born Charley Frank Pride on March 18, 1938, he is one of eleven children of sharecroppers who farmed near Sledge, Mississippi. Charley says that the lyrics of his 1974 hit "Mississippi Cotton Picking Delta Town" are an accurate description of his youth.

"That song was written about my hometown by a guy who grew up there. His name was Harold Dorman. He's passed away now. But he worked for the grocery store there in Sledge where we got our groceries every weekend. If you grew up at the time I grew up in Mississippi, you were cotton pickers. That's about the whole ball game there.

"Hard-luck backgrounds and poverty and such things, I've thought about that quite a bit. It's like the old adage, 'You never miss what you never had.' I think there's a lot of truth in that. I realized that other kids had bicycles and various different things that I never did get. But I just never believed in sitting around feeling sorry for myself. I always worked hard and felt that, yes, there was something else out there.

"I don't really look back on that as hard times, because I had a lot of brothers and sisters. We fought, and we loved, and we talked, and we grew up together. It was one of those things you just accepted and did the best that you could do. I dreamed, yes, and I still do. I was gonna be the greatest baseball player that ever lived."

He was captivated by the family's Philco radio set. It taught him that there was a world outside the Delta cotton fields. Charley was enthralled by the radio dramas and by baseball broadcasts. Inspired by the country music he heard, he taught himself to play guitar. But in those days, sports were his true focus. He left Sledge at age sixteen to pitch and play outfield in what was then called the American Negro League. One of the teams he played for was the Memphis Red Sox.

At a Memphis restaurant frequented by the team, Charley met Rozene. She was a cosmetologist. He was smitten. He visited her at the beauty shop, asked her out, and courted her. Rozene was as urban and sophisticated as he was rural and backward. Even more impressive to him was her love of baseball.

As Charley put it in his autobiography, "She was smart, beautiful, independent and could explain the infield fly rule. What else could a guy want?"

But their romance looked like it might be nipped in the bud. Charley was drafted into the army in November 1956. A month into basic training, the new recruits were given passes to go back home for Christmas. Worried that he would lose her, Charley proposed to Rozene. They were married by a justice of the peace in Hernando, Mississippi, on December 28, 1956. Charley was still in the army when son Kraig was born, in 1957. In 1960, the family relocated to Helena, Montana, where Charley worked in mining.

"I didn't work in any mines. I worked in the smelter that took ore from the mines and processed the zinc and so forth out of it. I was singing locally there. [At a Red Foley concert] I went backstage and asked could I play the guitar. The promoter had heard me sing, so he said to me, 'Would you like to do a couple of songs on the second half of the show?' So I did. The songs I did were 'Heartaches by the Number' that Ray Price had as a big hit and 'Lovesick Blues' by the great Hank Williams. Red Foley and Red Sovine looked at one another and said, 'It's odd, but you ought to go to Nashville. You're country.' So that's what I did."

Second son, Dion, was born that same year, 1962. If Charley had not met those Nashville stars, he believes he probably would have settled down in Montana and raised his family. He'd broken his ankle at the smelting plant. When it healed, Charley gave baseball one last shot. He went to the 1963 spring-training camp of the New York Mets in Clearwater, Florida. But manager Casey Stengel turned him away without even letting him try out.

On the way home, going north, Charley decided to stop in Nashville. Red Sovine (1918–1980) had told him to look up Cedarwood Publishing, where he would be welcome to audition. When he did, he was heard by Jack Johnson, who signed Charley to a management contract. Daughter Angela was born in 1965, and Charley's and Rozene's Mississippi families hadn't seen the new baby. While heading south to visit, he stopped to pester Jack about getting him a recording contract.

Jack Johnson convinced producer/songwriter Jack Clement to record Charley singing some tunes during the Prides' southern sojourn. Jack Clement took the tape to Chet Atkins at RCA Records. By year's end, Charley was an RCA recording artist.

"I guess when a history is written on country music years from now, I'll be remembered because I signed Charley Pride, which was a great civic thing to do in those days," recalled Chet. "There were no black country singers. Jack Clement came to me, my dear friend, and he said, 'You gotta hear my singer.' He used that 'N' word. A few days went by, and I thought, 'Boy, that would be really different, that would be great.' I called him and said, 'Where's that black guy you were gonna let me hear sing?' So he brought this demonstration record of 'The Snakes Crawl at Night,' and I thought he was great. He's got an edge to his voice. It sounded good on a bad jukebox. He had an edge like a Hank Snow or an Ernest Tubb.

"So I took the record to California and of course they thought it was great until I told them he was black, and then they still thought it was great. They said, 'This'll be very different.' The only determination we had to make was whether to put his picture on the sleeve of the record to let the people down South know that he was black, because we thought maybe they might boycott our records or something. And we were wrong. We were completely wrong. We never had one complaint.

"I asked Charley, 'Why do you just sing country? Do you sing anything else?' He said, 'No. My dad would tune in that Grand Ole Opry every Saturday night, and I liked it. I learned to sing like some of those guys, and that's the way it happened.' He pulled it off better than anyone ever could have. He's just such a great gentleman, and he's sharp, and he's a hell of a singer. And I'm so proud of that accomplishment. I think I'll be remembered for that if not anything else."

In early 1966, the Mel Tillis tune "The Snakes Crawl at Night" became Charley's first country single. Toward the end of the year, he made the charts with "Just Between You and Me," written by Jack Clement. Rozene was still working as a medical technician in Montana. Charley nervously resigned from the smelter to see if he could make any money singing his first songs.

"Royalty checks were a long way off and a long time coming," Charley recalled in his autobiography. "Rozene and I still lived as frugally as we had before, determined to pick our way slowly across this new terrain, taking nothing for granted, spending nothing until it was in the bank."

To everyone's surprise and relief, country audiences embraced

Charley warmly when he hit the road. His sincerity, solid country singing, and quips about having a "permanent tan" charmed fans everywhere.

"My first time that I appeared on the Grand Ole Opry was in 1967, January 1. I was elated, happy, scared, and nervous. I mean, all those in one. I appeared on the Opry many times after that, and every time it brought back those nervous butterflies I had back in 1967, when Ernest Tubb brought me on for that first appearance."

He was invited to join the Opry cast but had to decline because he was suddenly too busy to become a regular. In 1969, he landed his first number-one record, "All I Have to Offer You Is Me." In 1971 came his signature song "Kiss an Angel Good Mornin'." By the mid-1970s, Charley Pride was outselling every star on RCA's roster with the exception of Elvis Presley. Charley used his clout to help launch the careers of other million sellers, such as Janie Fricke, Neal McCoy, and Ronnie Milsap.

"In terms of helping country music to expand, I truly believe that I was part of that," says the thirty-million-selling Country Music Hall of Fame member.

His open-ended invitation to perform on the Opry remained in place until he was formally inducted into the Grand Ole Opry cast on May 1, 1993.

"I've done shows all over the world, but there is a special magic about stepping onto the Opry stage," says Charley Pride. "But I never thought I'd actually make it onto the stage at the Ryman Auditorium or become a member of the Opry, which is truly the icing on the cake."

# A Woman's Love

In 2007, Alan Jackson sang movingly of "A Woman's Love." His wife, Denise, gave him much more than her love—she gave him his career.

"I was thinking about coming to Nashville in 1985," Alan recalls. "I didn't know anybody. I'd never been to Nashville—I'd hardly been out of Georgia my whole life. I didn't even know what producers did or what publishers were. I didn't have a clue. My wife had just started flying with airlines [as a flight attendant], and she saw Glen Campbell and his band waiting for a flight in Atlanta. We'd never been around stars or anything. But she just walked up to him and introduced herself. She told him we were thinking about moving to Nashville and asked him if he had any advice.

"I wasn't the kind of person who felt comfortable approaching celebrities," wrote Denise in her best-selling book *It's All About Him,* "but I knew this opportunity wasn't going to come by again any time soon.

"He looked just as I remembered him from the *Glen Campbell Goodtime Hour* on TV when I was a child. . . . I knew what I had to do."

"She wasn't submitting a tape to him or anything," Alan recalls. "I didn't even have a tape. And Glen was real nice. He gave her the business card of Marty Gamblin, who ran his publishing company in Nashville. So she brought that home, and I thought, 'Boy, there's a connection!' I didn't have any others. So I came to Nashville, and that's the first place I went. Knocked on his door. Marty said, 'Well, I don't know what to tell you, but you're here. I guess you ought to get a job and start writing and singing demos and that kind of stuff.' So that's what I did."

It turned out that Glen had given Marty Gamblin's business card to many other aspiring country performers. But Alan is the only one who followed through and turned up on Marty's doorstep two weeks later.

Denise's "connection" paid off. Alan took a job in the mailroom at The Nashville Network (TNN) cable TV channel and applied himself to writing songs. In 1986, Marty Gamblin signed him as a $100-a-week songwriter, which enabled Alan to quit TNN and hit the road with his band. His publisher introduced him to music-industry figures up and down Music Row. He badgered record labels to sign Alan. He financed the recording session that led to Alan's signing a contract with Arista Records on June 26, 1989. The process took more than four years, but Alan and Denise never gave up and never lost hope.

Alan's subsequent success is all the more remarkable because there was so little in his upbringing in Newnan, Georgia, that pre-pared him for it. Born October 17, 1958, he was the fifth child and only son of an auto mechanic/assembly-line worker and his wife.

"We weren't starvin' poor or anything, but we weren't that well off," says Alan of his family. "We grew up more backwards than we did poor. I played with my cousins. My grandmother lived next door. It was like the Waltons. It was a real different kind of lifestyle than a lot of people had who grew up in that time. I think that helped me look at things a little different. I think that helps with your songwriting, and why a lot of people connect with some of the songs I write about everyday living."

Alan has frequently referred to his early lifestyle in his songwrit-ing. Hits such as "Chattahoochee," "Livin' on Love," "Where I

Come From," and "Small Town Southern Man" all refer, in various ways, to the roots of his raising. "Chasin' That Neon Rainbow" was the first of his hits that referred to his passion for country music.

"A lot of the artists in music that I liked were the older acts . . . what I call real country music. We listened to Conway Twitty and George Jones and Gene Watson and John Conlee and all of them people.

"When *Hee Haw* came out [in 1969], that was probably the earliest I remember being affected by real country music. My daddy watched that religiously. My daddy didn't say much, but I just remember this one time, Buck Owens was playing on that show and he said, 'You ought to be one of them singers,' or something like that. I don't know why it struck me. Even at that moment, it wasn't like, 'Okay, that's what I'm gonna do.' But I do remember that. And I'd always enjoyed music.

"I was a big Hank Williams Jr. fan, and I always sang his songs. I can do a ton of Don Williams songs, too, because I'm a big fan of his. I could do two albums' worth of Merle Haggard songs. I'm a huge fan of Charley Pride's."

He started taking guitar lessons in 1974. He began singing country music in public when he was in high school. He also landed a role in his high school's production of the cowboy musical *Oklahoma!*

"As I got to be a teenager, it was pretty pop-heavy at school. And disco, when I was in high school, and I survived all that. I started a little duo, singing with a girl who played guitar and sang harmony. We did all kinds of stuff. Most of it was kind of folky-country stuff.

"Then I hung out with a guy who was a little older than me, and we started our first little band. This little band played on the weekends. There really weren't hardly any clubs around the area. So it was more just playing little private parties, playing pizza joints or a little beer joint here and there. You'd play some current stuff that was on the radio. And you'd play some old stuff, and that's what I did. I sang Gene Watson, George Jones, George Strait, John Anderson, and John Conlee."

The band had been a rock group. But once group member Cody Deal heard Alan sing, the band completely changed its style to country. It was renamed Dixie Steel, after the brand name on a box of nails in Cody's basement rehearsal space.

In 1976, Alan Jackson spotted a pretty blonde sixteen-year-old at the Newnan Dairy Queen. He flirted with Denise by walking over to her table and tossing a penny down her blouse. When she drove away from the restaurant, Alan surprised her by popping up from the car's backseat, where he'd been hiding. Denise screamed and nearly drove off the road. She turned him down the first time he asked her for a date. She was captain of the cheerleading squad, the homecoming queen, a star tennis player, and a straight-A student. Alan wasn't on any sports teams. He just played guitar and worked on cars.

A few months later, he ran into her and asked her if she'd like a ride in his gleaming-white, fully restored 1955 Thunderbird convertible. The next time he called to ask her out, she said yes. Alan and Denise were married on December 15, 1979. At the ceremony, he sang Pat Terry's nuptial anthem "That's the Way" to her. Alan sold his beloved T-bird for $10,000 so that he could make a down payment on a house for them.

By this time, Dixie Steel had become regionally popular. The group came in second at a talent contest in Atlanta. People began telling the singer that he was as good as anyone in Nashville. But Alan was reluctant to give up job security to take a chance in Nashville.

He'd been working practically all his life. Alan's first job was cleaning up in a shoe-repair store at age twelve. He bought his own cars by working throughout junior high and high school. He worked as a carpenter and furniture salesman. He was a fork-lift operator at the regional Kmart warehouse on the night shift. In 1979, he began working at the Newnan Motor Company, selling Fords.

"I didn't really have a lot of friends. I didn't really socialize much until I got to be sixteen or seventeen. I kept to myself a lot and worked most of the time. That's all I did was work and try to save money to buy a car.

In fact, when the Jacksons first moved to Nashville, it was the first time that Alan didn't have a job. After his stint in the TNN mailroom, he worked at music full-time for the first time in his life. Throughout the first ten years of their marriage, Alan and Denise clung to their dreams. The reason his break in Music City was so long in coming was that everyone in power thought he was "too country."

"They always said that," Alan confirms. "It's pretty weird. When I moved to town, Randy Travis had just hit, and I thought, 'Man, this is it.' Because at that time, I felt like the country music that I was hearing was a lot more pop-based and a little slicker and middle-of-the-road. When Randy hit, I thought, 'This is it. They're opening up. Randy paved the way for me.' But I pounded around town for four, five years, and people just wouldn't sign me. A lot of the acts that were getting signed were more slick. So I always said, 'Well, I'm just too country for country music.'"

Even after signing with Arista, Alan faced an uphill battle. His first single, 1989's "Blue Blooded Woman," flopped. The label put him on the road to meet radio decision makers, so he wasn't making any money. It didn't look like the best time to be starting a family, but Denise was pregnant. Daughter Mattie was born in 1990.

On October 6, 1990, he sang "Here in the Real World," the song that catapulted him to stardom, at his debut appearance on the Grand Ole Opry. Coincidentally, that was the same night that Garth Brooks became an Opry member. A year later, Alan was invited to join the cast of the Grand Ole Opry, too.

"The Grand Ole Opry, the first time I walked out there it scared me to death. I'd been on the stage, because I worked over at The Nashville Network for about eleven months when I first moved to town. And I used to go over there and stand on that stage during the day when I was delivering their mail to them. I always thought it would be pretty cool to come out there and sing. But I never thought it would happen. But there I was.

"What I really think about the Grand Ole Opry is that it is the cornerstone of country music. It's made country music. It's the mother. And it's something I would like to see go on forever."

Randy Travis inducted Alan into the show's cast on June 7, 1991. Randy invited Alan to be his opening act on tour in 1992. The two cowrote Alan's hit "She's Got the Rhythm" and Randy's hits "Better Class of Losers," "Forever Together," and "I'd Surrender All."

On the road, fans responded powerfully to Alan's shy humility, dry sense of humor, drawling speech, lanky 6-foot 4-inch frame, and blond, blue-eyed good looks. His laid-back charm matched the honest simplicity of his music.

By 1993, Alan Jackson was headlining his own concerts and had welcomed his second daughter, Ali. For that year's Christmas gift, Denise tracked down Alan's 1955 Thunderbird, bought it back, and presented it to her delighted husband.

"Don't Rock the Jukebox," "Gone Country," and other block-buster hits led to ten million in record sales by 1994. *A Lot About Livin' (And a Little 'Bout Love)* sold six million more, and he was named the Country Music Association's Entertainer of the Year in 1995. Alan Jackson was as big as any star in Nashville in the late 1990s. But he was not a happy man. Shortly after the family moved to their Williamson County mansion, south of Nashville, and his third daughter, Dani, was born, Alan announced that he and Denise were separating. Just before Thanksgiving in 1997, he told his wife he was moving out. When Denise returned from a Christmas ski vacation, his things were gone. This painful time in their lives serves as the emotional centerpiece of her inspirational book.

"He had come to a point in his life," Denise wrote, "where he was realizing that all the material things in the world did not buy happiness. Everyone knows that . . . but it's another thing altogether to experience it. Alan had realized his greatest goals of music stardom, and enormous wealth and fame. But it didn't fill his heart.

"One day he stood in front of our 25,000-square-foot mansion, looking over the perfect house and the perfectly manicured grounds and the perfect garages full of cars and boats and airplanes . . . and he whispered, 'I'm still not happy.' In some ways, I became the focal point of Alan's unhappiness."

During the separation, he lost 25 pounds. Denise plunged into anger and depression, but then she found strength in a renewed religious commitment. After three months apart, Alan asked her out on a date. They went into marriage counseling. In May 1998, Alan Jackson returned to his home and family. The following Sunday was Mother's Day, and Denise and the girls returned from church to find Alan surprising them with a feast he'd cooked.

Through the remainder of the year, the Jacksons rebuilt their relationship. He confessed his infidelities. She continued to pray for reconciliation. On their nineteenth wedding anniversary, they exchanged new rings and renewed their vows. Alan again sang "That's the Way" to his bride.

In 2001, a few weeks after the terrorist attacks of September 11, Alan woke from a fitful sleep and began writing the moving ballad "Where Were You (When the World Stopped Turning)." People wept when he introduced it on the CMA awards show on November 7. Alan Jackson became the only artist, in any field of music, to create a lasting song of healing in the wake of the tragedy. "Where Were You (When the World Stopped Turning)" is a true testament to his power as a songwriter.

"God wrote it," he said humbly. "I just held the pencil."

The song earned him a Grammy Award and CMA Single and Song of the Year awards. An estimated 3,500 people attended a 2001 Music Row outdoor party to celebrate Alan Jackson's 35 million in record sales. Among them were his fellow Opry stars Jimmy Dickens, Trace Adkins, and George Jones.

The hits and awards kept coming for Alan, but in 2007, it was Denise Jackson who took the spotlight. She was not only featured in her husband's video for "A Woman's Love," she published her memoir *It's All About Him: Finding the Love of My Life.* Cowritten with Ellen Vaughn, the inspirational volume contained a foreword written by Alan, plus a CD containing his recordings of their wedding song, "That's the Way," and a new tune, "It's All About Him." On July 26, Denise's publisher celebrated the book's debut with a gala party at Nashville's Schermerhorn Symphony Center.

"She's always been the better half of this combo," said Alan. "I'm glad she's getting the chance to shine for a change. I've been in the spotlight too long, so I'm glad to be in the backfield. So many people are going to appreciate this book.

"She's a special person. We've always loved each other. We just didn't like each other sometimes. We grew up together and survived.

"So now you're thanking me for all that heartache you had to write about?" he kidded her at the event. "She's probably the reason God didn't strike me dead a long time ago. I'm obviously very proud of Denise and so happy that she finally gets the chance to step from the side of the stage to the center and enjoy her own accomplishment."

In its first week of release, *It's All About Him* reached number one on *The New York Times* best-seller list. Denise went on a whirlwind book tour. Requests poured in for her to speak to various women's groups.

"I commented to him, 'This is so exhausting,'" Denise told *The Tennessean* newspaper. "He just laughed and said, 'Welcome to the entertainment world. Now you see what it's really like.'"

As for Alan, "I just do what I like and what I feel I do best. Country music is America's music. It's America's common-man poetry. It always has been, and it's got to be preserved somehow. I'll just continue to do what I do, whether I keep selling records or not. I don't see any reason to change."

# Broken Duets

Of all the tragedies that have befallen the Grand Ole Opry's stars, few are as difficult to bear as beloved duet teams that are torn apart.

Opry star Emmylou Harris was devastated by the death of her singing partner Gram Parsons in 1973. In addition to intense grief, Emmylou was also facing the prospect of having her career end before it had truly begun. Gram was the reason she became a country singer in the first place.

Born on April 2, 1947, Emmylou Harris is the daughter of a marine corps officer who had been a prisoner of war during the Korean War. She grew up as a military brat on various military bases around the South. She attended the University of North Carolina and Boston University but became swept up in the folk-music boom of the 1960s. She moved to Greenwich Village in New York in 1967 and made a folk LP called *Gliding Bird* in 1969. After a brief sojourn in Nashville, she settled in suburban Washington, D.C., in 1970 as a divorcee with a baby daughter.

She started singing in folk clubs again in 1971. Chris Hillman, who later became a country star in The Desert Rose Band, heard her perform in D.C. and told Gram Parsons about her. Gram loved what he heard and a year later paid for her to fly to the West Coast to harmonize with him on his debut solo album, *GP*. She was even more prominently featured on a second collaboration with Gram, *Grievous Angel*, but he died from drug and alcohol abuse on September 19, 1973, at age twenty-six, four months before the record was released.

Although Emmylou had a brother who was a country-music fan, it was Gram Parsons who truly taught her to love the style. His vision was to take his passion for country to the rock audience. After his death, Emmylou made that mission her own. And that crusade is what took her from being a derailed duet partner to becoming a star.

Emmylou married record producer Brian Ahern in 1977. He produced the discs that were her early hits. Her second daughter is their child. After their divorce, in 1984, she moved to Nashville with her girls. Emmylou's third marriage was to British-born Nashville songwriter Paul Kennerley, a union that lasted from 1985 to 1992.

Her long string of hits, her reputation for musical integrity, and the universal respect she has in the Nashville entertainment community led to an offer to join the cast of the Grand Ole Opry. Emmylou Harris became an Opry member on January 25, 1992. In 2008, she was elected to the Country Music Hall of Fame.

THE OPRY CAST MEMBER whose shattered duet most resembles Emmylou's was the late Skeeter Davis. Like Emmylou, she was just beginning her career when her duet partner, Betty Jack Davis (1932–1953), was killed in an automobile accident.

Born Mary Frances Penick on December 30, 1931, she was dubbed "Skeeter" by her family because of her high-strung, energetic nature. When she formed a vocal duet with her high school friend Betty Jack Davis, Skeeter adopted her last name, and they began to record as The Davis Sisters. "I Forgot More Than You'll Ever Know" became a number-one country hit for the team in 1953. But the week it topped the charts, the girls were involved in a car crash in which Betty Jack was killed while traveling home to Kentucky from an appearance on the WWVA *Wheeling Jamboree* in West Virginia.

After she recovered from her injuries, Skeeter toured and recorded in 1954–1956 as The Davis Sisters with Betty Jack's sister Georgia. Then producer Chet Atkins suggested that Skeeter harmonize with herself in the recording studio. The sound was still that of a "duet," but Skeeter was now a solo star.

She had a big hit with 1959's "Set Him Free" and joined the Grand Ole Opry cast in August of that year. Skeeter's "The End of the World" was a massive pop and country hit in 1963, and she sang it on the Opry stage throughout the rest of her long career. Skeeter Davis died of cancer on September 19, 2004, at age seventy-two.

BROTHER-DUET SINGING REACHED ITS peak in the works of The Louvin Brothers. Older brother Ira Loudermilk was born April 21, 1924, and singing partner Charlie came along on July 7, 1927. They developed an electrifying vocal sound, with Charlie anchoring the melody and playing guitar while Ira sang sky-high harmony and played mandolin. The Louvin Brothers came from their native Alabama to Music City and became stars with such records as "When I Stop Dreaming," "I Don't Believe You've Met My Baby," "You're Running Wild," and "My Baby's Gone" in 1955–1959. The siblings joined the Opry on February 26, 1955.

But theirs was a volatile partnership. Like many brother teams, the Louvins grew to dislike one another. After a 1963 show with Ray Price in August in Watseta, Illinois, Ira announced to Charlie that it was their last. After attending a previously scheduled recording session back in Nashville, the team split up. Charlie continued on the Opry as a solo act. Ira formed a duet with his Canadian-born wife, yodeler Anne Young, and recorded a solo album.

Then a car crash ended Ira's life, dashing any hopes of a reconciliation between the brothers. Ira and Anne and a couple traveling with them were returning from shows they'd performed in

Missouri when they had a horrible head-on collision with another car on June 20, 1965. Everyone perished. Ira Louvin was forty-one years old.

Charlie Louvin went on to have a long solo career. He introduced songs from such stellar writers as Bill Anderson (1964's "I Don't Love You Anymore" and 1965's "Think I'll Go Somewhere and Cry Myself to Sleep"), Roger Miller (1965's "Less and Less"), Ed Bruce (1965's "See the Big Man Cry"), Dallas Frazier (1968's "Will You Visit Me on Sundays"), and Bobby Braddock (1970's "Something to Brag About" and 1971's "Did You Ever," both duets with Melba Montgomery). He enjoyed a career resurgence in the Americana field with his self-titled 2007 CD with the support of Elvis Costello, Marty Stuart, Jeff Tweedy, George Jones, Bobby Bare, and Tom T. Hall. Its standout track was the moving "Ira," a tribute to his departed brother and duet partner.

OPRY STAR RALPH STANLEY was the "junior" half of his duet team, too. And his older brother, Carter Stanley, died at age forty-one, just as Ira Louvin did. Guitarist and lead vocalist Carter, born on August 27, 1925, formed the bluegrass band The Clinch Mountain Boys in 1946 with his banjo-playing younger brother Ralph, whose birth date is February 25, 1927. The Virginia mountain duo recorded classic songs for Mercury Records, Rich R Tone Records, Columbia Records, and King Records in the 1940s through the 1960s.

Carter began to suffer from internal hemorrhaging. After he died on December 1, 1966, Ralph was uncertain about what to do. He'd never been the group leader, but music was all he knew, so he decided to carry on. He led a series of stellar Clinch Mountain Boys from whose ranks emerged such stars as Ricky Skaggs, Larry Sparks, Charlie Sizemore, and Keith Whitley.

The Stanley Brothers were elected to the Bluegrass Music Hall of Honor in 1992. As he aged, Ralph evolved into an icon of Appalachia. Ralph Stanley was made a member of the Grand Ole Opry on January 15, 2000—the first new cast member of the new millennium. His work on the acclaimed soundtrack of the film *O Brother, Where Art Thou?* earned him a Grammy Award in 2000, and in 2006 he was presented with a National Medal of Arts in Washington, D.C.

THE DELMORE BROTHERS WERE one of the earliest duos to join the Opry, entering the cast in the spring of 1933. Their gentle harmonies, fireside warmth, burnished songwriting skills, and deftly strummed dual-guitar accompaniment made this duo one of the most enchanting of all the old-time music acts. Alton Delmore was the older brother, born December 25, 1908. Rabon Delmore was born December 3, 1916. They hailed from rural Alabama.

The duo initially rose to fame with such softly crooned tunes as "Brown's Ferry Blues" and "Gonna Lay Down My Old Guitar" in 1933. Alton was also the creator of the country standard "Beautiful Brown Eyes." At the Opry, The Delmore Brothers were second only to Uncle Dave Macon in popularity. They loved the Opry but never got along with its leader, George D. Hay. In the fall of 1938, the Delmores left the cast. They eventually wound up at WLW in Cincinnati. That city's King Records label signed them and brought them to renewed stardom with 1946's "Freight Train Boogie" and 1949's chart-topping "Blues Stay Away from Me."

But this career revival was sadly brief. They returned to Nashville so that Rabon could be operated on at Vanderbilt Hospital, but he died of cancer on December 4, 1952, at the age of thirty-six. Alton wrote one of country music's most engaging autobiographies, *Truth Is Stranger Than Publicity,* before dying at age fifty-five of a liver disorder, on June 8, 1964. The Delmore Brothers were elected to the Nashville Songwriters Hall of Fame in 1971 and the Country Music Hall of Fame in 2001. Alton's son Lionel Delmore (1940–2002) became the successful songwriting collaborator of John Anderson's ("Swingin'," "Bend It Until It Breaks," etc.).

★　　　★　　　★

ANOTHER OPRY BROTHER DUO team, the Wilburn Brothers, grew up performing in a family band in Missouri and Arkansas. Doyle Wilburn was born on July 7, 1930, and Teddy Wilburn followed on November 30, 1931. Their pitch-perfect, close-harmony vocals attracted the attention of both the Opry and Decca Records, and they signed with both in 1953. Although they had a number of hits in the 1950s, the Wilburn Brothers' biggest successes came with such hits of the 1960s as "Trouble's Back in Town," "Hurt Her Once for Me," and "It's Another World."

They formed their Sure-Fire Music publishing company and Wil-Helm talent agency. Their most famous client became Loretta Lynn. Doyle got her signed to Decca Records. Teddy polished her songwriting and worked with her in the studio. The brothers also featured her on their syndicated television show. In 1973–1974, *The Wilburn Brothers Show* showcased Loretta's distant cousin, teenager Patty Loveless.

Doyle's health deteriorated during the 1970s. He died of cancer on October 16, 1982, at age fifty-two. For the next twenty years, Teddy carried on as a solo singer on the Opry, but he never really got over the loss of his brother and partner. Teddy was seventy-one when he died, on November 24, 2003.

THE LONGEST-LASTING BROTHER DUET in history was Jim & Jesse. The death of Jim McReynolds ended fifty-five years of togetherness. Guitarist-singer Jim was born February 13, 1927. Younger brother Jesse McReynolds, a singer and a dazzling mandolin innovator, was born July 9, 1929. They grew up in the mountains of Virginia and began their recording career in 1951. Jim & Jesse joined the Opry cast on March 2, 1964.

The team became superstars on the bluegrass-festival circuit. Every time the courtly Jim & Jesse appeared on the Opry stage, they were models of class and professionalism. Jim & Jesse were inducted into the Bluegrass Music Hall of Honor in 1993. Both brothers were diagnosed with cancer in 2002. Jim succumbed to the disease at age seventy-five, on December 31, 2002. Jesse has carried on, fronting a new edition of his band The Virginia Boys.

BOBBY OSBORNE, STILL SINGING more powerfully than many men half his age, has also continued as a solo artist after his long partnership with brother Sonny ended. The Osborne Brothers have immortalized such songs as "Once More," "Ruby (Are You Mad)," and, of course, "Rocky Top." The duo was somewhat controversial in bluegrass circles because of its willingness to use amplified instruments and Nashville Sound production touches. But it also created some of the genre's most exciting records and was justifiably inducted into the Bluegrass Music Hall of Honor in 1994.

Older brother Bobby Osborne is renowned for his piercing tenor vocals and driving mandolin work. He was born December 7, 1931. Sonny Osborne is much admired as a banjo stylist. He is also a walking encyclopedia of country-music knowledge. Sonny was born October 29, 1937. The Kentucky natives developed as musicians in various bands before joining forces in 1956. The Osborne Brothers joined the Opry cast in 1964 and were named the Country Music Association's Group of the Year in 1971. Sonny announced his retirement in 2005 and suffered a mild stroke in January 2007.

PERHAPS THE SADDEST OF all the Opry's broken duets was one that didn't have a hit collaboration until after one partner's tragic death. Following Keith Whitley's demise, widow Lorrie Morgan harmonized with a tape of his voice. "'Til a Tear Becomes a Rose" became a hit duet in 1990 and won a CMA award as the Vocal Event of the Year.

Lorrie Morgan has been on the Grand Ole Opry stage her whole life. She is the daughter of Opry crooner George Morgan (1924–1975), who sang such ballads as "Candy Kisses," "Room Full of Roses," and "Almost." Born in Nashville on June 27, 1959, Lorrie made her Opry debut at age thirteen, singing the Marie Osmond/

Anita Bryant favorite "Paper Roses." She was also at the Opry for its last performance at the Ryman Auditorium, on March 15, 1974, and its first in the new Opry House the next night. Her father George was the last Opry star to sing in the old hall and was one of the first to sing in the new one.

After her father's untimely death at age fifty-one from a heart attack, Lorrie Morgan sang at the Opryland theme park, at the Nashville Palace nightclub, on Ralph Emery's *Nashville Now* TV show, and on the Opry. On the road, she opened shows for Opry legend George Jones. She recorded a series of singles that went nowhere. Nevertheless, the Opry invited her to become a cast member, and she was inducted on June 9, 1984. Lorrie is particularly close to her fellow female Opry stars Jean Shepard and Jeannie Seely.

Lorrie Morgan first heard Keith Whitley sing at Acuff-Rose Publishing in Nashville. On April 12, 1986, they reconnected backstage at the Grand Ole Opry, where she was a regular and he was a guest, performing his new hit "Miami My Amy." The two recent divorcees were instantly infatuated with one another. Keith was a Kentucky native, born July 1, 1955, who became a teenage prodigy alongside boyhood friend Ricky Skaggs in Ralph Stanley's Clinch Mountain Boys band. After a stint singing lead for J.D. Crowe and The New South, Keith had come to Nashville in search of a country recording contract. Signed by RCA in 1984, he was on the verge of stardom.

Keith and Lorrie married on November 22, 1986. "Ten Feet Away" and "Homecoming '63" were on the radio airwaves as his first two top-ten hits. Lorrie got her own RCA recording contract. In 1988, Keith had massive hits with "Don't Close Your Eyes" and "When You Say Nothing at All." Everything seemed to be going the young couple's way.

But Keith Whitley had a dark secret. He was a binge drinker who downed huge quantities when he was by himself. Early in their relationship, he overdosed badly and would have died if she hadn't taken him to Vanderbilt Hospital's emergency room. Lorrie thought her love was strong enough to change him. She threw away his booze, entered him in treatment programs, and tied her leg to his in bed so that he couldn't sneak away to drink. But in 1989, Lorrie went on the road to promote her RCA single "Dear Me" and her upcoming album for the label. Alone in their house, Keith Whitley drank himself to death. The thirty-three-year-old's body was found on May 9, 1989. His single at the time was the prophetically titled "I'm No Stranger to the Rain." It became his third number-one hit and was named the CMA Single of the Year.

Lorrie was thrown into the painful position of grieving, yet having to provide for her children, a daughter from her first marriage and her son with Keith. She turned to her Opry sisters for solace, and the show's family warmly embraced her in her time of need. In addition to the duet "'Til a Tear Becomes a Rose," she honored Keith's memory with a devastating 1991 performance of the George Jones classic "A Picture of Me (Without You)." The fans rallied to her side and brought Lorrie a string of big hits throughout the remainder of the decade. But up to now, Lorrie Morgan has never found lasting love again.

# Outlaw's Prayer

**N**o one has ever had a more tumultuous country-music career than Donald Eugene Lyle, better known today by his stage name. Johnny Paycheck had a streak of country hits in Nashville but sank to being a homeless, alcoholic bum in Los Angeles. He climbed back to the top with "Take This Job and Shove It" and other successes. But then he was convicted of shooting a man in an Ohio tavern and was sent to prison. In the end, he found peace and contentment as a member of the Grand Ole Opry cast.

"Music saved my life and music governed my life," said Johnny Paycheck. "That's what really held me together through my problems and my troubles."

Few have sung country music with more hair-raising conviction. He wrapped himself in country music at an early age, and he seldom wavered from being a hard-core honky-tonk traditionalist. Born May 31, 1938, he was raised in the small town of Greenfield, Ohio, which is roughly 50 miles east of Cincinnati. Perhaps "raised" isn't quite the right word, since Paycheck was still a boy when he left home.

He began playing guitar at age six and was entering talent competitions at age nine. He dropped out of school in the seventh grade, landed his own local radio show at age thirteen, and began riding the rails as a vagabond at fifteen. He supported himself by singing in dives.

"I was not really a runaway," he recalled. "I just told my mom and dad I had to leave. I was just a gypsy, bummin' around the country."

He landed a job in a Columbus country nightspot at age sixteen, then traveled north to Toledo. That's where he joined the navy when he was eighteen. His nonconformity and against-the-grain independence made him ill suited to military discipline. He punched a superior officer and was court-martialed. He brazenly escaped from the brig twice. The navy released him in 1958, and he turned up in Nashville a year later.

"I didn't have any plan at all," he admitted. "I just wanted to play music and write songs and sing."

Tree Publishing executive Buddy Killen recognized his raw talent and signed him to write songs for his company. The youngster changed his name to "Donny Young." Killen talked Decca Records into signing him as a singer, but Paycheck vanished on the day he was to sign his contract with the label.

"Even in those days, he had a penchant for alcohol and drugs and was somewhat of a maverick," recalled Killen in what turned out to be a massive understatement. Six months later, Paycheck reappeared as suddenly as he'd disappeared. Killen took him back in, and "Donny Young" launched his recording career with Decca, then Mercury Records and smaller labels. Despite his talent, none of the resulting singles made the charts.

So Paycheck hit the road. He played bass and/or steel guitar for Porter Wagoner, Faron Young, Ray Price, and most famously, George Jones. The two rampaging honky-tonkers began touring together in 1960 and remained a team, on and off, for the next six years. Paycheck can clearly be heard singing harmony on such Jones hits as "The Race Is On" (1964) and "Love Bug" (1965).

"Actually, I formed George's band," Paycheck stated. "We started out in, I believe it was a '59 or a '60 Chevy. It was just him and me [playing with pickup bands in the clubs they visited], and we worked a long time that way. Then I quit and went out on my own, just ramblin' around the country. When I came back the second time, I formed The Jones Boys for him."

As a member of The Jones Boys, he performed on some fifteen Jones albums of the 1960s. There are some who contend that George Jones based his distinctive vocal style on Paycheck's phrasing, but the influence could have flowed just as easily in the opposite direction. Whatever the case, Johnny Paycheck's style would soon emerge as a model of stone-country singing.

Record producer Aubrey Mayhew discovered him in 1964. At this point, his billing changed from "Donny Young" to "Johnny Paycheck," a name the singer reportedly borrowed from a Polish boxer. The Jones Boys backed Paycheck in the studio in 1965. The result was the jukebox classic "A-11," which became his first single to make the popularity charts. In 1966, Paycheck earned his first top-ten hit, "The Lovin' Machine."

His Nashville career was on its way. The same year he scored as a singer, Tammy Wynette had her first single and first hit with the Paycheck-penned "Apartment No. 9," and Ray Price had a top-ten hit with Paycheck's "Touch My Heart." Johnny Paycheck also wrote "Once You've Had the Best," a 1973 smash for George Jones.

Paycheck was the opening act for the historic 1966 Carnegie Hall concert by Buck Owens and The Buckaroos. Following "A-11," he made the country charts eight more times in the 1960s. "Motel Time Again" (1966) and "Jukebox Charlie" (1967) were top-twenty successes.

Mayhew released Paycheck's records on their own imprint, Little Darlin' Records. In order to attract attention and to compete with bigger labels, the producer decided to connect his singer with some outrageous material. "The Cave" was about dreaming of a nuclear apocalypse. "You'll Recover in Time" took place in an insane asylum. In "The Ballad of Frisco Bay," the singer drowns after taking the blame for a murder committed by his wife. Most shocking of all was "(Pardon Me) I've Got Someone to Kill." But it was the title "If I'm Gonna Sink (I Might as Well Go to the Bottom)" that proved to be chillingly prophetic.

Johnny Paycheck did, indeed, sink to the bottom. He hit the skids and lived on the streets of Los Angeles in 1967–1970. He performed in sleazy bars to earn just enough spare change for his next drink or pack of cigarettes. His weight dropped to 103 pounds. He was destitute when Music Row executive Nick Hunter tracked him down and brought him back to Nashville.

"They'd been looking for me for a long time, and they finally got ahold of me out there in Los Angeles," Paycheck recalled. Producer Billy Sherrill signed him to Epic Records in 1971. "Billy said that if I'd get myself together, he'd give me another shot at it. So I got myself together, and I was with Billy for eleven years."

"She's All I Got" (1971) and "Someone to Give My Love To" (1972) returned Johnny Paycheck to the top ten on the country hit parade. He blossomed anew as a songwriter by writing such singles as "Mr. Lovemaker" (1973), "Loving You Beats All I've Ever Seen" (1975), "All-American Man" (1975), and "Friend, Lover, Wife" (1978).

Paycheck was a rebel all his life. So when the "outlaw" movement of musical mavericks hit Nashville in the mid-1970s, he enthusiastically embraced it. He swapped tailored suits for denim jeans, grew a beard, let his hair grow long, and donned leather vests and bandanas. His music acquired a new edginess as well.

"I think the outlaw movement came with people who got tired of being told what to do," he believed. "And because we did that, we became known as 'outlaws.' It's just another word for rebel, you know. But it was a very, very great thing to happen to this industry, because it let it progress.

"To me, an 'outlaw' is a man who did things his own way, whether you liked him or not. I did things my way."

"Outlaws" Willie Nelson and Waylon Jennings scored the biggest hits of their careers during this era. So did Johnny Paycheck. He issued the pounding "I'm the Only Hell (Mama Ever Raised)" as his manifesto in 1977. He followed it with the snarling "Take This Job and Shove It," and that disc became a phenomenon. Working people everywhere cheered the song. Written by Paycheck's fellow outlaw David Allan Coe, "Take This Job and Shove It" soared to number one. In 1981, the song became the basis and title of a Hollywood comedy film in which both Paycheck and Coe appeared. The cast also included Robert Hays, Barbara Hershey, David Keith, Martin Mull, and Art Carney.

"We had no idea how *big* a hit it was gonna be," said Paycheck of his most famous recording. "It became a movie, and it was number one worldwide in all languages. I guess it's because people work everywhere."

It was also huge because Johnny Paycheck was completely believable as the song's protagonist. He was a product of the working class and sounded like it. Throughout this period, his songs reflected his reality. The title of his single "11 Months and 29 Days" was said to be the length of the sentence he'd served in the navy brig. When he sang "Fifteen Beers," "Georgia in a Jug," "Drinkin' and Drivin'," and "D.O.A. (Drunk on Arrival)," you knew he'd been there. When he cautioned "(Stay Away From) The Cocaine Train," you knew he'd been there, too. "Me and the I.R.S.," "Colorado Kool-Aid," and much of the rest of his output of the late 1970s seemed like pages from his autobiography.

Not all of his music was rowdy, raucous, rebellious, and rambunctious. In his expressive 1979 recitation "The Outlaw's Prayer," for instance, Paycheck is barred from entering a fancy church because of his beard, jeans, and long hair. "Lord, I know I don't look like much," he says. "I believe you had a beard and long hair, too. . . . I'll be seeing you, Lord. I hope."

He teamed up with his old pal George Jones for a series of popular duets in 1978–1981. But then the renegade began to falter again. In the early 1980s came tax problems, bankruptcy, and a sexual-assault charge. In December 1985, he was back in Ohio visiting relatives for the holidays. One thing led to another in a barroom altercation, and he shot a man. The bullet only grazed the man's forehead, but a gunshot is a gunshot.

"It was an accident," the singer insisted. "I was a victim of circumstances."

Nevertheless, Johnny Paycheck was convicted of aggravated assault. While out on appeal, he came back to Nashville to record such 1986 landmarks as the rocking "Don't Bury Me 'Til I'm Ready" and the wistful, pensive "Old Violin" for Mercury Records.

"This will probably be my last time around," he said. "The fans have always taken me back. The fans, they've been with me for over thirty years, and if it wasn't for them, I would have been gone a long time ago. They've stuck with me."

At the time, his third marriage was unraveling. He readily credited wife Sharon for "keeping me as sane as I am." So he patched things up with her.

"My marriage is like the rest of my life. It goes haywire for a while, and then I'll get it back together. . . . My problems are the same as yours."

With his appeals exhausted, he was imprisoned in 1989–1991. One result of this was that he became, at last, free from drug and alcohol dependence. Another was that he earned his long-overdue high school diploma. As a condition of his release, he was required to do community service, and he frequently spoke to students and civic groups about the importance of education.

"In prison, you see the final product of what's produced by not having an education," Paycheck reflected. Using his life as a cautionary tale, he also spoke frequently against drugs and alcohol.

"An ordeal like that will put your priorities right," he said of his prison term. "It's a terrible place to have to go. . . . It's bad for that to happen, but it's been good for me. I'm drug-free, alcohol-free, and nicotine-free.

"The support from the people on the outside is what got me through. I'm very fortunate. I heard from fans constantly throughout the entire two years. The letters never stopped, from throughout the world. I looked forward to mail call every day. Country fans are the most loyal people in the world. They never stopped writing.

"When it came time for me to go up for clemency, I had so many supporters. George Jones, Waylon [Jennings], [Johnny] Cash, and so many of them wrote letters for me and stood up for me." Merle

Haggard visited Paycheck in prison and recorded a live album with him there (although it has yet to be released).

"It's a wonderful feeling to be free," Paycheck added. "I'm never going to do anything again to endanger my freedom. You never know what you've got until they take it away from you.

"I don't have anything right now. I'm starting over from the bottom, and that's fine with me. I'm bankrupt, but I'm working that out."

The battle-scarred honky-tonk survivor was invited to become a member of the Grand Ole Opry cast in 1997. This was unquestionably the highlight of his later years.

"The man was a singer's singer," observed Glenn Ferguson, who managed Paycheck during his hit-making years. "Did you know that whenever he played the Opry, the other artists would all gather at the edge of the stage to watch him?"

"I've played a Johnny Paycheck song on virtually every show I've ever done," said Opry announcer and WSM disc jockey Eddie Stubbs. "Every fan of country music deserves to know more about the career of Johnny Paycheck."

In the 1990s, new stars such as Garth Brooks, Tim McGraw, and Toby Keith praised Paycheck as a forefather. Texas singer Tracy Byrd revived "Someone to Give My Love To" in 1993 and scored a major hit with "She's All I Got" in 1997. Alan Jackson revived "Once You've Had the Best" in 1996, and Blake Shelton brought back "Georgia in a Jug" in 2003.

By then, Johnny Paycheck was gravely ill. Diabetes, asthma, emphysema, and their complications led to his confinement in a Nashville nursing home. Former manager Glenn Ferguson and the Opry Trust Fund supported the singer financially.

Singer Daryle Singletary was responsible for Johnny Paycheck's final recording. Singletary had recorded a new version of "Old Violin" in 2002 and wanted its songwriter to do its recitation. The request brightened the fading star's final months, and he agreed to be recorded from his hospital bed.

"There I saw an old violin, soon to be put away and never played again," ends the song. "That old violin and I were just alike—we'd give our all to music, and soon, we'll give our life."

The end came on February 18, 2003. Johnny Paycheck died in his sleep at age sixty-four and was buried in Nashville's Woodlawn Cemetery in a plot paid for by his faithful friend George Jones. Snow turned to rain on the cold day they laid Paycheck to rest. Jeannie Seely, Jimmy Dickens, Billy Walker, Trace Adkins, John Conlee, and his other Opry friends gathered to pay their last respects. When the star's 1986 recording of "Old Violin" was played in the funeral home, it got a standing ovation.

"I sing about things that have always been and always will be," said Johnny Paycheck. "I sing about the little guy who's been kicked around by the big guy. I like to sing about things that are universal and timeless.

"The definition of country music, to me, is life," he added. "When you say 'life,' you've said, 'country music.'"

# Pure Love

**B**eing born blind used to be a life sentence of poverty and dependence. But Ronnie Milsap turned what could have been a tragedy into professional triumph. By his side throughout his rise to stardom has been his wife Joyce.

He's a superstar today, but Ronnie's beginnings were anything but stellar. Born in the mountains of North Carolina on January 16, 1943, Ronnie was raised in abject poverty. His mother thought her blind baby was a curse and abandoned him when he was one year old. She visited him once when he was six, still rebuking him for being blind. She gave him a dollar, then took it back from the hurt little boy when she left, this time for good. Raised by his grandparents, Ronnie was taken to a series of faith healers to "cure" him.

"They'd lay their hands on you and shake you and shout, 'Heal!' at you," Ronnie remembers. "It'd scare ya! I never was healed, so I always felt a little bit guilty every time I'd go home, still blind. Felt like I'd let them down."

Lucky for him, his grandparents realized that if Ronnie was going to have any chance of making something of himself, he would need to be educated by experts. They took him to the Governor Morehead School for the Blind in Raleigh and left him there when he was six years old.

"My grandfather had read me stories from the Bible, and I particularly remembered Joseph and how he was sold to strangers as a slave. And I really felt like that at that time in my life. I felt I'd been just left. For the first two or three hours, I was just sittin' on the dormitory porch, just crying my heart out. That's all I can remember.

"The school in Raleigh was probably one of the highest academic schools at that time. It was the only school you could go to if you were blind, but you had to make good grades or you didn't stay. We lived in dormitories, probably three hundred kids there that lived on the campus. I grew up an institution kid.

"I was an institution kid, but those other blind kids were like brothers and sisters to me, and some of the teachers were like uncles and aunts. They felt like family.

"I learned to type in the fourth grade. The house mothers didn't want to write home for us, so they taught us to type. When I got out of high school, I was typing 100–125 words a minute. But I never could proofread anything! But I always knew it was basically right, because you know when you hit the wrong key and make a mistake."

Ronnie lived at the school for thirteen years, throughout his childhood. It taught him to be independent and self-sufficient and gave him the skills he would need to survive in a sighted world. The lessons were valuable ones, but they came with a price. The strict teachers often instilled discipline through beatings.

As a boy, Ronnie could detect certain shadows and light in one eye. But when a teacher struck him when he was fourteen, the resulting blood clot destroyed his "good" eye. Ronnie had always fantasized that an operation on that eye might have allowed him to see. With those hopes dashed, he plunged into depression and refused to eat or socialize.

"When I was at school and got hit over the head and lost my eye, I got down to 120 pounds. And I was as tall as I am now [6 feet 2 inches]."

He'd been playing piano since age eight. Now in total darkness, Ronnie Milsap plunged into music more than ever.

"It was okay when I was growing up to like all these different kinds of music. I mean, radio stations used to play Lefty Frizzell and Ray Price, and they'd follow it up with Little Richard. But at school, the only thing they'd let us play was classical music. Everything else was forbidden."

Defying the authorities, Ronnie listened to and emulated rock 'n' roll, country, gospel, bluegrass, and rhythm and blues. In high school, he and some other blind students formed a band called The Apparitions. The group played for a college fraternity party, and Ronnie earned $12 at his first paying music job.

The school for the blind was his home from 1949 to 1962. In it, Ronnie matured from being a terrified, ignorant, abandoned mountain boy to become a gifted, self-confident young man. His training was rigorous but invaluable.

Without the education, "I would've stayed up in the Smokies like all the generations before me. I'd have never gotten out of there. Any kind of talent I had in music would've died when I was a kid—there would have been nobody to encourage me and support me.

"A lot of parents will bring their [blind] children to my shows. They want to know certain things about what I'm doing and how I'm making things happen. I tell them that the key is education, because without the right skills, you'll never be able to participate." In 1985, he formed The Ronnie Milsap Foundation. It provides scholarships and/or job training for the blind and supports eye research.

After high school, Ronnie Milsap attended college with the intention of becoming a lawyer. But he never left music behind.

He settled in Georgia and joined a band called The Dimensions. He recorded a record in an Atlanta studio and enjoyed some local attention with it. "Total Disaster" backed with "It Went to Your Head" appeared on the dinky Princess Records label in 1963. An early newspaper review misspelled Ronnie's last name. He was born and educated as Ronnie Millsaps. When the reviewer trimmed it to "Milsap," Ronnie decided to keep the spelling and had his name legally changed to that for show-business reasons. Despite his musical aspirations, he continued his education.

Recalls Ronnie, "I had gone to Young Harris Junior College in north Georgia, where Zell Miller taught me. He later became governor of Georgia and is a dear friend of mine. Anyway, I had been accepted to Emory University to study law. The day that I was supposed to go over there and enroll, I had been hanging around a big radio station in Atlanta. A friend of mine there offered to fly me to New York that day. So I made the decision, we flew to New York [in the spring of 1965], and I made my first real record. It was for Scepter Records, which was a big R&B label at that time. They had Chuck Jackson and Dionne Warwick. And Maxine Brown—I did a lot of concerts with her. What a wonderful lady. Nick Ashford and Valerie Simpson wrote the first record that I had, 'Never Had it So Good.' They helped me a lot in the studio. I was twenty-two years old and in New York and scared to death.

"I went to a concert Ray Charles had in Atlanta and got backstage to meet him. I'd just recorded my first record, 'Never Had it So Good,' and on the back side of that record was a song called 'Let's Go Get Stoned.' Well, Ray heard that song and told me he was going to record it. He did. He wound up sellin' a million with it.

"This guy who was playing drums for me said, 'Ray, you won't believe this, but this guy sounds just like you.' Ray turned around and shook my hand and said, 'In all due respect, don't sing like Ray. Learn to sing like Ronnie.' At the time I thought, 'He ought to be glad I wanna sing like him!' What he was trying to say was, 'Find your own style.' He said, 'Do you know how many years I sang like Nat King Cole until I could find out who I was?'"

By this time, Ronnie had moved to Atlanta, where nightclub work was plentiful. One night at a party, he met Georgia native Joyce Reeves and was smitten. At a club on their first date, he impressed her by getting up onstage and singing the James Brown hit ballad "Try Me." They slow-danced to "Misty." They fell in love. Ronnie married Joyce on October 30, 1965. To this day, he calls her "the light of my life."

Ronnie's "Never Had it So Good" became a hit on the R&B

charts. Scepter Records expected him to travel to popularize the record, so he soon found himself on concert bills with the leading R&B stars of the day, including Sam & Dave, Maxine Brown, Little Anthony & The Imperials, Stevie Wonder, and James Brown. Joyce became his ever-present guide.

"Joyce was doing a lot of the show booking," Ronnie recalls. "She handled all the business, a bride of one year going in and out of the knife-wielding clubs of America's toughest inner-city neighborhoods. She handled the telephone negotiations, executed the contracts, drove me in a van to the shows, set up my VOX organ faster than anyone I'd ever seen, and collected the performance money."

He adds, "She's always taken care of me—my driver, booking agent, manager, and wife."

Joyce disagrees. "He doesn't depend on me. I depend on him. He's very strong. Beyond a doubt, the finest man I've ever met. It sounds trite, but he's a nice guy and a gentleman."

The early years of their marriage were lean ones spent in Atlanta and then Memphis, where Ronnie was hired to perform as a sideman on recording sessions.

"I worked on two albums with Elvis down there in Memphis. The big song 'Kentucky Rain' that Elvis did, I played piano and sang [high harmony] on that record with Elvis. At the time, I didn't know Eddie Rabbitt. He was the writer." Eddie later wrote Ronnie's first number-one hit, "Pure Love."

Joyce and Ronnie's happiest experience during the Memphis years was the birth of their son Todd, in 1970. One of the most unpleasant was a visit to their home by Internal Revenue Service agents in 1972. They burst into the Milsap home demanding payment for 1971 taxes, which Joyce had already paid. Ronnie was enraged.

"They're just bullies," says Ronnie. "I'd rather have a sister working for the Mafia than a brother working in the IRS."

By 1972, the music scene in Memphis was fading. Ronnie was so down on his luck that he was considering leaving his profession.

"There was a time in Memphis when I was thinking, 'I better go back to college and go to law school. I better go to radio school, or do something, because this thing isn't going to work out.' I'd been trying it for seven years.

"I was getting ready to go back to college. The [King of the Road Hotel] manager said, 'I want you to move from Memphis, move up here to Nashville.' That's all I needed, man, was for somebody to give me a job.

"But I wound up losing the house and everything in Memphis, because of managers that wind up taking everything an artist has. You find yourself signed to something. This guy and I had an agreement, and I was working at his nightclub. He had a management contract with me. He said, 'As long as you're working at my nightclub, you don't pay me any commission.' But once I got ready to move to Nashville, he said, 'You owe me all this back commission.' I said, 'But you said I didn't have to pay. . . .' He said, 'I don't care what I said. I'm going by what it says in the print contract.' We had to go to court. And I lost my house and everything. Came to Nashville $20,000 in debt."

Still, "I've always dreamed of living in this town. There's just something about being here. I just really get a big thrill out of it somehow. I used to think, 'Oh, if I could just be in Nashville' when I was struggling along with a career that went nowhere for years. I truly love it and what people here have done for me."

The Milsaps arrived in Music City on December 26, 1972. Ronnie immediately went to work at the King of the Road, where he, Todd, and Joyce also lived for their first three months in town. Founded by Roger Miller (1936–1992), the King of the Road Hotel had a rooftop nightclub that was the place to be and be seen in those days. In no time, Ronnie Milsap's soulful singing and well-honed showmanship were the talk of the music community. Faron Young, Ray Stevens, Porter Wagoner, Jack Greene, Charlie Rich, Jeannie Seely, Dottie West, Conway Twitty, and many other stars dropped by to hear the new Nashville sensation.

Charley Pride's manager Jack Johnson and song publisher Tom

Collins went to bat for Ronnie on Music Row. Jack took a tape to RCA Records, which signed Ronnie in April 1973. "I Hate You" became his first top-ten hit later that year. In 1974, "Pure Love" became the first of Ronnie's more than thirty-five number-one hits.

Hits such as "Please Don't Tell Me How the Story Ends," "(I'd Be) A Legend in My Time," and "Daydreams About Night Things" led to an invitation to join the cast of the Grand Ole Opry. Ronnie Milsap was inducted by Roy Acuff on February 6, 1976.

"Some nights I tune into the Grand Ole Opry and think, 'You know, all I ever really wanted was to be a country singer,'" Ronnie reflects. "I'm a huge radio fan. Why is that about blind people? They're all radio crazy, and I'm worse than the rest of 'em. I collect old radios and have thousands of hours of old radio shows on tape. [On the road] I had a satellite dish, so I could listen to Nashville radio—the Opry—and feel like I was at home."

The Opry's faith in him was well placed. "What Goes on When the Sun Goes Down," "(I'm a) Stand By My Woman Man," and "Let My Love Be Your Pillow" all became number-one hits later in the year he was inducted. To date, he has sold 25 million records and earned six Grammy Awards and eight Country Music Association honors.

Ronnie and RCA usually agreed on which songs could be hits. One exception was 1980's "Smoky Mountain Rain." Ronnie believed in it, but the label did not. Ronnie prevailed, and it became yet another of his chart-topping performances.

"When I first came to Nashville you could go over to a record company and hang out . . . just chat and hang out in somebody's office. They would let you do that then.

"One thing I'll never forget is [in 1981] we had already finished an album, and they were shipping its single, called 'It's All I Can Do.' They were literally stuffing the envelopes when I called [then–RCA boss] Jerry Bradley up and said, 'I've got something that you've got to hear. It's got to be on the album.' The next morning I took him my cut of '(There's) No Gettin' Over Me.' He listened and then turned around in his chair and got on the phone and stopped everything. And he let me put it out. I don't think you could do anything like that in Nashville today. Everything is really preset. It is a very big business. It's big money."

"(There's) No Getting Over Me" not only topped the country hit parade, it became a giant pop hit as well.

His enormous success as a hit maker enabled him to construct a full business complex on Music Row. Ronnie built his own studio, formed his own song-publishing company, and created enterprises to book and publicize his concerts.

His shows are legendary. Ronnie Milsap thrills audiences with his fiery vocals and boundless energy. He has been known to fearlessly leap from pianos and walk precipitously close to the edges of stages.

"I jump up on top of the piano," he comments. "But I'm not trying to prove anything. All I'm trying to do is just have a good time. I feel perfectly normal with it.

"I'm not serious about blindness. I'm so used to it. I don't think about it too much. I'd like to see Joyce and Todd and some other things. But I have never taken any of that very seriously. Even though I don't see her, I know Joyce is a very pretty woman.

"If I were given a choice between having 20/20 vision and music, I'd have to say, I'd never give up my music."

# The Red-Headed Stranger

**W**illie Nelson's Grand Ole Opry career went up in smoke.

On December 23, 1969, Willie was at a Christmas party at booking agent Lucky Moeller's office on Music Row when he was summoned to the telephone and informed that his house was on fire. He rushed home to his farm in Ridgetop, Tennessee, a small, rural community north of Music City. His wife and children were safe, but he dashed into the smoking debris nevertheless. He was worried that the firefighters would find his stash of marijuana and turn it over to the police.

"I wasn't being brave," he later observed dryly. "When I got there, it was burning pretty good. There were fire trucks, police cars, and a lot of other people. I ran in through the back door . . . down the hall to a closet, picked up my guitar and a bag of weed, and ran out the back door, giving the weed to a friend, who ran to the woods and hid it."

"It's the only time I've ever seen Willie rattled," observed his buddy and future duet partner Waylon Jennings (1937–2002).

The fire consumed hundreds of unpublished Willie Nelson songs. Ironically, the last song he'd written at the house was the prophetically titled "What Can You Do to Me Now." During that same year, Willie had wrecked five cars and his second marriage.

The family moved into a small trailer on the Ridgetop property. Daughter Susie and son Billy chopped down a scrawny little pine tree, stuck it in one of Willie's cowboy boots, and decorated it with ribbons and their father's socks. And that's what Willie woke to on Christmas Day. Soon after, Willie, his family, and his band moved to Bandera, Texas.

"When that [fire] happened, I didn't really have any reason left to stay here," says Willie of his decision to leave Nashville. "I'd been wanting to go back to Texas anyway. I was tired of driving back and forth between Texas and Ridgetop. I'd worked every beer joint in the state of Texas by that time."

In 1969, he let his Opry membership lapse. The time he spent at the Ridgetop farm and in the cast of the Opry in the 1960s marked the only span in Willie's life when he was "settled." After the fire, the road became his home. It still is.

"I sometimes pull over," he says of his gypsy lifestyle. "But I am out here on the bus more than I am any other place. I love the bus. It's my safe area, my halfway house. In Texas, even when I am off, I park it there in front of the house, and I spend as much time on it as I do inside my house."

Willie Nelson was born to wander. He has been on various stages performing for most of his life. Willie Hugh Nelson was born on April 30, 1933, in the small town of Abbott, Texas. His parents divorced, and he and his older sister Bobbie were raised by their grandparents. The household was highly musical. Both grandparents sang and played instruments. Bobbie practiced piano and learned to read music as a child. When he was six, Willie was given his first guitar.

Grandfather Nelson died of pneumonia in 1939, which plunged the family into poverty. Bobbie and Willie had to pick cotton alongside their grandmother to make ends meet. Making music at home continued to be a joy and a respite from hard times. Willie began writing songs on his little guitar. At age eleven, he fashioned his own songbook, using a brown paper sack for its cover.

Willie performed in a variety of bands, including one with his sister Bobbie and her husband, and eventually became a disc jockey. He married his first wife, Martha, in 1952, and a year later, after daughter Lana was born, the family moved to Fort Worth, where Willie worked at the radio station KCNC.

"I had a daily children's show from 1:00 p.m. to 2:00 p.m. as the kids got ready for their naps," Willie reminisced in his book *The Facts of Life.* "Every day I played 'The Red Headed Stranger.' Written by Carl Stutz and Edith Lindeman . . . this was by far my most requested song. I'd start off the show every day, 'This is your old cotton-pickin', snuff-dippin', tobaccer-chewin', stump-jumpin', gravy-soppin', coffee-pot-dodgin', dumplin'-eatin', frog-giggin' hillbilly from Hill County, Willie Nelson.'"

After a brief stint in San Diego, California, the family moved to Vancouver, Washington, in 1956. Willie talked his way into a disc jockey job at KVAN there and was soon one of the most popular broadcasters in the region. He sold thousands of copies of his self-financed debut single "No Place for Me" / "The Lumberjack." Daughter Susie was born in 1957, the year Willie was fired for demanding a raise.

Back in Fort Worth, Willie tried to quit show business and become a proper provider for his growing brood. He sold Bibles, vacuum cleaners, and encyclopedias door-to-door. He even taught Sunday school. But he was soon back to playing music in honky-tonks. His pastor dismissed him from teaching when he found out, even though Willie pointed out that many of the Sunday church-goers were, in fact, out listening to him on Saturday nights. This event led to Willie turning his back on organized religion and toward a spiritual quest that resulted in his belief in karma and reincarnation.

On the move again, he took the family to Houston. There, he took jobs playing in the Esquire Ballroom, spinning records on KCRT, and teaching guitar lessons. Son Billy came along in 1958, and the following year Willie began releasing tunes on D Records, starting with "Man with the Blues" and "What a Way to Live." He also became friends with music entrepreneur Paul Buskirk. Perpetually strapped for cash, he sold Buskirk the rights to his songs "Family Bible" and "Night Life." The latter appeared, and disappeared, on Rx Records, credited as being by "Paul Buskirk and His Little Men, featuring Hugh Nelson." As for "Family Bible," when it became a top-ten hit for Claude Gray in 1960, Willie didn't earn a cent in royalties.

But encouraged by that songwriting success, Willie decided to head to Nashville. His first contact in the city was Grand Ole Opry star Billy Walker (1929–2006).

"I knew Willie in Texas," Billy recalled. "I was on radio in Waco, Texas, and he came from Abbott, right outside of there. And sometimes he used to come and watch me perform live on the radio. Then I was a member of a show with Red Foley called *Ozark Jubilee*. And Willie came to Springfield [Missouri], and I was trying to get him a job up there. He was writing a song called 'The Storm Within My Heart Has Just Begun.' I told him I wanted him to finish it. I made him write me the song, which I recorded [in 1959] and which got in kind of the top twenty-five [in Texas].

"I came to Nashville. Willie Nelson came to Nashville. And I said, 'What are you doing here?' And he said, 'Well, there's nobody buyin' songs in Fort Worth, so I came here to see what I could do.' I said, 'Well, where are you livin?' And he said, 'Out there in that old '50 model gray Buick.' And I said, 'Well, get your gear and come on out to the house.' So he lived out there with me for about three months, and in the course of livin' with me, he wrote 'Funny How Time Slips Away' and several other songs that came to be standards."

Willie had been making a living playing music in Texas for years. But that wasn't so easy to do in a music-industry town like Nashville.

"There weren't that many places to play! There were no clubs or anything. I could never understand why the music capital of the world had no places for the players to play other than the Grand Ole Opry and a few clubs in Printer's Alley.

"I was an artist when I got here. I'd been playing in clubs around

Texas since I was twelve years old. So when I came here and didn't perform, that was different for me. Just sitting around trying to be a songwriter was not really what I wanted to do. As soon as I got to Nashville, I went immediately to Tootsie's Orchid Lounge."

The now-legendary Lower Broadway beer joint was then the major hangout spot for Nashville's small songwriting community. Its back door was opposite the Ryman Auditorium's stage door, so Opry stars often dropped in for a brew between shows. Among the songwriters at Tootsie's was Hank Cochran. Once he heard Willie's songs, he urged Pamper Music to sign the newcomer. Hank told owners Hal Smith and Ray Price they could pay Willie the $50 a week they had planned to give Hank as a raise.

"When Hank said I at last had a real job that paid a real salary for writing songs, I broke down and cried," wrote Willie in his autobiography. "Martha cried, the kids cried, Hank cried. We were so happy. It was a real big deal for me—my first job as a professional songwriter."

"Hank Cochran was and still is one of the best song pluggers in this town," says Willie. "He would pitch my songs; he would pitch Kris [Kristofferson's] songs; it didn't matter. Any time he had a good song or heard of a good song, he'd pitch it to somebody. It didn't matter whether it was his song, or my song, or a stranger's.

"I ran into Faron Young right away [at Tootsie's]. The next day, he recorded 'Hello Walls' and 'Congratulations.' Released 'em back-to-back on a single [in 1961]. 'Hello Walls' wasn't premeditated at all. I was just out there at the little Pamper Music garage. Hank [Cochran] went to answer a phone call, and by the time he got back, I'd written 'Hello Walls' by myself. Sorry, Hank."

Also in 1961, Billy Walker introduced Willie's "Funny How Time Slips Away." And he very nearly recorded "Crazy." Instead, Patsy Cline did later that year.

"He had written 'Crazy' a year or so before," Billy recalled. "I cut a demo of it over at Starday Studio, tryin' to show the guy what kind of songs Willie Nelson was writing. And this guy said, 'I don't think that song'll ever sell.' Willie had gotten a job with Pamper

Music, and so Hank Cochran came to me and he said, 'Owen [Bradley] wants to cut "Crazy" on Patsy Cline. Would you let the "hold" go that you've got on it?' I really didn't want to, but Hank promised me that he would find me another song, which he did. It sold a million records for me, a song called 'Charlie's Shoes.'"

After leaving Billy Walker's house, Willie rented a place in Dunn's Trailer Court. It was, in fact, the same mobile home that songwriters Hank Cochran and Roger Miller had once rented. Dunn's sign, "Trailers for Sale or Rent," was later used by Roger as the opening line of 1965's "King of the Road."

Although stars were having hits with his songs, Willie's royalty checks weren't coming in just yet. He needed cash, so he turned to performing once again.

"I was a songwriter at a publishing company that Ray Price was an owner of. He and Hal Smith owned it. Ray was traveling around, touring. Johnny Paycheck—or Donny Young as he was called—was playing bass for Ray at the time. Ray called me from the road and wanted to know if I knew a bass player, because Donny Young was leaving. I said, 'Sure.' He said, 'Who?' I said, 'Me.' Of course, I'd never played bass in my life, but I didn't figure Ray would notice for a while. But bass players around the world would know it immediately. On the way to the first gig, which was in Winchester, Virginia, Patsy Cline's hometown, [steel guitarist] Jimmy Day taught me to play bass on the bus from here to there . . . sort of."

Being on the road and carousing with his songwriter buddies when he was home didn't sit well with the fiery-tempered Martha. The couple's battles became the stuff of Nashville music lore. At one point she tied up the drunken Willie in a sheet and beat him with a broom handle. At another, she chased him over the tombstones at the Veterans' Cemetery, which was near the trailer park. Martha was wielding a butcher knife. Willie was in his underwear.

On the other hand, it was Martha who saved his life following a bizarre suicide attempt. Drunk and despondent, Willie laid down on Broadway in front of Tootsie's one night, hoping to be run over by a car. Martha and some friends dragged him to safety.

Despite his case of the blues, things were looking up for Willie Nelson. Songwriting success led to a contract with Liberty Records. He recorded "Willingly" as a duet with Shirley Collie. It became a top-ten hit in early 1962. Willie followed it with his solo top-ten hit "Touch Me." He quit Ray's band and hit the road with Shirley to promote their successes. When Martha found out that he was having an affair with Shirley, she took the children and left Nashville. Willie and Shirley both got divorces and married in 1963. They settled on the 400-acre farm in Ridgetop.

*And Then I Wrote* (1962) and *Here's Willie Nelson* (1963) were issued by Liberty as his first albums. Neither one sold particularly well. But his songwriting successes continued with Ray Price's recording of "Night Life" and Roy Orbison's recording of Willie's holiday classic "Pretty Paper." So Willie decided to quit the road, collect royalties, and try his hand at farming.

"I took a year off and went out to Ridgetop and raised hogs for a year. It was more or less to take myself off the market for a while, because I felt that I had been on the road for a long time and needed some rest. I didn't want to plug nothing. I just wanted to rest for a year and be a farmer. But unfortunately, I needed to make some money, too. I lost a lot of money raising hogs.

"It was sort of a casual type of thing. However, it was an expensive casual type of thing. I bought a lot of hogs for 25 cents a pound. Then I raised them for five months, put a lot of weight on them, and sold them for 17 cents a pound. So I found out immediately that farm profits are shaky." Shirley raised chickens. The children soon joined the couple at Ridgetop.

By late 1964, Willie was bored with farming and itching to return to music. He recorded a few tunes for Monument Records, then signed with RCA. On November 24, 1964, he agreed to join the Opry cast. Willie's debut as an Opry member was on November 28.

"I was very nervous the first time I played the Opry," Willie comments. "Because, you know, it's the Ryman Auditorium, it's the Grand Ole Opry, and it's where Ernest Tubb and Hank

Williams and my heroes had played. In fact, Ernest Tubb was across the street at the Ernest Tubb Record Shop. After I did the Opry, I got to go across the street and do his show [*The Midnite Jamboree*]. He treated me like I was really somebody. I said, 'Well, heck, I like ole Ernest.' He treated all of us that way.

"The Grand Ole Opry has been here for so many years that the local people have a tendency to take all that for granted. They don't realize what they're missing. I think they should get out and see the shows more often.

"When I lived in Ridgetop, I was 20 miles north of Nashville. I didn't come into Nashville except to go to the Grand Ole Opry."

Ernest Tubb had been one of Willie's boyhood heroes. In 1965, Ernest invited Willie to be the cohost of his syndicated television show. He wanted to help the struggling, fledgling artist, even though Willie wasn't talkative or comfortable in front of the camera. Willie never forgot the superstar's kindness to him.

"I'll tell you about Ernest Tubb. He called me just maybe a couple of weeks before he died [in 1984]. His band was breaking up, and at that time I was using two drummers and two bass players. He called me to see if I had any room anywhere in my band for any of his guys. Because he was trying to place everybody. And I thought that really said a lot for the man. That's exactly what he was like."

While Willie had only modest RCA successes through the 1960s, his singing and songwriting were hugely popular among his peers in the Nashville music business. However, that didn't translate into any national fame.

Kris Kristofferson, who arrived in Nashville in 1965, recalls that Willie was the hero of every young songwriter on Music Row: "We were a little underground bunch of songwriters who took songwriting very seriously. We happened to be guys who were just absolutely disciples of Willie Nelson. Every one of Willie's songs would be sung and analyzed for his emotion and his delivery and all this. It was a training ground for a whole bunch of us. We said, 'Willie will never make it because he's way too deep. He'll never make it, because they don't understand him.' Well, he proved us wrong."

Waylon Jennings was also a Willie fan. The two met in Phoenix in 1965.

"I was in Phoenix on tour doing one-nighters," Willie recalls. "Waylon was over there at a club named J.D.'s. He'd been there for many years, I think, and he had a great job, makin' a lot of money. We'd never met, but he called me and said, 'Since we're both from Texas, I thought we might have a little something in common. So you wanna get a cup of coffee?' I said, 'Sure.' So we went down to the Holiday Inn 24-hour restaurant and started talking. He wanted to know what I thought about him leaving Phoenix and going to Nashville and traveling around.

"I said, 'You've got to be crazy. You've got a good job. Stay with it.' Because I was out there traveling around with a six-piece band all over the world trying to make it. And I wasn't making as much money as he was, right there at J.D.'s. Of course, we all know that's not the important thing. He wasn't out where he needed to be. So naturally, he didn't pay any attention to me, went right on to Nashville . . . and did pretty good."

Willie was also on the road when he met his third wife, Connie. They met in Texas in 1968. She had their daughter Paula Carlene in 1969. Shirley left Willie when she found out. Willie and Connie married in 1971.

At the time of the Ridgetop fire, Connie was at home with their baby. The farm also housed a number of Willie's other relatives and many of his band members and their families. After the clan decamped to Texas, the house was rebuilt. In 1971, everyone returned to Nashville, where Willie recorded his masterpiece RCA LP *Yesterday's Wine,* a concept album about a dead man looking back on his life. Despite his lack of radio success, the label had never given up on him. RCA issued fifteen Willie Nelson albums between 1965 and 1972, though they considered *Yesterday's Wine* weird and noncommercial. After fulfilling his contract, Willie finally left the company.

Atlantic Records was starting a country division and signed Willie as its flagship artist. His albums for the company, *Shotgun Willie* (1973) and *Phases and Stages* (1974), were the most critically acclaimed and best selling of his career to date. "Bloody Mary Morning" and his "After the Fire Is Gone" duet with Tracy Nelson (no relation) became modest radio hits in 1974. Nevertheless, Atlantic decided to get out of the country-music business.

With the demise of his Atlantic contract, the Willie Nelson family, including his infant daughter Amy, left Nashville for good. This time, they headed for Austin, Texas. And that is where Willie found his future.

No one was more important in developing a hip, young audience for country music than Willie. In Texas, he discovered that he was popular with both rednecks and hippies.

"I think it was Big G's in Round Rock, Texas, which was a highly redneck place back in those days. But there were a few little long-haired cowboys that were coming in there, and of course they got the shit kicked out of 'em a couple of times. But they kept comin' back. They kept showin' up.

"Then I heard about a place called The Armadillo World Headquarters [in Austin], and they were also hangin' out over there, where they didn't get the shit kicked out of them. They were welcome over there. So I realized that there were young people who wanted to hear not only my music but a lot of good country music, but who weren't exactly being welcomed with open arms in the beer joints.

"So I said, 'Why don't I go down to the Armadillo and see how they like what I do?' The manager was real optimistic about it, and sure enough, there was a whole lot of people who showed up. A whole lot of young people. Plus, there were a few of the cowboys from Big G's who had ventured in there, just to see, because they'd never been around the hippies and the long hairs.

"Anyway, they came in there and they mixed around. They looked around, and they drank a beer and did whatever they did there together, and they wound up not disliking each other at all.

They found out that it's not hard to like Hank Williams and Ernest Tubb. They found a common ground."

A 1972 "country Woodstock" called The Dripping Springs Reunion also showed Willie and the other attendees that hippies and rednecks could coexist, at least in Texas. Willie began staging his Fourth of July "Picnics" in the Lone Star State the following year. Still much admired within the music industry, he landed a contract with Columbia Records. In 1975, he and his band went into an ad-jingle studio in Garland, Texas, and recorded an album in three days for a reported $12,000.

Like *Yesterday's Wine* and *Phases and Stages* before it, 1975's *Red Headed Stranger* was a concept album. Using his old radio kiddie show song as its title tune and thematic center, Willie wove together a western saga that fused original tunes with country golden oldies like "Remember Me," "I Couldn't Believe it Was True," and "Blue Eyes Crying in the Rain." His label executives thought the spare, simple recording sounded unfinished. But it sold millions, made Willie a superstar, and brought him his first number-one hit, his take on Roy Acuff's 1945 hit "Blue Eyes Crying in the Rain."

Comments Willie, "I wasn't doing anything at all except singing my songs the way I wanted to sing them. I had thirty albums of my own songs just sitting there. So I decided to do a song I knew everybody likes, 'Blue Eyes Crying in the Rain.'"

Around this same time, Waylon Jennings was demanding artistic control of his recordings at RCA. He once reportedly pointed to a photo of Willie on the wall at the company and told the label boss, "You blew it with him, hoss. Now just don't blow it with me." Waylon got his way. Journalist Hazel Smith described what Waylon and Willie were up to as being musical "outlaws." RCA packaged recordings by them, plus Jessi Colter and Tompall Glaser, on an LP titled *Wanted! The Outlaws* in 1976. It became country music's first million-selling platinum record.

"I don't know about the rest, but I am an outlaw," says Willie. "I don't know what the laws are, so I don't know when I'm outside one.

"We wanted to see the artist have a little more control. And that fight still goes on. I mean, every time you go to the studio, that's the big fight. Sometimes the artist knows what he wants and doesn't need a lot of help. A lot of times he knows what he's doing and doesn't get the chance to do it. And I think that's sort of sad."

Willie and Waylon became an award-winning duet team with "Good Hearted Woman" (1976), "Luchenbach, Texas" (1977), and "Mamas Don't Let Your Babies Grow Up to Be Cowboys" (1978). Willie issued his Lefty Frizzell tribute LP *To Lefty From Willie* in 1976 and scored a number-one hit with a remake of "If You've Got the Money, I've Got the Time." He suggested to Columbia that he'd like to make an album of pop standards. The company told him he was nuts. He made *Stardust* anyhow. After its appearance in 1978, it remained on the popularity charts for more than two years and sold in excess of five million copies. "Georgia on My Mind," "Blue Skies," and "All of Me" all became gigantic hits from the album.

Robert Redford cast Willie in his 1979 film *The Electric Horseman*. Willie scored another number-one hit by performing "My Heroes Have Always Been Cowboys" on its soundtrack. Next, the singer was cast in a film that was loosely based on his experiences, 1980's *Honeysuckle Rose*. While traveling together on a flight, the film's producer challenged Willie to come up with some appropriate theme music and was astonished when Willie wrote "On the Road Again" on an envelope then and there.

"I really think that's a good challenge for a writer, to come up with something to go with the story," says Willie. "And I enjoy the challenge.

"I'm not sure if 'fear' is the word. But I do wonder about myself, 'Well, have I written my last song? Is that it?' But so far, I've always been able to come up with more."

Many musicians find moviemaking tedious. Not Willie.

"They're a lot of fun," he insists. "There's a lot of waiting around, but that's what I do best. Everything else is waiting around, too, I've always felt."

Along with Grand Ole Opry star John Conlee, Willie founded the annual Farm Aid benefit concerts in 1985. He picked up six Grammy Awards and memorably returned to Nashville for his inductions into the Nashville Songwriters Hall of Fame (1973) and Country Music Hall of Fame (1993). Despite his early-career difficulties, he has never held any grudges or harbored any bitterness about Music City.

"This town hasn't really treated me worse than any other town. Geography really has nothing to do with it. What I was doing was a little bit different from what they were geared to sell. I understood what their problems were. I'm not sure they understood mine. I definitely knew the odds were stacked against me. They are any time a newcomer comes in. It's difficult for anyone to get started."

Willie has always carried his wounds with grace. One of his most difficult periods began in 1991, when the Internal Revenue Service announced he owed a staggering $16.7 million in back taxes. He'd earned hundreds of millions since his 1975 breakthrough. But Willie's generosity and cavalier attitude about material possessions are legendary. What he didn't give away was lost due to poor investment advice. He was warned by the IRS in 1984 and 1988. In 1990, the agency swooped down on his home, studio, and property near Austin, seizing anything that looked valuable, intending to auction off his assets. He hid his famous battered, autographed guitar, Trigger.

"When they came in and confiscated the studio, they also confiscated the tapes that I had recorded over the years," he reported. "So I thought a good way to pay them back was to put out an album—*The IRS Tapes*—with the songs they seized and use these songs to pay them back. And they thought that was a good idea.

"I've known eventually this was going to happen, so I had a long time to get over my first reaction: I screamed for the first six months.

"I've been broke before," Willie added serenely. "I've been a lot broker than this. I try not to worry. Worrying will make you old and gray. I like for other people to worry. That way I don't have to.

"Actually, I think it's the greatest thing that has happened in my career. I haven't had this much publicity in years. And the sympathy factor is great out there."

He did, indeed, sell *Who'll Buy My Memories: The IRS Tapes.* He also gave up all the profits from his 1991 "I.R.S. Tour."

After the tour was over, Willie stopped in Nashville to visit his son, Billy, who was back living in the Ridgetop cabin. It was shortly before Christmas. Billy was divorced and was struggling with drugs and alcohol. Willie invited him to come to Texas for the holidays, but his son declined. When he left, Willie thought everything was fine. Billy was found dead on Christmas Day. It was ruled a suicide. But Frank Oakley, who runs the Willie Nelson General Store in Nashville, isn't so sure.

"Billy had drank a bottle of liquor and had gotten drunk," Frank recalled in his book *The Nashville "Sidekick."* "Somehow a Venetian blind cord was wrapped around his neck, and he fell off of the loft, where his bed was above the living room, and somehow had hanged himself.

"I had forgotten about the New Year's Eve show coming up in Branson [Missouri]. When I spoke with Willie, I asked him what he wanted to do about the show. . . . I asked him if he wanted me to get someone to replace him on the show, or just cancel it. He said, 'Frank, let me call you back within the hour and let me think about it.' Within approximately ten minutes, Willie called back and said, 'Let's go pickin' . . . I think it will be better for me to get back to work instead of sitting on the beach, grieving over what has happened.'

"How Willie was able to stand up for the two-hour show and sign autographs for another two hours for everyone who gathered around the stage, just proves what a strong man Willie Nelson really is, physically and emotionally, after all he'd just been through."

At the time, Willie had started his third family. Son Lukas had been born in 1988 and son Micah came along in 1990. Willie married their mother, Annie, in that same fateful year of 1991.

He had also reinvented himself as a recording artist. Alongside Johnny Cash, Waylon Jennings, and Kris Kristofferson, Willie had been touring as one of The Highwaymen since 1985. The four issued Highwaymen albums in 1985, 1990, and 1994.

Willie dislikes long hours in the recording studio, preferring spontaneous and live performances for his records. Thus, he is able to record multiple albums in a year.

"I like to know what I'm gonna do before I go into the studio," he says. "I don't like to spend a lot of time in there, because, for me, that makes it get stale. A lot of times, the first take is the best. With multiple takes, I feel like I lose it. So I just like to go in and do it.

"It might be the ninth Willie Nelson album this month. But they all seem to be doing pretty well. So as long as they are selling, I'm not gonna worry about it. I'm gonna keep puttin' 'em out until they quit buyin' 'em. I guess that's what I'm supposed to do."

As he approached his seventieth birthday, Willie picked up a Grammy and a Country Music Association (CMA) Award for his "Mendocino County Line" duet with Lee Ann Womack and had a number-one record with his Toby Keith collaboration "Beer for My Horses." Both discs were issued in 2002. This American icon is still out there on the road, still singing, still writing, and still entertaining.

"I'm doing it as much for me as I am for them. Music is my medicine, my drug. And if I don't get it, I get sick. If I don't play music, I feel bad. You have to enjoy it more than you enjoy not doing it. And I do. I think going out and playing the guitar and singing releases some emotions, and that's why I do it.

"I'd sing anywhere that I could. If I couldn't find a job singing, I would sit in with someone [playing guitar]. I have to play music. And as long as I can, and as long as I'm healthy, I always will."

# Dating at the Opry

Singer-songwriter Dierks Bentley's special Grand Ole Opry moments have all been connected with his courtship and marriage to his wife Cassidy.

"She's really intertwined with my whole Opry experience," says Dierks. "The second time she came to Nashville, I took her to the Grand Ole Opry down at the Ryman Auditorium. It was February, and Martina McBride was the headliner, so to speak. That was such an important date, because to take her to a show like that was to have her see the Grand Ole Opry, see the Ryman, and see what I was passionate about. That was a gigantic thing to us."

Dierks dated Cassidy for more than a year before their marriage. During that time, the rising star became a member of the Opry's cast.

"She was there the night that Marty Stuart asked me to become a member of the family, a part of the Opry. It was on the Sunset Strip at the House of Blues. She was there when Marty surprised me on that stage.

"And she was there when I was inducted, on October 1, 2005."

Dierks and Cassidy grew up together. He was born November 20, 1975, and raised in Phoenix, Arizona.

"I met Cass when I was, I guess, thirteen. We both went to the same school and were in the eighth grade together back in Phoenix. I was attracted to her from the moment I met her. But I wasn't cool enough to date her. So I dated her best friend. I was dating her best friend, and she was dating my best friend."

After their high school graduation, they drifted apart geographically. Following her college education, Cassidy moved to San Francisco to work in advertising. He moved to Nashville at age nineteen, intending to pursue music.

In high school, Dierks had been "converted" to country after hearing Hank Williams Jr.'s 1990 recording of "Man to Man." By then, he'd been playing rock electric guitar for about two years, but the listening experience completely changed his musical direction. Dierks is entirely self-taught, and he made it his business to study everything he could about country music and Nashville.

When he arrived in Music City in 1995, Dierks went to work at the Country Music Association, where he learned about the inner workings of the music business. At night, he immersed himself in the bluegrass music scene at the famed Station Inn nightclub. He didn't perform there. He just sat and watched and listened.

His next day job was an education as well. Dierks was at The Nashville Network (TNN) working in the cable channel's tape library for a miniseries on country-music history called *A Century of Country.* He researched footage of old Porter Wagoner, Johnny Cash, and Grand Ole Opry television shows.

The TNN office was next to the Opry House. As an employee, Dierks was permitted to go backstage at Grand Ole Opry shows. In fact, he used this privilege so much that he was reprimanded and chased off by Opry executives.

In the evenings, Dierks played at songwriter showcases and had a regular performing slot at a dive bar called Springwater, near Centennial Park. Then he graduated to the nicer Market Street Brewery in downtown Nashville. He was playing there one night when Vince Gill dropped in, came up onstage, and played for an hour and a half with Dierks.

"Truly unbelievable is the only way to describe it. I thought that if my music dreams never went any further, that would be alright, because I got to share the stage with Vince Gill."

In 1999, he began recording his debut album. *Don't Leave Me in Love* appeared in 2000 on his own, homemade record label. Even though he was a complete unknown, Dierks got help from a stellar group of bluegrass players on the sessions.

It was around this time that he began thinking of Cassidy once again. He tried to establish a long-distance relationship with her but was not successful.

"I always kind of kept in touch with her through the years. We tried to date when I was, like, twenty-three or twenty-four and working at TNN. I'd send her songs and stuff I was working on. We tried to date a couple of times, but it was just hard. The distance made it difficult. At one point, I just kind of gave up on it and just assumed we'd always just be good friends but never work out."

Opry or no Opry, Ryman or no Ryman, it didn't look like Dierks and Cassidy were going to make it as a couple. At least not then.

"Actually, I cared for her enough that I didn't want her to be stuck. I just wanted her to be happy."

He dated others but was mainly focused on furthering his career. Dierks Bentley's drummer, Steve Misamore, took a copy of the homemade album to the Sony/ATV Tree Publishing office. Based on the tunes on the record, the company signed Dierks to a songwriting contract. Tree executive Arthur Buenahora teamed Dierks up with another Tree writer, Brett Beavers, and the new collaborators clicked instantly with one another. Brett began producing Dierks in the studio. The results were heard by the folks at Capitol Records, and the label signed Dierks to a recording contract in 2003.

The former backstage "pest" made his first appearance on the Opry stage on April 18, 2003. He introduced his debut Capitol single, "What Was I Thinkin'."

*Dierks Bentley* was released as his debut Capitol CD on August 19, 2003. "What Was I Thinkin'" rocketed to number one. "My

Last Name" and "How Am I Doin'" became his second and third hits. Superstar George Strait invited Dierks to be his opening act on the road in 2004. Romance was rekindled when Cassidy flew in to see her old flame at one of the shows.

"Her happiness, to me, most of all, was the most important thing," Dierks recalls. "So I just wrote her off as something that wasn't going to work out. That all changed on February 4, 2004. I was playing a show with George Strait in Las Vegas. She walked on the bus, and I just kind of knew, right away. I was like, 'Wow! I have got to find a way to make this woman happy, because I don't want someone else making her happy. I want to be the guy.'

"We dated for a year. It's weird how time flies. She moved to Nashville in August, and we got married in December."

The wedding, held December 14, 2005, was a private affair and a surprise present.

"I got engaged in Las Vegas, but I got married in Mexico. We had a trip lined up at the end of that year, so we were already going to Mexico. I went online and checked out the place we were staying. It had a wedding chapel. When you're passionate about something, you do things you otherwise might not have the guts to do. And that's certainly the case with arranging a wedding, which I did online and on the telephone with a wonderful Mexican woman down in Cabo San Lucas.

"Something special kind of came from carrying the rings and planning this whole wedding behind Cassidy's back. I'm not sure how I did it, but I guess when you're crazy in love, you just do things that normally you don't.

"I still think we did it the smartest way you could do a wedding. For us, it's like a real personal thing, memories that we get to share privately and have that between us. When the whole ceremony becomes bigger than the actual story itself, that doesn't sound like a whole lot of fun. It should be fun."

Afterward, he said very little to the press about his marriage. One story stated that his mother was upset about his eloping, but Dierks says that isn't true.

"My mom never had a problem with that. She always thought eloping was a great idea. She actually encouraged me to do that when I was younger. We shared the wedding with them through pictures we had taken while we were there."

To this day, Dierks Bentley is not comfortable talking about his private life. He insists that the media focus on his music above all else. He turned down a spread in *People* magazine because he thought the magazine was more interested in his personal life than his music. He also turned down a *Vanity Fair* photo shoot, because the publication wanted a frivolous shot of him lassoing country singer Miranda Lambert.

On the other hand, Dierks was pleased when music journalists recognized his musical tip of the hat to the late Waylon Jennings in the sound of "Lot of Leavin' Left to Do." The 2005 single was the first from his CD *Modern Day Drifter.* As a child, Dierks was a big *The Dukes of Hazzard* TV fan, and Waylon's "Good Ol' Boys" theme song was the first single he ever bought.

In 2005–2006, "Come a Little Closer," "Settle for a Slowdown," and "Every Mile a Memory" became his second, third, and fourth number-one smash hits. He won the 2005 Horizon Award from his old employer, the CMA.

After he played "Come a Little Closer" on the Opry stage on October 1, 2005, Dierks was joined by Marty Stuart and Opry manager Pete Fisher. "As country music has changed and grown through the years, the one thing that has remained steady is the Grand Ole Opry," said Marty. "I am proud to introduce the newest member of the Grand Ole Opry, Dierks Bentley."

"This here is the ultimate backstage pass," Dierks said to Pete, referring to his history with the executive. Then Jake came running out from the wings and jumped into his master's arms. The dog is well-known to country fans, since he often appears with Dierks at events and in videos. Dierks humorously describes his white, furry, mixed-breed pet as "half Spitz and half one-night stand."

Dierks Bentley cherishes his Opry membership and plays the show often. That is all the more impressive when you realize that he is one of the most aggressive touring artists in America. He spent three hundred days on the road during his first year of stardom. Even now, playing two hundred dates a year is not uncommon. He says that perfecting his live show is "an obsession" and admits that this might be hard on his bride.

"Being a 'road widow,' that's tough," Dierks comments. "I guess that's the truth, though. But Cassidy comes out with me sometimes. We try to do no more than three days apart. That means she's got to ride the bus. For a long run, she might fly out to meet us somewhere, do a couple of days on the road, and go back home.

"It's tough, because when I get off the road and get back to Nashville, that's when the work begins. I have to get up early and get stuff done, whether it be writing songs, meeting with the Web site people, meet with the record label. It's busy when I'm in town. But we try to schedule quality time together, like vacations."

Being married has brought stability to the singer's life. When Dierks was single, he and Jake the dog lived on a small houseboat anchored at a lake outside Nashville. The interior was about the same size as the space inside his tour bus—tiny bathroom, tiny kitchen and all. Now Dierks, Cassidy, and Jake live in a real house. A second dog, George, joined the family in 2006.

Dierks Bentley's female fans were up in arms when his "Long Trip Alone" video premiered in January 2006. For his role in the video as a prisoner, Dierks cut off his trademark halo of blond curls. He was shocked by the reaction and surprised that his image meant so much to them. "It's only hair!" he protested.

He'd much rather talk about music. "Free and Easy" became his fifth number-one hit in 2007. Dierks was so happy, he paid for a party at the Nashville Predators professional ice-hockey rink. He wanted to thank the Music Row community as well as have fun playing hockey with his buddies.

"It's not just a celebration of a number-one song," he told the party attendees. "This town is about community and relationships. It's so meaningful. I hope you guys take just as much pride in this as I do."

Although his style is thoroughly modern, Dierks loves traditional country sounds. Even before his debut CD was released, he enthusiastically signed up to sing the classic "I Don't Believe You've Met My Baby" with Harley Allen on a 2003 tribute CD to The Louvin Brothers. His own records have featured appearances by bluegrass stars such as the Del McCoury Band and The Grascals. He went out of his way to befriend traditional stylists such as George Jones.

"All those guys have different forms of advice. I got the standard money-management speech from Buck Owens. I got the lecture. I felt like I was going into an elite club when I got that speech.

"George's advice was to hit it while you're hot. He sees the money that people are making now in country music, and I think he sometimes gets a little bummed out about that. All the touring he did, it was a different deal. It was before money really entered the picture. I think his thing is always try to figure out where the music comes from. But also, hit it while it's hot and have fun out there.

"For a while there, I was so militant about country music and bluegrass music, I wouldn't listen to anything else. I really closed my mind off to anything other than those two genres. Cassidy has helped me open up my perspective a little bit to hear other music and other ideas.

"I feel like I know a lot about certain genres. But she knows a lot about music in general. She knows more about music than I do. She just loves music. She's one of those people who just gets moved by music of any kind.

"That is huge. I love that, because I learn from her. And she learns from me. I got to teach her about the Grand Ole Opry and teach her about the guys in country music whose music I love. I don't really see her as a Hank Jr. type, but she'll listen to him just to figure out why that music has an effect on me, why that music turned me on to country music. In return, I'll listen to her music."

The dedication on his 2006 CD *Long Trip Alone* reads "To Cassidy, whose smile I rest beneath." Dierks Bentley is a man in love.

"There's a lot of men I look up to," he comments. "They're the strong ones, the powerful ones. And those are always the ones who have a great love in their life, whether it be Johnny Cash or Bono of U2. Those are the guys that I respect the most. Those have always been the people I've looked up to. Having that great love, that's sexy and powerful to me. And it's tough to do."


DIERKS BENTLEY ISN'T THE only member whose love was with him for his Opry cast induction. Josh Turner's was not only there, she was onstage. That's because Jennifer Turner is the keyboard player in her husband's band.

Josh and Jennifer met when both were students at Nashville's Belmont University, majoring in music. Josh only went there to please his parents and because he knew the school was next to Music Row.

Born on November 20, 1977, Josh Turner was raised in Hannah, South Carolina. When he was fourteen, his mother signed him up to sing the Randy Travis hit "Diggin' Up Bones" at a church social. His impersonation of Randy was so perfect that many in the audience believed he was lip-synching to Randy's recording. To this day, Josh refers to Randy as "the man who taught me how to sing."

Galvanized by the applause he received, Josh decided he wanted to become a country performer. Guided by his grandparents' record collection, he studied the style and learned about its classic artists. When he was in college in South Carolina, he yearned to move to Nashville to pursue his dream. His parents wanted him to stay in school, so he transferred to Belmont.

Meeting Jennifer wasn't the only big event that took place while he was a Belmont student. Josh was so enthralled with the music of Johnny Cash that he drove his truck to the superstar's suburban home. The gate was open. He knocked on the door, and to his astonishment, there stood his idol. Although ill, Johnny spoke briefly with the infatuated youngster. After the encounter, Josh was so overcome that he broke down and cried in his parked truck.

The song that changed his life also came to him while he was a Belmont student. Josh listened to a boxed set of Hank Williams music in the library one evening. While walking home in the dark, he had a vision. Once he got to his room, he sat on his bed, and out poured the song "Long Black Train."

Josh's songwriting talent came to the attention of Music Row's executives even before he graduated. Within a few months of his 2001 graduation, Josh Turner was signed to his recording contract.

On December 21, 2001, Josh Turner stepped onto the Opry stage for the first time. Bill Anderson introduced him. After just one verse and chorus of "Long Black Train," the audience began cheering. By the end of the song, the crowd was on its feet.

"Josh, make that train a little longer," suggested Bill. Getting an encore so overwhelmed Josh that he choked up, began to cry, and skipped a couple of verses. Then he got another standing ovation.

In 2002, Josh Turner issued his debut single, the ballad "She'll Go on You." It flopped. "Long Black Train" was selected as Josh's second single. As predicted by its Grand Ole Opry reception, it emerged as Josh's first big hit.

While "Long Black Train" was climbing the charts, Josh married Jennifer in Atlanta on June 14, 2003. After her graduation from Belmont, she'd earned her master's degree in music at the University of Georgia and had begun teaching voice and piano.

Josh's deep, rich singing voice and boyish good looks were immensely appealing to country fans. The Long Black Train album eventually sold a million copies. In 2005–2006, "Your Man" and "Would You Go with Me" became back-to-back number-one hits. As a result, Josh's Your Man album sold two million copies. Two of his guests on the collection were Grand Ole Opry stars Ralph Stanley and Diamond Rio.

His career was exploding, but Josh and Jennifer took some time off when Jennifer gave birth to son Hampton Otis Turner on October 6, 2006.

In the six years following his debut on the show, the rising star made nearly one hundred guest appearances on the Opry. On September 29, 2007, Roy Clark surprised Josh by inviting him to become a cast member. After singing his hit "Firecracker," Josh was inducted by Vince Gill on October 27, 2007.

"Thank you, Grand Ole Opry," Josh responded. "Country music has always been a huge part of my life. I have always been willing and able to fight for it, and that's what I want to continue to do—and just continue to make great music for all these great country fans out there."

With his induction, Josh Turner replaced Dierks Bentley as the youngest member of the Grand Ole Opry's cast. The two share a November 20th birthday, but Josh is two years younger than Dierks.

With a happy, healthy baby, a wife who supports him both on and offstage, and cast membership in the Grand Ole Opry, Josh Turner is one contented young man. The title of his third album says it all: *Everything Is Fine*.

# The Harmonica Wizard

The first documented polio epidemic in America was in 1894, when 132 cases were reported in the state of Vermont. The disease is almost unknown in this country today, but throughout the first half of the twentieth century, it crippled and killed hundreds of thousands of young people.

Around 1900, localized paralytic polio epidemics began springing up in various U.S. communities. Three-year-old DeFord Bailey was afflicted in 1902, more than fifty years before a vaccine was developed to inoculate children against the paralyzing disease. The future Grand Ole Opry star turned what should have been a tragedy into musical triumph.

AMONG POLIO'S SURVIVORS HAVE been President Franklin D. Roosevelt, Olympic athlete Wilma Rudolph, golfer Jack Nicklaus, actors Alan Alda and Mia Farrow, painter Frida Kahlo, and photographer Dorothea Lange, as well as musicians such as Donovan, Neil Young, bluegrass star Mac Wiseman, and "The Nashville Nightingale," Dinah Shore. Like them, DeFord Bailey not only survived, he became a star.

He was born December 14, 1899, in rural Smith County,

Tennessee. His mother died when he was only a year old. He was taken in by his father's sister Barbara Lou and her husband Clark Odum, who raised him as one of their own. When he came down with polio, so did the son of the local doctor. Bedridden, he was able to move only his arms and head for nearly a year.

"My daddy would give me a harp [harmonica] or hang an old guitar or banjo around my neck and let me pick on it for hours at a time," DeFord recalled. "I couldn't do much else. I probably made more noise than music back then, but I've been playing my harp or something ever since then."

The physician gave up on DeFord, but Barbara Lou didn't. Day after day, she rubbed his legs with various folk remedies, including the grease cooked from an owl. One liniment, lubricant, or salve must have worked. Unlike many polio victims, DeFord was eventually able to walk without braces, though the disease did stunt his growth—he only grew to 4 foot 10 inches tall and 100 pounds.

DeFord's grandfather had been the county's champion fiddler. Various other Baileys played guitars, mandolins, banjos, fifes, drums, and harmonicas, and the family was often called upon to play what DeFord called "black hillbilly music" at church gatherings, fairs, barn dances, and other community events.

The frail little boy picked up traditional fiddle tunes, gospel songs, pop ditties, and blues numbers. He was a musical sponge who learned melodies quickly, easily, and flawlessly. He heard music all around him. There was something dreamy, almost mystical, about him. And he retained these qualities all his life.

"You know, there's some music in everything," DeFord believed. "Sheep. Cow. Chicken. Dog. They got music in 'em. All of 'em . . . I'm just like a microphone. I pick up everything I hear around me." He was particularly fascinated by the bells and train whistles he could hear from the tracks that were a couple of miles away from his rural home.

While he was growing up, the Odums moved to various communities in Williamson County, south of Nashville. His obsession with the harmonica remained constant, and he never did well in school.

"They tried to teach me reading, writing, and arithmetic, but I was only interested in arithmetic," he recalled. "I wanted to learn how to keep people from beating me out of my money. But they beat me anyhow. I did learn enough arithmetic to count my money and enough reading and writing to sign my name, but that was about it."

Essentially illiterate and handicapped by his condition, DeFord Bailey seemed destined for a life of poverty and dependence. But he had a number of skills that eventually proved to be invaluable. He was an excellent cook. He was extremely good with his hands, able to make toys and furniture out of cast-off materials. He was good with animals. He was neat, clean, and quite tidy. He could sew. He was highly inventive.

The family moved to Nashville in late 1918, when he was nineteen years old. Barbara Lou, the only mother he had ever known, died in 1923. Clark Odum moved to Detroit to find work. Now on his own, DeFord drifted through a number of occupations in Nashville. He ran errands for a pharmacy, cleaned and worked as a houseboy, worked in the kitchen of the Maxwell House Hotel, shined shoes, washed cars, took tickets at a silent-movie theater, was a delivery boy, and became an elevator operator. No matter the job, he always played his harmonica during any downtime.

In the big city, his musical palate expanded. DeFord was fascinated by the medicine shows that set up tents in his Edgehill neighborhood in Nashville. The Bijou Theater downtown catered to African Americans, and it became a favorite haunt of his. He even worked there for a time. This is where DeFord saw such greats as Bessie Smith, Ma Rainey, Butterbeans and Susie, Sara Martin, Clara Smith, and Sammie Lewis with his Creole Steppers jazz band. All of this would influence his ever-evolving repertoire.

He got around town on a bicycle he customized with a headlight, reflectors, and other features. He got parts for his bike at a hardware store called Dad's. When radio became popular in the early 1920s, the owner, Fred Exum, opened a shop selling parts to build receivers. To publicize it, he opened Nashville's first radio station, WDAD. When the station went on the air in September 1925, Fred remembered his bicycle customer's talent and invited DeFord Bailey to broadcast on it.

One of DeFord's fellow players on WDAD was the harmonica-playing Dr. Humphrey Bate (1875–1936), who led a string band. The two men became friends and mutual admirers. This relationship would lead directly to DeFord's stardom.

On October 5, 1925, WSM went on the air in Nashville. Unlike the tiny WDAD, the new station had a powerful signal and first-class studios. From the start, WSM wanted to be the best. George D. Hay at WLS in Chicago had been voted the most popular announcer in America in 1924, so WSM enticed him to come to Nashville. Hay knew how popular country music had been on WLS, so he immediately began to feature it on WSM. On November 28, he put old-time fiddler Uncle Jimmy Thompson (1848–1931) on the air, which began the station's tradition of broadcasting country music every Saturday night.

By the end of the year, "Judge" Hay, as he was known, had a cast of several other country acts. One was Dr. Humphrey Bate, who often went off the air on WDAD and walked up the hill to commence broadcasting on WSM. One night, he persuaded DeFord to go with him. The program was already in progress when they arrived. Dr. Bate told Judge Hay he wished to put DeFord on then and there, without an audition. When Hay objected, Bate persisted, "Judge, I will stake my reputation on the ability of this boy."

After DeFord played some tunes, Judge Hay tossed his trademark wooden steamboat whistle into the air in delight. He gave DeFord $2 and told him to return. At the time, the show's performers weren't paid. Thus, DeFord Bailey became WSM's first paid professional musician.

In addition to blowing his steamboat whistle and adopting the character of "The Solemn Old Judge," Hay came up with colorful names for his performers. Bate's string band, for instance, was renamed "The Possum Hunters." Fiddler George Wilkerson's group was dubbed "The Fruit Jar Drinkers." Mandolin and guitar player

Paul Warmack's band became "The Gully Jumpers." In 1926, Hay dubbed DeFord Bailey "The Harmonica Wizard," and beginning that summer, that is how DeFord was listed in every newspaper radio schedule.

Hay also had his acts costume themselves in overalls to convey a hayseed image, even though their occupations included policeman (Matthew Crook), auto mechanic (Warmack), jeweler (the Binkley Brothers), and barber (Howard Ragsdale). They might have had rural roots, but they weren't farmers. Still, Hay perpetuated the image in press releases that read like this:

> "During the week, most of these performers are farmers and hunters, men of the soil. When Saturday night comes, they take down their fiddles, banjoes, jugs, washboards, mouth harps, and the like, and come to the jamboree."

DeFord Bailey would have none of it. He refused to wear a rube getup and always appeared in a tailored suit, starched shirt, tie, and hat. He kept his clothes in immaculate condition and comported himself as a gentleman.

The Harmonica Wizard soon became a huge favorite with the station's listeners. Fan mail, telegrams, and phone calls arrived with praise and requests. His segments on what was then called WSM's *Barn Dance* or *Saturday Night Barn Dance* became longer and more frequent.

By 1927, DeFord Bailey and banjo-playing vaudevillian Uncle Dave Macon were by far the most popular performers on WSM's weekly show. Uncle Dave was already recording by then. Hay used his show-business contacts to arrange for his other star to record for Columbia Records in Atlanta that spring. The company recorded two songs but released neither. Angered, Hay cancelled the deal and sent DeFord to New York and Brunswick Records.

"They sat me down on a little seat," DeFord remembered, "and showed me three lights on the wall. One light was my signal telling me to get ready, one told me to start, and the last one was the signal to stop playing. I watched the lights and timed my tunes to fit 'em. Each record was three minutes. I stopped right on time for each one. I had played so long, I knowed right when to stop. One time was all it took, since I didn't make a single mistake on none of them. I recorded eight tunes, and I played every one perfect the first time. They couldn't get over that."

The first song he recorded was "Pan-American Blues," wherein his harmonica imitates a locomotive. "Dixie Flyer" was another of his "train" pieces. "Old Hen Cackle" was a fiddle tune he'd learned from his grandfather. "Evening Prayer Blues" also came from his boyhood. "Up Country Blues" and "Muscle Shoals Blues" were tunes he learned from seeing Bessie Smith at the Bijou Theater. The showplace was probably also where he learned "Alcoholic Blues," a tune that bothered him since he neither drank nor smoked. "The Fox Chase" was a tour de force in which he imitates dogs barking, riders' shouts, and fox howls associated with a hunt.

When he returned to Nashville, he introduced "The Fox Chase" and "Pan-American Blues" to WSM listeners. Both became wildly popular. In fact, "Pan-American Blues" was practically the *Barn Dance*'s theme song. It is the tune that inspired the name that the show has to this day.

In the fall of 1927, WSM was broadcasting a classical-music show from New York called *The Music Appreciation Hour*. Host Walter Damrosch introduced a piece by saying, "Most artists realize that there is no place in the classics for realism, nevertheless, I am going to break one of my rules and present a composition by a young composer from Iowa who sent us his latest number which depicts the on-rush of a locomotive."

Judge Hay was listening. When the classical show ended, he opened his country-music show by saying, "Friends, the program which just came to a close was devoted to the classics. Doctor Damrosch told us that it was generally agreed that there is no place in the classics for realism. However, from here on out for the next three hours, we will present nothing but realism. It will be down to earth for the earthy."

DeFord Bailey executed his dazzling "Pan-American Blues." Inspired, Hay added, "For the past hour, we have been listening to music largely from Grand Opera, but from now on, we will present The Grand Ole Opry." By December, newspapers were using the new name, and Hay was promoting it vigorously.

In 1928, DeFord Bailey performed on the Opry twice as often as any other artist. But he sometimes chafed at Judge Hay's paternalistic behavior. DeFord had been paid $400 for his Brunswick recordings, $50 a song. Hay had the money sent to himself, took 25 percent, gave DeFord $75, and doled out the rest in $10 increments. Moreover, the $10 replaced DeFord's usual Opry pay of $7 per show. At that point, he should have been getting $17 a week but wasn't. When the $300 was paid out, he was returned to $7 a night.

A second recording session took place that fall, when Victor Records came to town to record some of the Opry performers. The Binkley Brothers and their Clodhoppers kicked things off on September 28, 1928. Paul Warmack & His Gully Jumpers were next, recording both on that date and on October 1. Then it was DeFord Bailey's turn. On October 2, he recorded eight titles, three of which eventually appeared on disc, "Davidson County Blues," "Ice Water Blues," and "John Henry." Since DeFord didn't make mistakes, it is speculated that perhaps the wax masters of the other five titles were damaged or broken en route back to New York. This time, The Harmonica Wizard was paid a flat fee of $200 for his work.

Despite the increased income, DeFord still believed "I wasn't getting nowhere." So when WNOX in Knoxville offered him $20 a show, he moved there for three months. Hay agreed to match the $20 per appearance fee. DeFord returned to the Grand Ole Opry in early 1929.

His teenaged neighbor Ida Lee Jones loved music and danced while DeFord practiced. The two dated and decided to get married in 1929. Son DeFord Bailey Jr. was born in 1932, followed by daughters Dezoral Lee (1934) and Christine Lamb (1936).

In October 1929, the stock market crashed. Because of the ensuing Great Depression, WSM cut salaries for its performers and staff in half. Seeking extra income, DeFord built a cedarwood building designed to look like a log cabin and opened his Grand Ole Opry DeFord Bailey Barbecue Stand next to his house on Lafayette Street in 1930. He began renting rooms to both blacks and whites, essentially operating the first integrated hotel in Nashville. His shoeshine stand, which he opened in 1933, was also fully integrated.

He and the other Opry stars soon realized that they were going to have to tour to make ends meet. DeFord played hundreds of shows in the 1930s, traveling with Uncle Dave Macon, Sam & Kirk McGee, Sarie and Sally, Arthur Smith, and the other early Opry stars. Traveling in the then-segregated South was difficult. Uncle Dave insisted to hotel managers that DeFord was his valet in order to get him in his room. Sometimes DeFord had to sleep in the car while the others found lodgings. Often, he ate a sandwich outside while his touring partners dined in a restaurant.

Kindest of all were The Delmore Brothers. They refused to eat in restaurants if DeFord couldn't get a meal in the kitchen. They told him when he was being cheated financially. They let the diminutive Harmonica Wizard sleep between them in their hotel bed. They treated him like their younger brother.

"I've been studying people, two sets of people [blacks and whites], since I was eleven years old," said DeFord. "I remember sitting on a fence watching the stock in the field. They don't seem to notice no difference in the color of the other cows and horses. I wondered why it was different with people. That's when I first started trying to figure out people."

On the road, audiences were wild for DeFord Bailey. Because of his small stature—he stood on a crate to reach microphones—he wasn't a threat to anyone. He was deliberately not showy or brash in performance, so as not to appear "uppity." But he was a showman. DeFord devised a megaphone to increase his harmonica's volume. He also had a rack to hold it as well as a number of items for creating sound effects.

Roy Acuff came to the Opry in 1938. He knew of DeFord Bailey's drawing power and asked him to join his touring troupe.

"I was an unknown when I began touring with DeFord," Acuff later recalled. "He could draw a crowd, not me. He helped me get started."

When Bill Monroe came to the Grand Ole Opry in 1939, he did the same thing, taking DeFord along to ensure he'd have big audiences. "He was a good, decent man," said Monroe. "When we toured together, people even in rural areas knew that he was black, but it didn't matter to them."

The 1940s brought musical changes to the Grand Ole Opry. The old-time sounds were now joined by the modern country music of acts like Pee Wee King & The Golden West Cowboys. Segments by DeFord Bailey and the other Opry pioneers were shortened.

The Harmonica Wizard was also unwittingly trapped between the forces of the dueling musical-performance organizations American Society of Composers, Authors and Publishers (ASCAP) and Broadcast Music, Inc. (BMI). ASCAP collected music licensing fees from radio stations and distributed money to songwriters exclusively until 1940. When it raised its rates, broadcasters formed BMI to rival it. WSM invested in BMI and instructed its artists to perform only music licensed by the upstart company. DeFord's tunes were essentially folk songs, but they were licensed by ASCAP. In any case, he reasoned that his listeners wanted to hear "Pan-American Blues" and "The Fox Chase," not new, unfamiliar tunes.

Unable or unwilling to change, DeFord Bailey was dropped from the cast in May 1941. For the rest of his life, he was wary of the music business. But he remained friends with his old Opry cohorts.

During World War II, he returned to the Opry to perform in a film made to boost GI morale. In the early 1950s, he toured with WLAC bluegrass star Carl Tipton and appeared regularly on local television and the nationally broadcast Chicago radio show *Don McNeil's Breakfast Club*. Bill Monroe brought him back to the Opry as his guest several times, paying DeFord out of his own pocket.

In the 1960s, DeFord Jr. became a regular on the syndicated TV show *Night Train*, playing in a band that included the then-unknown guitarist Jimi Hendrix. At his son's invitation, DeFord appeared on the 1963–1966 series several times. In 1967, DeFord was also filmed for the syndicated TV series *National Life's Grand Ole Opry*.

By this time, the folk-revival movement was in full swing. It wasn't long before folk enthusiasts approached DeFord and other old-time musicians about making coffeehouse appearances. He did several shows in the late 1960s at a Nashville club called The Marketplace. On these occasions, he not only played harmonica but sang and played banjo and guitar.

In 1967, producer Mike Weesner had encountered the well-known blind Nashville street singer Cortelia Clark. *Blues in the Street,* the album that resulted, won a Grammy Award as the Best Folk Recording of the Year. Weesner believed that a record by DeFord Bailey should be the natural follow-up. Despite repeated requests by the producer, DeFord declined. He also passed on recording offers from folk star Pete Seeger, harmonica ace Charlie McCoy, and singer James Talley. He turned down $2,500 to perform three songs in the 1975 Burt Reynolds movie *W.W. and The Dixie Dancekings*.

Urban renewal closed DeFord's shoeshine parlor in 1971. It was torn down, and he moved into a federally subsidized high-rise for the elderly. Now divorced from Ida Lee, he lived alone in his memento-filled apartment.

Social worker David Morton became his friend and functioned as DeFord's manager. He booked a number of concerts for the living legend in the early 1970s. He made tape recordings of the old man's still-vibrant playing. DeFord returned to the Opry stage twice in 1974, celebrating his seventy-fifth birthday there on December 14, 1974. He appeared on the show again in 1975 and 1982.

His passion for music remained with him until his death. He played his harmonica daily and often picked on his banjo and guitar as well.

"A harp has been a mother and father to me," he said. "This harp has carried me places money wouldn't start to . . . and brought me back. It's worth a million dollars just to have and play around on. . . . It's company to me.

"I learn something new about a harp every day or two. You never learn everything about one. . . . Every day I'm alive, I hear a different sound."

He called the instrument his "best friend" and summed up his career by noting, "I was a humdinger."

DeFord Bailey died on July 2, 1982, at age eighty-two. But his fame survived him.

On June 23, 1983, a celebration of his life was held in Nashville. A commemorative plaque was installed at his address. Then a monument was dedicated in Greenwood Cemetery, where he is buried. At the ceremony, fellow Opry pioneers The Crook Brothers played old-time hoedown tunes. Bill Monroe plucked "Evening Prayer Blues" on his mandolin. James Talley performed "John Henry." After the tombstone etched with the image of a harmonica was unveiled, Herman Crook played "Amazing Grace" solo on his harmonica. At a subsequent reception at the Country Music Hall of Fame, the Bailey family donated a number of artifacts to the museum.

In 1988, David Morton's tapes became an album titled *The Legendary DeFord Bailey: Country Music's First Black Star*. In 1991, Morton and Charles Wolfe published The Harmonica Wizard's biography, *DeFord Bailey: A Black Star in Early Country Music*. In 2002 came the documentary film *DeFord Bailey: A Legend Lost*. In 2004, his remarkable life and music were saluted with a program at the Nashville Public Library.

On November 15, 2005, DeFord Bailey was inducted into the Country Music Hall of Fame during ceremonies televised nationally from Madison Square Garden in New York. Today, his plaque rests in the same room as those of his fellow Opry pioneers and touring partners Uncle Dave Macon (1870–1952), The Delmore Brothers, Roy Acuff (1903–1992), and Bill Monroe (1911–1996).

# Sure Love

Hal Ketchum had achieved country stardom and had found the "Sure Love" he sang about, but just when he seemed to have it all, he nearly lost it all.

"I woke up on my forty-fifth birthday—April 9, 1998—with little feeling in my right arm," Hal recalls. "I was admitted to Seton Hospital in Austin, Texas, on Easter Sunday. I was paralyzed from the neck down.

"Gina and I had only been married a couple of months. In a way, I think that was a bonding experience. Gina was there with me every second. They put a cot in my room. The nurses were opposed to it. They said, 'He needs absolute total silence and rest for these batteries of tests, until we know what this is. We're losing him.' Gina said, 'Well, take it or leave it—I'm staying.' She never left my side."

The singer credits his wife's steadfast love for his miraculous recovery. His medical condition was eventually diagnosed as multiple sclerosis in 2002. This disease involves the deterioration of nerve fibers in the brain and spinal cord. Some patients become permanently disabled. There is no cure.

Today, a rehabilitated Hal Ketchum remains one of the Grand Ole Opry's most charismatic performers and a widely beloved figure throughout Nashville's music community. Yet his road to Music City and the Opry's stage was anything but typical.

Hal was born April 9, 1953, and raised in Greenwich, New York, a hamlet of 2,500 in the shadow of the Adirondack Mountains, near the Vermont state line. His father worked as a production manager for a newspaper, played banjo, and was a member of the Buck Owens fan club.

"My mother had multiple sclerosis," Hal says, adding quickly, "Typically, it's not hereditary.

"She was sick all of my childhood. She was institutionalized—they thought she was nuts. They put her away, gave her shock treatments. In the dark ages of medical science, they didn't know what was wrong with her.

"She was in a wheelchair when I was in high school and then bedridden. It ended up she spent the last five years of her life in a nursing home. My father and my brother and sister and I were incapable of doing full-time nursing care."

Hal left home at age seventeen and moved to Florida to learn carpentry. He relocated to the Texas hill country to ply his trade in 1981.

Musically, Hal was a late bloomer. He'd played drums in local bands as a teenager but did not focus on music until he fell under the influence of the singer-songwriters of the Lone Star State. Captivated by troubadours such as Townes Van Zandt and Lyle Lovett, Hal taught himself to play the guitar and began writing tunes. Soon, that was all he thought about.

"I had to do it. There was never a day that I didn't wake up thinking about making a living as a songwriter and a singer. It was truly an obsession.

"My home life deteriorated because of my obsession. It cost me a marriage."

Hal Ketchum completely walked away from his steady profession of nearly twenty years as a cabinetmaker to enter the uncertain world of music making. In 1986, he recorded a small-label album called *Threadbare Alibis*. The following year, he was scouted by Nashville music executives when he performed at the Kerrville Folk Festival in Texas. Hal turned thirty-five in 1988. He figured it was now or never and headed for Music City.

The handsome, prematurely gray–haired Hal Ketchum burst on the country radio airwaves in 1991 with "Small Town Saturday Night." The national music-trade publication *Radio & Records* named it the top country single of that year. *Music Row* magazine named its clever video the Breakthrough Video of the Year. Inevitably, the giant hit led to an invitation to appear on the Grand Ole Opry. Hal made his debut on the Opry stage the day after Thanksgiving in 1991.

"I wasn't raised listening to the Opry," he admits. "I didn't really know that much about it, but my father was a huge fan of the Opry. It was through him and his record collection that I knew about it. The first time I was invited to play there and stood on that circle of wood on that stage . . . was the first time I felt like a star.

"It was a really spiritual thing. After that first time, I was completely hooked. I love being around all those guys. There are so many stories. For me, the essence of country music is there. So I really kind of lobbied to become a member. After I'd been there three or four times, I said to [then–Opry manager] Hal Durham, 'Look, if there's any way I can participate on a higher level, I'd be honored to.' I became a cast member on January 22, 1994.

"I can still remember every detail. It was the Standard Candy portion of the show. Marty Stuart, Jan Howard and, a surprise to me, Vince Gill were on with me. I sang 'Wings of a Dove' with Ferlin Husky. I had never met him. About three minutes before I went on, I saw him. My dad was in the wings, and he was a huge Ferlin Husky fan. So I asked Ferlin if he would join me on 'Wings of a Dove.' He said, 'I don't want to steal your thunder. This is your night.' But I insisted. So it was a great moment."

Hal's father was in a wheelchair that evening, terminally ill with lung cancer. Witnessing his son's induction was one of the last things he ever did.

"I finished up onstage and said, 'How'd I do, Pop?' He said,

'Good. Now take me home. I'm done.' And he died two days after I was inducted into the Opry cast. He stayed alive just so he could come and see it."

His father's memory was recalled in the poem that Hal wrote for his Opry induction. It was printed in that evening's program booklet:

A long time ago,
In my very childhood,
Marty Robbins told me
Of trouble in El Paso.
I was in the kitchen,
I remember it was wintertime.
Summer was for play,
Winter for reflection.
More time underfoot,
More time to listen.
The snow piled up,
The little house hummed and shook.
Ray Charles was Busted.
Buck and The Buckaroos
Had a Tiger by the Tail.
Patsy Cline descended like an
Angel on a staircase of strings.
I loaded Sixteen Tons with Ernie Ford,
And studied the written word
With Roger Miller.
My father brought these people home,
One by one,
And they all stayed.
They told me even then
That I was welcome,
They knew I understood.
A thousand souls and singers
Have reckoned me to this

Hallowed place,
And tho' some would say
I've come a long way,
I would say simply
That tonight, I arrive.

Hal's "Past the Point of Rescue" (1992), "Five O'Clock World" (1992), "Sure Love" (1992), "Hearts Are Gonna Roll" (1993), "Mama Knows the Highway" (1993), "Stay Forever" (1995), and other hits kept his career rolling. His personal life derailed again when his 1991–1997 marriage to a Nashville music publisher ended in divorce. Hal figured he'd stay single after that. But within weeks of his second divorce, he fell in love with Nashville stylist Gina Giglio.

"If I hadn't met her, I don't know if I would have ever married again," he comments. "She was doing hair and makeup for a Ricky Skaggs TV show at the Ryman Auditorium that I was on as a guest. I walked in, and there she was. She was the first person who walked up and said, 'Hi' to me. We just started a conversation. About five or six months ensued where we just talked every once in a while.

"I remember I was shooting a video ["Hang in There Superman"], and I wanted her to do the hair and makeup on it. I already had my sights on her. Then I asked for her again for a photo shoot, and that was it. We've been together ever since.

"I proposed to her in the Austin airport. I walked up to her holding a bunch of flowers with one iris in the middle. I had put a ring on the stem of the iris. I didn't say anything. I just handed her the flowers and made sure she did sniff from the iris.

"I'd asked her to marry me a few times before that, and she said, 'Where's the ring?' which apparently you're supposed to have when you propose—I'm a little slow."

They married on Valentine's Day, February 14, 1998. Almost immediately afterward came Hal's diagnosis of MS. Interestingly, it was not his first near-death experience. When he was twenty-two, he was in a construction accident that nearly killed him.

"I'd fallen on a pile of rocks from about 20 feet in the air. I fractured my skull and broke my collarbone and broke my arm in two places and broke my leg. The term 'multiple abrasions' doesn't even come close. I left my body, and I remember actually flying along behind a truck."

When he was in his thirties, he nearly drowned while snorkeling in the Caribbean. Again, he came back.

"I've come close a couple of times. But it's been important to stay. I wouldn't have the joys I have if I had left earlier.

"I've always healed remarkably well and quickly from any injuries. I've had some other illnesses in my life. I've always bounced back.

"Anyway, I faced the horror of that diagnosis. So I was traumatized and fearful of what was going to happen to me. Gina and the people she surrounded me with were so positive. She has a lot of holistic sense. This certain serenity of her presence was healing.

"I was taken home from the hospital after about a month. Gina would drive me to occupational therapy, physical therapy—things like learning to tie a shoelace, making a bow. Ironically, it feels exactly the same as it did when you were a child when you finally get the loop through the hole. It's the same feeling, and it's a beautiful feeling. When I learned to make a C-chord on the guitar again, it was exactly like being thirteen again."

During his recuperation, the Ketchums moved from Austin, where he had lived since 1997, to Chicago, and then to Santa Fe, New Mexico. There, Hal took up painting, and his works have been shown in Santa Fe galleries. The couple moved back to Nashville in 2001 and decided to start his second family. His children from his first marriage—Sarah and Graham—were both grown and living in San Antonio. Hal and Gina adopted Fani (born in 1997) and had daughters Ruby and Sophie in 2001 and 2004.

"Ruby was eleven days old the first time she was on the Opry stage. I had a Gibson guitar in a felt-lined case. I opened the case, built a little bassinet in it, and laid her in the case onstage while I performed. That's a pretty good introduction to the Opry.

"It's such a beautiful place for my girls. It's so welcoming. It's such a family environment. Where else in the world can you take your kids and let them run around backstage? Sophie kind of soaks it all in. She'll wander onstage. Fani has developed a real love of anybody with an upright bass. She loves going into the Riders in the Sky dressing room, because there's always music in there. Ruby's the one who really enjoys being onstage and singing with me.

"They're all really infatuated with Little Jimmy Dickens. They love The Whites—Buck White is kind of like a grandfather to them."

Gina and the girls have changed Hal Ketchum's personality profoundly. They give him hope and optimism, he says.

"Gina says, 'You *had* multiple sclerosis, and you don't have that now.' She is exceptionally strong. It's not denial. It's the power of mind over body. And I've always had that approach, myself."

Hal adds that Gina's grace and love are also responsible for his new outlook on life. Hal is much sunnier and far less subject to dark mood swings than he was ten years ago.

"I don't think I was ever really joyful before," he agrees. "I always felt like I was under a cloud in some way or other. That's my depressive nature, I guess.

"I think that being capable of being happy is being capable of being loved. I think those two things go hand in hand."

# Behind Every Great Man . . .

If it ain't broke, don't fix it.

Randy Travis has had the same record producer since 1985. Kyle Lehning was behind the country superstar's breakthrough hits two decades ago, and he is still producing Randy's records. Jeff Davis, the singer's road manager, has been with him for twenty years. Fiddler David Johnson was in Randy's band back home in North Carolina in the 1970s, and he's still there today. The star's lead guitarist is a veteran of more than twenty years. His bass player has also been a confederate since Randy's earliest days in Nashville, and his drummer has been with him for more than fifteen years.

Most significant of all is the steadfast love and dedication of Lib Hatcher Travis. She is both his wife and his manager.

"It's hard to believe, but we've known each other for thirty-two years," marvels Randy. "Can you believe that? We've been married seventeen years now.

"That working–together relationship is just another part of our everyday life. We have businesses together. I don't think it's any harder [to be both married and in business together]. I wouldn't say that. It boils down to truly loving one another and caring enough about making the relationship work and enjoying spending time with each other. All those things have to be there."

Lib is far more than his wife, manager, and life's companion. She practically saved his life. And she is definitely the reason he wound up with a career in country music, never mind one of the most wildly successful ones in history.

The star was born Randy Bruce Traywick in Marshville, North Carolina, on May 4, 1959. His father, Harold, was a farmer and construction worker. But he was also something else—an enthusiastic country-music fan and performer who coached all six of his children to be the same. Randy and his two brothers were given guitar lessons and put onstage at an early age. Harold Traywick's favorites included Hank Williams, Ernest Tubb, Lefty Frizzell, Gene Autry, and Roy Rogers, so they became Randy's as well.

Randy played his first show when he was nine years old. He and his older brother Ricky formed a duo and were regulars in local honky-tonks by the time they were fourteen and fifteen, respectively. Randy dropped out of school to become a full-time musician not long afterward.

"I didn't like school," he recalls. "I couldn't stand it, to tell you the truth. I started runnin' away from home, drinkin', and getting into trouble. After about the seventh grade, I just almost wouldn't go to school at all. I went into the ninth grade, and I never did finish that."

He was soon running wild, drinking, brawling, and committing crimes. By age seventeen, the juvenile delinquent looked like a sure bet for a prison sentence of one kind or another.

"When I look back to when I was a teenager, with the amount of drugs and alcohol, I wasn't much of a human. . . . It was drinkin' and drivin' and tryin' to outrun policemen. . . . I guess I would've straightened up sooner or later, but I probably would have gone to prison before I did. I may not have lived long enough to straighten out. . . . The way I was living, I was headed for jail or the local cemetery."

In early 1977, he entered and won a talent contest at a Charlotte nightclub called Country City USA. Club owner Lib Hatcher saw "something special" in him, as she later put it. He confessed to her that he was facing five years of jail time for breaking and entering. She went to the judge and talked him into giving her custody of the young hell-raiser. She also hired Randy as the club's full-time vocalist.

"With Mama and Daddy . . . I just didn't want to listen to them, didn't want to do what they said," Randy remembers. "But for some reason, I would listen to Lib. . . . She's such a good person. And when a person's like that, it kinda rubs off on you."

Lib was also fiercely dedicated to making him a star. Throughout the next few years, she tenaciously promoted him in every way she could. When Randy was eighteen, she financed a recording session that resulted in two singles that she badgered radio stations to play. One of them, "She's My Woman," actually made the national popularity charts. Because of her successful nightclub, Lib got to know many country stars who came through Charlotte on tour, including Dottie West, Gene Watson, and Loretta Lynn. She'd been a Grand Ole Opry fan since girlhood, and she eagerly tried to learn the country-music business from them.

Lib and Randy moved to Nashville in 1981. A year later, Opry star Ray Pillow recommended Lib for a job managing the Nashville Palace nightclub. She hired Randy as a dishwasher. He soon became the club's short-order cook. In between flipping burgers or grilling steaks, he'd take off his starched white apron and get onstage to sing. This went on for four long years.

The club's location proved to be advantageous. It was right next to the Opryland complex that contains the Opry House and, at that time, The Nashville Network (TNN) cable-TV studios. Opry stars often dropped by the Nashville Palace and were duly impressed by Randy's burnished baritone. The show's Jeanne Pruett recorded Randy's song "I Told You So." Opry stars like Johnny Russell (1940–2001) and Barbara Mandrell became boosters. Ralph Emery, the host of TNN's *Nashville Now,* invited him to sing on the TV show. As a gimmick, Randy would bring Ralph a meal he'd just cooked. Renamed "Randy Ray," he recorded an LP titled *Randy Ray Live at The Nashville Palace* in 1983.

"Sit back and listen to one of tomorrow's stars," wrote Jimmy Dickens for the liner notes. But down on Music Row, things weren't going so well. Lib had taken Randy's tapes to every record company in town. Every label turned him down, some more than once.

Now completely dedicated to leading a healthy lifestyle, Randy had begun working out with weights, eventually building the lean, muscular physique he maintains today. He also jogged up and down Music Row and worked at renovating Lib's home/office.

Record producer Keith Stegall had produced Randy's album, and he began to play it for various country executives. One was producer Kyle Lehning, who was intrigued enough to go to the Nashville Palace to hear Randy sing live. He, too, became a supporter. Although Warner Bros. Records had previously rejected him, the company relented and signed the singer in 1985. The label didn't like the name "Randy Ray" and renamed him "Randy Travis." Kyle and Keith coproduced his debut disc. Keith would later go on to produce Opry superstar Alan Jackson's records.

In June, Randy Travis sang "On the Other Hand" at Nashville's annual Fan Fair festival, and the crowd of twenty thousand went wild. In August, it became his debut single. It was at first deemed "too country" by radio programmers and fell off the charts. In December, the label issued a second single, "1982." This time, Randy Travis would not be denied. The tune became his first top-ten hit. In March of 1986, the singer fulfilled a lifelong dream by singing on the Grand Ole Opry. Next, his record company took the unprecedented step of re-releasing "On the Other Hand." This time, it became his first number-one smash.

*Storms of Life* was issued as Randy's debut Warner LP in June 1986. It contained both "1982" and "On the Other Hand," as well as his next two hits, "Diggin' Up Bones" and "No Place Like Home." *Storms of Life* eventually sold more than three million copies. Critics began hailing him as the leader of a "new traditionalist" movement in country music.

"Some people look at it like it's a new trend," he commented.

"But to me, it's just an old type of music that's being accepted by a wider group of people than it used to be."

No one was more elated by his success than the traditionalists at the Opry. On December 20, 1986, Randy Travis joined the show's cast.

By this time, he'd bought a bread truck and outfitted it with bunk beds for his band. He was opening shows for the likes of George Strait, Willie Nelson, and George Jones. But that didn't last long. Seemingly overnight, Randy Travis became a country-music headliner with his own gleaming tour bus instead of a bread truck.

Released in 1987, *Always & Forever* became an even bigger success than his debut album. Its four chart-topping singles propelled it to more than five million in sales. One of those singles, "Forever and Ever, Amen," was country's biggest hit of the year. By 1988, Randy Travis was the crown prince of country music, scoring hit after hit with tunes like "Deeper Than the Holler" and "Is It Still Over."

Despite the increasing pressure and the enormous workload, he remained unfailingly humble and polite. Randy still impresses people with his quiet dignity, easygoing charm, and soft-spoken grace.

By the dawn of the 1990s, Randy Travis was country music's top-earning concert star. At age thirty, he'd sold more than thirteen million records. (His tally is now in excess of 21 million discs sold.) Formerly struggling "nobodies" from North Carolina, he and Lib were now on top of the world. She invested their money in Nashville real estate, and they bought a home in Hawaii. He recalls proposing to her in 1991 by saying, "Well, we ought to get married now, I guess."

"Those aren't the exact words, but that's about as simple as it was. Heavy-duty romantic, huh? Lib will never let me live this one down, but our wedding took place in the backyard [in Hawaii] under a banana tree with a pastor and a stranger there to witness it. That's pretty much what it boiled down to, because I did not want a big anything."

Their wedding day was May 31, 1991. Tongues wagged in Music City because she was eighteen years his senior. But their relationship has endured. Randy was baptized around 1993, and the couple's journey together has been spiritual as well as romantic.

By the year 2000, Randy Travis was the veteran of more than thirty major hits. His classics include "Hard Rock Bottom of Your Heart," "He Walked on Water," "Better Class of Losers" (which he cowrote with Alan Jackson), "If I Didn't Have You," "Whisper My Name," "Spirit of a Boy, Wisdom of a Man," and "Look Heart, No Hands." Furthermore, he had branched out into acting. He has now appeared in more than forty theatrical films, TV movies, and episodes of television series.

In the early years of the new millennium, Randy turned out a series of religious albums that have resulted in six awards from the Gospel Music Association and have accounted for three of his six Grammy Awards to date. In 2003, "Three Wooden Crosses" became yet another of his number-one smashes.

Through it all, Lib has been by his side. In 1998, they moved from Nashville to Santa Fe, New Mexico. Their adobe mansion there resembles a southwestern pueblo. She loves decorating it and the guesthouse with Native American and western art. He enjoys the weight room, swimming pool, and horse stables. The two remain practically inseparable.

"We have disagreements, like anybody else," he admits. "There's no doubt about that. I'm the one who's usually going to get angry. That's the part of me that I have to pray a lot about. There's that redneck in me who still wants to get mad and yell. She walks away from the conversation at that point. So we just cease to talk for a few minutes. But as the years go by, that does not happen that often anymore."

So what is the secret to blending business with a lasting marriage?

"You do what she tells you," answers Randy Travis with a laugh. "Sometimes that's true, actually. But it's give and take. You can't always have your way. She can't always have her way. You have to truly have love for one another. If it's true love, you will show respect for each other. Your time together and the affection you show each other are important. You have to spend time, not just working [together] as we do, but laughing and enjoying other things outside of work.

"And let's face it, I finished the eighth grade. That's as far as I got. I have to look at it objectively here. I'm not dealing with a full deck in a lot of areas. I know I'm not the businessman here, so I've been fortunate to have people around me who are good at what they do and who care about me. I've been a blessed man."

33

# The Tragedy of Country Music's King

Everything you read about him will tell you that Hank Williams' death date was January 1, 1953. But he was almost certainly dead for hours before New Year's Day rolled around.

Thirty years after the superstar's death, a police report surfaced in Knoxville, Tennessee, that documented the last few hours of his life. For years, Hank's place of death has been listed as Oak Hill, West Virginia, because that is where his driver stopped, found him cold, and took him to a hospital. In the wake of the tragedy, the Knoxville police investigation was ordered.

Tennessee Highway patrolman Swan H. Kitts had stopped Hank's 1952 powder-blue Cadillac in the nearby town of Blaine, Tennessee, earlier that night. The driver, Charles Carr, was given a ticket after nearly running the cop's car off the highway. Swan Kitts was ordered by his superior, Captain John Davis, to fully investigate the time Hank spent in the Knoxville area the day before. The handwritten report lay forgotten in the Union County Courthouse for decades.

Swan Kitts wrote, "On Wednesday, Dec. 31, 1952, Hank Williams and his driver, Charles Carr, caught a plane out of Knoxville and left their car at the airport at 3:30 p.m. They returned to the airport at 5:57 p.m."

They'd driven to Knoxville from Hank's home in Montgomery, Alabama, en route to a New Year's Day concert in Canton, Ohio. A deep winter fog had halted them in the mountains of East Tennessee. The weather was too inclement to fly, so after the plane landed back at the airport, Charles Carr headed for a hotel with his nearly lifeless companion.

"At 7:08 p.m., Carr checked in Williams and himself at the Andrew Johnson Hotel," continues the police report. "Dan McCrary, assistant hotel manager for the night shift, said Carr seemed nervous. The hotel manager didn't see Williams as the porters helped him to his room. They carried him up. He spoke only a few words as he was so drunk that he was almost out. Carr ordered two steaks. Carr ate his, but Williams was out and couldn't eat.

"Dr. P. H. Cardwell arrived. He said Williams was very drunk and that he talked with him. He gave Williams two injections of morphine and B-12. He said he noticed Williams had some capsules, three or four, but didn't know what they were or if Williams had taken any of them. Dr. Cardwell stayed only a short time and left.

"In about an hour and a half or two hours, Carr talked with someone on the phone and said he and Williams had to leave for Canton, Ohio. The porters had to help him dress Williams. He was lifeless as they put his clothes on him. The porters carried him out and put him in the backseat of the car. Williams never moved at all. He seemed to make a coughing like sound as they carried him, but was lifeless and didn't move. Carr checked them out at 10:45 p.m., spending only three hours and 44 minutes at the hotel, after telling the manager that they planned to spend the night there.

"Carr, driving Williams' car, was stopped near Blaine, Tennessee, at about 11:45 p.m. by S.H. Kitts of the Tennessee Highway Patrol after Carr almost hit head-on with the patrol car.

"Carr said he was driving Hank Williams. I noticed Williams and asked Carr if he could be dead, as he was pale and blue looking. But he said Williams had drunk six bottles of beer and a doctor had given him two injections to help him sleep. He asked me not to wake him up as he was very sick and looked that way.

"I had him (Carr) to stop at Rutledge. I wrote him a ticket (for reckless driving) at 12:30. He was tried before a Justice of the Peace, O. H. Marshall, and was fined $25 and costs. I talked with him about Williams' condition in the presence of Sheriff J. N. Antrican and Marshall. We thought he (Carr) was a little nervous over paying the fine, and he asked us not to bother Williams. Carr had a soldier with him at the time he was in Rutledge. He paid the fine, thanked us and left at about 1 a.m.

"After investigating this matter, I think that Williams was dead when he was dressed and carried out of the hotel. Since he was drunk and was given the injections and could have taken some capsules earlier, with all this he couldn't have lasted over an hour and a half or two hours.

"A man drunk or doped will make some movement if you move them. A dead man will make a coughing sound if they are lifted around. Taking all this into consideration, he must have died in Knoxville at the hotel." For the record, Hank's driver has always disputed this conclusion.

Somewhere between Rutledge and Bristol, Tennessee, the soldier got out. An exhausted Charles Carr hired a taxi driver named Donald Surface to assist him when he stopped in Bristol. They arrived in Oak Hill, West Virginia, around 5:30 a.m. and stopped at a Pure Oil filling station. From there, they were directed to Oak Hill Hospital. Hank was pronounced dead there around 7:00 a.m. During the autopsy, nobody checked for drugs in his system. The cause of death was listed as "a severe heart condition." Hank Williams was twenty-nine years old.

Hank's funeral was held in Montgomery on Sunday, January 4, 1953. A crowd estimated at 20,000 gathered outside the Municipal Auditorium. Inside were 2,750 more. Roy Acuff led the singing of Hank's song "I Saw the Light." Red Foley sang "Peace in the Valley." Other Opry stars in attendance included Bill Monroe, Carl Smith, Jimmy Dickens, Ray Price, June Carter, Johnnie & Jack, Lew Childre, and Webb Pierce.

"It was almost impossible for the funeral procession to get from

Hank Williams' mother's home to the city auditorium where the service was," recalled Hank's Drifting Cowboys band fiddler Jerry Rivers. "It took probably two hours, and it was probably five or six blocks. . . . This was an event that I had never seen anything like and, of course, never will again. . . . Within ten years, he was bigger than when he was when he died. And his stature has continued to grow."

No Grand Ole Opry star's story is better known than that of country music's tragic king. Hank Williams remains the most influential singer-songwriter in country history, with classic songs that continue to inspire generation after generation.

He was born Hiram King Williams on September 17, 1923, in Mount Olive, Alabama. A congenital spinal-column defect called spina bifida was undiagnosed, and it caused him lifelong pain. Hank's musical style was influenced by his mentor, a black street performer named Rufus "Teetot" Payne. Hank was reportedly drinking by age eleven and was performing in honky-tonks by age fifteen. In 1943, he met the beautiful and ambitious Audrey Sheppard. They were married by a justice of the peace on December 15, 1944. Lycrecia, Audrey's daughter from her first marriage, remembers them both fondly.

"He's my father, as far as I'm concerned, the only father I ever knew," says Lycrecia. "My real father left Mother before I was even born.

"You know how the legend goes, that she caused him all this heartbreak. I guess people have to have someone to blame. But Mother was never interested in anything except helping Daddy get ahead. She had a lot of ambition. . . . He definitely would not have made it without Mother. And that's not taking anything away from him. She's the one who had the business sense, and Daddy had the talent."

In 1943–1948, Hank performed on WFSA in Montgomery, Alabama. He also sang in some of the roughest roadhouses in the state.

"My friends who grew up with Hank down there told me about

when they went to work with Hank," Jerry Rivers remembered. "He went into a pawn shop and bought everybody in the band a blackjack. He said, 'If you're gonna work with me, you'll need that a lot more than you will your guitar.' So that tells you something there about the atmosphere that Hank had to work in."

Audrey constantly looked for ways to get them out of Montgomery and into the big time. On September 14, 1946, they took the train to Nashville so that Hank could audition for songwriter/publisher/producer Fred Rose. Fred signed Hank as a staff songwriter for Acuff-Rose Publishing and got him a recording contract with a small label called Sterling Records. In 1947, Fred moved Hank up to the larger MGM Records. "Move it on Over" became Hank's first hit later that year. As Audrey had hoped, it got them out of Montgomery and secured him a cast position at the *Louisiana Hayride,* which was broadcast from Shreveport, Louisiana, by the powerful signal of KWKH.

"When Hank Williams came to the *Louisiana Hayride* [in 1948], I didn't know at the time that he was a drinker," recalls singer Johnny Wright. "His wife Audrey was pregnant. I guess they must have got into an argument. He tore up everything in the house, broke the furniture, the lamps, and everything. So she called my wife [Kitty Wells] and asked if she'd come over and stay the night. Hank was on one of his big sprees. So Kitty and I went over there and spent the night with them. Hank had gotten into Audrey's nerve pills. So I had to sleep with Hank that night, and my wife slept with Audrey. He'd stay on that drinking for about a week before you could get him off it."

"People talked about this young man from Montgomery, Alabama, who was absolutely stealing shows away from all the greats of that era," recalled singer-songwriter Merle Kilgore (1934–2005). "He had a slight little problem. That is, he liked to drink. He was a teenage drunk. They said he was coming down to see if he could work for a year in Shreveport, and then the Grand Ole Opry would consider him. He had a record out, 'Move it on Over,' that was played quite a bit. He had an early-morning show [on KWKH].

A teenage drunk—I'd never seen one of those. I wanted to meet this guy, so I was there waiting. About 5:30 in the morning, here came an old car. This guy got out. He had a white suit on. I said, 'You Hank Williams?' He said, 'Who are you?' I said, 'My name is Merle. The elevators don't work, and you have to carry your own instruments up. I'd like to carry your guitar.' He looked at me and said, 'Grab it, hoss.'

"I remember his wife Audrey was with him, and she was pregnant with Hank Williams Jr. I said, 'Are you going to sing?' She said, 'You're not kidding! I'll be singing right on the show today.' I remember Hank looking at me real funny, like he didn't want this to happen. But there she was, every morning."

Randall Hank Williams (Hank Williams Jr.) was born on May 26, 1949. Two weeks later, his father made the most spectacular Grand Ole Opry debut in history. Hank's success at the *Louisiana Hayride* and further hits like "Honky Tonkin'" and "Mansion on the Hill" led to his invitation to perform on the Opry on June 11, 1949. He sang his new record, "Lovesick Blues," and created pandemonium.

"I was in the audience," recalled Porter Wagoner. "It was electrifying. I think I was, like, fourteen years old. My sister and brother-in-law brought me down to Nashville [from Missouri]. My sister said, 'You know what would make this trip perfect? If Hank Williams was going to be on there.' I said, 'Well, he's not a member [of the Opry] yet.' But, God, I loved his music. We got in line early that day. We got a program, and it said, 'Special Guest Hank Williams.' And I lit up. I couldn't believe it, man. That night, I couldn't wait to see him come on. And then it was like a storm. People were just ecstatic. It was probably one of the most moving moments that I can remember. We were sitting behind this post, and I had a stiff neck the next day. It was wonderful, a great evening."

Between 1949 and 1952, Hank had twenty-seven smash hits, including "Cold, Cold Heart," "Hey Good Lookin'," and "Jambalaya." He eclipsed such established superstars as Roy Acuff, Eddy Arnold, and Bob Wills.

"Hank Williams was country music's first superstar," stated Jerry Rivers. "When we went to New York City to do a few of the showcase shows—Kate Smith's show, Perry Como's show—and I walked down 5th Avenue and out of one of the many camera shops, gimmick shops, along Times Square, I heard Hank Williams singin' 'Cold, Cold Heart' on a radio station or a record they were playing, and I thought, 'Hank Williams is known on Times Square, I can't believe that.'"

"He was on the Hadacol show," remembered former Opry bass player Buddy Killen about a tour sponsored by that patent medicine. "All the big stars in the country would get on the train, called the Hadacol Train, and they'd go around and play football stadiums. They had Bob Hope and Milton Berle and so many of the big pop stars of the day were on that show. Hank encored eight times in a row, and Bob Hope went back to the manager of the show and said, 'I will not go on after that hillbilly again. You put me on first.' That's how much of an impact that Hank had."

"I don't guess anybody can define charisma," mused former Opry steel guitarist Joe Talbot. "Whatever it is, he had it. I watched him work back in those days. He just absolutely laid the people out flat."

Jimmie Dickens reminisces, "I suppose I was as close to him as most people. He was a very moody person, and his moods changed quite a bit. You'd be talkin' to him once, he'd be laughin'. Then the next thing you'd know, Hank Williams would be in deep thought about something. But we were friends. We went rabbit huntin' with beagle dogs, and we went fishin' together. We'd go to one another's house and just visit. We'd sit around and talk, but not about country music. Just visiting."

"I met him when I first came to Nashville in 1950, and he was hot as a firecracker," recalled Chet Atkins. "I remember I was impressed by how slender he was and how dark his eyes were. He had real dark eyes. In a few days, he came to me and said, 'Fred Rose says you write songs. We should get together and try to write one.' We did, but I was too awestruck by his stardom and everything.

We tried to write a couple of songs, and nothing happened. But he would come up and say, 'Hey, hoss, listen to this.'

"You could smell the bourbon on his breath, and he'd sing 'Jambalaya' or one of those new songs he'd written. He was always nice to me, but he was pretty cruel to some of the people who turned down his songs. I remember he once played a song for Hank Snow, and Hank didn't like it. So he told Mr. Snow he could do some impossible physical things to himself. His songs were his babies.

"He was this funny guy, too. People think of Hank as being somber and writing all these sad songs, but he was very funny. He had some great comebacks. I guess he patterned himself in conversation a lot like Freddy Rose, because Freddy had a lot of great retorts. He was sharp as a razor, and Hank tried to be like that. A very funny fellow, I thought, and you never read that or hear about it."

"Hank was not actually a drunk," observed Drifting Cowboys bass player Hillous Butrum. "He was an alcoholic, 'cause he would go for months at a time and never take a drink. I've seen Hank buy the booze, but he'd sit there and drink a Coca-Cola because, he said, 'You know what would happen to me. If I take one drink, you all would wind up havin' to haul me on the rest of the tour.' And this would be what would happen, because he couldn't take one drink and leave it alone. He would just keep drinkin' 'til he completely knocked himself out. So then we'd go to an auditorium and pour coffee down him and get him straightened up to do a show. Then we'd come back to Nashville, put him in the hospital, and he'd dry out. Then he'd go for months and never take a drink."

But Hank's periods of sobriety became more and more infrequent. Everything began to unravel in 1952. He was recovering from a back operation as the year began and was dosing himself with pain medication. Unable to pay his band, he let The Drifting Cowboys go. He moved out of his house in January, probably at a fed-up Audrey's insistence. For a time, he shared a house with

Ray Price, who was then emerging with his first hits "Talk to Your Heart" and "Don't Let the Stars Get in Your Eyes."

"When Hank and I met, it was one of those instant-friendship things," Ray recalls. "He took me to the Grand Ole Opry the next day, and then we went to Evansville, Indiana, and wrote 'Weary Blues from Waitin'' together. We became very dear friends, close friends. I lived with Hank for almost a year before he moved [back] to Louisiana. Hank was my best friend, and he's the one that got me on the Grand Ole Opry. The house we shared is still there," a stone bungalow at the corner of Natchez Trace and Ashwood Avenue in West Nashville.

Hank traveled with The Carter Sisters, Mother Maybelle Carter, Roy Acuff, and Chet Atkins to appear on Kate Smith's TV program in New York. The shows were on March 26 and April 9, 1952. These shows are the only quality footage we have of Hank in performance.

As 1952 wore on, Hank began showing up drunk at shows more and more often, or not showing up at all. His reputation for unreliability meant that fewer and fewer people would take a chance on booking him to perform. When Audrey's divorce became final on July 10, 1952, Hank spent several days drinking relentlessly. Ray Price and Drifting Cowboys band member Don Helms arranged for him to be sedated and committed to a sanatorium. While he was gone, Ray moved out.

During his final year, Hank had an affair with a Nashville woman named Bobbie Jett. Then he took up with Faron Young's girlfriend, Louisiana native Billie Jean Jones. He went on another bender in August. As a result, he was dismissed from the Opry.

"I was there when he got fired," recalls Johnny Wright. "[Opry manager] Jim Denny called him and told him he was gonna have to leave the Opry. So Hank told him, 'Hell, you can't dismiss me—I've already quit.' Jim Denny said, 'Johnny, come by up here, and I will give you a check. He's got a little check coming.' So we loaded up everything Hank owned in his little Drifting Cowboys trailer. Kitty [Wells] and I had a '51 model Chrysler limousine. We put the reclining chair in the back, put Hank up in that chair, stretched him out, and took him home to Montgomery," towing the trailer.

"When we stopped at WSM [to pick up the check], Owen Bradley and Roy Acuff were up there. So they went down to my car to tell Hank good-bye. Then we stopped at a liquor store at 16th and Broadway. Hank wanted to get that check cashed and get him a fifth of whiskey. Hank's mother ran a boardinghouse in Montgomery. She met us at the door. We took him in, pulled his pants off, put his pajamas on, and put him to bed. The next time we saw Hank, he was back working at the *Louisiana Hayride*."

Fred Rose had come to Hank's rescue again by persuading the *Louisiana Hayride* to take him back. Hank married Billie Jean on the show's stage on October 19, 1952. Around this same time, he began to complain to *Hayride* performer Red Sovine that he was having chest pains. Hank's self-prescription was to take more drugs and drink more alcohol. During a December tour in Texas, Hank reportedly either overdosed or had a small heart attack or two. His time was running out.

Then came that winter ride down the "Lost Highway," to borrow a title from one of Hank's most chilling songs. Two days after Hank's burial in Montgomery's Oakwood Cemetery, Bobbie Jett gave birth to a daughter. The girl learned of her parentage as an adult and now performs as Jett Williams. Hank's son is superstar Hank Williams Jr. Grandchildren Holly Williams, Hillary Williams, and Hank Williams III are also singers.

In the aftermath of one of the greatest tragedies in music history, Hank had a string of posthumous hits. Indeed, "Kaw-Liga," "Your Cheatin' Heart," "I'm So Lonesome I Could Cry," and "Take These Chains from My Heart" remain some of his best-loved songs. As recently as 1989, he was on the charts and winning awards for "There's a Tear in My Beer," recorded as a "duet" with Hank Jr. A historical boxed set of his timeless recordings won two Grammy Awards in 1998. In 2008, Hank's radio broadcasts were released on compact discs, and his legendary family became the subject of a huge exhibit at the Country Music Hall of Fame.

Since his death, more than 250 tribute songs have been recorded about him. They include "The Night Hank Williams Came to Town" by Johnny Cash (1987), "The Ride" by David Allan Coe (1983), "Hank Williams, You Wrote My Life" by Moe Bandy (1965), and "Midnight in Montgomery" by the Opry's Alan Jackson (1992).

"It just felt like a little part of us died when Hank went," said June Carter Cash wistfully. "He was a great talent. We all grieved for Hank Williams."

# SOURCES

## Chapter 1: Johnny and June

Johnny Cash, interviews with Robert K. Oermann, July 1999, September 1994, April 1987.

June Carter Cash, interviews with Robert K. Oermann, July 1999, September 1994.

Cindy Cash, *The Cash Family Scrapbook* (New York: Crow Trade Paperbacks, 1997).

Johnny Cash, *Man in Black* (Grand Rapids, MI: Zondervan, 1975).

Johnny Cash with Patrick Carr, *Cash: The Autobiography* (New York: HarperCollins, 1997).

June Carter Cash, *Among My Klediments* (Grand Rapids, MI: Zondervan, 1979).

Marshall Grant with Chris Zar, *I Was There When It Happened: My Life with Johnny Cash* (Nashville: Cumberland House, 2006).

Peter Lewry, *A Johnny Cash Chronicle: I've Been Everywhere* (London: Helter Skelter, 2001).

Stephen Miller, *Johnny Cash: The Life of an American Icon* (London: Omnibus Press, 2003).

Michael Streissguth, *Johnny Cash: The Biography* (Cambridge, MA: Da Capo Press, 2006).

Steve Turner, *The Man Called Cash* (Nashville: W Publishing, 2004).

Hugh Waddell, compiler, *I Still Miss Someone* (Nashville: Cumberland House, 2004).

Mark Zwonitzer with Charles Hirshberg, *Will You Miss Me When I'm Gone: The Carter Family & Their Legacy in American Music* (New York: Simon & Schuster, 2002).

## Chapter 2: The Stringbean Murders

Anonymous, "Stringbean Buried Near Other Stars," *The Nashville Banner,* November 14, 1973.

Birthplace of Country Music Alliance, "David 'Stringbean' Akeman" online biographical entry, 2007.

Buddy Lee Attractions, *The Kentucky Wonder Stringbean* promotional biography (Nashville: Buddy Lee Attractions, 1971).

Warren B. Causey, *The Stringbean Murders* (Nashville: Quest Publishers, 1975).

Cousin Wilbur with Barbara M. McLean and Sandra S. Grafton, *Everybody's Cousin* (New York: Manor Books, 1979).

Bruce Eder, "Stringbean" online biographical entry on Allmusic.com, 2007.

Find a Grave, "David 'Stringbean' Akeman" online entry, 2007.

Linnell Gentry, *A History and Encyclopedia of Country, Western and Gospel Music* (Nashville: Clairmont Corp., 1969).

Bill Hance, "Shoe Box Banjo Start for 'String,'" *The Nashville Banner,* November 14, 1973.

Stacy Harris, "Stringbean Went a Lot Further," *The Tennessean,* November 13, 1973.

Louis M. "Grandpa" Jones with Charles K. Wolfe, *Everybody's Grandpa: Fifty Years Behind the Mike* (Knoxville: University of Tennessee Press, 1984).

Patricia Lynch Kimbro, "23 Years Later, Stringbean's $20,000 Found," *The Nashville Banner,* January 27, 1997.

Colin Larkin, *The Virgin Encyclopedia of Country Music* (London: Virgin Books, 1998).

Sam Lovullo and Marc Eliot, *Life in the Kornfield: My 25 Years at Hee Haw* (New York: Boulevard Books, 1996).

Barry McCloud et al., *Definitive Country* (New York: Perigee Trade, 1995).

John C. McLemore, "The Time Grandpa Jones Outwitted Perry Mason," *The Tennessean,* March 5, 1998.

Linda A. Moore, "Stringbean's Stash a Mouse Nest?" *The Tennessean,* January 28, 1997.

Musicweb Encyclopaedia of Popular Music, "Stringbean," biographical entry, 2005.

Randall Riese, *Nashville Babylon* (New York: Congdon & Weed, 1988).

Jeff Rovin, *Country Music Babylon* (New York: St. Martin's Press, 1993).

Richard D. Smith, *Can't You Hear Me Callin': The Life of Bill Monroe, Father of Bluegrass* (Boston: Little, Brown and Company, 2000).

Starday Records, *Stringbean and His Banjo: A Salute to Uncle Dave Macon* album liner notes (Nashville: Gusto Records, 1976).

Phil Sullivan, "More Than a Name," *The Tennessean,* April 1, 1962.

Wikipedia, "David 'Stringbean' Akeman" online encyclopedia entry, 2007.

## Chapter 3: A Lesson in Leavin'

Jan Howard interview with Robert K. Oermann, July 1993.

Wayne Oliver interview with Robert K. Oermann, July 1991.

Jeannie Seeley interview with Robert K. Oermann, July 1993.

Dottie West interviews with Robert K. Oermann, August 1990, November 1984, May 1983, April 1983.

Shelly West interview with Robert K. Oermann, July 1993.

Jim Albrecht, "The Wild West," *CountryStyle,* May 1981.

Michael Bane, "Dottie West: Country's Singing Swinger!" *Oui,* January 1983.

Judy Berryhill and Frances Meeker, *Country Sunshine: The Dottie West Story* (Nashville: Eggman Publishing, 1995).

Mary A. Bufwack and Robert K. Oermann, *Finding Her Voice: Women in Country Music* (Nashville: Vanderbilt University Press, 2003).

Scott Cain, "Dottie West: Happy Again," *Atlanta Journal*, April 17, 1981.

Rochelle Carter and Robert K. Oermann, "Trustee Seeks Out Dottie West Stash," *The Tennessean*, March 28, 1991.

Carol Davis and Sharon Curtis-Flair, "West Services Set for Saturday," *The Nashville Banner*, September 5, 1991.

Lois Ann Eagleston, "Events Leading to Dottie West Crash Pieced Together," *The Tennessean*, September 4, 1991.

Laura Eipper, "Country Music Warms Icy North," *The Tennessean*, April 2, 1978.

Thomas Goldsmith, "Fans, Friends Celebrate West's Life," *The Tennessean*, September 8, 1991.

Thomas Goldsmith, "Stars She Befriended Mourn Dottie," *The Tennessean*, September 5, 1991.

Dennis Hunt, "Dottie West Going Solo—On Record," *Los Angeles Times*, June 10, 1981.

David Kepple, "At 47, Beautiful Dottie Is Finding Her Best Success," *News* (Birmingham, AL), October 5, 1981.

Frances Meeker, "Bill, Dottie West Beat Hard Times," *The Nashville Banner*, January 26, 1967.

Bruce Minnigh, "Auction Brings Tears, Cash," *The Tennessean*, June 14, 1991.

Robert K. Oermann, "Manager: Dottie Endures Tough Times," *The Tennessean*, July 25, 1991.

Robert K. Oermann, "Dottie: Looking Up, Though She's Down," *The Tennessean*, August 4, 1990.

Robert K. Oermann, "Glamorous Dottie Remains a Role Model," *The Tennessean*, November 10, 1984.

Robert K. Oermann, "The Frizzell-West Dynasty," *Country Rhythms*, September 1983.

Robert K. Oermann, "Singer Dottie West Marries Steady Boyfriend," *The Tennessean*, July 2, 1983.

Robert K. Oermann, "Dottie, Shelly and Tess, West Gals Team Up," *The Tennessean*, May 7, 1983.

Jay Orr, "Stars Mourn West," *The Nashville Banner*, September 4, 1991.

Marty Racine, "At Her Peak," *Houston Chronicle,* August 30, 1981.

Joe Rich, "Dottie West Can't Pay Creditors," *The Tennessean,* August 21, 1990.

Dru Wilson, "West Was Raised on Cornbread and Fiddles," *Gazette Telegraph,* August 28, 1981.


## Chapter 4: Barbara and Ken

Barbara Mandrell and Ken Dudney interview with Robert K. Oermann, August 2007.

Barbara Mandrell interviews with Robert K. Oermann, September 1990, May 1988, December 1986, February 1984.

Mary A. Bufwack and Robert K. Oermann, *Finding Her Voice: Women in Country Music* (Nashville: Vanderbilt University Press, 2003).

Barbara Mandrell with George Vecsey, *Get to the Heart* (New York: Bantam Books, 1990).

Sandy Neese and Robert K. Oermann, "The Lady Is a Champ," *The Tennessean,* August 5, 1983.

Robert K. Oermann, "Mandrell's Life Story 'Gets to the Heart,'" *The Tennessean,* October 16, 1990.

Robert K. Oermann, "Mandrell's Candor Lands Her Best Seller," *The Tennessean,* October 7, 1990.

Robert K. Oermann, "Barbara Mandrell with Dolly: A Fantastic Comeback," *The Tennessean,* March 3, 1986.

Robert K. Oermann, "Choked Up Barbara Back: 'I Thank God I'm Alive,'" *The Tennessean,* January 4, 1985.

Robert K. Oermann, "The Barbara Mandrell Interview," *Country Rhythms,* May 1984.


## Chapter 5: Tribulation and Triumph

Bill Anderson interviews with Robert K. Oermann, July 2007, May 1999, September 1998, July 1996, August 1994.

Jan Howard interview with Robert K. Oermann, July 1987.

Bill Anderson, *I Hope You're Living as High on the Hog as the Pig You Turned Out to Be* (Marietta, GA: Longstreet Press, 1993).

Bill Anderson, *Whisperin' Bill* (Atlanta, GA: Longstreet Press, 1989).

Bill Anderson, *Poor Sweet Baby and Ten More Bill Anderson Songs* album liner notes (Los Angeles: United Artists Records, 1975).

Mary A. Bufwack and Robert K. Oermann, *Finding Her Voice: Women in Country Music* (Nashville: Vanderbilt University Press, 2003).

Larry Holden, "Full Circle," *Country Weekly,* October 23, 2006.

Larry Holden, "Penning Things Down," *Country Weekly,* January 20, 2004.

Jan Howard, *Sunshine and Shadow: My Story* (New York: Richardson & Steirman, 1987).

Robert K. Oermann, "Legendary Bill Anderson," *The Tennessean,* July 13, 1996.

Robert K. Oermann, "'Whisperin' Bill Stays in Biz," *The Tennessean,* July 21, 1989.

Robert K. Oermann, "Opry Star's Ups and Downs Make a Life of 'Sunshine and Shadow,'" *The Tennessean,* July 9, 1987.

Robert K. Oermann, "Life Buzzin' for Opry Star Bill Anderson," *The Tennessean,* January 9, 1987.

Robert K. Oermann, "'Whisperin' Bill' a Producer Deluxe," *The Tennessean,* May 24, 1985.

## Chapter 6: It's All Relative

Mel Tillis interviews with Robert K. Oermann, October 2007, September 1995.

Pam Tillis interviews with Robert K. Oermann, June 2007, July 1998, August 1997, July 1994, February 1993, March 1991, April 1987, January 1986, May 1983, June 1981.

Robert K. Oermann, "A New Chapter," *The Tennessean,* July 18, 1998.

Robert K. Oermann, "Slowing It Down," *The Tennessean,* August 2, 1997.

Robert K. Oermann, "Pam Tillis: It's Her Turn to Dance," *The Tennessean,* July 16, 1994.

Robert K. Oermann, "Defining Pam Tillis," *The Tennessean,* February 13, 1993.

Robert K. Oermann, "Pam Tillis: Mel's Rebellious Daughter," *The Tennessean,* May 11, 1991.

Robert K. Oermann, "Pam Tillis: Versatile Is Her Middle Name," *The Tennessean,* January 7, 1986.

Robert K. Oermann, "Pam Tillis Rocks on as Nashville's Kingpin," *The Tennessean,* July 10, 1983.

Robert K. Oermann, "Child of Nashville Opts for Rockin' & Rollin'," *The Tennessean,* December 5, 1982.

Mel Tillis with Walter Wager, *Stutterin' Boy* (New York: Rawson Associates, 1984).

Pam Tillis, "Thunder and Roses in Her Own Words," Arista Records press kit, n.d.

John Vasile, "Pam Tillis: Star Stats," *Country Weekly,* February 4, 2003.

Timothy White, "Pam Tillis' Talent: Telling it Like it Is," *Billboard,* September 26, 1992.

## Chapter 7: Fatherhood First

Eddy Arnold interviews with Robert K. Oermann, May 2007, June 2005, January 2002, August 2000, January 1987.

Eddy Arnold, *It's a Long Way from Chester County* (Old Tappan, NJ: Hewitt House, 1969).

Don Cusic, *Eddy Arnold: I'll Hold You in My Heart* (Nashville: Rutledge Hill Press, 1997).

James L. Dickerson, *Colonel Tom Parker* (New York: Cooper Square Press, 2001).

Beverly Keel, "Country Music's Eddy Arnold Is a Superstar at Real Estate," *The Nashville Banner,* September 10, 1987.

Alanna Nash, *The Colonel: The Extraordinary Story of Colonel Tom Parker and Elvis Presley* (New York: Simon & Schuster, 2003).

Robert K. Oermann, "'Tennessee Plowboy' Eddy Arnold Country Music's Humble Superstar," *The Tennessean,* January 18, 1987.

Jay Orr, "Arnold Giving Up Show Biz for 'Simple Things,'" *The Tennessean,* May 13, 1999.

Michael Streissguth, *Eddy Arnold: Pioneer of the Nashville Sound* (New York: Schirmer Books, 1997).

## Chapter 8: Garth and Trisha

Garth Brooks interviews with Robert K. Oermann, November 1997, November 1995, December 1994, July 1993, September 1990.

Trisha Yearwood interviews with Robert K. Oermann, April 2005, April 2001, September 1996, June 1995, April 1992.

Garth Brooks press conference, August 2007.

Peter Cooper, "Retired Garth Still Swings for Radio Hits," *The Tennessean,* August 19, 2007.

Peter Cooper, "Garth: That's a Wrap, Boys," *The Tennessean,* November 13, 2001.

Lorianne Crook with Garth Brooks, *Offstage with Lorianne Crook* televised interview, Great American Country, November 3, 2007.

Lisa Rebecca Gubernick, *Get Hot or Go Home: Trisha Yearwood: The Making of a Nashville Star* (New York: William and Morrow, 1991).

Larry Holden, "Facing Real Life," *Country Weekly,* May 16, 2000.

Chris Neal, "She Said Yes!" *Country Weekly,* July 4, 2005.

Chris Neal, "Squeeze Play," *Country Weekly,* April 16, 2002.

Chris Neal and Larry Holden, "Garth's Next Step," *Country Weekly,* December 31, 2007.

Robert K. Oermann, "Garth on Garth," *The Tennessean,* November 20, 1997.

Robert K. Oermann, "The Voice of Reason," *The Tennessean,* October 12, 1996.

Robert K. Oermann, "The Return of Garth Brooks," *The Tennessean,* November 20, 1995.

Robert K. Oermann, "The Girl Next Door," *The Tennessean,* July 1, 1995.

Robert K. Oermann, "Gartharama," *The Tennessean,* December 13, 1994.

Robert K. Oermann, "Garth's Back," *The Tennessean,* July 31, 1993.

Robert K. Oermann, "Trisha Yearwood: Move Over Boys, Here Comes a Star," *The Tennessean,* June 20, 1992.

Robert K. Oermann, "Garth Becomes Opry's 65th," *The Tennessean,* October 5, 1990.

Robert K. Oermann, "Garth Brooks Ranks a Country Contender," *The Tennessean,* August 8, 1990.

Jay Orr, "Yearwood Joins Cast of Greats as Opry's 71st Member," *The Tennessean,* March 14, 1999.

Jay Orr, "Old Opry Stage Greets New Member Yearwood," *The Tennessean,* January 17, 1999.

Bob Paxman and Chris Neal, "Hookups Breakups & Bliss," *Country Weekly,* August 19, 2003.

Deborah Evans Price, "Best of Both Worlds," *Country Weekly,* n.d. [2007].

Christine Reed, "Garth Brooks: Star Stats," *Country Weekly,* July 28, 1998.

Tom Roland, "Garth Brooks Announces He May Retire," *The Tennessean,* December 16, 1999.

Brad Schmitt, "Brad About You," *The Tennessean,* June 10, 2003.

Ray Waddell, "Trisha at Ten," *Billboard,* June 2, 2001.

## Chapter 9: Loretta and Doo

Owen Bradley interview with Robert K. Oermann, December 1997.

Waylon Jennings interview with Robert K. Oermann, August 1995.

Loretta Lynn interviews with Robert K. Oermann, June 2007, December 2000, September 1995, July 1993, July 1986, November 1982.

Mary Bufwack A. and Robert K. Oermann, *Finding Her Voice: Women in Country Music* (Nashville: Vanderbilt University Press, 2003).

Paul Kingsbury, *The Grand Ole Opry History of Country Music* (New York: Villard/Random House, 1995).

Loretta Lynn with Patsi Bale Cox, *Still Woman Enough* (New York: Hyperion, 2002).

Loretta Lynn with George Vecsey, *Coal Miner's Daughter* (New York: Bernard Geis Associates, 1976).

## Chapter 10: No-Show Jones

George Jones interviews with Robert K. Oermann, July 2007, February 1993, March 1984.

Nancy Jones interview with Robert K. Oermann, July 2007.

Peter Cooper, "On the Road to Redemption," *The Tennessean,* May 8, 2003.

James Hunter, "The Ballad of No-Show Jones," *The New York Times Magazine,* March 15, 1992.

George Jones with Tom Carter, *I Lived to Tell It All* (New York: Villard, 1996).

Paul Kingsbury, *The Grand Ole Opry History of Country Music* (New York: Villard/Random House, 1995).

Barry McCloud et al., *Definitive Country* (New York: Perigee Trade, 1995).

Robert K. Oermann, "George Jones: I Start All Over Again," *The Tennessean,* February 27, 1993.

Robert K. Oermann, "George Jones Finds a Haven in Tyler County, Texas," *The Tennessean,* April 4, 1984.

Robert K. Oermann, "George Jones Surprises All, Gets Hitched," *The Tennessean,* March 5, 1983.

Tom Roland, "Keeping Up with the Joneses," *Country Weekly,* April 27, 2004.

Tom Roland, "I Just Kind of Live the Story of the Song," *The Tennessean,* June 20, 1999.

Walt Trott, "George Jones Still Charting in Sixth Decade," *The Nashville Musician,* January–March 2000.

## Chapter 11: An Opry "Curse"

June Carter interview with Robert K. Oermann, July 1993.

Charlie Dick interviews with Robert K. Oermann, November 1986, October 1985.

Ralph Emery interview with Robert K. Oermann, August 1995.

Emmylou Harris interview with Robert K. Oermann, July 1993.

Jan Howard interviews with Robert K. Oermann, July 1993, July 1987.

Loretta Lynn interview with Robert K. Oermann, July 1993.

Jean Shepard interviews with Robert K. Oermann, August 1995, May 1988.

Bill Anderson, *I Hope You're Living as High on the Hog as the Pig You Turned Out to Be* (Marietta, GA: Longstreet Press, 1993).

Mark Bego, *I Fall to Pieces: The Music and the Life of Patsy Cline* (Holbrook, MA: Adams Publishing, 1995).

Larry Brinton and Clay Hargis, "4 Opry Stars Die in Crash," *Nashville Banner,* March 6, 1963.

Meredith S. Buel, "Hillbilly with Oomph," *The Washington Star,* March 18, 1956.

Mary A. Bufwack and Robert K. Oermann, *Finding Her Voice: Women in Country Music* (Nashville: Vanderbilt University Press, 2003).

Gary Copas, *The Cowboy Copas Story* album liner notes (Madison, TN: Starday Records, n.d.).

Ralph Emery with Tom Carter, *More Memories* (New York: G.P. Putman's Sons, 1993).

Ralph Emery with Tom Carter, *Memories: The Autobiography of Ralph Emery* (New York: Macmillan Publishing, 1991).

Ralph Emery with Patsi Bale Cox, *50 Years Down a Country Road* (New York: HarperCollins, 2000).

Doug Hall, *The Real Patsy Cline* (Kingston, Ontario: Quarry Music Books, 1998).

Hallway Productions, *The Real Patsy Cline* video documentary (Nashville: Hallway Productions, 1986).

Jan Howard, *Sunshine and Shadow: My Story* (New York: Richardson & Steirman, 1987).

Margaret Jones, *Patsy: The Life and Times of Patsy Cline* (New York: HarperCollins, 1994).

Rich Kienzle, "Hawkshaw Hawkins," *The Journal,* August 1995.

Paul Kingsbury, ed., *The Encyclopedia of Country Music* (New York: Oxford University Press, 1998).

Paul Kingsbury, *Patsy Cline Live at the Cimarron Ballroom* album liner notes (Nashville: MCA Records, 1997).

Paul Kingsbury, *The Patsy Cline Collection* boxed-set booklet essay (Nashville: MCA Records, 1991).

Otto Kitsinger, *Hawkshaw Hawkins* boxed-set booklet essay (Vollersode, West Germany: Bear Family Records, 1991).

Barry McCloud et al., *Definitive Country* (New York: Perigee Trade, 1995).

Bob Millard, "Patsy Cline: Owen Bradley Remembers," *Goldmine,* December 4, 1987.

Ellis Nassour, *Honky Tonk Angel: The Intimate Story of Patsy Cline* (New York: St. Martin's Press, 1993).

Robert K. Oermann, "Documentary Tells Patsy Cline's 'Real' Story," *The Tennessean,* November 19, 1986.

Robert K. Oermann, "Patsy's Mate: Lives Not That Violent," *The Tennessean,* October 6, 1985.

Robert K. Oermann, "Back in the Country 1963: Tragedy Strikes the Country Music World," *Country Song Roundup,* September 1985.

Jay Orr, "Patsy Cline's Musical Legacy Lives," *The Nashville Banner,* March 5, 1993.

Don Pierce, *Cowboy Copas: Songs That Made Him Famous* album liner notes (Madison, TN: Starday Records, n.d.).

Don Pierce, *Opry Star Spotlight on Cowboy Copas* album liner notes (Madison, TN: Starday Records, n.d.).

Ray Reeves, *16 Greatest Hits of Hawkshaw Hawkins* album liner notes (Nashville: Gusto Records, 1977).

Chris Skinker, *The Melody Ranch Girl: Jean Shepard* boxed-set booklet essay (Hambergen, West Germany: Bear Family Records, 1996).

Jonathan Guyot Smith, "Cowboy Copas: One of Country Music's Finest," *DISCoveries,* November, 1993.

Ivan M. Tribe, *Mountaineer Jamboree: Country Music in West Virginia* (Lexington: The University Press of Kentucky, 1984).

Walt Trott, *The Honky Tonk Angels* (Nashville: Nova Books, 1993).

Walt Trott, *Johnnie & Jack* boxed-set booklet essay (Vollersode, West Germany: Bear Family Records, 1992).

Ginger Willis, "A Shepard Catches a Hawk," *Country Song Roundup,* May 1961.

## Chapter 12: Gentleman Jim

Chet Atkins interview with Robert K. Oermann, August 1994.

The Jordanaires interview with Robert K. Oermann, September 1994.

Buddy Killen interview with Robert K. Oermann, November 2005.

Cindy Walker interview with Robert K. Oermann, July 1999.

Maxine Brown, *Looking Back to See: A Country Music Memoir* (Fayetteville, Arkansas: The University of Arkansas Press, 2005).

Pansy Cook, *The Saga of Jim Reeves* (Los Angeles: Crescent Publications, 1977).

Colin Escott, *The Essential Jim Reeves* liner notes (Nashville: RCA Records, 1995).

Rich Kienzle, *RCA Country Legends: Jim Reeves* liner notes (New York: RCA Records, 2002).

Buddy Killen, *By the Seat of My Pants* (New York: Simon & Schuster, 1993).

Paul Kingsbury, ed., *The Encyclopedia of Country Music* (New York: Oxford University Press, 1998).

Tracy E.W. Laird, *Louisiana Hayride* (New York: Oxford University Press, 2005).

Horace Logan and Bill Sloan, *Elvis, Hank and Me* (New York: St. Martin's Press, 1998).

Barry McCloud et al., *Definitive Country* (New York: Perigee Trade, 1995).

Tracy Pitcox, *Legendary Conversations* (Brady, Texas: Heart of Texas Country, 2007).

Ronnie Pugh, *Gentleman Jim 1955–1959* boxed-set booklet essay (Vollersode, Germany: Bear Family Records, 1989).

John Rumble, *Welcome to My World: The Essential Jim Reeves Collection* boxed-set booklet essay (Nashville: RCA Records, 1993).

Michael Streissguth, *Jim Reeves and Friends: Radio Days Vol. 2* boxed-set booklet essay (Hambergen, Germany: Bear Family Records, 2001).

Michael Streissguth, *Like a Moth to a Flame: The Jim Reeves Story* (Nashville: Rutledge Hill Press, 1998).

Cindy Walker, *The Jim Reeves Way* liner notes (Nashville: RCA Records, 1965).

## Chapter 13: Dolly's Mystery Man

Dolly Parton interviews with Robert K. Oermann, October 2007, May 2007, May 2002, August 1999, July 1998, August 1996, December 1990, April 1989, March 1987, June 1984, October 1983, April 1982.

Porter Wagoner interviews with Robert K. Oermann, May 2007, May 2000, July 1988, January 1985.

Mary A. Bufwack and Robert K. Oermann, *Finding Her Voice: Women in Country Music* (Nashville: Vanderbilt University Press, 2003).

David Cantwell, "Hillbilly Deluxe," *No Depression,* July-August, 2007.

Ivory Jeff Clinton, "Musical Tribute," *People,* November 12, 2007.

Steve Eng, *A Satisfied Mind: The Country Music Life of Porter Wagoner* (Nashville: Rutledge Hill Press, 1992).

Alanna Nash, *Dolly* (Los Angeles: Reed Books, 1978).

Dolly Parton, *Dolly: My Life and Other Unfinished Business* (New York: HarperCollins, 1994).

## Chapter 14: Marty's Greatest Treasure

Ricky Skaggs interviews with Robert K. Oermann, November 1997, July 1987.

Connie Smith interviews with Robert K. Oermann, October 1998, September 1992, October 1986.

Marty Stuart interviews with Robert K. Oermann, July 2007, December 1999, January 1993, September 1989, July 1986, July 1985.

Sharon White interview with Robert K. Oermann, July 1987.

Mary A. Bufwack and Robert K. Oermann, *Finding Her Voice: Women in Country Music* (Nashville: Vanderbilt University Press, 2003).

Michael A. Capozzoli Jr. and Marianne Horner, "Spirits of Marty Stuart and Connie Smith Finally Unite," *Country Weekly,* August 12, 1997.

Kathleen Gallagher, "Connie Smith: 'I've Had a Chance to Live My Life Over,'" *Country Music,* December 1973.

Darryl E. Hicks, *God Comes to Nashville* (Harrison, AR: New Leaf Press, 1979).

Paul Kingsbury, *The Grand Ole Opry History of Country Music* (New York: Villard/Random House, 1995).

Mary Ellen Moore, "Connie Smith: A Traditionalist Comes Back to the Fold," *Country Music,* March–April 1985.

Robert K. Oermann, "Cinderella Déjà Vu," *The Tennessean,* January 3, 1999.

Robert K. Oermann, "Country Legends Marty Stuart's Models," *The Tennessean,* December 2, 1989.

Robert K. Oermann, "Ricky and Sharon Chart Marital Bliss," *The Tennessean,* August 1, 1987.

Robert K. Oermann, "Connie Smith's in Quest of Her Crown," *The Tennessean,* October 11, 1986.

Robert K. Oermann, "Marty Stuart Keeps Country Rockin'," *The Tennessean,* July 26, 1986.

Robert K. Oermann, "'Boy Wonder' Marty Stuart Grows Up to Solo Stardom," *The Tennessean,* July 14, 1985.

Robert K. Oermann, "Ricky Skaggs Balances Family Life and Fame," *The Tennessean*, July 13, 1985.

Robert K. Oermann, "Electrifying Connie Smith Back at Last," *The Tennessean*, April 27, 1984.

Christopher Reed, "Star Stats: Connie Smith," *Country Weekly*, August 24, 1999.

Marty Stuart, *Pilgrims: Sinners Saints and Prophets* (Nashville: Rutledge Hill Press, 1999).

Eddie Stubbs with Marty Stuart and Connie Smith, *An Intimate Evening with Eddie Stubbs* radio interview, WSM, July 2, 2007.

## Chapter 15: Vince and Amy

Vince Gill interviews with Robert K. Oermann, July 2007, December 2005, June 1998, May 1998, June 1997, May 1996, June 1990, April, 1984.

Amy Grant interviews with Robert K. Oermann, July 1991, October 1988, December 1986, March 1986, July 1985.

Mark Bego, *Vince Gill* (Los Angeles: Renaissance Books, 2000).

Larry Holden and Gerry Wood, "The Marriage and the Music," *Country Weekly*, April 18, 2000.

Beverly Keel, "To Amy, Happy Valentine's Day, Love, Vince," *The Tennessean*, February 14, 2007.

Bob Millard, *Amy Grant* (Garden City, New York: Dolphin/ Doubleday and Company, 1986).

Wendy Newcomer, "Girl of His Dreams," *Country Weekly*, June 26, 2001.

Robert K. Oermann, "Tried and True," *The Tennessean*, June 22, 1997.

Robert K. Oermann, "Just Faxing with Amy Grant," *The Tennessean*, August 2, 1991.

Robert K. Oermann, "Vince Gill Finally Gains Own Spotlight," *The Tennessean*, July 28, 1990.

Robert K. Oermann, "Gusty Amy Wings Way into Maturity," *The Tennessean*, October 15, 1988.

Robert K. Oermann, "Any Grant's 'Tennessee Christmas' Goes

Nationwide, Like Her Pop Hits," *The Tennessean,* December 14, 1986.

Robert K. Oermann, "Vibrant Amy Grant Stands at Gospel/Pop Crossroads," *The Tennessean,* March 16, 1986.

Robert K. Oermann, "Christian Vocalist Amy Grant 'Finds a Way' to Pop Success," *The Tennessean,* October 20, 1985.

Robert K. Oermann, "Vince Gill Packs a 'Quadruple Threat,'" *The Tennessean,* September 14, 1985.

Robert K. Oermann, "Amy Grant: Her Music Speaks of Her Faith, *The Tennessean,* August 3, 1985.

Jay Orr, "Amy Starts Over," *The Tennessean,* October 7, 1999.

Jay Orr, "Behind Amy's Eyes," *The Nashville Banner,* September 12, 1997.

Bob Paxman, "New & Improved," *Country Weekly,* April 1, 2003.

Brad Schmitt, "Amy, Vince Nuptials Low Key," *The Tennessean,* March 11, 2000.

George Zepp, "Amy Grant's Granddad Owned Burton Farm," *The Tennessean,* September 6, 2006.

## Chapter 16: Funny Love

Henry Cannon interview with Robert K. Oermann, October 1992.

Minnie Pearl interviews with Robert K. Oermann, April 1989, January 1986, May 1984.

Anonymous, "Hats ON for Minnie Pearl," *National Jamboree,* June 1949.

Teddy Bart and Carlin Evans, "Off Mike," *The Nashville Banner,* March 11, 1996.

Paul Bryant, "The Belle of Grinder's Switch," *The Mountain Broadcast and Prairie Recorder,* October 1946.

Mary A. Bufwack and Robert K. Oermann, *Finding Her Voice: Women in Country Music* (Nashville: Vanderbilt University Press, 2003).

Mona Collett, "Sarah Ophelia Colley Cannon Leaves Many Timeless Pearls of Wisdom," *Belmont University Circle,* Spring 1996.

Ralph Emery with Tom Carter, *Memories: The Autobiography of Ralph Emery* (New York: Macmillan Publishing Company, 1991).

Carrie Ferguson, "Life's Worth of Minnie's Memories on Sale to Highest Bidders," *The Tennessean,* December 18, 1998.

Thomas Goldsmith, "Sarah, Minnie Share Golden Anniversary," *The Tennessean*, November 14, 1987.

Ren Grevatt, *Laugh-Along with Minnie Pearl* album liner notes (Long Island City, NY: Hilltop Records, n.d.).

Jack Hurst, "Minnie Pearl Edits Out 'Seamy Details,'" *Cincinnati Enquirer,* January 21, 1980.

Kevin Kenworthy, *The Best Jokes Minnie Pearl Ever Told* (Nashville: Rutledge Hill Press, 1999).

Rich Kienzle, "Minnie Pearl," *Country Music,* November–December 1991.

Paul Kingsbury, ed., *The Encyclopedia of Country Music* (New York: Oxford University Press, 1998).

Barry McCloud et al., *Definitive Country* (New York: Perigee Trade, 1995).

Judy Mizell, "Minnie Pearl: Grand Ole Opry's Crown Jewel," *Inside Opryland USA,* November 1990.

Alanna Nash, "A Thoroughly Nice Person," *Country Weekly,* August 6, 1996.

Alanna Nash, *Behind Closed Doors: Talking with the Legends of Country Music* (New York: Alfred A. Knopf, 1988).

Robert K. Oermann, "Minnie Pearl," *New Country,* April 1996.

Robert K. Oermann, "Back in the Country, 1940: Minnie Pearl Joins the Grand Ole Opry," *Country Song Roundup,* October 1983.

Robert K. Oermann, "Minnie's 70th Birthday Brings Out the Stars," *The Tennessean,* October 26, 1982.

Jay Orr and Michael Gray, "A Final Refrain for Life Filled with Love, Music," *The Nashville Banner,* March 7, 1996.

Jay Orr, "Just So Proud You Were Here, Minnie," *The Nashville Banner,* March 5, 1996.

Minnie Pearl, "Mule Is Too Tall, Turkey Is Too Tough!" *Country America,* November 1990.

Minnie Pearl with Joan Dew, *Minnie Pearl* (New York: Simon & Schuster, 1980).

Don Pierce, *Howdee! Cousin Minnie Pearl* album liner notes (Nashville: Starday Records, n.d.).

Don Pierce, *America's Beloved Minnie Pearl* album liner notes (Nashville: Starday Records, 1966).

Tom Roland, "Opry Honors Miss Minnie," *The Tennessean,* March 10, 1996.

Tom Roland and Carrie Ferguson, "Minnie Pearl Remembered," *The Tennessean,* March 7, 1996.

Leah Rozen, "Minnie Pearl," *People,* October 26, 1987.

Sandy Smith, "Minnie Says 'Howdee' to Comedy Hall of Fame," *The Tennessean,* April 6, 1994.

Sandy Smith, "How-Dee, Minnie!" *The Tennessean,* October 25, 1992.

Sandy Smith and Robert K. Oermann, "She Was Country Music's Pearl," *The Tennessean,* March 5, 1996.

Gerry Wood, Catharine Rambeau, Clif H. Dunn, and Bruce Honick, "Minnie's Heart Was as Big as Her Talent," *Country Weekly,* March 26, 1996.

## Chapter 17: For the Rest of Mine

Trace Adkins interviews with Robert K. Oermann, July 2007, March 2003, October 1997, May 1996.

Jimmy Dickens interviews with Robert K. Oermann, April 1999, October 1998, September 1995, December 1987.

Trace Adkins with Keith and Kent Zimmerman, *Trace Adkins: A Personal Stand* (New York: Villard Books, 2007).

Peter Cooper, "Sizing Up the Opry," *The Tennessean,* August 23, 2003.

Beverly Keel, "Shooting Straight," *The Nashville Scene,* April 17, 1997.

Rich Kienzle, *I'm Little But I'm Loud: The Little Jimmy Dickens Collection* album liner notes (Cooper Station, NY: Razor & Tie Entertainment, 1996).

Richard McVey, "Catching Up: Little Jimmy Dickens," *Music City News,* April 1998.

Robert K. Oermann, "Grand Ole Opry—Jimmy Dickens Marks a Half-Century Milestone," *Journal of Country Music,* August–September 1999.

Robert K. Oermann, "Adkins Does Romance 'Big Time,'" *The Tennessean,* December 6, 1997.

Robert K. Oermann, "Hard Workin' Man Oils (Singing) Career," *The Tennessean,* August 24, 1996.

Robert K. Oermann, "Jimmy Dickens Video Asks Santa's Forgiveness," *The Tennessean,* December 25, 1987.

Bob Paxman, "Little Jimmy's Got the Dickens of a Home," *Country Weekly,* June 24, 1997.

Catherine S. Rambeau, "Little Jimmy Dickens Casts a Giant Shadow," *Country Weekly,* November 3, 1998.

David Scarlett, "Firing on All Cylinders," *Country Weekly,* January 17, 2005.

David Scarlett, "It's Always Today," *Country Weekly,* n.d. [2003].

## Chapter 18: Small-Town Gals

John McBride interviews with Robert K. Oermann, June 2005, July 1992.

Martina McBride interviews with Robert K. Oermann, June 2005, July 2001, July 1997, February 1994, January 1993, July 1992.

Reba McEntire interviews with Robert K. Oermann, May 2001, April 1989, July 1988, December 1986, November 1986, February 1986, October 1984.

Paul Worley interview with Robert K. Oermann, June 2005.

Mary A. Bufwack and Robert K. Oermann, *Finding Her Voice: Women in Country Music* (Nashville: Vanderbilt University Press, 2003).

Bob Cannon, "Pistol Packin' Mama," *Country Weekly,* March 6, 2001.

Peter Cooper, "Welcome to Planet McBride," *The Tennessean,* November 2, 2003.

Steve Dougherty and Kate Klise, "Martina with a Twist," *People,* January 12, 1998.

Shannon Heim, "Reba," *Close Up,* June 1999.

Beverly Keel, "Blackbird Studio Produces Top 3 Albums in Nation," *The Tennessean,* June 28, 2007.

Paul Kingsbury, *The Grand Ole Opry History of Country Music* (New York: Villard/Random House, 1995).

Martina McBride, "Blessed Indeed," *Country Weekly,* April 2, 2002.

Reba McEntire with Tom Carter, *Reba: My Story* (New York: Bantam Books, 1994).

Chris Neal, "Is TV Ready for Reba?" *Country Weekly,* October 2, 2001.

Wendy Newcomer, "Martina's Love Secrets," *Country Weekly,* February 14, 2005.

Robert K. Oermann, "Martina McBride," *The Tennessean,* October 11, 1997.

Robert K. Oermann, "Divined," *Twang,* Holiday 1996.

Robert K. Oermann, "Driving Martina," *The Tennessean,* February 19, 1994.

Robert K. Oermann, "Martina McBride: Will Lightning Strike Twice?" *The Tennessean,* November 28, 1992.

John Vasile, "Star Stats: Martina McBride," *Country Weekly,* August 6, 2002.

Gerry Wood, "Revved Up Redhead," *Country Weekly,* November 11, 1999.

## Chapter 19: It Takes Two

Patty Loveless interviews with Robert K. Oermann, July 2007, November 1998, February 1996, March 1993, November 1988, June 1987.

Mary A. Bufwack and Robert K. Oermann, *Finding Her Voice:*

*Women in Country Music* (Nashville: Vanderbilt University Press, 2003).

Clif H. Dunn, "Domestic Harmony Pays Off for Patty," *Country Weekly,* March 19, 1996.

Bill Friskics-Warren, "Down from the Mountain," *No Depression,* July–August 2001.

Brenda Lee with Robert K. Oermann and Julie Clay, *Little Miss Dynamite* (New York: Hyperion, 2002).

Wendy Newcomer, "Soil & Soul," *Country Weekly,* October 24, 2005.

Robert K. Oermann, "No More Trouble with the Truth," *The Tennessean,* March 23, 1996.

Robert K. Oermann, "Patty Loveless: A Honky Tonk Angel," *The Tennessean,* May 8, 1993.

Robert K. Oermann, "Patty Loveless: Today She's the Latest Honky Tonk Angel," *The Tennessean,* November 12, 1988.

Robert K. Oermann, "Patty Loveless Eyes Country Queendom," *The Tennessean,* September 1, 1987.

Tom Roland, "Georgia on Her Mind," *Country Weekly,* April 30, 2002.

## Chapter 20: Some Memories Just Won't Die

Marty Robbins interview with Robert K. Oermann, August 1982.

Ronny Robbins interviews with Robert K. Oermann, March 2006, April 1988, November 1987, August 1986.

Bob Allen, "Marty Robbins," *Country Rhythms,* January 1983.

Bob Allen, "Marty Robbins Doesn't Sweat the Small Stuff," *Country Music,* October 1981.

Bob Allen and Robert K. Oermann, "Marty Robbins: 1925– 1982," *Country Song Roundup,* July 1983.

Jim Bessman, "The 'El Paso' Connection," *Billboard,* August 6, 2005.

Ralph Emery with Patsi Bale Cox, *50 Years Down a Country Road* (New York: HarperCollins, 2000).

Ralph Emery with Tom Carter, *Memories: The Autobiography of Ralph Emery* (New York: Macmillan, 1991).

Colin Escott, *Marty Robbins Country: 1960–1966* boxed-set booklet essay (Hambergen, Germany: Bear Family Records, 1995).

Colin Escott, "Marty Robbins: The Early Years—Rockin' Rollin' Robbins," *Goldmine,* July 10, 1992.

Colin Escott, *Marty Robbins Country: 1951–1958* boxed-set booklet essay (Vollersode, West Germany: Bear Family Records, 1991).

Bob Garbutt, "Marty Robbins: Twentieth Century Drifter," *Goldmine,* March 1981.

Greg Hall, *Marty Robbins: Seems Like Yesterday,* PBS-TV special, 2006.

Rich Kienzle, *The Essential Marty Robbins* boxed-set booklet essay (New York: Columbia Records, 1991).

Red O'Donnell, "Opry Pals Will Miss Marty," *Nashville Banner,* December 9, 1982.

Robert K. Oermann, "Marty Robbins Home Video to Be Released," *The Tennessean,* April 8, 1988.

Robert K. Oermann, "Ronny Robbins Remembers Famous Dad for TV Special," *The Tennessean,* August 10, 1986.

Robert K. Oermann, "Marty Robbins Remembered as Ambassador," *The Tennessean,* June 16, 1985.

Robert K. Oermann, "The Death of Marty Robbins," *Country Rhythms,* April 1983.

Robert K. Oermann, "Hundreds Pay Tribute to Robbins at Funeral," *The Tennessean,* December 12, 1982.

Robert K. Oermann, "Country Superstar Marty Robbins Dies," *The Tennessean,* December 9, 1982.

Robert K. Oermann, "Superstar Marty Robbins in Critical Condition," *The Tennessean,* December 3, 1982.

Barbara J. Pruett, *Marty Robbins: Fast Cars and Country Music* (Metuchen, NJ: Scarecrow Press, 1990).

Joel Whitburn, comp., *Joel Whitburn's Top Country Songs 1944 to 2005* (Menomonee Falls, WI: Record Research, 2005).

Larry Woody, "On or Off the Race Track, Robbins Was True Champ," *The Tennessean,* December 10, 1982.

## Chapter 21: Live Fast, Love Hard, Die Young, and Leave a Beautiful Memory

Faron Young interviews with Robert K. Oermann, July 1994, May 1985.

Mae Boren Axton, *Country Singers as I Know 'Em* (Austin, TX: Sweet Publishing Company, 1973).

Diane J. Diekman, letters to Robert K. Oermann, March–June 2000.

Ralph Emery with Patsi Bale Cox, *50 Years Down a Country Road* (New York: HarperCollins, 2000).

Ralph Emery with Patsi Bale Cox, *The View from Nashville* (New York: William Morrow & Company, 1998).

Colin Escott, *Faron Young. The Classic Years* boxed set booklet (Vollersode, West Germany: Bear Family Records, 1992).

Bob Garbutt, "Faron Young," *Goldmine,* September 1982.

Lydia Dixon Harden, "A Duet with Willie Fuels His Career," *Music City News,* October 1984.

Pat Harris and Danny Proctor, "Faron Young: 1932–1996," *Music City News,* February 1997.

Rich Kienzle, "Faron Young: 1932–1996," *Country Music,* March/April 1997.

Barry McCloud et al., *Definitive Country* (New York: Perigee Trade, 1995).

Tom Normand and Patricia Lynch Kimbro, "Faron Young 'Didn't Realize How Much He Is Loved,'" *Nashville Banner,* December 11, 1996.

Robert K. Oermann, "Faron Young: Still Making Headlines," *Country Music,* October/November 2000.

Robert K. Oermann, "Faron Young Hopes for a Revitalized Career," *The Tennessean,* May 18, 1985.

Jay Orr, "Of Faron Young: Lore, Laughter and No Apologies," *Nashville Banner,* December 11, 1996.

Charley Pride with Jim Henderson, *Pride: The Charley Pride Story* (New York: William Morrow & Company, 1994).

Tom Roland and Ken Beck, "Sun Goes Down on 'Singing Sheriff,'" *The Tennessean,* December 11, 1996.

Walt Trott, "Faron Young: Feb. 15, 1932–Dec. 10, 1996," *Country Music News,* January 1997.

Faron Young, "Reflecting on 30 Plus Years of Recording," *Music City News,* May 1989.

## Chapter 22: The Houston Cowboy and the Hollywood Star

Clint Black interviews with Robert K. Oermann, July 2007, June 2007.

Lisa Hartman Black interview with Robert K. Oermann, June 2007.

Mary A. Bufwack and Robert K. Oermann, *Finding Her Voice: Women in Country Music* (Nashville: Vanderbilt University Press, 2003).

Celeste Fremon, "City Girl, Country Boy," *Good Housekeeping,* January 2008.

Beverly Keel, "How Fatherhood Gave Paisley His Muse," *The Tennessean,* June 17, 2007.

Paul Kingsbury, *The Grand Ole Opry History of Country Music* (New York: Villard/Random House, 1995).

The Internet Movie Database, "Biography for Lisa Hartman," online biographical entry, 2008.

The Internet Movie Database, "Lisa Hartman Filmography," online entry, 2008.

Star Pulse, "Lisa Hartman Black Biography," online biographical entry, 2008.

Star Pulse, "Lisa Hartman Black Filmography," online entry, 2008.

TV.com, "Lisa Hartman," online biographical entry, 2008.

Wikipedia, "Lisa Hartman Black," online biographical entry, 2008.

Wikipedia, "Kimberly Williams," online biographical entry, 2008.

Chris Willman, "Spotlight: Brad Paisley," *Entertainment Weekly,* August 24, 2007.

## Chapter 23: Kiss an Angel Good Mornin'

Chet Atkins interview with Robert K. Oermann, September 1995.

Charley Pride interviews with Robert K. Oermann, February 1998, September 1995.

Country Music Hall of Fame, "Charley Pride: Country Music Hall of Fame Medallion Presentation" press release, March 13, 2001.

Lorie Hollabaugh, "Charley Pride," *CMA Close Up,* July–August 2003.

Paul Kingsbury, *The Grand Ole Opry History of Country Music* (New York: Villard/Random House, 1995).

Nike Krewen, "Still in the Game," *Country Weekly,* November 9, 2004.

Pam Lewis, "Together Over 40 Years," PLA Media press release, February 12, 1999.

Diana Melz, "Charley Pride Kicks Off New Year with Two Big Milestones," PLA Media press release, January 3, 1997.

Diana Melz, "Charley Pride Kicks Off New Year with Two Big Milestones," PLA Media press release, December 10, 1996.

Robert K. Oermann, "Pride a Mentor to Young Black Performers," *The Tennessean,* February 23, 1996.

Neil Pond, "Charley Pride Didn't Want to Hurt Anyone," *Music City News,* May 1988.

Charley Pride with Jim Henderson, *Pride: The Charley Pride Story* (New York: William and Morrow, 1994).

Christine Reed, "Charley Pride: Star Stats," *Country Weekly,* January 19, 1999.

Unknown author, "Charley Pride and Wife Reveal Secret of Their 40-Year Marriage," *Jet,* February 10, 1987.

## Chapter 24: A Woman's Love

Alan Jackson interviews with Robert K. Oermann, July 2007, September 1999, August 1999, September 1995.

Peter Cooper, "Alan Jackson Takes His Honky-Tonk to Church," *The Tennessean,* March 12, 2006.

Peter Cooper, "A Driving Force," *The Tennessean,* February 2, 2002.

Jennifer Gerlock, "Alan Jackson: Money Doesn't Buy Happiness," *Country Song Roundup,* April 1999.

Holly Gleason, "Hard Country Soft Heart," *New Country,* March 1994.

Larry Holden, "Loving Somebody," *Country Weekly,* November 28, 2000.

Denise Jackson with Ellen Vaughn, *It's All About Him: Finding the Love of My Life* (Nashville: Thomas Nelson, 2007).

Beverly Keel, "Book's Popularity Overwhelms Singer's Wife," *The Tennessean,* December 1, 2007.

Beverly Keel, "Glamorous Book Party Is All About Denise Jackson," *The Tennessean,* July 27, 2007.

Paul Kingsbury, *The Grand Ole Opry History of Country Music* (New York: Villard/Random House, 1995).

Brian Mansfield, "Satisfaction Jackson," *New Country,* November 1996.

Alanna Nash, "The Private Alan Jackson," *Country Weekly,* October 9, 2006.

Alanna Nash, "God Country Family: Alan Jackson," *USA Weekend,* November 1, 2002.

Chris Neal, "Making Marriage Work," *Country Weekly,* December 17, 2007.

Chris Neal, "Alan Jackson: Why I Do What I Do," *Country Weekly,* September 28, 2004.

Chris Neal, "All About Alan: Hidden World," *Country Weekly,* September 2, 2003.

Bob Paxman, "Living on Love," *Country Weekly,* August 22, 2000.

Deborah Evans Price, "The Love of My Life," *Country Weekly,*
August 13, 2007.

Kristin Russell, "Star Stats: Alan Jackson," *Country Weekly,* May
16, 2000.

David Scarlett, "Where He Comes From," *Country Weekly,* May
27, 2003.

David Scarlett, Chris Neal, and Bob Paxman, "Putting Family
First," *Country Weekly,* November 5, 2007.

Laurie Werner, "Fast Track Jackson," *USA Weekend,* October 5,
1990.

## Chapter 25: Broken Duets

Mary A. Bufwack and Robert K. Oermann, *Finding Her Voice:
Women in Country Music* (Nashville: Vanderbilt University
Press, 2003).

Skeeter Davis, *Bus Fare to Kentucky: The Autobiography of Skeeter
Davis* (New York: Birch Lane Press, 1993).

Alton Delmore, *Truth Is Stranger Than Publicity* (Nashville:
Country Music Foundation Press, 1977).

Paul Kingsbury, *The Grand Ole Opry History of Country Music*
(New York: Villard/Random House, 1995).

Barry McCloud et al., *Definitive Country* (New York: Perigee
Trade, 1995).

Lorrie Morgan with George Vecsey, *Forever Yours, Faithfully: My
Love Story* (New York: Ballantine Books, 1997).

Joel Whitburn, compiler, *Joel Whitburn's Top Country Songs 1944
to 2005 Billboard* (Menomonee Falls, WI: Record Research,
2005).

Charles Wolfe, *In Close Harmony: The Story of The Louvin Brothers*
(Jackson: The University Press of Mississippi, 1996).

John Wright, *Traveling the High Way Home* (Urbana: University of
Illinois Press, 1993).

Laurence J. Zwisohn, *Loretta Lynn's World of Music* (Los Angeles:
John Edwards Memorial Foundation, 1980).

## Chapter 26: Outlaw's Prayer

Glenn Ferguson interview with Robert K. Oermann, February 2003.

Johnny Paycheck interviews with Robert K. Oermann, July 1994, January 1991, May 1986.

Lyn Aurelius, "Johnny Paycheck," *CMA Close Up,* February 1998.

Jim Bagley, "Obituary: Johnny Paycheck, Country Singer," *Goldmine,* April 18, 2003.

Don Baird, "Paycheck Looks Beyond Trial," *The Columbus Dispatch* (Columbus, Ohio), May 14, 1986.

David Cantwell, "Johnny Paycheck, 1938–2003," *Nashville Scene,* February 27, 2003.

Daniel Cooper, *Johnny Paycheck: The Real Mr. Heartache* album liner notes (Nashville: Country Music Foundation Records, 1996).

Kevin Gepford, "Johnny Paycheck Sings Praises for Adult Education," *The Daily Citizen-News* (Dalton, Georgia), July 17, 1991.

Craig Havighurst, "Singer Johnny Paycheck Dies at 64," *The Tennessean,* February 20, 2003.

Rich Kienzle, "Johnny Paycheck, 1938–2003," *No Depression,* May–June 2003.

Buddy Killen, *By the Seat of My Pants* (New York: Simon & Schuster, 1993).

Aubrey Mayhew and Tom Kittypaw, *Johnny Paycheck on His Way* album liner notes (Nashville: Little Darlin' Records, 2005).

Richard McVey II, "Johnny Paycheck Back on Track," *Music City News,* April 1997.

Robert K. Oermann, "Paycheck Freed to Sing," *The Tennessean,* January 23, 1991.

Robert K. Oermann, "Battle Scarred Paycheck Returns to the Ring," *The Tennessean,* May 31, 1986.

Robert K. Oermann, "Country Stars Bail Out Paycheck," *The Tennessean,* May 23, 1986.

Robert K. Oermann, "Royalties to Help AIDS Research When Paycheck Is Serving Time," *The Tennessean,* February 8, 1986.

Bob Paxman, "Death of an Outlaw," *Country Weekly,* April 1, 2003.

Jim Ridley and Michael McCall, "Jukebox Hero," *Nashville Scene,* September 26, 1996.

Phyllis Stark, "Johnny Paycheck Dead at 64," *Billboard,* March 1, 2003.

Jonny Whiteside, *The Soul & The Edge: The Best of Johnny Paycheck* album liner notes (New York: Columbia Records, 2002).

## Chapter 27: Pure Love

Joyce Milsap interview with Robert K. Oermann, June 1983.

Ronnie Milsap interviews with Robert K. Oermann, June 1997, September 1993, August 1991, March 1991, August 1990, November 1986, July 1984, June 1983.

Brian Mansfield, ed., *Grand Ole Opry 80th Anniversary Picture History Book* (Nashville: Gaylord Entertainment Company, 2005).

Ronnie Milsap with Tom Carter, *Almost Like a Song* (New York: McGraw-Hill Publishing Company, 1990).

Robert K. Oermann, "Ronnie Milsap's Secrets," *The Tennessean,* September 11, 1993.

Robert K. Oermann, "Milsap Shines Light on Dark Beginnings," *The Tennessean,* August 25, 1990.

Robert K. Oermann, "Ronnie Milsap Brings His Music, His Heart, Home," *The Tennessean,* November 30, 1986.

Robert K. Oermann, "Living in Nashville Has Always Been 'The Big Dream' for Ronnie Milsap," *The Tennessean,* April 17, 1983.

## Chapter 28: The Red-Headed Stranger

Kris Kristofferson interview with Robert K. Oermann, September 1995.

Willie Nelson interviews with Robert K. Oermann, June 1999, September 1995, November 1992, May 1990, February 1987, October 1984, September 1984, May 1983.

Billy Walker interview with Robert K. Oermann, October 1995.

Bob Allen, *Waylon & Willie* (New York: Quick Fox, 1979).

Michael Bane, *Willie* (New York: Dell Publishing, 1984).

Jim Brown, *Willie Nelson: Red Headed Stranger* (Ontario: Quarry Press, 2001).

Bill DeYoung, "Willie Nelson: Funny How Time Slips Away," *Goldmine,* January 6, 1995.

Robert Draper, "Poor Willie," *Texas Monthly,* May 1991.

Lana Nelson Fowler, *Willie Nelson Family Album* (Amarillo, TX: H.M. Poirot & Company, 1980).

Rich Kienzle, *Country & Western Classics: Willie Nelson* liner-note booklet (Alexandria, VA: Time-Life Records, 1983).

Susie Nelson, *Heart Worn Memories* (Austin: Eakin Press, 1987).

Willie Nelson, *The Facts of Life and Other Dirty Jokes* (New York: Random House, 2003).

Willie Nelson with Turk Pipkin, *The Tao of Willie* (New York: Gotham Books, 2006).

Willie Nelson with Bud Shrake, *Willie: An Autobiography* (New York: Simon & Schuster, 1988).

Frank Oakley with Patsi Bale Cox and Virginia Robicheaux, *The Nashville Sidekick* (Nashville: Frank Oakley, 2006).

Robert K. Oermann, "Who'll Buy Willie's Memories?" *The Tennessean,* May 29, 1991.

Robert K. Oermann, "Willie Accepts Roy Acuff Award," *The Tennessean,* February 4, 1987.

Robert K. Oermann, "Superstar Willie Christens New Show," *The Tennessean,* October 16, 1985.

Robert K. Oermann, "Willie & Kris All Smiles About 'Songwriter,'" *The Tennessean,* October 8, 1984.

Robert K. Oermann, "Willie & Merle's 'Pancho & Lefty' Premieres on the Silver Screen," *The Tennessean,* May 29, 1983.

Robert K. Oermann, "Willie Takes to TV for Cablecast But Hankers for the Big Screen," *The Tennessean,* May 13, 1983.

Robert K. Oermann and Brad Schmitt, "Willie Nelson's Son

Found Dead in Apparent Suicide," *The Tennessean,* December 26, 1991.

Steven Opdyke, *Willie Nelson Sings America* (Austin: Eakin Press, 1998).

Christine Reed, "Willie Nelson: Star Stats," *Country Weekly,* July 7, 1998.

Lola Scobey, *Willie Nelson: Country Outlaw* (New York: Zebra Books, 1982).

## Chapter 29: Dating at the Opry

Dierks Bentley interviews with Robert K. Oermann, December 2007, June 2007.

Heather Byrd, "Josh Turner Tells About Breaking in on Man in Black," *The Tennessean,* September 5, 2006.

Peter Cooper, "Sure He's Cute, But That's Beside the Point," *The Tennessean,* November 5, 2006.

Beverly Keel, "Josh Turner Surprised with Invite to Join Opry," *The Tennessean,* September 30, 2007.

Beverly Keel, "Josh Turner Sounds Off," *People,* March 13, 2006.

Brian Mansfield, "'Regular Guy' Enjoys Ride Up Country Charts," *USA Today,* September 5, 2003.

Chris Neal, "Love Train," *Country Weekly,* January 20, 2004.

Chris Neal, "Finding His Voice," *Country Weekly,* December 12, 2002.

Bob Paxman, "Dierks Elopes," *Country Weekly,* January 30, 2006.

Deborah Evans Price, "Steady Chug of 'Train' Pays Off for Turner," *Billboard,* February 21, 2004.

M. B. Roberts, "Water Works," *Country Weekly,* October 26, 2004.

David Scarlett, "Good Times, Tough Times," *Country Weekly,* November 2007.

David Scarlett, "A Long Trip, But Not Alone," *Country Weekly,* December 18, 2006.

David Scarlett, "Road Warrior," *Country Weekly,* August 1, 2005.

## Chapter 30: The Harmonica Wizard

Ken Beck, "Remembering a Wizard," *The Tennessean*, May 7, 2002.

Ralph Duncan, "Had You Heard DeFord Bailey: A Legend Lives," *The Morning Press* (Murfreesboro, TN), July 12, 1982.

Pamela E. Foster, *My Country: The African Diaspora's Country Music Heritage* (Nashville: Pamela E. Foster, 1998).

John Hartley Fox, "I Was a Humdinger," *Bluegrass Unlimited*, December 1982.

Frye Gaillard, "An Opry Star Shines On," *Country Music*, March 1975.

Peter Guralnick, *Lost Highway* (Boston: David R. Godine Publisher, 1979).

George D. Hay, *A Story of the Grand Ole Opry* (Nashville: George D. Hay, 1945).

Paul Hemphill, *The Nashville Sound: Bright Lights and Country Music* (New York: Simon and Schuster, 1970).

Dwight Lewis, "Country Music Changes Its Tune on DeFord Bailey," *The Tennessean*, September 1, 2005.

Dwight Lewis, "This Country Music Great Is Still in Need of Deserved Recognition," *The Tennessean*, March 11, 2004.

David Morton, "Every Day's Been Sunday," *Nashville!* March 1974.

David C. Morton with Charles K. Wolfe, *DeFord Bailey: A Black Star in Early Country Music* (Knoxville: University of Tennessee Press, 1991).

Robert K. Oermann, "Country Music Commemorates DeFord Bailey," *The Tennessean*, June 24, 1983.

Bengt Olsson, "The Grand Ole Opry's DeFord Bailey," *Living Blues*, n.d.

Paul Reddick, *Harp Blowers (1925–1936)* album liner notes (Vienna, Austria: Document Records, 1993).

Tony Russell, *Blacks, Whites and Blues* (New York: Stein and Day, 1970).

Brian Rust, *The Victor Master Book* (Highland Park, NJ: Walter C. Allen, 1969).

Edmund J. Sass, George Gottfried, and Anthony Sorem, *Polio's Legacy* (Lantham, MD: University Press of America / Rowman & Littlefield Publishing Group, 1996).

Reginald Stewart, "Death of Black Opry Pioneer Leads to Disharmony in Nashville," *The New York Times,* August 22, 1982.

Charles K. Wolfe, *A Good Natured Riot: The Birth of the Grand Ole Opry* (Nashville: Country Music Foundation/Vanderbilt University Press, 1999).

Charles K. Wolfe, *The Legendary DeFord Bailey: Country Music's First Black Star* album liner notes (Murfreesboro, TN: Folklore Society Records, 1998).

Charles K. Wolfe, *Tennessee Strings* (Knoxville: University of Tennessee Press, 1977).

Charles K. Wolfe, *Nashville the Early String Bands* album liner notes (Floyd, VA: County Records, 1976).

Charles K. Wolfe, *The Grand Ole Opry: The Early Years 1925–35* (London: Old Time Music, 1975).

Ron Wynn, "Harmonica Legend Honored," *The City Paper,* March 12, 2004.

Ron Wynn, "Pan American Blues," *No Depression,* January–February 2002.

Gwendolyn C. Young, "Family, Others Still Fighting to Get Opry Pioneer into Hall of Fame," *The Tennessean,* December 5, 2002.

## Chapter 31: Sure Love

Hal Ketchum interviews with Robert K. Oermann, June 2007, May 1993, December 1992, December 1991.

Keith Ryan Cartwright, "For Hal Ketchum, Lady Luck Is Smiling," *The Tennessean,* October 9, 2001.

Marianne Horner, "Back on Track," *Country Weekly,* August 31, 2004.

Robert K. Oermann, "Hal Ketchum: Living His Dream," *The Tennessean,* May 1, 1993.

Robert K. Oermann, "Hal Who? Late-Blooming, Hit-Making Hal Ketchum," *The Tennessean,* December 28, 1991.

Jay Orr, "Illness Couldn't Catch Him, Now Ketchum's Coming Back," *The Tennessean,* December 4, 1998.

Jay Orr, "Ketchum's Drug Woes Behind Him," *The Tennessean,* June 16, 1998.

Tom Roland, "Heart," *Country Weekly,* February 4, 2003.

Tamara Saviano, "Hal Ketchum's Happy He's Seen the Light," *Country Weekly,* May 5, 1998.

## Chapter 32: Behind Every Great Man . . .

Randy Travis interviews with Robert K. Oermann, August 2007, January 1998, November 1997, July 1996, September 1995, March 1994, April 1991, June 1987, August 1986.

Jay Cocks, "Trippin' Through the Crossroads," *Time,* July 25, 1988.

Thomas Goldsmith, "Laid-Back Randy Travis Learns to Live with Peaks and Valleys of His Career," *The Tennessean,* October 22, 1989.

Thomas Goldsmith, "Country's Paying Off for Randy Travis," *The Tennessean,* February 8, 1986.

Kim Heron, "Randy Travis: Making Country Music Hot Again," *The New York Times Magazine,* June 25, 1989.

Larry Holden, "Walking on Faith," *Country Weekly,* August 5, 2003.

Robert K. Oermann, *Randy Travis Anthology* album liner notes (Los Angeles: Warner Bros., Records, 2002).

Robert K. Oermann, "He's Back!," *The Tennessean,* September 7, 1996.

Robert K. Oermann, "Randy Travis," *The Tennessean,* April 23, 1994.

Robert K. Oermann, "Travis Points to Future," *The Tennessean,* June 8, 1991.

Robert K. Oermann, "Randy Goes Public with His Romance," *The Tennessean,* April 13, 1991.

Robert K. Oermann, "Randy Travis Praised for Hard Work," *The Tennessean,* March 30, 1990.

Robert K. Oermann, "He'll Sing Country Forever and Ever, Amen!," *The Tennessean,* June 27, 1987.

Robert K. Oermann, "Randy Travis Set to Become Opry Member," *The Tennessean,* November 28, 1986.

Robert K. Oermann, "Country with a Capital C Suits Hit Maker Randy Travis to a T," *The Tennessean,* August 23, 1986.

Randy Travis, "She's My Woman," *Guideposts,* June 2001.

John Vasile, "Star Stats: Randy Travis," *Country Weekly,* October 16, 2001.

## Chapter 33: The Tragedy of Country Music's King

Chet Atkins interview with Robert K. Oermann, June 1994.

Hillous Butrum interview with Robert K. Oermann, August 1995.

June Carter Cash interview with Robert K. Oermann, September 1994.

Jimmy Dickens interview with Robert K. Oermann, September 1995.

Merle Kilgore interview with Robert K. Oermann, August 1995.

Buddy Killen interview with Robert K. Oermann, August 1995.

Lycrecia Morris interview with Robert K. Oermann, February 1987.

Ray Price interview with Robert K. Oermann, September 1995.

Jerry Rivers interview with Robert K. Oermann, September 1994.

Joe Talbot interview with Robert K. Oermann, September 1995.

Porter Wagoner interview with Robert K. Oermann, July 2000.

Johnny Wright interview with Robert K. Oermann, September 1995.

Jay Caress, *Hank Williams: Country Music's Tragic King* (New York: Stein & Day, 1979).

Bob Claypool, "Hank Williams' Last Ride," *The Houston Chronicle,* January 1, 1989.

Peter Cooper, "Retracing a Ghostly Night Ride," *The Tennessean,* January 1, 2003.

Colin Escott, *Hank Williams* (Boston: Little, Brown & Company, 1994).

Colin Escott, "Hank Williams: Long Gone Lonesome Blues," *Goldmine,* June 14, 1991.

Colin Escott, *Hank Williams: The Original Singles Collection* album liner notes (New York: PolyGram Records, 1990).

Colin Escott and Kira Florita, *Hank Williams: Snapshots from the Lost Highway* (Cambridge, MA: Da Capo Press, 2001).

Rush Evans, "The Last Temptation of Hank Williams," *Goldmine,* February 1, 2008.

Chet Flippo, *Your Cheatin' Heart* (New York: Simon & Schuster, 1981).

Tim Jones, *The Essential Hank Williams* (Nashville: Eggman Publishing, 1996).

George William Koon, *Hank Williams: A Bio-Bibliography* (Westport, CT: Greenwood Press, 1983).

Robert K. Oermann, "Only Lycrecia Remembers Hank Williams as 'Family,'" *The Tennessean,* February 18, 1987.

Robert K. Oermann, "Old Report Tells of Hank Williams' Last Hours," *The Tennessean,* December 16, 1982.

Jerry Rivers, *Hank Williams: From Life to Legend,* second edition (Goodlettsville, TN: Jerry Rivers, 1990).

Jerry Rivers, *Hank Williams: From Life to Legend* (Denver: Heather Enterprises, 1967).

Arnold Rogers and Bruce Godell, *The Life and Times of Hank Williams* (Nashville: Butler Books, 1993).

Bruce Sylvester, "Country Music's Tortured Genius," *Goldmine,* February 7, 2003.

Lycrecia Williams and Dale Vinicur, *Still in Love with You* (Nashville: Rutledge Hill Press, 1989).

Roger M. Williams, *Hank Williams* album liner notes (Alexandria, VA: Time-Life Records, 1981).

Roger M. Williams, *Sing a Sad Song: The Life of Hank Williams* (New York: Ballantine Books, 1975).

# Index